Dad

With love at Christmas,
Trina
xx ♡

This Turbulent Priest

This Turbulent Priest

A LIFE OF CARDINAL WINNING

STEPHEN McGINTY

HarperCollins*Publishers*

HarperCollins*Publishers*
77–85 Fulham Palace Road,
Hammersmith, London w6 8jb

www.harpercollins.co.uk

Published by HarperCollins*Publishers* 2003
1 3 5 7 9 8 6 4 2

A catalogue record for this book
is available from the British Library

ISBN 0 00 274083 4

Set in PostScript Linotype Minion with Photina display by
Rowland Phototypesetting Ltd,
Bury St Edmunds, Suffolk

Printed and bound in Great Britain by
Clays Ltd, St Ives plc

For Lori, my 'Elektra'

CONTENTS

LIST OF ILLUSTRATIONS

Charles Canning (*courtesy: Margaret McCarron*)
Thomas Winning senior (*courtesy: Margaret McCarron*)
Agnes Canning (*courtesy: Margaret McCarron*)
Winning aged four (*courtesy: Margaret McCarron*)
Thomas and Margaret Winning as children (*courtesy: Margaret McCarron*)
A Sunday promenade (*courtesy: Margaret McCarron*)
Thomas Winning, the seminarian (*courtesy: Flourish*)
Family gathering in Rome (*courtesy: Flourish*)
Students on the Spanish Steps (*courtesy: Flourish*)
Winning as Lady Macbeth
Winning as parish priest (*courtesy: Flourish*)
Winning ordained as bishop (*courtesy: The Scottish Catholic Observer*)
The new archbishop (*courtesy: The Archdiocese of Glasgow*)
With Archbishop Scanlan (*courtesy: The Scottish Catholic Observer*)
Addressing the General Assembly of the Church of Scotland (*courtesy: The Scottish Catholic Observer*)
Greeting Pope John Paul II in Scotland (© *The Scotsman Publications Ltd*)
Receiving the cardinal's hat (© Osservatore Romano)
As cardinal (*courtesy: The Archdiocese of Glasgow*)
With Bishop Roderick Wright (*courtesy: The Scottish Catholic Observer*)
With Donald Dewar (*courtesy: The Scottish Catholic Observer*)
With cardinals Cahal Daly and Basil Hume (*courtesy: The Scottish Catholic Observer*)
On pilgrimage in Jerusalem (*courtesy: Flourish*)
Cartoons (© *Steve Bright/Mirrorpix* and © *David Austin*)
With Melinda Cox (*courtesy: The Scottish Catholic Observer*)

ix

Family pictures (*courtesy:* Edward McCarron)
Princes of the Church (© Osservatore Romano)
With Henry McLeish, John Reid and the Pope (© Osservatore Romano)
With the Pope after Mass with the new cardinals (© Osservatore Romano)

ACKNOWLEDGEMENTS

Writing a book is a little like climbing a mountain – you're pretty much on your own, and without the encouragement and support of so many people, I would not have reached the summit. First, I would like to thank those who gave generously of their time and knowledge to further this project. The late Mgr Tom Connelly was an early supporter, as was Ronnie Convery, Director of Communications at the Archdiocese of Glasgow, and Peter Smith, Chancellor of the Archdiocese. Then there are the members of Cardinal Thomas Winning's family – his sister Margaret McCarron, his nephew Edward McCarron, his niece Agnes Cameron, and his cousin, Sister Mary Canning. I would also like to thank his housekeeper, Isobel McInnes. I'm indebted to the members of the Bishops' Conference of Scotland who gave freely of their time: Joseph Devine, Bishop of Motherwell, Keith O'Brien, Archbishop of St Andrews and Edinburgh, Vincent Logan, Bishop of Dunkeld, Maurice Taylor, Bishop of Galloway, John Mone, Bishop of Paisley, and the Secretary of the Bishops' Conference, Mgr Henry Docherty. At Glasgow archdiocese I would like to express my thanks to Mary McHugh, the archivist, Vincent Toal, editor of *Flourish*, his secretary, Mary McMahon, and Louise Devine, Director of Finance. I would also like to thank Campbell and Rebecca Armstrong, T.M. Devine, Fr George Donaldson, Michael Kelly, Bishop Richard Holloway and Ron Mackenna.

Whilst many priests preferred to speak to me off the record, I would like to thank those who were happy to be quoted, including Fr Paul Conroy, Fr Paul Murray, Fr Bob Bradley, Fr Brian Logue, Fr Neal Carlin, Fr Angus MacDonald, Fr Philip Tartaglia, Fr Eugene Matthews, Fr Ronald

MacDonald, Fr John Fitzsimmons and Mgr John McIntyre. I was assisted invaluably in my research by a whole host of others who include Frank Cullen, Pat Connelly, Alan Draper, Hugh McLoughlin, Rennie McOwan, Jack Irvine, Brian Souter, Sir Tom Farmer, Hugh Farmer, Gerry O'Brien, George Galloway, Sir Ian Lang, Dr Anna Murphy, Susan McCormack, and Harry Conroy, who, as editor of the *Scottish Catholic Observer*, was as generous with his time as with his publication's pictures. I would also like to thank Paul Chitnis of SCIAF, John Wilkins, editor of *The Tablet*, Clifford Longley, and, for an astute critique, Peter Stanford. In Rome I would like to express my thanks to Dr Joaquin Navarro-Valls, John L. Allen of the *National Catholic Reporter*, Archbishop John Foley, Cardinal Lopez Trujillo, Duncan MacLaren of Caritas and Christopher McElroy and Raymond Breslin, rector and vice-rector of the Scots College in Rome. Many others offered assistance and off-the-record insight – to those who must remain nameless, I also extend my thanks.

The last few years would have been even more difficult without the support of the staff at the *Scotsman* newspaper: the publisher Andrew Neil, my editor, Iain Martin, Charlotte Ross, Will Peakin, John McGurk, all the library staff and all those fellow toilers in the Glasgow office, Jim McBeth, Tracey Lawson, Andrew Denholm, James Doherty, James Reynolds and Alastair Dalton. Also, my agent Giles Gordon. For the title, I would like to thank Allan Brown and for general enthusiasm and encouragement I would like to thank David Wylie, Chris Deerin, Thomas Quinn and Carmen Reid. At HarperCollins I thank my editors Richard Johnson and Marian Reid.

I would like to thank my brother Paul, my sisters Claire and Alison, my nephew Charlie, and especially my parents, Margaret and Frank, for the faith they gave me.

Last in my acknowledgements but first in life, I would like to thank my wife, Lori, who knows all the many reasons why.

Stephen McGinty, May 2003

INTRODUCTION

If ever an incident encapsulated the character of Cardinal Thomas Joseph Winning, it was a meeting with Derry Irvine, the Lord Chancellor. The Archbishop of Glasgow had travelled to London in 1999 to meet Britain's most powerful lawmaker, in order to raise concerns over the issue of bioethics. After a long wait in the outer chambers of the Lord Chancellor's office at the House of Lords, the Cardinal spotted Irvine striding towards him, woollen wig flowing, ruffled shirt tucked in place, breeches and silk stockings meeting neatly at the knee, and patent leather shoes buffed to a brilliant shine, offset by silver buckles. As Irvine breezed past, offering the Cardinal the briefest of nods, Winning nudged Ronnie Convery, his current affairs adviser, and said: 'If that's the Lord Chancellor, can you imagine what God looks like?'

So much of this anecdote gives a flavour of the man: he was a humorist who pricked pomposity with wit, he was an outsider, suspicious of the corridors of power, and he was a critic of the government, whether it came wrapped in the blue ribbon of the Conservative Party or wore the red rose of New Labour. As a Prince of the Church, Winning possessed a wardrobe of scarlet robes and red birettas capable of matching the Lord Chancellor stitch for embroidered stitch, but instead he preferred the anonymity of a dark suit and white collar, the garb of a common priest. Derry Irvine famously proclaimed himself in the mould of Cardinal Thomas Wolsey, the Lord Chancellor under Henry VIII, whose power and pomp in the early sixteenth century was legendary. Winning, in comparison, was closer to St Thomas à Becket – 'this turbulent priest', as Henry II christened his Archbishop of Canterbury, so painful had he become to the government of the day.

Yet Cardinal Winning was no saint. He could be arrogant, a bully

1

and a sexist. He disliked homosexuals, distrusted many politicians, and considered Donald Dewar, then First Minister of Scotland and 'Father of the nation', a 'bigot' – a charge to which he himself lay open. In financial matters, he was at best woefully uninterested, and at worst incompetent, and his tenure as Archbishop of Glasgow coincided with the creation of a £10 million debt that almost bankrupted the diocese. On the flip side of the coin, he was warm and personable. He cared deeply for his priests and his people and, throughout his career, he fought both poverty and social injustice. In a secular age, he managed to make the Church relevant. He battled against Prime Minister Tony Blair over the issue of abortion and startled the country by offering money to women in crisis pregnancies. This is the story of a miner's son, raised in a crucible of anti-Catholicism, who went on to become arguably the most powerful religious leader of his day in Britain.

I was a six-week-old infant cradled in my mother's arms when I first met Thomas Joseph Winning. He was then an auxiliary bishop in the archdiocese of Glasgow who had been sent, against his will, to the parish of Our Holy Redeemer in my hometown of Clydebank, the shipyard town that bequeathed the world the Singer sewing machine and the QE2. A reluctant parish priest, he appeared to spread the misery around by decreeing that all baptisms be carried out before nine o'clock Mass on a Sunday morning. I was born in the January of a bitter winter and my mother feared I would catch pneumonia if brought out at such an early hour. Winning never actually baptised me – he was too busy fighting a turf war with his fellow auxiliary bishop – but he did peer into my swaddling clothes and I repaid his interest by praying for him every Sunday until the day he died.

It was customary during the Eucharistic prayer of the Mass for Catholics in Glasgow to pray 'for our bishop Thomas', but I was unaware of him as public figure, looming larger than his five feet six inches. Later, as an altar boy, I served at Masses at which he concelebrated. My interest in him deepened once I had exchanged

2

the soutane of an altar boy for a journalist's mackintosh. I literally bumped into him on the Glasgow-Edinburgh train shortly after he had received the red hat of a cardinal, and I was surprised that he was travelling alone, without a bag carrier or assistant. We chatted for an hour and I marvelled at his approachability.

It was not until I returned to Scotland after eighteen months working for the *Sunday Times* in London that I began to consider him as a subject for a biography. The idea flowed from a profile of the cardinal I wrote for the Scottish edition of the paper in May 1998. I flew to Rome to speak with Cardinal Lopez Trujillo, the president of the Pontifical Council for the Family. The previous year, Winning had launched his pro-life initiative and became a cause célèbre, and I expected steady praise from the leader of the Vatican department on which he served. Instead I received nothing. In a strange, almost jealous turn the Colombian cardinal refused to discuss Winning at all, in spite of my varied attempts to lever him into the conversation. After a particularly blunt segue he simply stood up, offered me a chocolate from a box on his desk, kissed both my cheeks and showed me to the door. 'Winning is one man,' he said and shrugged.

True, Winning was *one* man, but a man rapidly growing in stature and influence. If Basil Hume, the Archbishop of Westminster, was for the Establishment the soft, pious face of Catholicism, then Winning was the hard man, a poster boy for the traditionalists who welcomed his fight back against a secular society. The *Sunday Times* profile left me nursing more questions than answers. Why did he provoke such extremes of emotions? What drove him on? Had he ever fallen in love? What did he think about when alone in the dark? I began to see his role less as a spiritual leader than as a minister in a world government, pushing through policy, dealing with egos and jealousies, juggling crises, attempting to keep the faith in an uninterested world. To touch his soul is too melodramatic a phrase; instead I wished to prise open the armour Thomas Winning had constructed around himself during a half a century as a priest.

*   *   *

When I first approached the late Mgr Tom Connelly, then press spokesman for the Catholic Church in Scotland, with the idea of a biography, he was enthusiastic. 'It's got to be warts and all,' he explained over lunch at his favourite Italian restaurant. He viewed previous books on Scottish Church figures as anaemic hagiographies, well intentioned but principally the efforts of fans with typewriters. I planned a more robust and in-depth project and the idea was discussed with Ronnie Convery, Winning's adviser, before being pushed up the line to 'the Boss'. After both men prepared the way, I was invited to lunch in the Cardinal's private dining room in the diocesan offices in Glasgow, overlooking the River Clyde. Winning sat at the head of the table, ladled out the spaghetti, and listened to my pitch. After five minutes he agreed: 'I'd have no problem with that, Stephen,' he told me, and once lunch was over, we walked to his office to inspect his diary and plan the first of over forty interview sessions which would spread out over the next two years.

The going was tough, the terrain unfamiliar. The Catholic Church in Scotland has for so long been ignored or reported simply at face value. Winning was a natural raconteur, an experienced interviewee, but the key was to strip away the tired and worn answers and somehow reach a deeper truth. It was not easy. Painful memories were shuttered behind 'I can't remember', personal feelings required careful teasing out – and even then were swiftly converted into the third person and immediately generalized, so that 'you would feel' took the place of 'I would feel'. Friends, family, politicians and old foes provided an alternative record and a process of checks and balances distilled the facts from fondly remembered fiction. I was the first journalist to enjoy access to Winning's sister Margaret, who explained their childhood. His niece and nephew described the various visits, dinners and football matches that comprised their uncle's only relaxation.

My interviews were regularly one hour long. I would arrive at The Oaks, the wonderful Arts and Crafts-style villa in the leafy suburb of Newlands on Glasgow's south side, promptly at 9.25 in the morning. I discovered that arrival any earlier disturbed his daily recitation of the divine office, the prayers of a priest which he performed each morning in the small oratory just off the hall. Our discussions took place in the living room, he on the sofa, myself in an armchair, and the glass table that lay between us became the net over which questions and answers were batted. At ten-thirty, Mrs McInnes, Winning's housekeeper of thirty years, would arrive with tea and biscuits and a further fifteen minutes would be idled away on current events or personal pleasantries.

We wrestled with the years from his birth in 1925 to the present day, arguing, me prodding and he resisting. For the majority of our sessions we were alone; only when we crossed into his years as a cardinal (1994–2001) was he joined by Ronnie Convery. Far from blocking or fielding questions, Convery sat, listened, and even assisted as we discussed Winning's duels with the government, the launch of the pro-life initiative and the Roddy Wright affair, when the errant Bishop of Argyll and the Isles abandoned his post for a divorcee.

The rules for the book were clear from my first approach. I wished to enjoy the access of an 'authorized' biography but none of the controls or manipulations often inherent with 'official' status. I happily agreed that I would allow Winning to read the finished book before publication to allow the correction of factual errors. Any views, opinions and matters of interpretation were to be mine alone. I knew this would be difficult. Winning was a man un-schooled in the acceptance of constructive criticism. He shared an attitude with Margaret Thatcher, his bête noire, during the 1980s for bracketing people either as 'one of us' or 'one of them'. Those who were not for him, he felt, were against him. At one point our relationship skittered over an icy patch when I arrived for an appointed interview and was presented with a formal letter that insisted he receive a written document and be given the opportunity to read the work completed so far; the continuation of any further interviews hinged upon my acceptance. A compromise was reached when I wrote a letter, putting our previous oral agreement on paper. Winning was a clever manipulator. 'Stephen,' he said, smiling his crinkled Robert de Niro smile, 'I want you to be as welcome in this house once the book is published as you are today.' I knew this would be unlikely and steeled myself for the inevitable battle which would take place once the book was completed.

It was a battle never fought. Winning's death on Sunday, 17 June 2001 closed our collaboration, but not our relationship. When the news editor of the *Scotsman* called me at home, alerting me to the announcement by the Press Association, I felt physically sick. The Cardinal had suffered a heart attack eight days previously but had returned home and was described as 'recovering well'. A 'get well' card and a wrapped present rested on my kitchen table. That afternoon I sat in the *Scotsman*'s offices and wrote a lengthy appreciation with time spent in the toilet in tears. I was troubled by the turbulence of my emotions, and it took a few days to trace the source to the obvious: an obsessional analysis of a life now lost. As any man in a public and powerful position, Winning had a number of sides, one witnessed by family, another by friends; priests saw a third, brother bishops a fourth, and so on. For two years, I had attempted to meld these separate sides, like frames on a negative, into a single, moving picture. The early summer of 2001 was to be a curious time. His death had occurred during my sabbatical when I was finishing a first draft of the book. A strange sensation occurs when you witness a man in his coffin, then return to your study to re-animate him on the page.

When I first embarked on the writing of this biography, I was aware that a previous book by Vivienne Belton, a Glasgow school teacher, had been completed, but had as yet been unable to find a publisher. When in March 2000 the *Daily Record* first revealed that Winning's life was to be the subject of a 'controversial' biography by myself, it had the fortunate effect of galvanizing Ms Belton into asking for Winning's assistance in finding a publisher for her manuscript. *Cardinal Thomas Winning: An Authorised Biography* by Vivienne Belton was published by Columba Press in the autumn of 2000. *The Cardinal: An Official Tribute*, published by the Glasgow archdiocese and the *Scottish Catholic Observer*, joined it on the shelves a few months after Winning's death, together with *Always Winning*, a book of tributes and photographs published by Mainstream. I have read all three books, yet the principal source for my account remains the hundred hours of interviews with Winning, his friends, family, colleagues, contemporaries, priests and politicians: all buttressed by newspaper reports, both secular and religious.

In the jargon of Hollywood, every story has an arc and progresses through 'action beats', dilemmas and troubles the hero overcomes which fuel him through the next phase of his development. Thomas Winning never overcame all of his troubles. He remained a poor judge of character and was let down by a number of close associates; his director of social work ran up large debts in highly ambitious but slackly managed projects, his spin doctor was unspun by a love affair, a court case and a bawdy limerick, while his beloved Pastoral Plan was at one point in the hands of a priest later revealed to be a drunk who hired a former topless model as a housekeeper and paid the inevitable price. The popular view propagated first by the Scottish media and latterly by the British media, was of Winning as the man of the people. This was a convenient pigeonhole, grounded in truth and weary with repetition, but one which ignored Winning's inevitable loneliness. He was a man severed by the weight of position and responsibility from the people. As a young teenager, he had undergone a harsh transformation to become a priest when there was little room for the personal. What constituted Winning the priest and Winning the man was to be a dilemma with which he wrestled for the rest of his life. The garb of a priest was a suit of armour in which he clanked uncomfortably. He found the expression of love beyond the strict confines of his family to be difficult, afraid that the emotion might veer from the platonic.

If the suit of armour retarded his emotions, it lent him protection during his long campaign to drag Catholicism in Scotland out from under the parapet and into the mainstream. This was not to be achieved by ducking issues or diluting dogma. In his twenty-nine years as a bishop, Winning branded Britain a nation of 'spiritual dwarfs', accused Prince Charles of 'woolly theology', wrestled with the Conservative Party over nuclear weapons, condemned the Gulf War, and spent the last six years of his life staring over a 'no man's land' littered with issues such as abortion, student fees and bioethics, at Tony Blair, the Labour leader and pseudo-Catholic who had the potential on paper to be his greatest ally.

The life of Thomas Joseph Winning, a journey from poverty to a position as a prince of the Church, is an inspirational tale of one man's struggle with himself and his surroundings to achieve what he genuinely believed was God's will, in an age when self-will has increasingly become the only currency which counts. At the height of his popularity Winning was to be touted as one of the *papabile* – a candidate for Pope. Although it was a ridiculous suggestion – he lacked both the intellect and standing in Rome – and he was already too old, he was flattered by the suggestion. On one occasion, when I accompanied him to Rome, we walked across St Peter's Square late in the evening after dining in the Via Condotti. Winning was dressed in an anorak from C&A, while the Roman clergy were elegant in their long black frock coats. As we both looked up at the light burning from the papal apartment, I asked if he was not proud to have climbed up to be a candidate.

'Sure,' he said, before triggering another vintage moment. 'I wouldn't want to score the goal, but I'm glad I've made it to the penalty area.'

The Priestly Years

ONE

In the Beginning . . .

'The papists [are like a] rattlesnake, harmless when kept under proper restraints, but dangerous like it, when at full liberty; and ready to diffuse a baleful poison around.'[1]

JOHN ANDERSON, PROFESSOR OF NATURAL PHILOSOPHY,
GLASGOW UNIVERSITY, 1770

It is not known exactly when Patrick Win arrived on the boat from Belfast at the docks of Glasgow in search of a better life and a fuller belly. Born in 1834 among the hills of Fermanagh in the counties of Ulster, he survived the terrible potato famine of the following decade that killed one million of his countrymen and emerged, like his father John, a hardy survivor and itinerant labourer. Ireland at the time was a ravaged country, where food was scarce and what little work there was offered scant prospect of betterment. Tired of farm work and the quiet desperation of his fellow workers, Patrick decided to strike out for a brighter future 'across the water'. A lack of formal schooling had left him illiterate, a barrier which forced him to live on his wits and by the sweat of his brow.

In the middle of the nineteenth century, Scotland was a country in the grip of the Industrial Revolution. Railways, quarries, ironworks, mines, canals, docks and factories were consuming working men, women and children like so much coal in a furnace. The centres of heavy industry such as Glasgow and Dundee were drawing immigrant workers from Ireland at a tremendous rate. By 1851, Patrick Win was just one of over two hundred thousand first-generation

Irish immigrants who had arrived in Scotland over the past fifty years, the majority bedding down along the west coast of the country. While most were Catholic, a proportion of the Irish visitors were Protestants from Ulster, whose ancestors had gone to Ireland to colonize the country in the sixteenth and seventeenth centuries. Many had been tempted back by the notices placed in Belfast newspapers looking for skilled workers to replace those Scottish employees drawn away to Canada, America or Australia. The owners of steelworks, ironworks and coal mines offered them sweeteners such as comfortable accommodation and education for their children. The Irish Catholics could expect no such welcome.

Those who arrived in Scotland were quickly saddled with several unshakeable problems, namely poverty and Catholicism; Scotland may have been expanding its industries, but wages were low and the city of Glasgow offered an example of both boom and bust. Shipbuilding on the Clyde was the cornerstone of its prosperity and accounted for a third of all the world's merchant fleet before 1912. The flourishing tobacco and cotton trades only added to its success. Yet the city had a tradition of high death rates eclipsed by even higher birth rates. The population explosion had been fuelled by the influx of immigrants and refugees fleeing the depopulation of the Scottish Highlands. In 1850, over 50 per cent of the population of 400,000 were born outside the city, resulting in severe overcrowding over a long period in pitiful accommodation which, on average, did not extend beyond one room. Outside the houses open sewers flowed freely and so disease was rampant.

The distress caused by low wages and poor, unhygienic living conditions was compounded by the attitude of locals to Catholicism. In Scotland in the middle of the nineteenth century, the Catholic faith was abhorrent to the Protestant population. For over two hundred years, since the Reformation of 1560, Catholicism had been illegal. Priests were prosecuted and celebration of the Mass was forbidden; the remaining small outcrops of believers who refused to convert were despised. A relaxation in the law came with the

Catholic Relief Act of 1793, once again allowing freedom of worship, and the Emancipation Act which followed thirty years later loosened the bonds further still, but the attitude of the public remained fixed.

Catholics were viewed as a problem to be contained, an attitude encapsulated by John Anderson, Professor of Natural Philosophy at Glasgow University in 1770. While debating with a colleague the merits of repealing laws against Roman Catholics, he compared them to a rattlesnake: 'harmless when kept under proper restraints, but dangerous like it, when at full liberty; and ready to diffuse a baleful poison around'.

The population of Glasgow had always kept a watchful eye on their Catholic neighbours. It was claimed that during the 1790s the city housed forty-three anti-Catholic organizations at a time when the total Catholic population was just thirty-nine. By 1850, the Catholic population in the city had risen to over seventy thousand. In response, anti-Catholic organizations such as the Scottish Protestant Association formed and printed journals such as the *Bulwark* and the *Scottish Protestant*. Members and readers were of a view that Scotland was under attack by an 'inferior race' threatening disease, crime and degradation.

In a short, hard life, Patrick Win witnessed them all. After arriving in the city he moved to the south side of the river Clyde and settled in the village of Pollokshaws. The construction of the Glasgow, Paisley and Johnstone Canal in 1808 had brought a large number of Irish Catholic labourers, or navvies as they were known, into the area and Win was just another to add to their number. Instead of finding work with the large cotton mills, the principal employers in the area, he succeeded in obtaining a job as a railway surfaceman. In such a hostile atmosphere the Catholics invariably spent time with their own countrymen and women at the Irish clubs whose music and dancing offered an opportunity to forget for a few hours the misery of their lives. Win was to meet a young woman by the name of Ann Maguire, a bleacher by profession and a fellow exile from Fermanagh, and on 19 October 1855, the couple wed.

The location for the service was an old smithy in Skin-mill Yard, named after the nearby chamois factory that had been quietly purchased in 1849 for use as a church. Previously, Catholics in Pollokshaws had been forced to walk en masse into the city centre to attend Sunday services at St Andrew's Church by the banks of the Clyde, a six-mile return trip that invariably involved being showered with stones by bigots aware of their destination. In 1840, the city council granted permission for Mass to be celebrated in Pollokshaws and an upstairs room on the village main street became the first venue. The converted smithy that opened nine years later was an improvement by comparison.

The marriage was conducted by Fr Adam Geddes, who at the age of twenty-five was just three years older than the couple clasping hands before him. He was privately furious at such a humble structure and had vowed to see an impressive church replace it. However, a fatal dose of typhus fever contracted the following year ensured that he would never live to see one built. Three close friends, Thomas McGovern, Charles Reilly and Ann MacManus, who took on the role of bridesmaid, witnessed the ceremony.

Patrick Win's work on the railways was enough to pay the rent on a small one-room flat on Main Street for himself and his wife and three years later, on 3 October 1858, the couple's only child, a boy called James, was born. Following his birth, a generous clerk called Will Sewell in the local Registrar's office added an extra 'n' to the family name, a note of little consequence to his illiterate parents who spelt both their names with a humble 'X'. The family name, in fact, was probably Wynne, but it was very likely rendered in the most remedial manner as they were unable to spell it themselves. Anxious that their child achieve a modicum of education, Patrick and Ann enrolled James in the local school. In 1868, by the time he was ten and could read and write, his mother had died. She was thirty-five, and had lived five years beyond the city's average life expectancy, so teeming was Glasgow with tuberculosis, cholera and typhoid. Her husband Patrick lived a further seven years as a widower, looking after his son between long shifts in a variety of jobs including quarry labourer and coal pit roadsman. A nervous cough that began in 1874 developed over the next two years into phthisis, a wasting disease that attacks the lungs in a manner similar to tuberculosis. For his final few months, Patrick Win was bedridden in their tiny flat, tended by his son who would view his father's passing on 14 October 1876 as a blessing.

The death of his father severed any ties that held James Winn to Glasgow, the city of his birth, at least for the next twenty years. At the age of seventeen, he headed to the town of Motherwell in the blasted landscape of Lanarkshire, and the life of the pit. The town lay twelve miles south-east of Glasgow, with the river Clyde to the west and the river Calder to the north, and while the town's name may have been derived from the Celtic expression for 'the level place above a river', its modern identity was less romantic and came caked in soot and coal dust. Motherwell was a mighty industrial town at the heart of an extensive array of coalfields, and James Winn was to find employment at Parkhead colliery.

The work was brutal, back-breaking and extremely dangerous. Subsequently, the men took their brief pleasures where they could, primarily in the alehouses that lined Motherwell High Street. Winn, meanwhile, had an alternative form of recreation. In the spring of 1889, when he was thirty-one, he began a relationship with Mary Weir, a twenty-six-year-old domestic servant. Mary Weir discovered she was pregnant in the late autumn of 1889 and, faced with the prospect of being dismissed from her work and expelled from her home, as they were one and the same, she turned to her lover for support. In such circumstances, the most convenient solution was a swift marriage in front of a frowning priest before the bride's condition began to show. The mother would be saved the shame of being labelled a 'fallen woman' and the baby would be spared the ignominy of being born a bastard. Why this did not occur is unknown, but James Winn's subsequent behaviour in the years that followed intimate that he was a feeble character, unable or unwilling to take on the burden and responsibility of parenthood. Abortion, though available in the crudest of forms from midwives of dubious reputation, was not considered an option.

As a result of her lover's initial reluctance to marry, Mary Weir had little choice but to abandon her job, leave her hometown and travel fifty miles to Edinburgh where in the anonymity of the capital her 'disgrace' was more tolerable. There, in a small rented room at 382 Lawnmarket, an anonymous tenement block a few hundred yards from Edinburgh Castle, she awaited her child's birth. On 15 July 1890, the father of Cardinal Thomas Winning was born. He was named Thomas Weir after his mother, and marked by the registrar, as was the tradition, illegitimate.

Mother and child returned to Motherwell a few weeks after the birth to be greeted by a man transformed. James Winn, perhaps moved both by the sight of his infant son and guilt that the child's mother had suffered as a result of his own unwillingness to wed, now attempted to mend Mary's reputation. The couple were married on 10 September 1890 at Our Lady of Good Aid, the local Catholic Church. The ceremony was small, attended only by two close friends, Maggie Brown and Felix Mullan, who acted as the legal witnesses, and the bride's mother, Agnes Weir. Her husband, a miner like her son-in-law, was long dead. By the following year, the couple had moved to 9 Camp Street, a solidly working-class area of Motherwell, and when the census collector visited, Thomas, now nine months old, finally received his father's name. The illusion of a happy family was enhanced in 1892 by the birth of a daughter, Anne, but it was not to last: five years later, the death of Mary Weir robbed the children of their mother while James Winn's fecklessness was to deprive them of their father. Shortly after burying his wife, Winn deposited Thomas, then seven, and Anne, five, into the care of his mother-in-law, departed for work, and never returned.

Why Winn chose to abandon his two children when they needed him most is not known. He was certainly a reluctant candidate for marriage and fatherhood, but it is unimaginable that a deep bond did not exist at some level between this insecure, dithering Irishman and his young children. Yet any such tie was severed for ever in 1897 when he abandoned his family in Motherwell and returned to Glasgow, the city of his youth. The next three generations of his family – his son, grandson and granddaughter, and great-grandson and great-granddaughter – all believed that he died shortly after his departure. When his own son Thomas finally wed in 1924, James Winn was listed as dead on the marriage papers.

There is evidence however, that Winn was alive and living under an assumed name in his native Glasgow. At some point after the abandonment of his family, he appears to have changed his name from Winn, a name that was uncommon and eminently traceable, to Mullan, an exceedingly common Irish name, and one he now shared with his former best friend. Fifteen years after the death of his first wife, his new name allowed him to marry for a second time, but as a bachelor, as opposed to a widower. This new identity spared him any awkward questions from Mary Wylie, the fifty-year-old woman he chose as his new wife. Winn subsequently spent the remainder of his life working as a labourer in a lace factory, and his true identity was only discovered long after his death at the age of seventy-five in 1933.

The childhood of Thomas and Anne Winn was fraught with death and change. The demise of their mother and departure of their father were followed by death once again when, a few years later, their grandmother passed away and they were passed, like inherited heirlooms, into the care of their mother's two bachelor brothers, James and John Weir, with whom they grew to adulthood in relative contentment. The final element of change arrived courtesy of the classroom. Just as the family had seen their name mutate from 'Win' to 'Winn', it now reached its final apotheosis when, according to family tradition, an inattentive schoolteacher misheard young Thomas at primary school and wrote the corruption 'Winning' on the blackboard. The new name increased the distance between the children and the father who had abandoned them, as now they no longer even carried his name, but by now neither did he.

Thomas Winning grew into a young man who embraced his responsibilities where his father had shirked them. When his sister's new husband died in a railway accident while working in Canada, leaving Anne without a pension, Thomas moved into their small room and kitchen in John Street, Craigneuk, and provided for her by working as a miner at the Camp Street Pit in Motherwell. It was during this time that he met Agnes Canning, a local girl who worked in the jam factory in nearby Carluke. Agnes was a quiet, shy girl whose introspective personality mirrored Thomas's own but whose long dark hair, which she wore in an elegant velvet bow, ensured she attracted her share of admirers. The second youngest of thirteen children from an Irish Catholic family, Agnes had the distinction of being the daughter of one of the most successful Irish immigrants in the district.

Charles Canning was a handsome man who dressed in a dark three-piece suit; a white hankie sprang from his breast pocket, and the ensemble was completed by an elegant tie pin and silver watch and chain. He wore a full beard and walrus-style moustache that was draped long over his mouth like the ventriloquists of the day. He had every reason to take pride in his appearance for, despite the extreme prejudice prevalent at the time, he had attained the position of Bailie in the Wishaw Parish Council. The title accorded him the right to sit in judgement over those who came before the parish court on charges of drunkenness or debt. He also owned a popular pub on Dryborough Road in Wishaw, an irony not lost on the locals, who coined a saying. 'Canning gets them drunk on a Friday night and sentences them on a Monday.' His achievement was all the more impressive for his background. Canning had arrived in Scotland in the late 1870s after his family had lost their farm in Kilmacrenan, County Donegal. His father had paid his rent, but either failed to obtain a receipt or lost it on the walk home from the landlord's. When the landlord appeared and demanded Canning repeat his payment, he refused, and so was forced from the home which had been in the family for generations. The eviction forced the family to pursue a new life in Scotland. In one of the Irish clubs in Glasgow, Canning met his future wife, Margaret Boyle, an immigrant from Ramelton, ten miles south of his parents' former farm. Together the couple moved to Lanarkshire where Canning swiftly rose from miner to pit contractor and later a local councillor.

*   *   *

The Canning family home was tiny for such a large family, but it was located in an area of relative respectability. The Whitegates was named after the coloured gates that closed off the road to allow the trains laden with coal to crawl from the pits to the main connection line at Wishaw. The house sat at 515 Glasgow Road and this was where Thomas Winning would collect his intended before the pair would stroll down to the parish hall for a dance on a Saturday night. Agnes Canning's weekday evenings were quietly taken up baking, knitting and embroidering table covers. It was from her home in 1914 that she bid farewell to the man who was now her fiancé as he embarked for the Great War.

The outbreak of World War One was viewed by Thomas Winning, as it was by so many of his generation, as an opportunity to exchange his soot-smeared clothes for the glamour of the military uniform – in his case, the pleated kilt and black tam-o'-shanter of the Gordon Highlanders. As the British government urged every able man to do his duty and defend his country, the call to arms was given a dramatic impetus across Scotland by the leaders of the Catholic community. The archbishops of both Glasgow and Edinburgh urged men to sign up for active duty, an attitude questioned by many for whom Scotland remained a nation that had so long treated their community with an intense disrespect, yet the hierarchy believed the war in Europe offered a wonderful opportunity to unite the country's disparate groups and fuse them together. Catholic or Protestant would soon lose their distinctions in the muddy trenches of the Western Front.

Thomas Winning was to return unwounded and with little visible display of the mental trauma that comes with witnessing such carnage. For the duration of his military career, he kept in close contact with his fiancée through regular postcards from places such as Mons, the Somme and Ypres; locations that would become synonymous with the slaughter of hundreds of thousands of British soldiers but whose postcards arrived with a lace trim and cartoon effigies of moustached Germans, and caricatures of tanks and guns.

Winning did not drink, so he would accept the traditional 'tot of rum' given to the men before the officer's whistle urged them over the top, and would exchange it for cigarettes or chocolate. During one military push along the trenches, Winning and a comrade crawled out into no man's land to retrieve a wounded officer. Afterwards, both soldiers tossed a coin to see who would receive a decoration. His colleague won the toss but later lost his life in the Dardanelles, while Winning escaped bullets and bombings and the only injury he received was from an attack of mustard gas.

In later years, Thomas Winning senior never discussed the bleakness of his role in the war with his children. When they asked him to take down the old tin containing the dozens of postcards he told humorous tales of his fellow soldiers and their attempts to be discharged as shell-shocked – how they would unfurl their Balmoral hats, stare into space and blow on the ribbons that hung down. A silly tale to a young boy and girl unaware of the horrors their father had experienced. Even the darkest tale was very funny to a child, and it involved the soldiers marching down the line after a big push, past a dead German soldier lying with his hand outstretched, into which someone had wedged a tin of bully beef.

Thomas Winning was discharged after the war but despite his feelings for Agnes he felt unable to return directly and marry her. He regarded himself as unworthy. She was the daughter of a man of property and respect while his father existed in only the vaguest of memories, and despite his heroic labours in the trenches, he was now unemployed, and Lanarkshire had little to offer. Instead, he was determined to better himself so as to provide for his fiancée and set sail from the Glasgow docks to Chicago and the promise of the American dream. It was a strange and difficult time for Thomas. He spent four years travelling, from low-paid job to low-paid job, from the city of Chicago to Canada and Alberta and Winnipeg.

By the time he left, all he had accrued was a familiar nickname: Scottie. Fortunately, it was still enough to secure the hand of Agnes in marriage and so, on 17 July 1924, after more than twelve years of courtship, they were wed in a ceremony at St Patrick's Church in Shieldmuir. After a decade of conflict, travel and broken dreams for Thomas Winning, the time had come to raise a family.

The couple moved into a small room and kitchen near the railway in the village of Craigneuk, and, in among the din of the trains, they were happy together. Thomas had secured himself a job as a miner and Agnes would prepare the tin bath for his arrival home after a twelve-hour shift. Eleven months later their son Thomas Joseph was born on 3 June 1925 and baptized two weeks later at St Patrick's Church. The birth of their son was followed eighteen months later by the birth of a daughter, Margaret, by which time her father was already unemployed, a victim alongside thousands of others of the General Strike of 1926. He was to remain unemployed for more than twenty years.

A younger sister was to provide Winning's earliest memories, for when he was just four, Margaret was stricken with scarlet fever: 'My mother was sitting on a stool in the kitchen, cradling Margaret who was bawling, and I remember trying to console her, trying to stroke her little head.' Around this time a photograph was taken of the pair of them and an older cousin, Lucy Canning. Margaret is propped up in a wooden armchair wearing a light-coloured woollen dress, and Lucy, at the age of eight, stands at the back with her hair in ringlets. But the most striking presence is Winning: just four years old and dressed in a dark-coloured Russian-style top, shorts, long woollen socks and polished black boots, he carries the confident stare of a little prince.

The young Thomas's early confidence was tested a few months after the photograph was taken, when he began to suffer symptoms similar to Margaret, whose life had been saved by a visit to the local fever hospital. Winning spent a total of three weeks in isolation at the hospital as the scarlet fever ran its course. Every few days, his mother arrived at the hospital and would wave outside his bedroom window, but this was little comfort to a five-year-old who felt himself victimized by the nursing staff. A particular nurse had taken to sticking her tongue out at him, no doubt in an effort to make the child laugh, but with the opposite result. He began to believe she genuinely disliked him, an attitude confirmed in his young mind by the fact she fed him a disgusting daily diet of castor oil mixed with orange juice.

The house to which Winning returned after his hospitalization was slightly bigger than their previous accommodation. In 1928, the family moved a few hundred yards to Glasgow Road and a tenement house at number 511. The house offered little extra comfort, but had the benefit of being only two doors away from Agnes's brother and sister who had never married and who had remained in the family home at 515. The house was a typical working-class property. The front door opened on to Glasgow Road, while inside a short lobby ran to the front room; behind this was the kitchen, while the toilet was outside in the dry green, the concrete area where the washing was hung. The kitchen also had two recessed alcoves in which the family slept, separated by a thin white curtain. Winning slept with his father in one bed, while in another Margaret slept with her mother.

The sleeping conditions were common for an ordinary family at this time but a search for the reticence that Winning junior would attach to sex, even within the confines of marriage, should begin on the thin mattress of his sleeping arrangements. Winning never minded sleeping with his father, irritated only by his steady snoring, but the lack of room and, more crucially, privacy meant he rarely saw his parents kiss or even embrace. It was a subject Winning was always reluctant to discuss; in his family, sexual intercourse was strictly for the services of procreation. 'There is something in that,' Winning was to explain later. 'They never had a holiday. I would say they were in their thirties before they were married. Two kids were as much as they could manage. If you were unemployed, two kids were as much as you could afford.'

In spite of their poverty both children were always smartly dressed, with Agnes foregoing personal clothes or pleasures for the benefit of Thomas and Margaret. The lack of physical contact between husband and wife extended to their children. In the Winning family home, emotions were rarely physically expressed and instead love was illustrated by actions. Yet while Margaret reacted to her upbringing by becoming, as she believed, overly emotional, her brother followed his mother's example and would grow up to keep his emotions tightly suppressed. Margaret explains.

> None of them went in for hugging at all. Emotions and things like that were done with their actions. You could hug anybody, but they showed you more love through their actions than by hugging. My mother kept her emotions under rein – it seems to be a failing of the Cannings. They did not show emotion. Thomas was like that. He did worry about things, but he kept them to himself.

Winning could not miss what he had not received but when his mother did show great physical affection, he adored the experience. Unfortunately this came at a time of great personal peril. At the age of seven, Winning developed a case of pneumonia after sitting on wet grass while on an outing to the local park with his father. His mother returned from a religious talk organized by the Catholic Woman's Guild to find her son sitting next to the fire, shivering violently. Over the next two days his condition worsened as he rolled under the heavy woollen sheets, drenching them in sweat. The condition was grave, dozens of children in the village had died of diphtheria, cholera and pneumonia, and both parents feared he might succumb. His mother, who had previously measured out her emotions as carefully as a ration-book recipe, was in turmoil, weeping at his condition.

A young neighbour, Mary Cromwell, who worked as a nurse, prepared a mustard poultice, which was tightly bound round the boy's back in an attempt to reduce the inflammation. When he did not improve, the extended family of aunts and uncles organized a collection to pay for the services of a doctor, which, prior to the creation of the National Health Service, were billed per visit. After administering treatment, the doctor could not guarantee the boy's survival, and so the parish priest was called for.

Father Bartholomew Atkinson arrived with a vial of holy water from Lourdes, blessed the boy, and left instructions that the contents be sipped, like any strong medicine, three times a day and that Winning was to direct his evening prayers to St Bernadette. That evening, after the priest's departure, Agnes Winning was distraught and prayed in a manner that disturbed her daughter: 'My mother prayed that he would not die, but that she would give him back to God if he wanted him,' remembered Margaret. 'At one point, she shouted aloud that if God wanted him, He could have him.' The future priest, bishop, archbishop and cardinal was unaware of his mother's pact. Thomas drifted in and out of consciousness, but that evening a corner was turned and he began to recover.

Winning's memory of this time was not of pain or discomfort or fear of an early death, but of the transformation that he had witnessed taking place in his mother and the softness of her touch. 'My mother showed me a great deal of affection then. I would lie in the dark, pretending to be asleep, and she would stroke my forehead and kiss me.'

The infancy and early childhood of Winning was spent in a contented state, cocooned in a strong family, loved – though in a distant manner – and protected from a poverty he did not see or yet understand. The task of raising two young children on the few coins provided by the State was a feat of miraculous ingenuity, but a feat made easier by a generous aunt and uncle. Agnes Canning's brother and sister had no children of their own, and would lavish their attention and shillings on their niece and nephew, paying for treats their mother and father could not afford.

In order to increase the family's allowance, Thomas Winning began to make and sell sweets, an idea suggested by his wife's cousin, Bob Purdy, during a routine visit. At first the former soldier laughed off the idea as ridiculous, but Bob was persistent and insisted on giving a personal demonstration. In the kitchen the men's jackets were thrown off, their sleeves rolled up and mixing bowls and bags of sugar were commandeered for an initial experiment with candy balls. In those few moments, Thomas Winning recognized a golden opportunity. Sweet aromas began to waft through the house as he developed recipes for tablet, candy balls and an array of boiled sweets. Sales were initially to children at tuppence a bag, but soon local shops had taken an interest and Mr Winning had generated enough money to buy a small piece of machinery. The gadget resembled a mangle with a roller impregnated with hollowed shapes such as stars, fish and cars, into which the boiling candy was poured. The most popular line was marzipan walnuts – so sweet, light and irresistible to the taste that the parish priest, Fr Bartholomew Atkinson, would send his housekeeper round to fetch a dozen at a time, in spite of his diabetic condition.

The greatest indignity of Agnes Canning's married life was the visits by the 'Means Test Man', the government official whose job it was to visit families on welfare with the purpose of checking whether or not they were living beyond their means, funded by illicit employment. Thomas Winning's confectionery business had attracted their attention, even though he was scrupulous about earning only four shillings, the maximum sum permitted if he wished to retain his welfare aid. 'My mother hated the indignity of those visits. She was house-proud and felt it was a form of invasion and yet there was nothing she could do,' Margaret recalled. Agnes dreaded each visit and would always weep after the official had left.

The persistent unemployment of Thomas Winning had nothing to do with indolence; instead, his religious identity prevented him from walking through the factory gate. In the past, when work was plentiful, employers did not enjoy putting a Catholic on their payroll but strong backs were required. Now, in the Depression years of the 1930s, they could pick and choose. This was the era when an employer's first question was: 'What school did you go to?' Those who had been educated at a Catholic school were told there was no work available. On numerous occasions, Thomas Winning would re-christen his school, but his background was always uncovered. While he accepted wave after wave of rejection with stoicism, forged in the knowledge that as a veteran of the Somme he was lucky to be alive, it ignited a burning resentment within his son. Winning was moulded in a crucible of anti-Catholicism, the consequences of which were a deep distrust and even dislike of Protestantism and an unswerving loyalty to the Catholic Church. He remembered: 'It was a time that left its mark. My main memory was watching my father always on the look-out for work, always asking for a chance, but always being knocked back because of his religion. It ingrained something in you. It builds harshness, and so you always side with other Catholics.'

Winning's earliest experience of hostility towards Catholics was on the small football field that lay at Shepherd's Park, a few streets away from his home. Although his group of friends was mixed, it was not uncommon when picking sides for players to glare at him and declare: 'I don't want an Irishman on my side.' He would insist he had never set foot in the country but ethnic subtleties did not matter, the equation was simple: a Catholic equalled an Irishman. On other occasions, Winning would deny he was even a Catholic when he was pounced upon by a teenage gang who often lurked along Glasgow Road and hauled up against a wall as they demanded to know if he was a 'Fenian'.

The attitude was repeated by the Winnings' neighbours, the Russells, who at least had the civility to restrict their behaviour to one day each year. On 12 July, the anniversary of the Battle of the Boyne, when William of Orange vanquished his Irish enemies, protest songs would roar from the window and Mr Russell would refuse to speak to the Winnings. For the remainder of the year, the family was good natured and brought presents for the children from their annual holiday in Portobello, on the east coast. (The Winnings could not afford a holiday and when Thomas asked why, he was told that if he ate margarine instead of butter all year, they could afford a trip. Thomas said he would rather stick to butter.)

What the family experienced was common across the country as Winning's formative years covered the most dynamic and difficult period of the twentieth century for the Catholic Church in Scotland. The Catholic population had almost doubled during the past forty years to over six hundred thousand and in 1918 the community had benefited from the Education Act that saw the government fund Catholic schools. Previously, they were funded by collections from among the parishioners. Flush with extra capital, the Church leaders embarked on an extensive building programme, yet outside the stone gables and away from the scent of incense, trouble was brewing.

The Education Act triggered a backlash as Protestants argued against what they saw as 'Rome on the Rates'. The Church of Scotland, the country's official Church, whose annual General Assembly was viewed as the conscience of the nation, increased the pressure when, in 1923, the Church and Nation Committee prepared a report entitled 'The Menace of the Irish Race to our Scottish Nationality'. Their conclusion was that the immigrant Irish and their subsequent generations were stealing jobs from native Scots and dragging the country down into a gutter of crime, drunkenness and thriftlessness. The solution was the exclusive employment of Scots Protestants and the deportation of those Irish on poor relief or in prison.

The following decade saw the rise of two potent anti-Catholic groups. The Scottish Protestant League was based in Glasgow and led by Alexander Ratcliffe, a former railway clerk and son of a minister. He was an eloquent speaker who secured five seats for the League on Glasgow City Council by telling packed meetings salacious tales about renegade priests, vicious nuns and the true villainy of the Vatican. The problem had an uglier face in Edinburgh, where John Cormack, a Baptist and veteran of the First World War, formed Protestant Action in 1933, an organization that advocated the withdrawal of the vote for Catholics and their eventual expulsion from the country. Their campaign reached its height in the spring and summer of 1935, when they rallied ten thousand protestors to picket the City Chambers where a reception for the Catholic Young Men's Society was in progress. A detachment of Gordon Highlanders was placed on standby to secure the CYMS's safe departure. The treatment of Catholics attending a Eucharistic Congress, an assembly of devotion, in the city a few weeks later led the Archbishop of St Andrews and Edinburgh, Joseph McDonald, to write to Stanley Baldwin, the Prime Minister, to complain:

Priests were savagely assaulted, elderly women attacked and kicked, bus-loads of children mercilessly stoned and inoffensive citizens abused and assailed in a manner that is almost unbelievable in any civilized community today. The disgraceful scenes have become known in every quarter of the globe, and have sullied the fair name of a city which once was justly regarded as a leader in all culture, thought and civilization.[2]

Across the country, parishioners were in a state of readiness, organizing around the clock watches on their churches against what was considered the worst outbreak of anti-Catholic fervour since the Reformation. The summer of 1935 was to prove the zenith of violent anti-Catholicism, but the insidious boil remained and would take decades to lance.

The red sandstone church of St Patrick's was the beating heart of the Catholic community in Craigneuk. Built in 1891, it was here under the high arches that an oppressed people came for spiritual succour, here they brought their newborn and recently dead, here they confessed their sins, pledged their love during marriage, prayed for the strength to cope with life in this world and for a better life in the next. In an environment hostile to their faith, life revolved around the church in ways unimaginable today. The church hall was a leisure centre, open in the evening and equipped with a library, games room and a tea bar to act as an alternative to the public house. Concerts and amateur productions were performed regularly, but the highlight was the weekly dance organized to introduce the young men and women of the parish under the watchful eye of the clergy. On a Sunday morning, all three Masses were packed, the wooden pews straining to contain the villagers in their smartest clothes. The parish supported a range of organizations popular enough to operate by invitation only. Thomas Winning was a member of the St Vincent de Paul Society, the Scottish branch of a French organization founded after the French Revolution by a Catholic lawyer to aid the poor.

Each Sunday, Thomas Winning would appear at Mass, wearing a bright yellow sash embroidered with the organization's name, and work as an usher, supervise the collection, afterwards count the takings, and then decide on its distribution among the poor and elderly. Johnny Kelly, a burly Irishman who worked at the Etna Steel Plant and devoted his spare time to charity work, led the Shieldmuir conference of St Vincent de Paul. It was a generous act for which he was cruelly rewarded. He was the father of eight children and, with his wife, watched helpless as each one contracted tuberculosis and died, a tragic event he blamed on the great bundles of old clothes, probably contaminated, that he stored in the house, prior to distribution.

The young Winning was involved in the Church from the moment of his baptism. At home each evening the family gathered to say the rosary, with his father using a set of keys instead of beads. On the morning of his fifth birthday, he began classes at St Patrick's primary school, a mile from his house, where the four Rs were taught instead of the usual three, religion being regarded as important as reading, writing and arithmetic. The Catholic faith was taught by rote before and after lunch using the penny catechism, a dark hardback book whose questions and answers were to be memorized. The idea was to provide Catholics with ready answers for anyone who might question their beliefs.

Winning was quick to display his intelligence. He memorized large chunks of a book on biblical history, and so was asked to visit the other classrooms to demonstrate his skill. When a new headmaster was appointed, he asked to speak to the brightest boy in the school and Winning was sent forward. Unfortunately, he panicked and answered every question put to him incorrectly. 'I have never forgotten that day,' he was to say later. 'I felt ashamed. I felt that I had let everybody down and I felt humiliated.'

The primary school was a natural extension of the church, and three times each year both were united with the entire Catholic community for public processions. The largest procession was the feast of Corpus Christi, the Body of Christ, in June, when the consecrated host was carried aloft by the priest around the village.

In preparation, the families in tenements which looked on to the church and school playing fields dressed their windows like altars, with lighted candles and statues of Our Lady. On two occasions, Winning was given the role of carrying a basket of rose petals for a classmate, Maureen Hoban, who scattered them like a carpet of flowers over which the gathered community processed while singing hymns and saying the rosary.

At the age of seven, Winning joined his class in preparing to receive the sacraments of Confession and Holy Communion. One night, Winning went home to his mother and asked if it was acceptable to inform the priest that he had disobeyed her five times. 'Five times! *Five* times? Fifty times, more like,' she replied. Winning was not a particularly naughty child, but he did enjoy teasing his younger sister to the point of tears by insisting on calling her 'the Cat's Auntie' instead of by her name. Then there was the occasion when he climbed up on to the dresser to find football tickets and toppled the whole structure down. Winning made his confession, told the priest that he had disobeyed his mother fifty times, and was forgiven his sins. In the classroom, his teacher explained that the host, the little wafer of bread, would be transformed through the mystery of transubstantiation into the actual body of Jesus Christ; a concept that struck Winning as truly wondrous, but which built expectations the Catholic Church could not match. On the day of his first Holy Communion, neat in pressed trousers, white shirt and ironed tie, Winning stuck out his tongue and received the bread to a crushing disappointment: 'I was so disillusioned by the host. I thought it would be much thicker, crunchier, and much more fleshy.' Afterwards, he received a hot breakfast in the school and a penny from the parish priest, but even this could not make up for the earlier let-down.

While pennies were spent on gumballs, cinnamon sticks or twisted paper pokes of boiled sweets – unavailable in his father's pantry – the week's pocket money was spent on the cinema. Every Saturday morning, Winning would travel to Motherwell, to the Rex cinema.

There, in the gloom of the cinema, he and his friends would watch Westerns and gangster films starring James Cagney and Humphrey Bogart. The local cinema was deemed too rough for Winning, who once had his hat stolen by some boisterous lads, and watched as his younger sister fought to retrieve it. Eventually the cinema was closed and renamed. 'All the kids thought it was called the R 10, and couldn't work out what it meant. Eventually we learned it was called the RIO. I loved the cinema, and the way every kid felt he could be a cowboy or Indian,' said Winning. While the cinema provided the necessary escapism, the Church was to offer him a possible career.

As a teenager, Winning never glimpsed a burning bush, heard the voice of God, or walked a road to Damascus. Instead, he was quietly drawn towards the altar by the magnetic example of the parish priests. Before becoming eligible to be an altar boy, prospective candidates had to spend a period of penance in the choir loft. The 'Lord of the Loft' was Fr James Cuthbert Ward, a priest from Edinburgh, who had been banished to the west coast as two older brothers were already priests in the city and the Archbishop feared a cabal. Ward was a chubby man who wore thick glasses, the size and depth of lemonade bottles, and Winning initially considered him soft on account of his frequent homilies about his mother. It was a notion the priest quickly dispelled by regularly beating altar boys and choirboys for errors and cheek. If Ward meted out punishment and strict discipline, his devotion to the high hymns and Latin chants that made up the sung Mass redressed the balance. To Ward they were a reflection of God's beauty and a way of softening the harshness of the parishioners' lives. Winning was no nightingale, but the effort he exerted was appreciated by Ward and the choir loft offered him a better view of the panoply below.

The elevated role priests held in the Catholic community was never emphasized more than on a Sunday when they led the parishioners in prayer. Winning would watch in quiet awe as they paraded across the altar in rich, embroidered vestments of purple, gold, green, red and white. At the age of eleven, he was finally allowed to join the priests on the altar, carrying the large brass cross, swinging the long steel thurible, the elaborate holder for the incense that perfumed the air, and holding up the priest's cope during weekly devotions. Winning was hard-working and diligent and his duties were expanded to include the sale of religious booklets door-to-door. Often people would take one out of pity and promise to pay later, a promise seldom kept, forcing Winning to contribute his pocket money to correct the balance. He also had to maintain a steady supply of religious pamphlets for display and sale at the back of the church. This involved taking the bus to Glasgow and the Renfrew Street offices of the Catholic Truth Society. It was while browsing amongst the lives of saints and booklets on personal morality that Winning picked up a copy of *The Imitation of Christ* by Thomas A Kempis, a text that was to deepen his faith to a greater degree than the shallows usually inhabited by schoolboys. The author was born in Kempen in the German Rhineland in 1380, and was responsible for the training of novices, but his posthumous work, published a century later, would became almost as widely read as the Bible. The book is constructed as a series of proverbs, designed to overcome vices, develop virtues and nurture a private prayer life, and Winning saw it as 'a great précis on how you should live your life as a Catholic'. The enthusiasm other schoolboys reserved for football, Winning ploughed into the stern and demanding nature of the book, but kept the practice utterly private. Priests may have been admired and held up as pillars of the community, but anyone who wished to join them was a 'Holy Joe' fit to be pilloried by their young peers.

The only two people to whom Winning disclosed his interests were Fr James Ward and his superior, Fr Alex Hamilton, the parish priest of St Patrick's. Alex Hamilton had arrived three years previously, in 1935, and was a quiet, reserved man whose mother had died when he was very young; the reason given for his emotional distance. When Winning first raised the idea of becoming a priest and the possibility that he might attend junior seminary at Blairs College in Aberdeen, Fr Hamilton had been surprisingly cautious.

As a veteran of Blairs from the age of ten, he had no wish for Winning to suffer the poor food and intense homesickness that he himself had endured. Instead, he advised Winning to complete his secondary education and allow his true calling, if it was so, to deepen.

At no point did Winning discuss his thoughts with either his mother or father and it would be a further three years before the issue emerged into the open. In the intervening years, Winning continued his education at Our Lady's High School, the local Catholic secondary school for boys, based two miles away in Motherwell. He had been accepted for the school after the successful completion of the Eleven-Plus, the examination designed to separate children with academic promise from those viewed as possessing a lesser ability, more suited to an early entry to the work place. The fact he passed one year earlier than most, and that many of the school friends he believed cleverer than himself should fail or be prohibited from sitting by parents anxious to secure another wage, seemed a great injustice. This feeling was later compounded by guilt when Winning did not fulfil his scholastic potential. 'I did not feel that I fared particularly well at school,' said Winning. 'I have always felt it is a mistake to push kids on.'

At primary school Winning had been taken to the local swimming baths where he had stepped off the side, expecting to find steps, and sank. He spluttered to the surface, but it would be almost sixty years before he tried to swim again. After the familiar warmth and relative ease of primary school, secondary education was a shock and once again Winning felt he was drowning. The problem was understanding the art of studying; he was unfamiliar with the secret of dividing work into sections, organizing study timetables and structuring revision. His parents were supportive, offering the sitting room and dinner table for his books, and ensuring a silence suitable for study descended on the house, but, left on his own, Winning would panic. Maths was a particular chore. He missed numerous classes while serving as an altar boy at funeral services, and had a natural blind spot for numbers which was exacerbated by the maths master, John Bancewicz, whom he disliked intensely and viewed as a 'bully'. On a number of occasions, Winning asked his father, who had taken a correspondence course in mathematics, to complete his homework, which he would then copy into his jotter and present as his own work. Trial and error in methods of revision finally paid off and the perseverance he would display during the course of his life began to take root. During those early years of secondary school, his vocation to the priesthood began to deepen, but it was not the contemplative or spiritual aspect of the job that he desired. 'There was a glamour in the priesthood. I would imagine myself running for sick calls and looking after people in road accidents or during emergencies.'

The persecution of Catholic priests and nuns in Spain, upon the outbreak of the Spanish Civil War in 1936 and over the next three years, galvanized Winning's ambition to be a priest. What the astute observer viewed as the beginning of a titanic struggle between Fascism and Communism was reduced to the simplest level in Winning's mind. The machinations of Franco and his coup against an elected government were immaterial to a young Catholic boy in Lanarkshire who saw the conflict in black and white: Godless Communists against the nobility of the Catholic Church. Each Sunday, Winning would lie in front of the coal fire in the family's living room and read the *Catholic Observer* and the *Universe* for reports on the atrocities being carried out against priests and nuns in towns across Spain. He was riveted by a picture that appeared in the *Universe* of the execution of a Jesuit priest who, just before he was shot by a firing squad, called out '*Viva Christo Rey!*' – 'Long live Christ the King!' The Scots Catholics who supported Franco were against the tide of public opinion that sided with the Republicans, sending men, money and supplies to support the International Brigade. The sight of the co-op store collecting money for the war in Spain sickened him, and he considered smashing the window, but fear of being caught and of his parents having to pay for the damage changed his mind.

I was a staunch Francophile. I felt great resentment at the way the British government supported the Republicans. The co-op store had a milk-for-Spain campaign, it involved milk bottle tops and the money was to go towards the International Brigade. It was the way they were treating the Church that coloured my attitude. They were anti-Catholic and so I hoped they would be defeated. I discussed it with my father. We all felt the same way. To me it was simple: it was murderers versus the rest.

Winning remembers hearing about the end of the siege of Madrid on the radio and the whole family cheering Franco's victory. 'It was a real joy and a pleasure for us to hear that the Republicans had been defeated.'

The annual retreat organized for the boys of Our Lady's High School and St Aloysius Boys' School, a private school based in Glasgow city centre, was a great influence on Winning. Each year the two schools would travel to Craighead Retreat Centre in Bothwell for an overnight retreat. Winning enjoyed the walks around the expansive gardens and the clandestine game of cards after light's out, but he would return home with a personal mantra, a prayer written by St Ignatius, the founder of the Jesuits, which was said before each talk:

> Lord, teach me to be generous, to serve you as you deserve.
> To give and not to count the cost,
> To fight and not to heed the wounds,
> To toil and not to seek for rest,
> To labour and not to ask for any reward
> Save for knowing that I do God's Holy Will.

On 3 September 1939, as Prime Minister Neville Chamberlain announced to the British nation that war had been declared on Germany, Winning was tossing balls at a coconut shy at Craigneuk fair with Patrick Macmillan, the son of the local doctor. World War

Two was to bring mixed fortunes to the family. Rationing meant the closure of Thomas Winning's confectionery sideline, but after twelve years of unemployment, he was given a job on the nearby Belhaven Estate. On the farm the unemployed men were put to work planting crops, tending sheep and milking cows for a set number of hours each day for which they were paid in farm produce.

Each 'pay day' Thomas Winning would return to his family laden with eggs, butter and buttermilk, prized possessions when the average family were entitled to just one egg a week. Conscious of the generosity of his in-laws over the past decade, he insisted on sharing the food around. The war effort also increased Winning's responsibilities. As the fighting drained the parish of able-bodied men, sent to serve overseas in the various armed forces, Fr Ward set up a monthly newsletter to keep them informed of parish life. Winning was conscripted to update and log all the addresses on file index cards and spend one day each month churning out copies using an early version of the Xerox machine.

In his fifth and sixth years at school, Winning remained reluctant to reveal his ambitions for the priesthood. He brushed away questions about his future plans and when once asked by a teacher what he wanted to do after leaving school, his surly response was, 'Get a job', an attitude that was swiftly admonished as cheek. In truth, he remained embarrassed by his ambition. Despite his doubts and poor start, he passed higher qualifications in English, German, Latin, and, incredibly, Mathematics. He followed these up by taking the prospective teacher's exam, a qualification similar to an A-level in religious studies and which acted as a convenient cloak for his true intent.

His choice of vocation had also clouded his relations with girls. In the 1930s and the early 1940s, very few boys of fifteen or sixteen had girlfriends but the prickly hormones of puberty meant the interest was there even if the contact was not. Winning was friendly with girls in the neighbourhood, pulled pigtails and even took to the floor when Our Lady's High met up with its sister school for girls for monitored dances, but there remained a certain careful detachment. 'He knew what he wanted to be and knew girls didn't come into it,' said Margaret.

When he was sixteen, Winning finally broke the news to his parents of his plan to study for the priesthood. Their response was quiet and subdued. They had expected this day to arrive. His role as an altar boy, his interest in Latin, his weekly chores for the church, were all part of a religious mosaic. His mother said very little, while his father asked only if he was sure of his plan and when Winning replied that he was the matter was closed.

Equipped with his parents' permission and the blessing of his parish priest, Winning's name was sent forward to the archdiocese of Glasgow and in early June 1942, Winning was invited for an interview. His father accompanied him on the bus trip to the large Victorian town house in the Park Circus area of Glasgow. Mr Winning waited outside while his son was questioned in the drawing room. The panel of five elderly priests charged with scrutinizing candidates asked him to read a passage of Latin prose by Cicero, the great Roman orator, and though they took exception to his pronunciation, it was deemed a pass. When asked why he wanted to become a priest, Winning replied sanctimoniously but effectively: he wished to leave the world a better place. Three weeks later he received a formal letter of acceptance and notification that his training would begin at St Mary's College, Blairs, the following autumn.

Winning was delighted and as the summer weeks crawled by his dreams and ambitions expanded to fill those empty days. One evening towards the end of the holidays, he sat on the step of his house beside his young cousin of seven, Mary Canning, turned to her, and said with (as she recalled) 'absolute certainty': 'I'm going to be the first Scottish pope.'

TWO

Blairs Bound

'They drained my self-esteem. I simply didn't have any.'
THOMAS WINNING

On the afternoon of 27 August 1942, Platform Two of Buchanan Street railway station in the centre of Glasgow resembled a convention of apprentice undertakers. Three dozen boys dressed in black suits, black coats and soft trilby hats stood waiting for the one o'clock train to Aberdeen. Ahead lay their first year at Blairs, as St Mary's seminary was commonly known, and around them hung an air of acute trepidation. Thomas Winning had perhaps more to fear than his fellow students. This was his first trip away from home and the thought of leaving behind his family had left him quite sick. His aunts and uncles had paid for his new wardrobe, the highlight of which was his first pair of football boots; but only his immediate family had come to wave him off. Before arriving at the station, Fr James Ward had taken them to Luigi's Fish and Chip Emporium as a final treat. The farewell on the platform was short and strained. Afterwards, the priest bought Winning's mother, father and sister tickets to see the film *How Green Was My Valley*, a popular weepy about a Welsh mining disaster, and told Margaret: 'You can get your tears out in the dark.'

On the train, Winning had the same emotions, but no such opportunity for release. Instead, he took a seat beside Maurice Taylor, a quiet boy one year younger than himself, with whom he had become friendly during his previous two years at Our Lady's

High School. The carriage was filled with boys who enjoyed the easy camaraderie that accompanied a secondary education at Blairs, a clique that left Taylor and Winning with the feeling of being outsiders. As the others talked, the pair mainly stared out of the window at the countryside's blur of browns and greens.

At five o'clock in the afternoon, the party arrived at Aberdeen's Central Station and spilled out for what was a Blairs' tradition – a high tea of scones and cress sandwiches at Kenaway's, the renowned delicatessen. A fleet of taxis was then organized to carry the boys and their trunks to the college, which sat five miles west of the city centre on the south Deeside Road. Rattling in the back of the black hackney, they crossed the bridge over the river Dee and, looking back, saw the spires of Aberdeen disappear into the distance. For many boys, the brief walk from the station to Kenaway's would be as much as they would see of the Granite City during their northern education. The temptations of Aberdeen were strictly out of bounds.

Father Stephen McGill greeted the party at the doors of the college. A small man with a clipped and careful manner and a pious spirituality many found sickly sweet, McGill had trained as a priest in France with the Order of St Sulpice, a group dedicated to the formation of aspirant priests, and would boast of having escaped the German invasion with only his typewriter and a pair of socks. He ushered them inside for a tour and what would become their traditional supper: a sweet tea, bluish in colour, and slices of bread and jam. The customary strict decorum was suspended for that first evening as the party were shown around their new home. Each student was allocated a plywood cubicle, seven feet by five feet, each with a bed and a small wooden stool. There was no door and only a curtain for privacy. The centre of the room also acted as their main recreational area and this meant that throughout the year the boys slept in the smoke-filled atmosphere. Winning sat on his bed and listened as the 'Decano', a senior student, shouted over the tops of all the cubicles that the following day they would be expected to dress in Roman collars and soutanes. The lights were then suddenly switched off, leaving Winning and his fellow students to unpack in the dark. He felt utterly alone. 'The first night was hellish,' said Winning. 'There was a certain harsh loneliness to the place.'

Winning and his fellow students were awoken at six o'clock by the morning bell and queued in silence for the 'jakes', as the toilets were called. Then, dressed in their black soutanes, they headed to the oratory for morning prayers and meditation, followed by Mass. Over a breakfast of porridge, tea and toast they were introduced to the Redemptorist priest who would lead them through their first few days. The priest, from a religious congregation founded in Naples in 1732, specialized in the administration of spiritual retreats, and each new intake of students began their formation at Blairs with a three-day silent retreat. As well as the traditional monastic vows of poverty, chastity and obedience the Redemptorists included a fourth, perseverance, an attribute they were keen to impress on the students at a time of confusion and doubt. Winning was reluctant to listen. 'If there had been a correspondence course I would have taken it. I found those days an ordeal.' The problem was the silence, a void that was quickly filled with doubts, unease and uncertainty. The long periods of contemplation and prayer were separated by a series of religious talks, opportunities for confession, and walks around the 'bounds' – a circuitous route through the attractive parkland in which the college sat. For Winning, it was the beginning of a long period of adjustment where he had to balance his desire to be a priest with the emotional rigours of the training.

Preparation for the priesthood at Blairs was run along monastic lines. Each day would begin and end enfolded within *magnum silencium*: the 'Grand Silence'. This restful time, when students were freed from the tug and pull of daily life and were thought to be more open to God's call, started with night prayers in the oratory and ran through until the beginning of breakfast. To break the silence was considered a grave error, one indicative of a lack of self-restraint, and grounds for the guilty student's dismissal. The college's regimented timetable was an attempt to ingrain discipline into the very hearts of the students.

Their days ran as follows:

6 a.m.	Rise, wash and bathe
6.30 a.m.	Morning prayer and meditation
6.55 a.m.	Mass
8 a.m.	Breakfast
9 a.m.	Lessons
12.40 p.m.	Spiritual talk
1 p.m.	Lunch
1.45 p.m.	Recreation
3 p.m.	Lessons
4.45 p.m.	Tea
5.30 p.m.	Private study
7.30 p.m.	Rosary
8 p.m.	Supper
8.30 p.m.	Free time
9.30 p.m.	Night prayers
10 p.m.	Lights out

At the time of Winning's formation, the priesthood retained an exalted and highly respected position both within the Catholic Church and across mainstream society. Priests were untarnished by scandal, unquestioned and reverently deferred to. As a spiritual descendant of his leader, Jesus Christ, a priest was no longer of the world; he had moved beyond it. He enjoyed a unique position, able to straddle both the ordinary and the divine. The power to transform unleavened bread into the actual body of Christ, and to administer or retain God's forgiveness at will was bestowed on him. A priest was not only in a position of patriarchal privilege, deferred to in society and enjoying great influence, sometimes even adoration, he was viewed as physically closer to God, and capable of wielding the supernatural. As Winning had read previously in *The Imitation of Christ*, 'High is the ministry and great the dignity of priests, to whom is given that which is not granted to the angels.' But such a privilege comes at a heavy price as Thomas A Kempis later explained: 'You have not lightened your burden; you are now bound by a stricter bond of discipline, and are obliged to a greater perfection of sanctity.'

There was little place for the individual in the role of the priest; through their training, seminarians were to be melted down and re-cast in a uniform mould. Priestly celibacy was viewed as both a practical necessity for men who were, in essence, married to God and to the Church, as well as an opportunity to radiate purity. As Fr Ronald Knox, a popular contemporary author, wrote in *The Priestly Life*, a priest should not have:

> the insensitivity of the bachelor who finds women a nuisance, not the furtive horror which tries to forget that sex exists, but something unapproachable, blinding, on a different plane from thoughts of evil. What a waste of God's gift, when the life that's pledged to celibacy is not a life irradiated by purity. What brooding regrets or cheap familiarities tarnish the surface of the mirror, which ought to reflect Christ?[1]

In the opinion of Fr Knox, the ground on which a priest's feet trod should be 'a part of the soil of heaven transplanted to earth'.

Before such a feat could be performed, seminarians would undergo a five-year course, two years of philosophy, followed by theology. Philosophy, it is said, is the handmaiden of theology, and before studying the latter, student priests were given a solid grounding in the former. At Blairs, the first-year class had four lecturers in the subject, led by Fr Philip Flanagan, who had spent two years until 1940 as vice-rector of the Scots College in Rome. Although the youngest of the lecturers, he was the most senior, taking lectures in ethics and cosmology. A second escapee from Europe was Fr Stephen McGill. He was assisted by Fr Hugh Cahill, lecturer in logic and psychology, a likeable man, nicknamed

'Domine' Cahill after his habit of addressing students by the Latin for 'Mr'. The faculty was completed by Fr John Sheridan, a brilliant academic whose only complaint was that his typewriter would not keep pace with his constant flow of essays and articles. He was an erudite speaker who would often spend an entire lecture on areas of cosmology and natural philosophy which were beyond even the brightest boy. For the first few months, Winning found the classes wearisome and a distraction from what he had in mind (which was the active service of others), but over time, he appreciated the clarity that the discipline brought to his life.

When his class was taught the works of René Descartes, the seventeenth-century French philosopher who stated: 'I think, therefore I am', Winning and the other students began to counter-argue, using the rules of logic to prove that they did not exist. Discussions during meals or what little social time was available had previously been light and casual, but now they took on a competitive edge. Loose talk was scrutinized for philosophical faux pas and anyone coming to a conclusion greater than the evidence will support was accused of breaking the laws of minor logic. Winning's teachers impressed upon him that a firm grasp of philosophy would allow him to discuss the deepest problems of human life with men and women of any (or no) religious persuasion. It also gently led to a clearer understanding of Catholic theology. Through the study of general metaphysics and ontology, Winning learned to probe below surface appearances and physical characteristics to the nature of being. He learned how to distinguish between matter and form and was able to explain the mystery of why the host, which after consecration becomes the body of Christ, doesn't taste of flesh, but remains instead brittle bread: in the language of metaphysics the 'accidents', the taste, the shape and texture, remain the same while the 'substance' is transformed by the power of God, working through his priest.

Winning grew to enjoy his philosophy classes, but the same was not to be said of his spiritual studies under the tutelage of Fr McGill, the year's spiritual director. 'I didn't particularly take to McGill as a spiritual director – he was just too sickly sweet for me. I didn't like his manner and he seemed to have absolutely no sense of humour.' McGill's field was viewed as the 'inner forum', the cultivation of the spiritual life. Each day, for twenty minutes, he was responsible for a series of religious talks that quickly became known as the 'starvation talks' among the students. Prayers were often said for the bell that signalled the beginning of lunch and the end of McGill's lecture.

Winning viewed McGill as a patron of popular psychology from their first meeting. Over later decades, the two men, as brother bishops, would become friends, in spite of their less than auspicious beginning.

Winning did not take easily to the more progressive methods of prayer. Although he experimented with both the Sulpician method which involved a rigid schedule of prayer, spiritual conferences and study, and the spiritual exercises of St Ignatius of Loyola, neither system truly matched his temperament. He found piety and overt holiness distasteful, almost insincere, and in many ways this was a throwback to his fear of being viewed as a 'sissy' or 'Holy Joe'. Instead, the rosary, the Our Father, daily attendance at Mass and periods of quiet contemplation, became the cornerstones of his early spirituality.

After the exercise of both the mind and the soul, the body came third. Every pupil was encouraged to walk for one hour each day in the company of two other students, chosen at random to prevent the curse of 'cronyism'. Wednesday and Saturday afternoons were set aside for football, and although Winning was delighted by his football boots, they were seldom worn, as he preferred the role of spectator to that of participant. He viewed the game of billiards as the sign of a misspent youth and would instead practise the piano while others played.

In Fr Flanagan's view, an appreciation of the arts was an important element in the education of a priest. He also believed that the charisma required to attract young people to Jesus Christ and the ability to project one's voice from the pulpit could best be nurtured on the stage. So each year the students were required to perform a play or musical from the canons of either Shakespeare or Gilbert and Sullivan. During Winning's time at Blairs *The Merchant of Venice* was chosen and he was cast in the role of Portia, the intelligent heroine but calculating deceiver, a casting coup he attributed to his good looks. Frank Cullen, who was cast as his Antonio, said: 'Tom wasn't a great actor, he was like the rest of us – we managed to mug through.'

Not everyone was as successful as Winning at masking their initial unhappiness. One morning in the spring of 1943, Winning discovered at breakfast that a fellow student was to abandon his studies. The doubts that everyone developed and so often brushed away had dragged Hugh Heslin down and he announced his immediate departure by slamming a tin of syrup on to the breakfast table and declaring, 'I'm off.' Heslin's departure had a shattering effect on Winning's confidence. His decision had appeared as if from nowhere and Winning began to wonder how firm were the foundations of his own vocation. Hadn't Hugh Heslin once thought the priesthood was his calling? Over the next few weeks, he grew increasingly concerned about the strength of his vocation.

The doubts coincided with the collapse of the water system at the college and the students returned to their homes for an unscheduled six-week break. The family house at Glasgow Road had been given up and Winning's parents and sister had moved to a larger property in Stewart Crescent, a ten-minute walk away. The house had originally been built by the husband of Kate Canning, sister of Winning's grandfather. While James Stewart and his wife lived in one section, the remainder had been rented out. For many years, Winning's father had acted as handyman for the elderly couple, and upon their death, he was rewarded with joint ownership, along with his cousin Patrick Canning.

The move, though unsettling, had its benefits. Winning was given the front parlour as his own private room for the duration of his stay, which he largely spent in study and visiting his various relatives.

He maintained the practice of daily attendance at Mass, but made his sister walk a few paces behind, lest gossips, unaware of their relationship, report his behaviour. He was grossly overreacting, but it was an action which illustrated his concerns and the need to tighten his grip against any possible lapse in his conduct.

The impromptu break was quickly followed by the summer holidays, and by the time of his return to Blairs at the end of August 1943, Winning had so long wrestled with his doubts that he had gained the upper hand. He returned to Blairs equipped with a new-found piety and determination, illustrated by his decision to start a diary. Throughout his life, Winning would regularly start a diary with the best of intentions only to abandon it after a few entries. A whole year would have only one or two entries, offering an odd isolated insight in a sea of empty pages.

A diary entry for 27 and 28 August 1943 contains the following: 'The master has recalled me to another year of prayer and labour but one of sweetness, for what sweeter thing is there than the knowledge that one is carrying out the will of Jesus Christ.'[2]

He continues in the purplish prose of the newly inspired:

> Soon autumn will arrive, if it has not already done so. The trees will be stripped of their foliage and they will stand desolate and naked against the cold winter blasts till spring invites them to don their former robes of healthy green and ripening fruit. So also must I strip myself of all my little tendencies to things of earth, the master has invited me to do so by calling me back. Then I must let grace enter my soul freely without hindrance and in the summer of my spiritual life of 1943–44 I will bear the fruits of my mortifications, my prayers and my labours which, unworthy though they be, will store up treasures for me in the land of the living . . .

If Winning was dwelling on God's infinite love, the rest of the world was engulfed by man's hate. In the evening during their hour of leisure time, the students listened to the BBC News and devoured the local Aberdeen *Press and Journal* for reports on the success of Montgomery in North Africa as well as the Americans' increased involvement. German bombers regularly flew on sorties from Norway, and although their principal targets were the shipyards of Glasgow and the west coast, they would regularly dump any remaining armaments on the northeast. When Aberdeen was targeted, the boys would retire to the bomb shelter built in the basement, while each student took it in turn to act as a fire watcher, staying up all night in order to keep track of enemy planes and report on any bombing close to the college.

For the first year and a half of Winning's stay at Blairs, the war in Europe carried the added fear that he might yet be called up to fight. Under the terms of an agreement negotiated by the Catholic Church at the beginning of the conflict, student priests were placed on the list of reserve professions. However, this was dependent on each student having clearly demonstrated his desire for a vocation prior to the outbreak of war. Technically, Winning should have been protected from the prospect of being forced to follow in his father's footsteps, but for the public-spirited contrariness of Archbishop Donald Mackintosh of Glasgow. He believed, in defiance of every other Scottish diocese, that only those admitted to the clerical state, following tonsure, the ceremonial cutting of hair after the third year of study, should be excused.

During Winning's first year, Mackintosh made a visit to the college, raising hopes that he might have changed his position. However, during an inspection of the Glasgow students, where he paraded past them delicately carrying a hankie, he said: 'I wish you joy', before asking how many had been tonsured. When only a few raised their hands, he sighed and said: 'The rest of you know the rules.' In other words, on their eighteenth birthday, they would be eligible for conscription and were expected to do their duty and fight for their country. Winning had no desire to exchange his soutane for combat fatigues, his meditation and studies for armed combat and the likelihood of an early death. He was proud of his father's contribution in the previous war, but had no desire to follow his lead. Winning turned eighteen in June 1943, but did not advertise the fact, on the grounds that if called up he would serve, but he would not volunteer his services. For six uncomfortable months he held his breath, then, in December 1943, Mackintosh died. With the unyielding archbishop removed, Fr James Ward was able to persuade the Diocesan Administrator that Winning should be exempt under the government's agreement. Ward was backed by Fr Alex Hamilton and together both men explained that Winning had wanted to train for the priesthood since he was a schoolboy in 1937, but that this had been postponed on their advice.

Maurice Taylor was not so fortunate. His parish priest was unable to vouch for his vocation prior to 1939 and so, in 1944, Taylor received his commission. However, it was with the medical corps, and the war was over by the time he was sent to India. Instead of tramping across the beaches of northern Europe with kit and gun, Winning was rolling the clay tennis courts at the college when news broke of the Allied invasion of Europe, but an endurance test of another sort lay ahead.

In the autumn of 1944, Winning and his class switched the relative comfort of Blairs for the harsher, more ramshackle facilities at St Peter's College in Bearsden, five miles to the north-east of Glasgow. After completing their two-year philosophy course, they were to begin their studies in theology. They had reached the Holy Land. Unfortunately, there was nothing virtuous about St Peter's College, as Winning quickly discovered. The building was decrepit and the staff critical to the point of abuse. It was to be a miserable year, the repercussions of which unfurled far into the future.

After the striking architecture of Blairs, St Peter's appeared rather bland by comparison. The college was approached off a main road, through a lodge gate, where it stood at the end of a long, curved drive. The atmosphere was set by the hill behind the college, branded the 'Hungry Hill' on account of its poor soil. The college was packed and rooms were scarce. The strict rule of seniority meant that older students enjoyed the luxury of rooms, while Winning and his friends studied in a disused cupboard. The actual sleeping quarters, or 'slum clearance' as they were known, had shaky walls, inadequate lighting and, along with the rest of the college, a feeling of decay. Dry rot was discovered in the refectory and so all meals were taken in the common room.

Tuberculosis had also begun to take grip. The stuffy atmosphere produced by the blackout conditions created a breeding ground for the bacillus, and a number of students fell seriously ill. In an attempt to combat the condition, the college gardener kept a goat and the sickest students were fed its milk. Frank Cullen secured his own room after the previous occupant died of the disease. As fresh air was the remedy recommended by staff, the students spent long hours out of doors working in the gardens or hiking along the 'Khyber Pass', the circuitous thirteen-mile walk along the foot of the Campsie Hills and back via the town of Milngavie.

Winning spent the time reflecting on his rapidly diminishing self-esteem. As a schoolboy on his front step, it had seemed impregnable, but any thought of achieving the papacy was replaced by the idea that at best he would be an inadequate priest. The cause of the crisis of confidence was that his education now took on a dismissive and caustic edge. At Blairs, the regime was rigorous and disciplined, but the lecturers remained friendly and encouraging. At Bearsden, there was a total separation of staff and students, they no longer joined each other at dinner, on the football field, or for a smoke over a game of billiards. The attitude of the staff was encapsulated by an incident later that winter when Winning returned from a walk in the snow and slipped in the corridor from ice on his heel just as he was passing a member of staff. Sprawled on the ground, he looked up just as the priest looked down, sneered, and walked away. 'You were a worm. They were distant, unsympathetic, and they failed to offer any encouragement,' said Winning.

Condemnation became standard teaching practice. The priest whom Winning found most ill-tempered and contemptuous was Fr John Conroy, a lecturer in moral theology, who viewed the world in terms of black and white. Frank Cullen described him as possessing a 'sneering and supercilious manner' and although he was tough on himself, the students believed he reserved his true bile for them. In classes, he dismissed them as lazy and ignorant. If the priesthood was already held in an exalted regard, Conroy cranked it a few notches higher. He inspired fear and conjured up a spectre of trouble. Winning felt that at any moment he could be branded an unsuitable candidate and sent home. Instead, he and the entire college were sent to London.

By the summer of 1945, the college in Bearsden was in such a state of disrepair that the hierarchy decided to close it down and allow the myriad faults to be tackled simultaneously. With space at a premium across Scotland, the students and teachers were forced to relocate to St Joseph's Missionary College, close to Hendon aerodrome in the Mill Hill area of London, twelve miles from the city centre. The disconsolate air of Bearsden was unfortunately also packed up and shipped south.

The college was the principal centre of education for the Mill Hill Fathers, a religious order founded a hundred years earlier by Bishop (later Cardinal) Vaughan, and the Scots were blamed for the current overcrowding. The students were unpopular with their hosts. Talk during breakfast was banned and instead they were forced to listen in silence as a senior priest read out chunks of *The Imitation of Christ* in French, followed by an English translation, which was scarcely an aid to digestion.

Father Conroy, meanwhile, grew increasingly dictatorial; he launched a series of talks each Sunday evening, which Winning believed served no greater purpose than to censure the clergy. Each student was also expected to spend thirty minutes every day in manual labour. When given a choice, Winning opted for tailoring in the belief that he would be stitching 'loin clothes for wee black kids'. Instead, he had to darn holes in trousers belonging to members of staff. Even visits to central London were prohibited, along with any visits to private homes. On one occasion, Winning broke the rule. Their daily constitutionals took Winning and his two colleagues to Edgware, close to the home of his mother's cousin, William Canning. The three boys paid a visit, but Winning was unable to enjoy the reunion for fear that the visit would be discovered. On this occasion he was lucky. But three other friends who decided to sneak a visit to Madame Tussaud's waxworks were less fortunate. Riding on the tube home, the trio were spotted by the vice-rector and promptly expelled.

On 13 May 1946, a workman, tackling repairs to the roof of St Peter's College, accidentally set it alight. The fire quickly spread, gutting the main building but providing a spark of good fortune for the brighter students. In order to combat overcrowding, the decision was taken to reopen, as quickly as possible, the foreign colleges in Spain, France and Rome. Two weeks after the fire, Fr James Ward wrote to Winning with the promise of escape:

My Dear Tom,
By now you will have heard the sad news of the destruction of Bearsden College – to us here it was like the death of a dear friend. Fortunately no lives were lost, the chapel is saved – it is a strange affair, but God's will [and] that is exactly how His Grace has accepted it. Now, let me whisper something in your ear (not for anybody else) – I'm glad you want to go to Rome because you are definitely going, along with seven others – you see, my undercover man has really been busy, eh? You do know that I would not joke about this, don't you? I am thrilled that you have been chosen to go to Rome and am really proud of your success – thank the Good God for his kindness to you, thank him to keep you humble as you have always been – that virtue is the secret of your success. I am sure that Jack will be delighted when I tell him and will be able to give you some knowledge of the life there ... Congratulations on your good fortune – don't forget your dear pal!
Best love and prayers,
Jim

Winning was delighted. He was bound for the centre of the Catholic universe. Rome carried not only a reputation as the training ground for the brightest of students, but held out the promise of a wonderful cultural experience. The basilica of St Peter's, the frescos of Michelangelo, the presence of the Pope – what he had previously only read about in the inky pages of the *Catholic Observer* he was about to witness for real. The question he continued to nurture in his mind, however, was: could he cope?

THREE

To the City by the Tiber

'Perhaps the most intimate quality of Roman formation is the personal love and loyalty it nurtures for the Vicar of Christ and the Holy See.'[1]

THOMAS WINNING

When Pope Clement VIII founded the Scots College in Rome in the year 1600, his goal was more than just the provision of education for the sons of Catholic noblemen condemned to a strictly Protestant schooling since the Reformation forty years before. A leading pope of the Counter-Reformation, Clement VIII now wished for a foundry for casting Catholic agents whose ambition was to overthrow the might of Protestantism in Scotland and return the nation to the faith of their fathers and their fathers before them.

At first the Scots College, which opened in 1602 with eleven students on its roll, was principally an educational establishment where the sons of noblemen were taught good morals, piety, sound doctrine and Christian values without having to make any promise to join the priesthood. Yet when control came into the hands of the Jesuits a decade later, it took little over a year to convert the college into a seminary. The catalyst was the first anniversary in 1615 of the execution of John Ogilvie, a Jesuit hanged at Glasgow's Tollcross for refusing to swear allegiance to the Crown.

At the time, the students were asked to sign an oath promising to receive holy orders and return to Scotland as missionaries. The popular story is that the anniversary was enough to galvanize all fifteen students to sign up, but in truth only five oaths were ever discovered. Over the past three centuries, many students have taken advantage of the college's excellent education, but failed to emerge with a clerical collar.

By the eighteenth century, the college became a hotbed of Jacobitism as hopes of a restoration of a Catholic monarchy ignited. They rested on Prince Charles Edward Stuart, Bonnie Prince Charlie, who was born and educated in Rome. A legitimate heir to the throne, he was prevented from ever succeeding by the Act of Settlement, put in place in 1701 to ensure the Protestant Hanoverian succession passed over the Stuarts, though his ill-fated campaign in 1745 carried the hopes of the college students. When he returned to the city in 1766, following the death of his father, Prince Charles, he received a welcome befitting a monarch from the college rector, later summarily dismissed by the Pope, who, on grounds of *Realpolitik*, refused to recognize the Young Pretender.

From almost its earliest days, the Scots College has enjoyed a desirable address, sitting close to the Quattro Fontane, the road of the Four Fountains, high on the Quirinal, one of the seven hills that make up the Eternal City. The original property was knocked down and in 1869 a new college was built a few hundred yards away on a street with the gradient of a toboggan run. As the Quattro Fontane was the principal route to the papal palace, for over three centuries Scots students would watch as kings, queens and the royalty of Europe arrived to pay their respects.

In the early twentieth century, the palace was home to Italy's King and, just before the Second World War, students watched as Hitler and Goebbels drove towards a meeting with Mussolini. One contemporary diarist at the college commented how easily he could have lobbed a bomb. It was a thought shared by the Italian partisans, who, in March 1944, planted a bomb in a bin at the college's back door on the Via Rasella. The device detonated and killed thirty-two passing members of the Waffen SS. Upon hearing the news, Hitler demanded that the entire quarter be razed, but Field Marshal Kesselring, the country's commander-in-chief, insisted on a more emotive act of retribution. He had 320 men rounded up from the surrounding streets, marched to the Ardeatine caves outside the city, and shot – ten men for every dead German. At the time, the college's caretaker, Lorenzo Martinelli, narrowly escaped with his life after hiding among the Italian orphans, now based within the college.

The lynching of Mussolini, Germany's defeat and the triumph of the Allies in 1945 left the college's rector, Mgr William Clapperton, anxious to return to Rome from his exile in Scotland. Appointed in 1922, Clapperton was almost sixty and could be cantankerous and brisk with underlings but he was proud of his achievements at the college. The son of a Justice of the Peace from a Catholic enclave in Banffshire, he earned a First in Classics at Durham University before studying in Rome, a city he would never truly leave. At the Scots College, he bounded up the career ladder from head boy to vice-rector, then rector at the age of thirty-six.

The death of Archbishop Mackintosh of Glasgow in 1943 had robbed him of his great supporter and left the Archbishop of St Andrews and Edinburgh, James McDonald, the senior cleric in the country. A man with little respect for the college, McDonald preferred instead to send promising students to Cambridge. His intention was to maintain the college as a distant outpost populated by a few egg-headed postgraduates, but Clapperton's resistance and a strongly worded letter from Cardinal Pizzardo at the Vatican's Congregaton of Seminaries produced the desired effect. In May 1946, it was finally agreed to reopen the college and in July, Clapperton was flown by the British Government's Transport Command to Rome to make the necessary arrangements.

The essence of the Scots College is contained in the lyrics of the college song, written in 1900 as part of the institution's tercentenary celebrations. The author was John Gray, a published poet, novelist and Englishman. Gray had been a former lover of Oscar Wilde, who named his most celebrated character, Dorian Gray, after him in order to capture his affections. Accepted by the college as a mature student, Gray put away what he viewed as the errors of his youth and rose to be a canon and secretary of the Scots College society. The song runs:

> From the land of purple heather, from the dear and distant north,
> Scotland casts our lot together, Bonnie Scotland sends us forth,
> To the city by the Tiber, to the height of St Peter's Dome,
> To bear the bright tradition back of everlasting Rome.
>
> Here's a hand and faith behind it, here's my love till death shall
>   part;
> Give yours and I will bind it, with the dearest of my heart.
>
> So land and kin forsaking, for Scotland's faith grown cold
> For her valiant spirit aching, with the wound they wrought of old:
> In faith and heart united all in happy exile one,
> That Scotland's wrong be righted, so that Scotland's work be done.
>
> We foot the fervent traces of those that went before,
> Adorned with gifts and graces from our Alma Mater store:
> So sing the Careful Mother for a tribute to her worth,
> For to find so good another we might journey all the earth.
>
> For aye the gaps supplying she draughts her study bands,
> To keep her colours flying in the best of bonnie lands:
> The men she taught to cherish all she knows or ever knew;
> The hope that cannot perish Romans all and Scotsmen true.

To the accompaniment of these words, Winning and thirty other students arrived, under the supervision of Fr Philip Flanagan, at Rome's Stazione Termini on the afternoon of 18 October 1946. The college's vice-rector had taught them the words as an antidote to the tedium of their three-day journey – by rail from Glasgow to London, by boat from Dover to Calais, and by train once again via Paris to Rome. The devastation of central Europe, following six years of war, was visible from the carriage windows and the volume of ruined bridges and rail lines buckled by bombs reduced their progress to a crawl. Winning was to spend the first leg of the journey attempting to cheer up a fellow student, who would become one of his dearest friends. Charles 'Donny' Renfrew had been raised by two aunts, following the death of his mother, and the day before departure one of them had been killed by a passing tram. With the date of departure fixed and the journey viewed as impossible for a solitary seventeen-year-old, Renfrew was prohibited from attending the funeral. When not attempting to raise Renfrew's spirits, Winning was at work on his own. A painful stomachache, written off as a bad case of nerves by his parents, developed during the course of the journey into a series of stabbing pains that left him pale and withdrawn. The train's arrival in northern Italy was accompanied by a splitting headache, one that powdered Asket mixed with Vichy water was unable to tame. The party then stopped in the city of Turin to visit the tomb of St John Bosco, founder of the pious Society of St Francis de Sales (the Salesians). John Bosco was the patron saint of youths and author of many of the pamphlets Winning had previously sold door to door. It was while in Turin that Winning first encountered Italian food. What was in fact to develop into a lifelong love affair did not begin well: he was unable to twirl the spaghetti, the veal Milanese was mistaken for fish in breadcrumbs, and the spicy tomato sauce exacerbated his tender stomach.

The party's final approach to Rome was heralded by one student's cry that he had spotted the Colosseum, which later turned out to be a gasometer.

On the platform to greet them stood Mgr Clapperton and Fr Gerry Rogers, a tall, handsome priest from Glasgow who had arrived in Rome for further study in the field of canon law at the Roman Rota. Together as a happy band they made the short trip to the college by bus, along the Via Volturno, where British troops in khaki uniforms and bolt-action rifles patrolled the streets. At the Scots College, Lorenzo Martinelli had dusted down the cassocks he had hidden for the duration of the war. Winning was now to experience his own taste of Italian style, a uniform that consisted of a purple soutane, red sash, and black university-style gown called a soprana, an ensemble that was then topped by a black broad-brimmed hat, nicknamed the soup bowl.

Once dressed, the boys were given a tour of their new home. The kitchen and refectory were on the ground floor, the first floor housed both the library and the offices of the rector, while the second floor contained red damask-covered chairs and the valuable paintings of the drawing room. The student rooms were tucked away on the third floor. Winning's room was small, basic and tiled in black and white. Its only accoutrements were a bed, a wardrobe, desk and chair, and an enamel basin, jug and pail. There was a solitary light in the ceiling and a cube of sunlight would sneak in through the window high in the wall. A shower room sat at the end of the hall, where each day he would collect water to wash.

Over the next few days, Winning began to familiarize himself with his new surroundings. A trip was organized by Fr Rogers to the catacombs of San Callisto and Winning, along with a few other students, wandered through the ancient passageways where the first Christians and early popes were buried. As impressive as the frescos and stucco work of San Callisto were the contents of the bakers' windows to students starved of cakes and éclairs and subsisting on meagre food with little charm. Rationing was in force and the rector was struggling to secure adequate provisions; a situation that led to the Vatican sending over supplies of bread and pasta. Yet still the students would retire to bed hungry.

The cold was another persistent problem. The students arrived in the middle of October, when the days should have remained sunny and warm, but the worst winter that century had arrived for a long stay. The long cassocks worn by the students were valuable insulation against the cold, as were the silk stockings into which their trousers were tucked (as the college rules insisted). Until his death, Winning still possessed the silk stockings bought at great expense by his mother. He said: 'It was so cold that first year and the building was so old that the cold seeped into your bones. I remember wrapping anything I could find round my legs to keep me warm.'

*   *   *

In 1946, Pope Pius XII, christened Eugenio Pacelli, had resided on the throne of St Peter for seven years, since the very eve of war. A skilled diplomat, he had previously worked as papal secretary of state and negotiated concordats with both Austria and National Socialist Germany, agreements which lent Hitler international prestige at a crucial time, but which the dictator would later break. Throughout the war, Pius XII had repeatedly argued for peace, but refused to condemn the specific genocide of the Jews, preferring to protect the Vatican from possible destruction by the use of the broadest of strokes. Yet for all the condemnation that would accrue after his death, Pope Pius XII attracted universal devotion during his long life. He would become Winning's favourite pope, a relationship triggered by the student's first glimpse of the ethereal pontiff, who more than any previous incumbent offered a glimpse of the divine.

The first time Winning saw Pius XII was on the Sunday after his arrival in October 1946. The students had been informed that a beatification ceremony was to take place that evening at St Peter's, and those who chose to could attend. Winning made his way to St Peter's Square accompanied by three other students, where they were recognized as Scots through the purple of their tunics by an elderly priest. 'Wonderful! You are back in Rome,' he commented, before introducing himself as a retired bishop of Malta and insisting they all accompany him as his 'secretaries' to the front of St Peter's Basilica. As they walked along the vast, marble-encrusted interior, crammed with chapels, altars and precious works of art, Winning was visibly taken aback, an emotion that would only deepen with the appearance of the Pope.

They waited almost an hour in the pews, where the bishop interspersed his prayers with a brief history of the building. Both students and host fell silent when hundreds of crystal chandeliers throughout the church unexpectedly sparked into life, to be followed a few seconds later by sonorous peals from silver trumpets. The Pope's arrival was further heralded by the choir singing 'Tu es Petrus' (You are Peter), while musicians played the pontifical march written by Vittorino Hallmayr, an Austrian regimental band director. The crowds then cheered. The first thing Winning saw was the plumed steel helmets of the Swiss Guard, advancing with raised halberds, the striking combination of spear and axe, and a chamberlain in traditional ruff. Then, high above their heads, seated on the Sedia Gestatoria, the great portable chair carried on the shoulders of robed men, was Pius XII. He had a rake-like appearance and the ghostly pallor of one who eats frugally. His fixed stare, shuttered behind round wire-rimmed glasses, was that of a man who could see past his audience, beyond this world and into the next. For the duration of his carriage, he was fanned by ostrich feathers and he in turn continually blessed those present by making a rigid sign of the cross. 'He had an almost mystical image. I felt overawed by the experience,' said Winning. He remembered the evening and the many future audiences he would attend, when he wrote in 1964:

> Perhaps the most intimate quality of Roman formation is the personal love and loyalty it nurtures for the Vicar of Christ and the Holy See. In Rome the student lives under the shadow of Peter, close to Christ's visible head. Every student has his favourite Pope; it is usually the one he first saw and knew on coming to Rome. Instead of being simply a man or a catechism answer, the Holy Father is a living person.

Two years later, in 1948, Winning and a group of Scots students attended a private audience with Pius XII. They were not permitted to speak but instead they each knelt before him and kissed his ring as a sign of loyalty and devotion; in return, they received an individual blessing and a group photograph. Fifty-one years later, Winning fulfilled his vow when John Cornwell, the Cambridge scholar and author, published *Hitler's Pope*, a critical biography of Pius XII that viewed him as an anti-Semite who did little to protect the Jews. In a robust defence in the opinion pages of the *Daily Telegraph*, Winning argued that Pius XII had been fearful of further antagonizing the Nazis who would then turn the screws tighter on the Jews. 'Would history have judged Pius differently if he had hurled anathemas at Hitler's regime, and wallowed martyr-like in the blood of his own people and the Jewish people?'[2] He went even further and contacted the priest in charge of furthering Pius XII's beatification and offered every assistance in the defence of his hero's crumbling reputation. This was to become a typical response from Winning who would mentally edit evidence, dismissing or reducing Pius XII's obvious anti-semitism and embracing the line that best supported the Church: a position that painted him as an ultra-loyalist, prepared to swallow the party line and regurgitate it when so called upon.

Winning and his colleagues departed the ceremony at around five o'clock and spotted seminarians in the scarlet cassock of the German College. Winning took the lead in approaching them in a gesture of peace, but his noble effort was unnecessary; each student was from Hungary, though based at the German-Hungarian college. As Latin was the only common tongue they began to quiz each other as they walked home. Josef Bistyo, one of the Hungarian students, explained how he had deserted from the army and walked for weeks until he reached Rome. Unable to speak the language he would rub his stomach when hungry. Winning and Bistyo became friends and for the duration of their university years they spent each morning break talking in Latin, so that they would become fluent in the language of the classroom and their textbooks.

If Winning's devotion to the papacy was fuelled by his first sight of Pius XII, his template for the priesthood was formed by the lecturers at the Gregorian University, the West Point of the Catholic Church. If Oxford University in England had a propensity to produce prime ministers, the Pontificia Universita Gregoriana produced popes; ten during the previous four hundred years, including Pius XII. Originally founded as the Collegio Romano by Ignatius of Loyola, it was upgraded to a university by Pope Gregory XIII in 1582 and became an incubator for the Church's elite. The original building, constructed from a handsome honeyed stone, and situated in the old town, was confiscated during the Reunification of Italy in the 1880s. Mussolini granted permission for a new building to be built in 1929, a feat completed with Fascist punctuality in

1931. So it was to the Piazza della Pilota, a ten-minute walk from the Scots College along the Via Rasella, that Winning arrived in November 1946. The Scots College was comparable to a contemporary hall of residence, with Winning's actual education taking place at the university under the tutelage of the Jesuits.

The first day brought a problem. After examining the Scots students' previous course of study, the authorities decided that it was necessary for Winning to repeat a year of theology. It was a decision which meant the misery of Mill Hill was compounded by being regarded by Rome as a waste of time. He was initially disappointed, but grew to be grateful for the extra time, relishing the dynamism within the university. Each day, 2,500 students drawn from over 200 colleges and religious orders or communities gathered at the 'Greg' to learn from 110 professors. The lecture theatres had raised banks of seats, each with a hinged desktop, and on the ground floor stood the professors who led them through dogmatic theology, fundamental theology and moral theology. A German student who sat in front of Winning in a number of classes was so enamoured with particular lecturers that he would sneak a camera from his leather satchel and take their picture. Winning said: 'He never bothered with the boring ones. Rome and the Greg were so full of great people he did not need to.'

Their teachers were contemporary stars such as Heinrich Lennerts, a German who taught dogmatic theology and explained to Winning the nature of the Trinity, the power of grace and the workings of the Holy Spirit, while also writing speeches for Pius XII. Maurizio Flick was an Italian Jesuit who taught moral theology and focused on the theology of the cross, a subject on which he would later write a celebrated book. Winning's personal favourite was Sebastian Tromp, a Dutch Jesuit who was the principal author of Pius XII's encyclical, 'Mystici Corporis', issued in June 1943. During classes Tromp would joke, 'As we said in our encyclical . . . excuse me, as the Holy Father said in his encyclical.' Winning was inspired by their quiet and usually humble nature, unexpected from men of such intelligence and achievement. On one occasion, he bumped into Charles Voyers, the French Jesuit who was an acclaimed humanist and pioneer of the ecumenical movement. Winning was able to give him a spare ticket for a papal event. 'He thanked me profusely and I would think these are the kinds of guys I want to be. He was a world-famous theologian, but very humble.'

Winning's attempts to become such a 'guy' were aided by his tremendous stamina for work, combined with a comprehensive style of study. He would never use three textbooks, where a fourth might offer a more illuminating passage. At the college he would consistently study past midnight, despite the threat of a five o'clock rise. Eugene Matthews, a postgraduate student of canon law, said: 'I thought he was very unwise and pushed himself much too hard.' Since Rome was regularly bedevilled by power-cuts, this meant most of Winning's studies were conducted by candlelight. Commenting on his study methods, Charles Renfrew said: 'He read a lot in bed at night. The rest of us would have one or two books ... Tom would have fourteen books and they'd all have markers sticking in them. I used to say: "Can I take away thirteen of those and let you finish one?"'[3]

For all the breadth of his study and the depth of influence brought to bear by the current pope and the teachings at the university, Winning was still able to carry his own personal experiences into the classroom. One unmarked exam paper was to have a growing consequence for his concept of social justice, which became more radical as he aged. During Winning's second term, a lecturer asked the question, was it right to steal if you were starving? Winning drew on the poverty of his childhood and viewed the answer as simple: clearly it was better to save your life than die in obedience to the law. Outside of the class, he discussed his answer with other students and discovered that he was the only one to answer yes. Yet as the papers were never corrected his position was never challenged. 'I asked the older fellows and they would shake their heads; but I felt they damn well needed to experience it.'

The experience of a Roman education was one of the gifts for which Winning would most often thank God. After the demoralizing drudgery of his British education, his experience in the Italian capital was one of levity and an unexpected liberalism. True, there were strict rules regarding many of the quintessential Italian experiences: the smoky bars of Trastevere, the chic restaurants of the Borgo Pio, the Opera House and theatre were all proscribed under threat of expulsion. But the museums, the churches, the Colosseum and the millennia of culture remained on permanent display and through the mandatory daily walk, designed to ensure the body remained as fit as the mind, Winning witnessed them all.

The Scots College, under the firm reign of Mgr William Clapperton, was reasonably contented. The rector preferred one rule for all, rather than having exceptions, and Winning found the college the most relaxed of all the establishments he had been in. 'If you were caught smoking in Bearsden, you would be fired. But if you were caught smoking in Rome, the rector would just say: "Don't put the cigarettes down the washbasin sink."'

Clapperton could be boorish at times with his own staff, but he was remembered fondly by students for the balance he brought to their education. For instance, students were encouraged to drink wine with their meals; a pleasure denied to Winning who was now nursing the beginnings of a stomach ulcer that would trouble him for the next twenty years. Should a student become 'puggled' through drink, it would pass once without comment but a lesson was considered learned. However, as the wine was consistently watered down, such an occasion occurred only rarely.

Winning was called before Clapperton a number of times and reprimanded for his untidy dress and tardy arrival at morning prayer, but he held him in some affection. The rector was at his most unpopular during the monthly film nights, organized by Eugene Matthews with the assistance of Warner Brothers and MGM, who had offices in Rome. As a result of Clapperton's poor hearing, he would ask for a running commentary. Rome was the type of city that attracted Hollywood stars and on one occasion, shortly after watching a Tyrone Power picture, Winning spotted the actor with Linda Christian, a leading actress of the day, posing for pictures by the Trevi fountain.

Clapperton reserved his most spectacular outbursts for the college football team. Before the war the Scots never lost their annual match against the English college; after the war they never won. Winning was an ineffectual player and rarely strayed on to the pitch; instead he preferred to remain on the sidelines and revelled in the Celtic match reports sent from home. He once took the opportunity to canonize Celtic's entire first team. Each day at 12.45 p.m., the students filed into the college chapel to perform the Litany of Saints, a prayer in which they petitioned the help of the Church's saints and martyrs. As Winning was leading the chant, and in the absence of either rector or vice-rector, he substituted the names of the saints for players such as George Hazlett, Konrad Kapler and William Gallacher.

Winning was frequently late. His tardiness provoked the ire of Clapperton, and caused his fellow students to moan with frustration. The amateur dramatics common at Blairs had been revived in Rome. Rehearsals were scheduled between eight o'clock and nine-thirty each evening, and Winning was perpetually late, reluctant to don a frock once again.

During his three years in Rome he would go on to perform as Calpurnia and Lady Macbeth, but he was allowed to retain his own sex in the operas of Gilbert and Sullivan. 'We all assembled at the right time, but he was always late. He would get impatient and he'd say, "Why the hell do we have to say this?"' said Charles Renfrew. Roddy Macdonald, another contemporary, said, 'He wasn't Laurence Olivier, but he worked hard, he made an effort.' The productions were performed each Christmas when, for a few nights, the English-speaking colleges in Rome became a cabaret circuit with the students performing one evening, spectating the next. The life of a 'poor player' had its downside, when on more than one occasion Winning had to visit a chemist, dressed in his soutane, to request nail-polish remover.

In July 1947, in a tradition dating back over three hundred years, the college closed down and everyone, staff, students and servants, travelled the twelve miles from the baking heat of the city centre to the relative cool and shade of the mountains. A stone house had been purchased in 1654 in an idyllic spot outside the hill town of Marino, which offered wonderful views out across the Sabine Hills on one side, and the blue of the Mediterranean on the other. The original Villa Scozzese had long since crumbled and had been replaced in 1925 with a modern two-storey structure, complete with an elegant courtyard and a bell tower which commanded views across the parched plains to Rome and up to the summit of Monte Cavo. The leisure facilities were those of an upmarket country hotel and included a swimming pool, tennis court and acres of vineyards, where, as Winning remembered, 'you could pick bunches of grapes as big as a bucket'.

Upon arrival, the students' and staff's first priority was to inspect for any war damage, as the villa had been rented by the Italian Air Force before being converted into a German command post for the local area. It was in this capacity that Field Marshal Kesselring, commander-in-chief of Italy, had visited. Monsignor Clapperton discovered that what the Germans had lent with their right hand, they had stolen back with their left: new pumps had been fitted to ensure a steady water supply, the roads had been kept in good repair, and a mechanical wine press had been installed in the cantina. Upon their retreat, however, they had taken all the beds and mattresses, and ripped out the stoves they had fitted, leaving, as Clapperton recalled, 'only the holes in the walls to greet us'.[5] The compensation the college eventually received failed to cover the cost but, as Clapperton felt, 'It was summer, we were back at the villa, and it felt good to be alive.'

In previous centuries, summer visits to the Villa Scozzese had been restricted to just six weeks, but now with exams over, the university closed until October, and visits to Scotland restricted to just one every three years, the house was to be home for almost three months. The students settled into a long summer of hiking, swimming, tennis and only the lightest of studies. The rector ran a morning class, studying Dante's *Inferno* in the original Italian and there was the rosary and Benediction each evening. Yet Winning was to tolerate his visits to the villa as opposed to truly enjoy them.

A lifetime's fear of indolence was born during the two summers he spent at Marino. On future holidays for the rest of his life, he would plan and pack each day with excursions or visits, unable to simply slouch. 'I felt it made you soft,' said Winning, of his drowsy Italian summers. He was also stricken with pangs of homesickness and would climb the bell tower to watch the planes he imagined were bound for Scotland. To keep himself busy, Winning began teaching a daily German class for any students who could muster the enthusiasm to attend.

Some days, however, were easier to endure than others. The rector enjoyed the sea and regular trips were organized to Netuno on the coastline. A lorry was hired and the students would climb into the back for the short trip. The villa's servants would also travel down to prepare a large lunch at a beachside restaurant that they would take over for the day.

One incident Winning remembered with bemusement was the arrest of Constantino, the villa's chef. He had already embarrassed himself by making a drunken speech in honour of dead Fascists. This took place when the students had attempted to pray before a memorial to the Gordon Highlanders who fell at the Anzio beach-head. A few days later, a second incident occurred on the occasion of Marino's annual festival, when the townsfolk travelled the neighbouring vineyards collecting grapes so that the town's fountain would spout wine. After the ceremony, Constantino returned to the villa to prepare supper, but instead of simply serving the meat dishes and departing, he insisted on blowing a kazoo repeatedly in the rector's face. He was arrested the next day with two stories circulating (both of which may or may not be true), one that he had killed a man while serving Mussolini during the war, another involving the theft of a cow.

In the summer of 1947, the students were joined for a few weeks by the Scots bishops, who had arrived in Rome for the Ad Limina, the report they deliver every five years to the Pope and the various Vatican departments. Their arrival had an effect on Winning's future as he learned that the archdiocese of Glasgow would be split to create two smaller dioceses, centred around the towns of Paisley in the west and Motherwell in the east. Although Winning remained a student for the diocese of Glasgow, he now knew he would not serve there as a priest, as his address lay within the new diocese of Motherwell. The students returned to the college in October, narrowly missing the collapse of the top-floor ceilings.

In the autumn of 1947 and spring of 1948, Winning was an interested spectator in an unprecedented campaign by the Catholic Church in the national politics of Italy. The cause was in opposition to the growing strength of the Communist Party under the remarkable leadership of Palmiro Togliatti, a native Italian who had spent the war years sheltering in Moscow. Togliatti was a natural politician, aware that Italians had no desire to swap Mussolini for Stalin, and so he developed a distinctly Italian form of Communism, one capable of drawing ten thousand spectators to hear him speak. He had already been expelled from the coalition government during the spring, at the behest of Washington, and now with a general election planned for May 1948, he stood as a potential Prime Minister.

While the American government publicly threatened to withdraw the benefits of the Marshall Plan from Italy, in the event of a Communist victory, privately they pumped in $5 million through the fledgling Central Intelligence Agency to the Christian Democrats and anti-Communist trade unions to prevent any such victory occurring. Hundreds of thousands of posters began appearing for the Christian Democrats, showing a skeleton in a Soviet uniform with the shoutline: 'Vote – or he'll be your boss.' A pastiche of such posters appeared on walls of the Scots College, during the election of the new debating chairman. Yet it was the power of the Pope which arguably swung the election. On 8 February 1948, Pius XII met with Professor Luigi Gedda, leader of Catholic Action, a Vatican-backed lay movement, which operated in a number of European countries to educate men (and a few women) about Catholic social teaching with the idea that they would influence society for the better, and charged him with the task of preventing a Communist takeover.

Pius XII denounced the Communists whom he detested for their atheism, and threatened any Catholic who sided with the party with excommunication, and Gedda set up a Civic Committee in 1,800 parishes across the country. These distributed propaganda posters and screened films depicting the Communists as godless and evil. From the balcony of his papal apartment, Pope Pius asked the gathered crowds, which included Winning, 'Do you want to live under the atheism of Russia? Do you want to be disciples of Christ?' A week prior to the election, while Winning was on a short break in Siena with Charles Renfrew and Eugene Matthews, Italian seminarians across the country removed their cassocks, dressed as laity, and actively campaigned for the Christian Democrats. On 18 April 1948, the Church's pressure bore fruit: the Christian Democrats proved victorious. The Church's achievement would resonate with Winning, who would never forget the potential for influence which existed within the Catholic Church, though at the time he questioned the effects on democracy. His conclusion, however, was that a Communist victory would have had even greater, more serious consequences.

The date of Winning's ordination as a priest was set for 18 December 1948. As he was still only twenty-three years old, one year below the permitted age, a special dispensation was sought and granted. Prior to the ceremony, he embarked, as was customary, on a one-week retreat to reflect on the honour and burden about to be bestowed on him. Winning and Hugh McEwan, a fellow Scot whose ordination was set for the same date, spent their retreat at the Jesuit headquarters a few hundred yards from St Peter's Square. There they met their former scripture professor, Fr Josef Mochsi, a Hungarian Jesuit, who was composing a report for the Vatican on Communist Hungary. The priest wished them both well, but asked that they pray for him as he would be returning to Budapest shortly and arrest was inevitable. Winning promised to offer his first Mass for the priest, who one month later was imprisoned by the Communist authorities.

Maurice Taylor had reconvened his priestly training in Rome on the completion of his military service, and it was he who visited the Jesuits' headquarters and told Winning the location of the ordination. Unfortunately, the Church of the Twelve Apostles was an ordinary, unflattering site – entirely undesirable in the opinion of Winning – for hosting such a service. He insisted Taylor change the mind of the bureaucrat at the Vatican office who had made the decision. Winning wanted the ceremony to take place at the Basilica of St John Lateran, the grandest church in Rome after St Peter's, and the site where he had previously received his minor orders. The self-regard of such a statement is one that verges almost on arrogance and illustrates that behind Winning's doubts and occasional crises in confidence, there actually lay a strong bedrock of self-confidence. It is hard to imagine any Scots seminarian before or since who would deem a particular venue as unsuitable for his own ordination. Incredibly, Taylor was successful and Winning's presumptuous wish was granted. On the appointed day, he arrived before dawn for a ceremony that began at half past six and would last over six hours.

Among the packed congregation was an extended delegation from Winning's family. Thomas Winning senior had decided to sell his sweet-making machines in order to raise the necessary funds for himself, his wife and daughter to attend. Eight other relatives, including aunts, uncles and cousins, decided to make what was in 1948 a once-in-a-lifetime opportunity, not only to witness Winning's ordination, but also to see the sights of Rome. The church, with its stunning marble statues and fourteenth-century frescos, did not disappoint. In total, thirty-nine priests and a whole host of minor orders were ordained that morning by Archbishop Luigi Traglia.

Winning attempted to focus all his attention on what was to come. God, working through the Holy Spirit, was only moments from descending upon him. At the altar, the elderly archbishop laid both his hands on his head and began to utter the prayers of ordination which stretch back two thousands years to Christianity's earliest days. After praying that the Holy Spirit would touch Winning with his gifts, Traglia anointed his hands with the oil of

Christ, the sacred oil of olives once used in the coronation of kings and a symbol of the Holy Spirit. It was these hands which would now be able to administer the sacraments of the Church, turn wine into blood, and unleavened bread into the body of Christ.

In the most dramatic part of the ceremony, Winning lay flat on the floor of the sanctuary, his face pressed into the marble and his arms folded under his head – a form of surrender to God and a symbol of his rebirth. 'He is waiting there like a dead thing, for the Holy Spirit to come and quicken him into a new form of life,'[6] wrote Ronald Knox of the ordination ceremony. After a moment of silent contemplation, Winning rose as a priest and accepted the chalice and paten, the cup and plate used during the Mass for the bread and wine.

Outside after the service he embraced his mother and sister and shook hands with his father. It was the first time they had seen each other in over two years and the delight was evident. Although students were prohibited from missing classes to witness their friends' ordination, Charles Renfrew had attended and gave his warm congratulations. Again, according to tradition, the rector was absent and so Winning returned to the college to give Clapperton his first blessing as a new priest. After this he retired to a local restaurant for a family lunch, which he followed with a visit to Vatican Radio in order to broadcast his blessings and good wishes to Scotland.

A highlight, not only of his ordination but also of his life, followed two days later when he and his family enjoyed a brief audience with Pope Pius XII. In contrast to Winning's previous encounters with the Pope, this time he was able to speak with him, even though very briefly. He exchanged a pledge of loyalty for the Pope's blessing and promise of his thoughts and prayers. It signified the closure of a remarkable two years. Though his final exams at the Gregorian would not take place until June and his fine grades, a cum laude, were not yet known, that meeting on 20 December 1948 contained the essential ingredients of his future life and career: a fierce loyalty to the Pope, a deep love of the family, and an unflinching devotion to his duty as a priest.

FOUR

A Curate's Tale

'Gerry Rogers was a father figure to me.'
THOMAS WINNING

Ecclesiastical politics and their secular cousin are very similar. In both, any change in leadership frequently corresponds to a change in personnel. In 1947, Fr Gerry Rogers, once the indispensable troubleshooter of the previous Archbishop of Glasgow, Donald Mackintosh, discovered that his successor, Donald Campbell, was a far brisker, ruder character. Where Rogers had once sat at Mackintosh's right hand, advising on a range of issues from Church law to liturgical matters and changes of personnel, he now found himself distanced from and no longer welcome within the confines of the inner circle.

Donald Campbell did not care much for Gerry Rogers. He disliked his popularity among his fellow priests and was jealous of his easy manner and his reputation as a 'man's man', as comfortable on the eighteenth hole as he was uttering Latin prayers or cradling a child beside a baptismal font. As president of the Glasgow Archdiocese's Marriage Tribunal, Rogers spent office hours sifting through the detritus of buckled marriages and would never have become Thomas Winning's close friend and valued mentor were it not for Campbell's irrational desire to rid his archdiocese of a brilliant mind whose face he felt no longer fitted. Campbell's solution was cunning; in 1947, Rogers was appointed chaplain to a congregation of nuns in the town of Bothwell. In 1948, the archdiocese of Glasgow was broken up to create two new dioceses, and as Bothwell fell within the boundary of the new Motherwell Diocese, Rogers was excluded from the diocese of his birth.

The reason for the formation of the new dioceses was not simply to facilitate Rogers' departure. It was the culmination of five centuries of antagonism and jealousy between the country's rival cities – Glasgow on the west coast and Edinburgh on the east – over where the Church's power lay and who best had the ear of Rome. Glasgow had enjoyed an early lead in the Dark Ages when in 1175 the diocese was granted the title *specialis filia Romanae ecclesiae*, Special Daughter of the Roman Church, by Pope Alexander III; this was a cloak of protection which defended the diocese from the long crook of the Archbishops of York and Canterbury who wished to see it pulled within their empire.

Seventeen years later, the title was stretched to cover the whole of Scotland, and Glasgow lost her exclusive status. Her fortunes tumbled further when, in 1472, the Vatican chose to elevate St Andrews to a metropolitan archbishopric, an arrangement which placed every other diocese, including Glasgow, in a subordinate role to the east of Scotland and incensed both bishops and King alike. James III initially refused to allow the new Archbishop Patrick Graham access to the town of St Andrews. So deep was his fit of pique at not having been consulted over the appointment that it took Graham's promise of extra taxation for the Crown before the King agreed to lift his blockade. In Glasgow, Bishop Robert Blacader sank into a petulant sulk over his inferior position and refused to recognize the east's new status; he went on to petition the Scots parliament who, in 1489, passed a law stating that: 'the honour and welfare of the realm demanded the erection of Glasgow into an archdiocese'. Two years later, the bishop travelled to Rome and successfully pleaded his position before Pope Innocent VIII. Glasgow's honour was restored on 9 January 1492 when a papal bull announced the area's elevation to an archdiocese with its own suffragen sees of Dunkeld, Dunblane, Galloway and Argyll. Yet hostilities continued between Blacader, now Archbishop, and William Scheves, the Archbishop of St Andrews and Edinburgh.

Scheves was attempting to seek redress at the Apostolic Signatura, the Church's highest court, for what he considered Blacader's repeated violations of his metropolitan authority. After a further year and a half, King James IV had cause to bang their mitres together in an attempt to seek a solution to a problem that was draining the country of money as rents and dues were now being sent to Rome to fund the lawsuit. The squabble was never resolved and decades later the Archbishop of Glasgow and the Archbishop of St Andrews and Edinburgh were still fighting over supremacy. On one occasion during the 1540s, the cross bearers of Cardinal David Beaton of St Andrews and Edinburgh and James Dunbar, the Archbishop of Glasgow, were reduced to fighting each other outside Glasgow Cathedral to ensure their respective Archbishop entered the cathedral first.

The situation in reality was comparable with tussling over a deck chair on the *Titanic*. The Catholic Church was viewed as corrupt and heretical by the new reformers led by John Knox. The religious houses were perceived to be swollen with the contents of the people's purses, parish priests were often absent, having abandoned the work to low-paid, poorly trained and ill-educated curates, and, as a result, parishes fell into neglect. A distinct lack of discipline rippled across the Church, leading to accusations of sexual immorality. While the Church leaders were rarely as promiscuous as presented in the accounts of Protestant historians, any sexual relations at all were hypocritical among men sworn to celibacy. In their defence, they believed the Church was on the cusp of recognizing a married clergy, and characters such as Cardinal Beaton, who had eight children by the same woman, Marian Ogilvie, with whom he lived for twenty years, considered themselves to be pre-empting progress. Progress, however, lay in the hands of Protestantism. The reforming theologies of Martin Luther and John Calvin, with their emphasis on scripture and condemnation of the way in which the Catholic Church conducted itself, had arrived in Scotland in the 1520s and begun to exert their influence. The burning of reformers such as George Wishart in 1545 and Walter Myln on 28 April 1558 did nothing to cauterize calls for change; instead, the first death led directly to the revenge slaying of Cardinal Beaton in his own room at St Andrews in 1546, while the execution of Myln triggered rioting in Edinburgh.

In reaction to increasing hostilities, the Church held a number of provincial councils between 1547 and 1559 to introduce reforms but, by the close of the final council, Catholicism was already doomed. A coalition of Lords and Lairds, hostile to Scotland's French Queen, Mary of Guise, now christened themselves the Lords of the Congregation and vowed to rid the country of both Queen and Catholicism. In 1557, a bond was issued vowing to 'renounce the congregation of Satan' and to 'establish the most blessed work of God and his congregation'. John Knox was invited back from Geneva and within two years the group had raised an army, with the patronage of Elizabeth I, the new Queen of Protestant England, and defeated the forces of Mary of Guise.

At the Reformation Parliament which took place in Edinburgh in 1560, the Confession of Faith, a document written by John Knox, was produced to state Scotland's new intent: the country was to be Protestant, and Catholicism was now illegal. The Mass was forbidden, priests were arrested and locked in the stocks, children born following a Catholic marriage ceremony were classified as illegitimate and the Church sank underground. Tufts of Catholicism remained in the north of the country and in the more remote islands where the Reformation failed to penetrate but the organized Church as it was known withered and died. Priests were pensioned off and married, parishioners converted, and attendance at the Kirk was mandatory.

Glasgow lost out once again in 1878 when the hierarchy of the Catholic Church was finally restored to Scotland. For 275 years the country had been without dioceses or bishops; instead, it was branded as a mission country and carved into three districts, northern, eastern and western, which were overseen by vicars apostolic. An argument was made that Glasgow, then the second city of the empire, the chief centre of commerce, manufacture and industry and crucially home to three times as many Catholics, priests and churches as Edinburgh, should be made the new metropolitan archdiocese.

Unfortunately, sense gave way to sentimentality. John Strain, the

Vicar Apostolic of the eastern Crichton-Stuart district, supported by powerful lay patrons including John Patrick, the third Marquess of Bute, then one of the richest men in the world, argued that the Church should favour continuity and over time reanimate the dead dioceses. St Andrews may once have been the ecclesiastical centre of medieval Scotland, but in 1878, the town housed only two Catholic families and had no Catholic place of worship. Despite the drawbacks, John Strain won his way and was crowned Metropolitan Archbishop of St Andrews and Edinburgh with a bejewelled mitre purchased by the Marquess of Bute, a generous gesture he extended to each new bishop.

The restoration of the hierarchy had triggered violent religious tensions in England when it took place in 1850, but Scotland was for once more fortunate. The *Glasgow Herald* was surprisingly supportive and argued that it would give the Pope pleasure and do Scotland no harm. The Free Church of Scotland was more aggressive, but overemphasized the strength of Scots law when one member sent a telegram to the Vatican threatening legal action in the Court of Session should the Pope have the temerity to persist, while the Episcopal Church, recognizing a credible threat to the size of its congregations, many of whom would subsequently drift to the Catholic Church, described it as 'a violation of the law of unity and a rendering of the Body of Christ'. Neither opinion, however, led to bloodshed on the streets.

In recognition of Glasgow's size and history, the city and the surrounding towns and countryside were made an archdiocese, responsible directly to Rome and operating without ties to Edinburgh, but also without the prestige of any suffragan sees. The Vatican had always planned to rectify this, but delay was followed by delay and once the archdiocese of Glasgow had embarked on a huge building programme it was thought imprudent to launch any new diocese until the books were balanced. This was achieved by the work of Archbishop Mackintosh, working closely with William Daley and Gerry Rogers.

*   *   *

During the course of his career as Archbishop and Cardinal, Winning would swivel both the media's spotlight and the balance of power away from the metropolitan archdiocese of St Andrews and Edinburgh to a permanent anchor within the confines of the archdiocese of Glasgow. In the space of one lifetime he would succeed where a dozen bishops and archbishops spread across eight hundred years had failed, by making Glasgow the undisputed capital of Catholic Scotland. Yet such achievements lay in a distant future; Winning, twenty-three years old, newly ordained and back living at home with his parents, said Mass daily at St Patrick's where he had previously served as an altar boy, and waited for an appointment to a parish.

A new diocese requires a new bishop and in late December 1948, one was appointed. He was a poor choice. In later years, parishioners would joke that the Holy Spirit was on holiday when Fr Edward Douglas was appointed as their spiritual shepherd, others that the appointment was less the result of a rigorous search of the viable candidates than the activities of a blindfolded altar boy, armed with a list of names and a hat pin. The responsibility lay with Archbishop William Godfrey, the papal delegate to Britain, who developed a reputation for his controversial appointments. The new Bishop of Motherwell was certainly that. Edward Douglas was a small man, with a long crooked nose and a stoop, and if some heads are made for the mitre, others are crushed by the weight, and during the next six years, he was slowly flattened. For the past eighteen years, Douglas, who was forty-six, had been a diligent teacher at Blairs, where he was better equipped to deal with books, lessons and students than he was to deal with the administration, priests and stress that now lay ahead. In spite of his own deep reservations, he accepted that Rome – or at least the London branch office – had spoken, and on 21 April 1948, Douglas was ordained a bishop at Our Lady of Good Aid in Motherwell, a large Gothic church which would now serve as the diocese's new cathedral.

What Douglas lacked in qualities of leadership was compensated for by his eye for talent developed during twenty years in the classroom. Among his first decisions was the appointment of Gerry

Rogers as his Vicar General, a choice that irritated Archbishop Campbell who had no wish to see the adversary he had thought he had rid himself of return. In a traditional diocese the 'VG', as he is commonly known, acts as the Bishop's deputy or chief of staff, assisting with appointments, liaising with priests and attending functions in his absence, but in the case of Motherwell, an infant diocese with a nervous, inexperienced leader, Rogers' influence and power were magnified. It was a testament to his character that he never exploited his position, and instead did his best to support his wilting boss.

The new diocese's office was a detached bungalow in Bothwell from where Rogers began to organize staff. His position meant he was unable to oversee the marriage tribunal which each diocese required, so a new recruit was needed to be trained in canon law. As Rogers was a graduate of the Gregorian University and believed this was where the brightest students would reside, he contacted the rector of the Scots College asking him to recommend a suitable candidate. Clapperton suggested Winning, who had recently graduated with high honours, as someone possessing the necessary intelligence to complete the postgraduate course in canon law. A few weeks after returning from Rome, Winning was called into Rogers' office and informed that he would be heading back the following year. The news was initially unwelcome. Rogers explained that knowledge of canon law was an invaluable aid in climbing the Church's career ladder, that it would open up new opportunities, but Winning could only see a return to the familiar pattern of study, one he was glad to have left behind. Before recommencing his studies, he needed to complete a year as a curate. This was to be his first opportunity to practise as a priest and he was sent to the tiny village of Chapelhall in Lanarkshire.

In August 1949, Fr Thomas Winning stood in his vestments at the altar of St Aloysius, smiling as Fr Peter Murie, the parish priest, introduced him as the church's new curate. 'He'll only be here a year,' explained Murie from the pulpit, 'so don't you be muttering that I can't keep a curate.' Duly warned about his short shelf life, the parishioners still embraced the new priest as one of their own.

As his first parish, St Aloysius was an exhilarating introduction to Winning's chosen career. First, there was the church itself which enjoyed an enviable position on top of a hill, overlooking the rows of tenements that housed the village's two thousand residents, and backed on to a blanket of green fields. On a Sunday, Winning would stand outside the church door, ring a hand bell and watch as children aged from four to fourteen ran from their houses and up the hill for a weekly bible lesson. Father Murie was an erudite man and talented pianist who, although he suffered persistent ill health, remained a fine conversationalist and was only too happy to entertain his young charge with show-tunes after supper. Finally there was the work, which Winning found as rewarding as it was at first frightening. One week after his arrival, Murie took three weeks holiday leaving Winning in charge.

For almost a year, Winning revelled in his new role. He worked hard to set up a variety of groups such as the Union of Catholic Mothers and a Catholic Young Men's Society. The children's Sunday school was a source of great humour; he dubbed one boy the 'heathen' as his enthusiasm for putting up his hand was never matched with the correct answer. He organized a football team for the older boys of the parish, who proved as poor in the penalty area as their younger siblings were at Sunday school. Winning remembered the team in an interview for the book *Faith, Hope and Chastity*, a compilation of interviews with priests around Britain. 'We were beaten 10–1 the first time we played. During the game one of the team got a bad gash in his knee – one minute I was studying it and cleaning it up, the next minute I was having a cup of tea in somebody's house. I was twenty-four, and I'd fainted at the sight of his blood.' A remarkable aversion for a man with the ability to transform red wine into the blood of Christ.

In the evenings, he conducted home visits and discovered that the dozen demanded by Fr John Conroy at Mill Hill was both impractical and ineffective. Instead, Winning settled on three or four visits per night and applied the tips suggested in the works of

Fr Ronald Knox: speak with the father about work, the mother about her children, and always listen more than you talk. Although the area was poor, a visit from a priest remained an occasion for the best china and the provision of the comfiest seat. The only disappointment came within the confessional box. After seven years in the study of philosophy and theology, Winning was eager to flex his new knowledge, to wrestle with great moral issues, counsel the confused and guide those in doubt. Instead, his long hours behind the metal gauze and thick velvet curtain which separated the priest from the penitent were a tedious litany of adults continuing to confess the 'sins' of a child. When one old man confessed that he had been 'disobedient' to his sister, Winning asked him if he was not 'a wee bit old for that'. The man, taken aback by what he perceived as the priest's impudence, replied by asking Winning if he was not 'a wee bit too young for this', then walked out, and from then on went to Fr Murie for confession. Winning felt it was crucial to dissuade parishioners from repeating in rote form what they had said, once a month, for decades. Confession, he insisted, was about liberation from sin – not simply turgid repetition. This was to be the only blip in an enjoyable year that drew to a close too soon.

Winning returned once again to Rome in the autumn of 1950, exchanging his previous freedom for the rigid discipline of a student, for although ordained with experience in a parish he was still expected to follow the same strict timetable as the youngest student. The rector found it easiest to apply a universal set of rules and so Winning slipped back into a routine of a five-thirty rise, followed by prayers, Mass, breakfast and university. It was as if Scotland and St Aloysius were now little more than a blurred, half-remembered dream. 'In the library, I saw the same bookcase with the same panel of broken glass, and it felt like I had never been away,' he explained.

As soon as Winning arrived, he was given over to doubts which tore away at his confidence and ability. It was hardly surprising, for the task that lay before him was daunting. To achieve a doctorate in canon law was considered a stiff challenge to those familiar with the subject. John McQuade, an Irish priest who accompanied Winning and was also destined for Motherwell diocese, had studied the subject for three years, while another student on the same course had taught it for twelve years at an Irish seminary. In comparison, Winning's experience to date with canon law was restricted to a couple of lectures at the Gregorian University three years previously. Winning likened the situation to being sent to complete a PhD in chemistry at Cambridge University when 'you hadn't made it past cleaning out the test tubes at school'. Privately, he was terrified of failing, and in order to avoid such humiliation, examined his strengths and plotted what he recognized was the only route to success: a working routine of Stakhanovite proportions. His fluency in Latin was a tremendous aid, one which allowed him to understand the lectures with a precision which other students lacked, but closing the huge gulf required a daily programme of study which continued until one o'clock in the morning and permitted little more than four hours sleep each night, having serious consequences for his health.

In November 1950, a new Catholic dogma on the assumption of the Blessed Virgin Mary was announced.

A joke is perhaps the simplest way to illustrate the depth of devotion many Catholics have towards the mother of Jesus Christ: while Michelangelo was painting the ceiling of the Sistine Chapel, he looked down to see a peasant woman, kneeling in silent prayer. Bored with his work, he decided to brighten his morning by playing a trick at the old woman's expense, and so as she bent her head in prayer, unaware of the artist's presence, Michelangelo began to speak in a deep, resonant voice: 'I am Jesus Christ, speak and your prayers will be answered.' Slowly the woman's head tilted up towards the heavens and she began to answer. 'Hush! Can't you see I'm talking to your mother?'

The Blessed Virgin Mary or Mary, the Mother of God, has for almost fifteen hundred years inhabited a deep place in the hearts of Catholics across the world. The reason for her popularity and the piety directed towards her is that she was entirely human, but one who, through her acceptance of God's will and the virgin birth of her son, became blessed with the divine. For centuries, Mary has been viewed as an intermediary, a postmistress who ensures the petitions and prayers of the faithful reach the correct destination, namely God.

The concept of Mary as a mediator between God and his sinners on earth developed in Western medieval piety around the eighth century, with the translation of the legend of Theophilus. The story is a predecessor of that of Dr Faustus and tells of a man who exchanged his soul for well-paid employment; when he was near to death, he begged Mary to save him from eternal damnation, which she achieved after pleading with the Devil. As the story spread out across Europe, so developed the idea of Marian devotion and the theological concept that God's grace could flow through Mary to earth. The belief was comforting to those who felt unworthy to pray directly to Jesus, the son of God, for they believed Mary's maternal nature would intercede with her son on their behalf. By the eleventh century, pilgrimages had sprung up in her name, her image appeared on icons, and miracles were attributed to her hand, while the prayer the Hail Mary and the prayer cycle known as the rosary were becoming increasingly common. So powerful was the concept of Mary to become that in 1854, the Church proclaimed the dogma of the Immaculate Conception, the assertion that she had been born without original sin. Less than a century later, in 1950, just two months after Winning's return to Rome, a second dogma was to be defined. Pope Pius XII announced the doctrine of the Assumption, in which it was stated that at the end of Mary's natural life she was raised body and soul into heaven.

In truth, Winning had never had much time for Mary. He said the rosary, appreciated that May was a month devoted to her memory, but that was as far as it went. In Winning's mind, Mary was not a principal player and so was relegated to the role of extra. In the autumn of 1950, the theologians at the Gregorian University were deep in debate on the merits of Mary's new status. A series of Saturday morning debates had been organized to articulate the arguments for and against the Pope's plans. The ecumenists were concerned that it would further distance the Catholic Church from the Protestants for whom Mary was no more than a vehicle for Christ's birth. Since the Reformation they had been critical of any devotion to Mary on the grounds that it demonstrated a lack of trust that salvation would come through Christ alone. The Eastern Orthodox Church was in disagreement of the doctrine, for they felt the move distanced Mary from the human race, while the Mariologists were convinced of the hope such a dogma would provide to the world, namely that one day all the faithful would be similarly raised up.

Winning had attended the talks, but remained indifferent; it was his passion for Pius XII and his desire never to miss a public appearance that brought him to St Peter's Square on 1 November 1950 where the Pope was preparing to address a crowd of almost one million people. The square was packed so tightly that Winning could scarcely move his arms, and had to strain his neck up in an attempt to peer over the shoulders of his fellow pilgrims. The setting was most uncomfortable for what Winning marked as a profound spiritual experience: looking across the sky above Rome, he noticed that although it was now early morning, the moon was still visible and was carved in a deep crescent – the same shape common to many illustrations of Mary as Queen of Heaven in which she stood perched on a crescent moon, smiling down on her charges below. The image startled Winning, and the crowds appeared to melt away. It was as if he had found a point where the membrane that separates the world from God was particularly thin and he was able to push through. In his heart he now knew Mary was real. 'Previous to that moment, she had been a statue or a figure or a face flat on a wall. I don't know what it was, but it came to me that she was real. It has remained in my memory as a very powerful image.'

Pius XII had his own reasons for announcing the doctrine of the Assumption. While Winning had been moved by the moon, the Pope had been struck by the sun, for while walking in the Vatican gardens, he had witnessed the phenomenon of the spinning sun, a sight associated with the visions of Our Lady of Fatima in 1917. He also wished to make a statement about the preciousness of life. In his text *Munificentissimus Deus* (God the Most Generous), he reaffirmed the importance of the body as a sacred vehicle of God, following a decade in which over fifty million lives had been lost during the Second World War. When the Pope finally appeared on the balcony and began to speak, Winning borrowed pen and paper from a neighbour and began to transcribe his comments, so anxious was he to capture the moment. Over the next few weeks, he was to re-examine the text and arguments concerning the Church's new teaching, and it was to strengthen his understanding of eschatology – the theology of death and mankind's final destiny. Later, Winning was to develop a dreadful fear of death, one he felt was unbecoming for so senior a religious figure, and this moment was one he would frequently return to for solace during private moments of prayer.

In the Catholic Church, it is said that the politicians study canon law, while the spiritual are drawn to study the liturgy. As lawyers proliferate in the secular world of politics, so are they found in the upper reaches of the Catholic Church. Though Winning had no choice in the matter, there is little doubt that his intellect and aggressive personality were better suited to grappling with the practical application of rules and regulations than the esoteric flights of fancy required for pioneering work in theology. He was interested in the law, and if the field had been easily accessible to him in Scotland (it was for the most part a Protestant clique) he might have considered it as a career. In later life, he talked about alternatives to the priesthood he might have pursued as being those of 'a doctor or lawyer, something with a bit of bite'.

The law of the Catholic Church – or canon law, drawn from the Greek word for 'rule' – had been passed on through the centuries from AD 95, when the first 'Church orders' were written down in order to clarify the organization of the early Church and the manner in which the sacraments were to be celebrated. The writings of Church Fathers such as St Augustine and St Ireneus had produced further ideas that required legislation, while the growth of the

Church led to a proliferation of rules governing everything from doctrinal issues and public worship to the disciplinary proceedings for priests and religious. Canon law became divided into *universal* laws, applying to Catholics throughout the world, and *particular* laws which held force within a given territory such as a diocese. Winning was to learn that the laws themselves were derived from three areas: Church law, which covered such matters as disciplinary measures or the length of the fast prior to communion; natural law, which concerned itself with issues such as the insistence of monogamy and correct heterosexual behaviour, as they were discovered in the natural order and were considered irreversible; and a third area, known as divine positive law, found in the revelation or the self-disclosure of God, and which included the indissolubility of marriage and the sacrament of confession. In 1140, Gratian, a noted canonist, produced a common text of the Church's rules and regulations, a collection of five volumes which was swollen over the centuries with new additions, but not until 1917 were all the volumes comprehensively codified. The man largely responsible for codification in 1917 was Fr Pietro Gasparri, but among his closest assistants was Padre Cappello, a diminutive Jesuit whose lectures Winning grew to love. In many ways, Cappello was a character the young priest could have found disagreeable; he had almost no sense of humour and refused to engage the class outside of the parameters of the discussion. Gifted with a prodigious memory, Cappello used neither textbook nor notes while speaking and could quote entire pages of canon law with ease. Laws and rules, he was keen to impress on his students, were for the safety and benefit of mankind, they were the boundaries on a straight road to heaven. Outside of the university, Cappello had a reputation as a wise and considerate confessor, a latter-day Solomon who sat for hours each day hearing confessions at the Church of St Ignatius. 'When he died, his body lay in the chapel of the Greg and thousands came to see him, later they introduced his cause for canonization. He couldn't help but be a living role model of who you were trying to be,' said Winning.

*   *   *

Although Winning had just three lectures daily, each lasting fifty minutes, the period between the autumn of 1950 and the summer of 1951 was the hardest period of his academic life. John McQuade offered assistance where possible, but had his own concerns as he struggled to develop a working knowledge of Latin. Month after month, Winning worked seven days a week, from dawn until after midnight; his only breaks were morning and evening prayers and the daily queue to say Mass in one of the college's small oratories. By the time of his summer exam, the punishing regime had shattered his health; so exhausted was he by his labours that he had to take a taxi to the university as he was unable to walk. After focusing for the length of the oral exam he took a taxi back to the college and spent the next ten days in bed. When a doctor was called he was diagnosed as suffering from rheumatism and although he had planned a trip to Lourdes, en route home for the summer, he was forbidden to take a dip in the waters in case it exacerbated his condition. After treatment at a Glasgow clinic for nodules in his joints, Winning returned to Rome in September 1951 for an academic year that was only slightly easier.

Among the friends Winning made that year was Paul Marcinkus, a huge American who had the build of the football player he once had been. Marcinkus was a postgraduate student at the US college who drove a Cadillac and spoke, as Winning observed, 'from the side of his mouth, like a gangster'. Winning's friend would rise to become the most senior American in the Vatican and the centre of one of the Church's biggest contemporary scandals. In 1982, 'the chink' as Marcinkus was dubbed by Winning, was head of the Institute for the Works of Religious (IoR), otherwise known as the Vatican Bank, when it became tangled in the collapse of the Banco Ambrosiano, a large Italian bank. Marcinkus was friendly with Roberto Calvi, the chairman of Banco Ambrosiano, and in order to assist him as he attempted to sort out the bank's finances he provided Calvi with letters of patronage which stated that the IoR backed his activities. However, in order to protect the Vatican, Marcinkus insisted Calvi provide him with a letter indemnifying the IoR from any financial responsibility, a fact hidden from Calvi's creditors, who would later consider this to be fraud. When the bank collapsed owing $1.2 billion, Calvi apparently hanged himself from Blackfriars Bridge in London, a scene that inspired Francis Ford Coppola who a decade later incorporated the death into *The Godfather Part III*. Many still believe he was murdered. The Italian authorities later convicted thirty-three people over the bank's collapse, while Marcinkus spent two years trapped within the Vatican City after the police threatened him with arrest in spite of his diplomatic immunity. The matter was finally resolved in 1984 when the Vatican's secretary of state, Cardinal Agostino Casaroli and the Pope agreed to pay $244 million compensation to Banco Ambrosiano's creditors against Marcinkus's opposition. At the time, Winning stood by his old college friend and believed Marcinkus's defence that he himself had been misled and was innocent of any wrongdoing. This position was, frankly, ridiculous, extending as it did a greater degree of leeway and understanding to Marcinkus than either the Pope or Cardinal Casaroli could muster, but it still fitted Winning's pattern of deliberately choosing to believe the best about Church personnel, in the face of compelling evidence to the contrary.

In order to graduate, Winning was required to complete a body of original research that would further the study of canon law and so in the summer of 1952, he began to search for a suitable subject for his thesis. There were two reasons why he settled upon 'Tithes in Pre-Reformation Scotland' as the completed manuscript was titled; the first was proximity – he was to spend the summer at home and it made sense to focus on an aspect of Scottish Church history when libraries and research facilities were so easily to hand; the second reason was more basic and primal – a desire for revenge. In the past so much research had been carried out by Protestant historians who Winning believed had twisted and distorted the facts in order to better justify the Reformation. This would be his opportunity to redress the balance, and so he set to work with the words of the college song whispering in his ear: 'that Scotland's wrong be righted, so that Scotland's work be done'.

He was aided in his research by the discovery just four years before of a manuscript copy of lectures delivered in the sixteenth century by William Hay, the Scottish theologian and canonist at King's College in Aberdeen. Although it had not yet been edited, Winning found inside its worn and faded pages a wealth of original information which he fashioned into crucial ammunition in his battle against what he perceived as the errant forces of Protestantism. Over the summer, he buried himself in the libraries of Scotland, working through a variety of sources including diocesan registers, the chartularies of monastic houses, and as many ecclesiastical documents as had survived the destruction of reformers. Where previous historians had found a corrupt system of arbitrary taxation of the poor by the Catholic Church, Winning uncovered a carefully regulated and organized system that funded hospitals and poor houses. In the preface to his work, he set forth his agenda to treat the subject from a Catholic point of view for the first time and to correct erroneous perceptions made by Protestant historians who, he wrote, 'manifest an appalling lack of understanding of the canon law which regulated the payment of tithes to the clergy'.[1] Winning wrote with a clear, simple style topped with the occasional literary flourish and over the course of 236 pages, he traced the origin, development and decline of the tithe system, crossing swords wherever possible in defence of the faith and within only a few pages skewering opposing views: 'Scotland has never recovered from the calamity of the Reformation and over three hundred years were to pass before she could boast once more of a properly constituted hierarchy. The great hatred of the priesthood engendered by Knox and his unruly mobs has been kept alive by generations of bigoted historians who have slandered the pre-Reformation Church without respite and continue to do so today.'

Among the historians taken to task by Winning's research was Sir John Connell, and advocate and procurator of the Church of Scotland, who in 1850 had published a book entitled *A Treatise on the Law of Scotland respecting Tithes*. Winning was dismissive of his work, accusing him of 'fundamental errors' in the very nature of tithes. While Connell argued that it was not clear who received the money, Winning corrected him, insisting that it was for the care of souls. Withering lines such as 'had the writer been more conversant with Church law' appear with increasing frequency. Another error pointed out and corrected with visible relish was the belief that tithes were first introduced in Scotland and then England, when in fact the chronology was reversed with Scotland among the last countries in Europe to adopt the tithe system. Although Winning conceded abuses had taken place, he disagreed with his Protestant counterparts on the extent of them. 'There were abuses [but] all medieval religious and clergy were not as rapacious as Scottish historians would have us believe.' Winning was also to reveal a mild disregard for the monastic orders; the feelings were common among diocesan priests of his day, who felt they were consistently being compared unfavourably to their more 'saintly brethren' in the orders. At the time he wrote: 'Perhaps Scotland has never been able completely to restrain her love of monastic institutions, a weakness which in earlier centuries had retarded her development as a Christian community.' Winning was to end his thesis with a clarion call: 'Nevertheless, an institution Catholic in origin and Protestant in fact, survives today to remind thoughtful men of how the Protestant Church robbed the True Church of her temporal possessions in Scotland ... We trust that this work will be a modest contribution to the ever-increasing volume of information on the past glories of Catholic Scotland.'

His examiners obviously agreed. When combined with his successful completion of a final exam and a forty-five minute talk in front of five professors on a subject chosen only one day previously, Winning once again emerged from the Gregorian University cum laude. In the previous three years Dr Winning, as he was now known, had further demonstrated his abilities. As he left Rome, bad news waited at home: his mother was dying.

FIVE

A Time to Die

'When I was walking behind the coffin, I felt very proud that she had been my mother.'

THOMAS WINNING

When the specialist emerged from his office, having just seen Agnes Winning, and approached her son, his first few words told the whole story: 'Excuse me, are you the next of kin?' Winning rose from his seat in the waiting room of the Glasgow Royal Infirmary, where his mother had been booked for a series of tests the results of which, judging by the doctor's expression, were not good. He had returned from Rome in July 1953 to discover his mother looking pale, weak and suffering severe lower-back pain. It had been a persistent problem since she returned from a trip to Lourdes with her daughter Margaret in May. As the local doctor had admitted to being baffled at the cause, Winning had urged her to seek further medical attention.

The cause, he was told, was a cancerous tumour growing in her rectum. Exploratory surgery was now required to determine how far the disease had spread, but the description the doctor used was 'hopeless'. The operation was scheduled for the following day and as Agnes had no wish to spend an unnecessary night in hospital, they travelled home to Craigneuk by bus and in silence.

Winning, with the doctor's agreement, had chosen not to reveal the diagnosis to his mother and she had not asked. Cancer was treated like a curse in the 1950s, the word was rarely uttered. The operation the following day was pitifully swift: no sooner had the surgeons opened her up, than the decision was made to close on the grounds that there was little they could do. When told by a lady in the neighbouring bed that she had been absent scarcely an hour, Agnes Winning took this as a sign that nothing had been found. Winning and his father had no intention of disavowing her of such comfort, even after Patrick Macmillan, the son of the doctor who had treated Winning as a child for pneumonia, and who was now working as a registrar at the Royal, explained that she might last no longer than three weeks. He explained that all they could do was administer a colostomy in an attempt to relieve the pain from the tumour pressing on the nerves of her legs.

Agnes Winning was to live for one more year, lulled for the first six months by the belief that the colostomy had corrected the complaint and for her final few months cushioned by the new happiness her daughter had discovered. The truth of her mother's inoperable cancer had been hidden from Margaret by her father and brother and she was left under the delusion that Agnes would one day recover. At twenty-six, Margaret was now a qualified schoolteacher and had recently fallen in love. Edward McCarron, or Eddie to all, had been a fellow pupil with Margaret at Our Lady's High School, he had worked as a lorry driver for the armed forces during the war and was currently working as a grocer. The couple had first met through the Catholic Young Men's Society (CYMS) where Eddie was a member and Margaret belonged to the Associates of the CYMS, a women's group which organized dances and prepared any food the men might require. It is an indication of the exalted position in which Winning was placed that prior to his return home, she had been fretful about his opinion of Eddie. Since childhood, her brother had been her hero; even when the truth emerged about her mother's condition Margaret was not angered by the deception, believing instead that her brother had been protecting her from unnecessary anguish. Her fears over Eddie were to prove groundless as both men struck up a firm friendship, with Eddie agreeing to teach his future brother-in-law how to drive. An evening excursion with Eddie at the wheel was to constitute the Winnings' final outing as a family. On Easter Monday 1954, Agnes and Thomas senior were joined by their son and daughter on the back seat of a hired car for a short trip to Largs, a scenic little town that looked out on to the Firth of Clyde and boasted the finest Italian café in the country. Nardini's Café was owned by a family of Italian immigrants and drew visitors from across Scotland to sample their unique blend of ice cream and revel in the culinary delight of their knickerbocker glories. Winning impressed his family by ordering in Italian and together the five scraped their glasses clean and watched the sun set.

Agnes Winning was to die hard. After the outing to Largs, she was unable to leave the house again and was confined to a bed made up in the living room. Although Ellen Donnelly, a cousin who was a night nurse, visited each morning to administer morphine injections, the pain in her legs proved interminable and the distress turned her dark hair white. Agnes knew she was dying but refused to discuss her condition or even acknowledge the colostomy; all she did was plead for the pain to cease. Winning found his mother's slow, unsightly death to be a crucifixion. Where possible he visited every day to bring her Holy Communion and each day off or week's holiday was spent by her side or supporting his father, for whom the experience was equally unbearable. On 22 August she slipped into a coma and one week later, on 29 August 1954, she died at the age of sixty-two while surrounded by her family. In a curious twist that sustained the family's belief that she had at last found peace her hair, once so white, turned back to black and the lines that riddled her face faded. 'It was weird,' remembered Margaret. 'But then I suppose all the pain had gone.'

While father and daughter wept openly, Winning remained stoical. 'Thomas didn't cry. He was devastated, but he didn't cry. I guess he thought he had to do it for my sake,' said Margaret. Emotions, though painfully felt, were left unexpressed as he attempted to support his father and sister in the manner of a priest as well as that of a son and a brother. It was he who organized the funeral at St Patrick's, the church his mother had supported for so many years, and it was he who, in a remarkable feat of self-control, presided over the funeral Mass, something he described as a 'great honour'.

> I can remember the funeral well. It is a terrible experience [the death of your mother]. The gap is never filled. I felt very proud that she had brought me up because I could not point to anything other than she had done her level best. By all the social standards we were poor, but you never knew it. I never had a patch on my trousers. When I was walking behind the coffin I felt very proud that she had been my mother.

His mother's death marked the conclusion of a difficult year in which Winning's life both personally and professionally had seemed to conspire against him. When not fretting over her health and the terrible toll it was taking on his father, Winning was consumed by his work which over the past twelve months had been less than comforting. Monsignor Alex Hamilton, who had been parish priest at St Patrick's while he was an altar boy, had suggested to Gerry Rogers, the Vicar General, that Winning join him at his new parish of St Mary's in the neighbouring town of Hamilton and serve as one of his three curates. On paper, it appeared a perfect plan, one that conjured the image of an old mentor taking a young charge under his wing, and so Rogers agreed but Winning was to find the new dynamic extremely difficult. The problem was that Hamilton's view of his former altar boy had frozen with Winning still in short trousers. While he had gone on to develop into a determined, opinionated and ambitious young priest, the monsignor continued to treat him in the dismissive manner of a child. Winning came to believe that the older priest was emotionally stunted, unable or unwilling to either give or receive affection; a characteristic he attributed to Hamilton's loss of his mother while he was just an infant. As parish priest, Hamilton kept a similar distance from his parishioners. A shy man, he rarely made home visits and relied heavily on his curates for information. Winning said: 'You were a functionary for him. You did not get the feeling that you had a personable relationship with him. He never gave you any great support or enthusiasm.'

Sharing the parish house and the task of home visits, daily Mass and the organization of community groups such as the CYMS were two other curates – John Murray, an older priest in his late forties who was desperate for promotion to a parish of his own, and John Boyle, a chubby pioneer, who as a member of the Irish temperance movement was sworn to abstinence for five years. Winning did not bond with Murray, but developed a great affection for Boyle, with whom he would later holiday among the vineyards of France once his 'sentence', as Winning described the pledge, was complete. Hamilton had little time for tittle-tattle or parish gossip so the dinner table where the four dined each evening became a forum where discussions on theology, politics and the morality of nuclear weapons were passed around with the green beans and boiled potatoes. This was one aspect of Hamilton's cold character that Winning enjoyed and it was here that his strong lifelong opposition to nuclear weapons hardened. By 1954, the Second World War was scarcely a decade past but fears of a new nuclear holocaust were growing.

A mini-mushroom cloud had risen over the diocese in February 1954 when the announcement was made that Bishop Edward Douglas was to retire on health grounds. Douglas's leadership of the diocese had been little short of disastrous; he was nervous, inarticulate, and wore a perpetual frown of concern. He had also developed a drinking problem in response to the pressures of office, and Gerry Rogers had increasingly been forced to deputize on occasions when Douglas was physically unable to perform his duties. Although his vicar general remained as supportive as possible, the situation was untenable and the farce collapsed when the bishop was found drunk on the kitchen floor by the Apostolic Delegate, who had agreed to pay a visit to the diocese to quietly review his continuing suitability for office. Douglas was swiftly removed from the diocese, appointed titular Bishop of Botri, an ancient Holy Land diocese, and retired to the diocese of Aberdeen, where he attempted to recover through attending meetings of Alcoholics Anonymous, an American society that had arrived in Scotland only a few years earlier.

The true reason for his departure was hidden from the public but remained an open secret among the clergy and was another destabilizing factor in Winning's work. He had only met Bishop Douglas once but the loss of a bishop was always preceded by an air of uncertainty and unease prior to a new appointment. And then there was the marriage tribunal: two days each week, Monday and Wednesday, Winning joined John McQuade at a detached redbrick villa in the more salubrious end of Bothwell, an attractive and leafy suburb of Hamilton. Between nine o'clock in the morning and six o'clock at night when they returned to their respective parishes, Winning and McQuade attempted to convert the theory learned in Rome into what was an often difficult practice. There are few areas of Catholicism as misunderstood as the Church's prohibition of remarriage after divorce without a declaration of nullity, better known as an annulment. To the unaware, there exists a troubling double standard, but to the Church, the procedure remains utterly consistent with her belief in the indissolubility of a true marriage. The key is to understand that marriage in the eyes of the Catholic Church is a sacrament made between two people and witnessed by God; it is a knot tied by two willing individuals who promise to accept children if so fortunate and to nurture one another until death. The indissolubility of marriage is predicated on the words of Jesus in St Matthew's Gospel: 'Whomsoever My Father has united, let no man put asunder.' Annulment is based upon the fact that the exchange of consent brings marriage into existence. Therefore if consent is faulty, no marriage occurs. If it can be shown, for example, that consent was obtained by force or given by someone who was incapable of doing so, or given with conditions affecting permanence, children, fidelity, or the nature of marriage itself, then it might be possible to obtain a declaration of nullity. So, while a marriage may have taken place, a ceremony held, and vows and rings exchanged, the sacrament may not neces-sarily have occurred and God has 'united' no one. If a girl was forced to marry against her wishes there could be no consent; if a man knew he was homosexual there may be no consent; if demands or conditions were placed on the marriage by either party, a common occurrence in Italy where a husband would often make his wife promise that her mother would never live with them, there could be no true consent. The same principles applied if a wife agreed to marry on the condition that the couple not have children: once again there could be no true consent. One of Winning's jobs was to sift through a marriage that had collapsed for any evidence that would support an application for annulment.

> The work taught me about human nature. It opened up a completely different world about people's behaviour and how they think and act. I would be wrong if I said it didn't shock me. You can be disappointed that people can be so twisted. It gave you an awful strong compassion for people who had to suffer at the hands of other people, especially the women. There were some bad cases. What I could never understand was how someone could love a woman so much that he wanted to marry her and then turn out to be a right swine. You developed a tremendous sympathy for people who had to live with people who were abnormal.

At the time, very few cases involving two Catholics constituted grounds for annulment. If couples could not live together they were expected to live apart with no hope of remarriage in the Church, and if they should marry outside the Church, in a registry office or within another denomination, they were barred for ever from receiving holy communion and were viewed by the Church as 'living in sin'; any sexual relations with their new husband or wife were branded as 'adultery'. On many occasions, Winning had to turn away desperate women (there were few men) who wished an annulment but for whom no chinks in their marriage could be found, both partners having been baptized Catholics who had willingly entered into the marriage which was considered sacramental. Winning had compassion for their situation, but lost no sleep over their plight; the Church was powerless and unable to defy or change what was understood to be God's law. On one occasion, a woman visited Winning at St Mary's parish house and refused to believe his statement that there was no case. She finally accepted Mgr

Hamilton's agreement with Winning after she sought what she described as an 'older and wiser head'.

A more palatable part of Winning's work was issuing approvals for mixed marriages. At the time, a marriage between a Catholic and a non-Catholic was permitted but not supported; a bride or groom were more likely to fall away from their faith in such a marriage and so, in an attempt to prevent this, certain agreements were secured before permission was granted. The non-Catholic partner was required to swear an oath that any children born of the marriage would be raised as Catholics; this was in operation until 1970, when the onus and oath were switched to the Catholic partner. The marriage itself usually took place at a bare side altar on a weekday morning, as if God had agreed to attend but did not wish for any witnesses.

Yet another part of his towering workload involved the dissolution of a non-baptized person's previous marriage to allow him or her to remarry a Catholic and therefore for the Catholic to be able to continue to practise their Catholic faith. This was achieved using a rule known as the Pauline Privilege and hinged upon the previous marriage being viewed as 'non-sacramental' by proving that neither party had been baptized at the time of the ceremony. In order to prove this point, cases evolved like mini-detective stories with Winning having to track down and interview the petitioner's parents and those of his or her former spouse as well as check Church records. If one member of the couple was baptized, the dissolution could still take place using a second rule, the Petrine Privilege, however, while a local bishop could act on the first rule, the second rule was at the discretion of the officials of the Holy Office – now called the Congregation for the Doctrine of the Faith. The preparation for even the simplest case involved bulging files and a myriad reports that had to be rendered into Latin, which remains the Church's official language. Two days each week was never enough and the work sloshed into Winning's evenings and flooded his weekends.

It was not uncommon for cases to involve a spouse from another country and this meant liaising with that nation's appointed tribunal and then translating witness statements back into English. One such case led to Winning being introduced to a teacher who would become one of his closest female friends. Susan McCormack was a language teacher who specialized in German and Italian and taught at a small private school, run by some Franciscan nuns in Bothwell. A diminutive figure, she possessed a determined character which surpassed her height and intelligence which Winning came to admire especially as she refused to pander to his position as a priest, an outlook he found distinctly refreshing. They were introduced by John McQuade, whose own family in Ireland were friendly with Susan's parents, and who was a regular visitor to their council house at 25 Alexander Avenue in the Viewpark area of Hamilton, where Susan (who was and would remain unmarried) also lived. After assisting with a complicated translation, Susan and both priests became regular dining companions. 'The basis of my friendship, and this is going to sound snobbish, was that we were educated and interested in educational things,' explained McCormack. In order to protect their reputations from gossip, neither priest dined alone with her and if one was visiting without the other it was always at her parents' house.

The diocese of Motherwell had been leaderless for over a year when in May 1955 a new bishop was appointed. During the intervening period Archbishop Donald Campbell of Glasgow had visited once a week to ensure diocesan affairs progressed, but now his presence was no longer required. Bishop James Scanlan, the former Bishop of Dunkeld, who was based in Dundee, was the new leader, a promotion which found no favour with Gerry Rogers. Tensions had existed between the Rogers and Scanlan families drifting back a genera-tion when both men's fathers had vied for the title of first family of Glasgow's East End. Frank Rogers was a talented sports journalist while Thomas Scanlan was reportedly Glasgow's first Catholic doctor. Each family had a different view of the faith; while the Rogers sup-ported their son in his vocation, Scanlan's father was so critical of the clergy that his son travelled to Westminster to pursue his vocation.

Both men were opposites: Rogers had little time for airs and graces and no desire to separate himself from parishioners, and in comparison, James Scanlan would become known as the 'last of the prince bishops', never setting foot in public unless dressed in the finest purple robes, complete with gloves and elegant ring of office. To signify his influence, he had Ronald Knox, then one of the most celebrated Catholic speakers in Britain, lecture on the role of the bishop at his enthronement on 8 September 1955. Winning was impressed, as he was already an admirer of Knox's work. Rogers was less so. Shortly after Scanlan's arrival, he moved Rogers from his home in Bothwell, which he took himself, and placed him in charge of the cathedral parish. Previously, Rogers had been free to run the diocese unhindered by the responsibility of a parish, but the arrival of a confident bishop had redressed the balance. Both men went on to work well in partnership but there was no doubt who was in charge.

Winning's admiration for Rogers grew when the priest was billeted at St Mary's for three months while his new quarters at the cathedral were prepared. Both men spent hours in conversation on matters of canon law, parish business and the role of the priest, and Winning became quite taken with Rogers' relaxed, off-the-cuff manner. Rogers had an innate ability for problem solving which permitted him to cut through bureaucratic difficulties, and intelligence which saw him juggle his workload as vicar general with the completion of a degree in civil law at Glasgow University.

Winning's first encounter with the 'prince bishop' was in the confines of Bertrand's Barber Shop in Hamilton's town centre. Scanlan had never tired of the traditional short, back and sides he wore as a young soldier and was seated for his fortnightly trim. As Winning stepped through the door he recognized him and said, 'Hello, my lord.' Scanlan replied, 'Hello, Father.' Then added, 'You are just the very man I have been looking for. Come tomorrow at four o'clock.' He then turned back to his paper. The invitation was a concern as bishops were distant figures to fear. Winning had only met the previous bishop once, when Douglas told him that he did not expect to see him in his office ever again or, as he explained, 'it will be for a very unpleasant reason'. Douglas believed the only reason to meet his priests in person was to discipline them. Scanlan's reason was actually benign. When Winning arrived, he was presented with a paper on marriage and canon law which the bishop had written and which he now wished edited and subbed down to size. Winning returned the paper two days later suitably corrected. Rogers had already spotlighted Winning for Scanlan as a talent to watch and for once the two men were in agreement.

The late Derek Worlock, Archbishop of Liverpool, who died in 1996, once described the role of the bishop's secretary as follows: 'A good, efficient secretary is a priceless jewel. He must be a diplomat, magician, martyr, mind reader and psychologist. He must be able to spell, punctuate and write correct English. He must have the patience of Job, the wisdom of Solomon and the physical endurance of a mule.'[1] When in 1958 Thomas Winning was asked to take on the role of secretary to Bishop Scanlan, he was unaware of the attributes required, but would have three years in which to learn. Worlock, however, had missed one crucial characteristic: the bishop's secretary must be able to drive. Scanlan had never mastered the skill, believing the idea of driving oneself to be vulgar. So initially, while Scanlan's gardener was taking driving lessons, it fell on Winning's shoulders to act as chauffeur. The job was claustrophobic. For the first three months the new secretary lived with the bishop at his Bothwell home, a situation that was to have a lasting influence on Winning's future living habits. 'It was such a bind. It's why I would never have another fellow living with me,' he explained. He found it impossible to relax; although the housekeeper was civil to him, he felt that his presence jolted the smooth running of the house. When Scanlan asked for his 'usual' drink after work, Winning agreed to the same, imagining a fine Chardonnay, but instead tasted tonic water for the first time. The next night Winning simply asked for a glass of milk.

Even a birthday visit to his sister offered no relief. Just as he was sitting down to dinner and his favourite dessert of clootie dumpling, the phone rang with Scanlan asking Winning to collect him and his friend Mgr William Heard and to drive them around the district visiting elderly friends. Margaret advised him to tell the bishop to take 'a running jump', but instead Winning collected his car keys and left. He had sworn an oath of obedience at his ordination and he would never break it, regardless of how tedious or inconvenient the request. 'I had always felt that a priest was ordained for people and for pastoral work, not to be a flunky for a bishop.'

The majority of Winning's work was desk-bound, collecting statistics for Rome, answering letters, and putting forward requests for marriages. Scanlan could be difficult to deal with. He had a strong temper and he would threaten those who displeased him by saying he would 'blow out their brains'. He could also be deeply insensitive. When a priest of the diocese – who had been a close friend of Bishop Douglas – died, he issued instructions that his predecessor not attend the funeral on the grounds that it would cause embarrassment to the diocese to be reminded of past mistakes. The decision was reversed when Fr Vincent Cowley, a friend of both Douglas and the deceased, strode into Scanlan's office against Winning's protestations and berated the bishop for his behaviour. Douglas subsequently attended the funeral.

Winning was soon sent to stay at the cathedral house alongside Gerry Rogers, before he was given a more permanent appointment as chaplain to the Franciscan convent in Bothwell where Susan McCormack taught. The work was low maintenance, requiring only Mass each morning in the oratory, confession, and regular visits to the school. The position also offered accommodation in a small flat above the lodge gate at the entrance to the school. The role of bishop's secretary was an education for Winning. 'I learned you should treat your fellow priests with concern and that you are there to help, not to boss them. There was an opportunity to store up these experiences. You can become too bureaucratic and autocratic. You can treat people like bits of paper with no more importance than a form.'

*   *   *

The 1950s were a decade characterized by loss and success. The death of his mother had been followed by Winning's promotion to bishop's secretary, and further advancement would follow the death of his father. Thomas Winning senior had repeatedly said after his wife's death that he wished God would take him to join her. Instead he remained alive to witness his daughter's marriage (officiated by his son) in 1955, and the birth of his two grandchildren, Agnes, born on 26 August 1956, and Edward, born on 3 January 1958 – three events which brought a great happiness to his twilight years. He would regularly stroll with each child in its pram and commented that he had never spoken to so many women in his life as when he was accompanied by his infant granddaughter or grandson.

His daughter and son-in-law and the two children had moved into the family home and as Thomas Winning suffered from angina, he was encouraged by Margaret to stay in bed each morning while she fed and dressed the children. On 2 March 1959, he had been suffering from flu, and when Margaret came up to his room with a breakfast of porridge and toast, she found him confused and distressed; Agnes was playing on the floor and the window was wide open. 'He kept saying: "When will Thomas be here?"' said Margaret. 'Every time I spoke to him it was "When will Thomas be here?"' He knew it was his son's day off, but Winning, as usual, had been delayed. He had popped into the office to check if everything was satisfactory and had been sent to the bank. Meanwhile, Margaret had visited her cousin, who lived next door, and asked for assistance in shutting the bedroom window but when John Canning climbed the stairs he found Thomas senior unconscious. Scooping Agnes from the floor he ran downstairs to call a doctor and a priest from a neighbour's telephone. After returning from the bank, Winning received a telephone call urging him to return home at once.

By the time I got home he was dead. He had died of hypertension. It was a brain haemorrhage. It was quite upsetting that I was not there when he died. I had quite a lot of time that morning. I could have been round at Scanlan's earlier and then got over to the house.

I don't feel guilty, but I wish I had been able to speak to him before he died. He was a stout wee fellow and we used to tell him to go easy because of his heart, but he would just start to laugh as I got angrier and angrier with him.

That day the anger was directed at himself and internalized. When Margaret told him how his father had been pleading for him, he felt nauseous with grief and regret that, however unwittingly, the Church had taken him from his father when he required him most. As with the death of his mother, Winning pulled down the shutters and grieved for his father in privacy and silence. The following morning he was standing at the gates of the church speaking to parishioners as they arrived for 7.30 a.m. Mass and Susan McCormack and her sister, unaware of his loss, approached and exchanged idle conversation for a few moments before moving inside. 'His father had died the day before and he never said a word. He was so full of hurt he could not say so to anyone.'

It was not until later that day when McCormack passed him in the school corridor that he broke the news. 'I could have dropped dead myself. I said, "Why didn't you tell us? May and I would have just been so sorry to hear it." But he never gave it away.'

Unable to be at his father's deathbed, Winning took what little comfort he could in providing the funeral he had always wanted. Born illegitimate in a dingy Edinburgh tenement, Thomas Winning wanted to depart a gentleman under the guidance of a bishop, and Scanlan was only too happy to assist in his young secretary's wishes. The funeral took place at St Patrick's, where the pews were packed with men young and old who remembered with affection Thomas Winning's kindness and Christian charity.

Less than a year after Winning lost his father, he lost, for the moment, his mentor. Gerry Rogers was now bound for Rome to replace Mgr William Theodore Heard on the Roman Rota following Heard's elevation to the college of cardinals. Originally a priest of the English diocese of Southwark, Heard had been born in Edinburgh and is now known as Scotland's forgotten Cardinal. He had been rewarded with a red hat for his decades of service to the Vatican, latterly as Dean of the Roman Rota, a role that involved weekly meetings with the Pope to brief him on recent cases and disputes. The Catholic population of Scotland was delighted, though few had ever met him, that a Scottish cardinal had been appointed, the first in over four hundred years since the assassination of Cardinal Beaton in 1546. Scanlan was overjoyed and travelled to Rome for the consistory, where it was also announced on 6 February 1960 that Rogers would take his place in Rome. At a private farewell dinner in Motherwell, Rogers explained his doubts about the task ahead: 'You can imagine a dedicated life of this kind cannot go on with human resources alone. These brilliant men who are among the best jurists in the world have given themselves completely to this work. The atmosphere is one of complete self-sacrifice. That is why I ask for your prayers so that I can persevere and that I may not let anyone down.'[2] Winning raised his glass and said a prayer.

By 1960, Winning was still employed as the bishop's secretary and spent his dwindling free time organizing Catholic scout troops. The extent of his interest in Baden-Powell's organization could have been stitched on the back of a first aid badge, but Scanlan believed the Scouts were crucial to integrating Catholics back into the ranks of the establishment and so encouraged his secretary's work. The life of the outdoorsman failed to enamour Winning who, despite taking part in a variety of weekend camps, failed to secure the required number of badges. The Scout work remained a source of great amusement to his friends. Susan McCormack remembered taking the salute from his troop and stifling laughter at Winning 'in shorts with the nobbliest pair of knees you've ever seen'.

At the time, Winning was living alone in a small flat at the entrance to the convent, a situation he never wished for and did not enjoy. A gregarious person by nature, he missed the camaraderie of the seminary and parish house and would feel lonely and dispirited when he returned each night. One evening, as he sat by the fire, he began to feel queasy and rushed to the bathroom and was violently sick. In the dim light the toilet bowl appeared black and he cursed the Bovril he had taken earlier in the day; it was not until he came back into the living room and noticed how weak he felt that he realized he had vomited blood. The doctor confirmed his ulcer was bleeding again and he was advised to adjust his diet. Stress seemed to exacerbate the condition and though his health improved over the next year it collapsed in October 1961 following his latest promotion.

A vacancy had emerged at the Scots College in Rome for a spiritual director and Mgr Conway, who worked in the diocesan office alongside Winning, said he had discovered the name of the new appointment. Winning regrettably insisted that he be allowed to guess and fired a series of names at Conway who shook his head at each suggestion. 'So who is it, then?' asked Winning, to which Conway pointed his finger at him. His appointment had been requested by his old vice-rector, Mgr Flanagan, and Scanlan had agreed. Initially Winning was asked to fly out the following week, but he requested, and received, almost a month to prepare himself and say goodbye once again to friends and family. The appointment was a terrible blow to Winning for it targeted his Achilles' heel, his spirituality, and was compounded by the decision, made a condition on his release by Scanlan, that he complete extra studies at the Roman Rota. Almost immediately, his health began to falter. 'I do believe it was the pressure and the strain of wondering how I would cope,' he reflected.

The night before his departure for Rome, Margaret and Eddie invited him to dinner and to stay over in an attempt to calm his nerves, but after dinner Winning became so weak and sick the doctor was called and he was advised not to fly. Unwilling to delay his departure any longer, Winning insisted he be driven to the airport the following morning, where he took off towards the largest storm in the Catholic Church's recent history: the Second Vatican Council (Vatican II) was now beginning to unfold.

SIX

No One is Far Away

'We were the Church of Silence.'
FATHER JOHN FITZSIMMONS

'I was out of my depth.'
CARDINAL GORDON GRAY

On 11 October 1962, Pope John XXIII was carried aloft on the Sedia
Gestatoria, to the blasts of silver trumpets. Slowly, the Swiss Guard
in plumed steel helmets and yellow, blue and red striped uniforms
bore the Holy Father up the central aisle of the Basilica of St Peter.
Tracing the sign of the cross in the air, he gazed around at a sight
last witnessed ninety-eight years ago: a Vatican Council. But where
in 1870 the attendance was just 737, this time the 2,600 bishops
drawn from the farthest corners of the globe had turned St Peter's
into a forest of mitres; a living testament to the growth and power
of the Roman Catholic Church.

The fact that they were now here, sitting on giant tiers of seats
on either side of the main aisle, like so many spectators at a baseball
game, was evidence of the power of the new pontiff who had been
elected in 1958 after the death of Pius XII. Cardinal Angelo Guiseppe
Roncalli, the Patriarch of Venice, was seventy-six years old and
considered a caretaker whose sole role was to keep the Sedia Gestatoria warm for Giovanni Battista Montini, the Archbishop of Milan.
Roncalli had other, very firm ideas. Just six months after his election,
on 25 January 1959, he announced to the world that there would

be a second Vatican Council, 'to let some air in', as the Pope later explained, gesturing to the open windows. His predecessor, Pius XII, had considered a second Council, but he allowed himself to be dissuaded by the cardinals of the Roman Curia, the senior civil servants of the Church by whom all change was to be resisted. John XXIII, a Vatican diplomat for twenty-five years, was aware of their Machiavellian ways and had sprung the announcement on them, instructing key people to applaud on cue. The Pope now wished the Holy Spirit to circulate through the lead-lined windows of the Vatican City. During his career, he had perceived the Spirit's '*pneuma*' in changes such as the end of the great empires of Britain and Germany, the freedom of the working classes and increased rights for women. The time was now right for the Church to succumb to the Spirit's grace.

The previous twenty-one general councils of the Catholic Church had principally righted perceived wrongs, defined dogmas, overthrown emperors and condemned heresy. In the mind of John XXIII, the Church needed to dispense not severity, but the medicine of mercy. The approach fitted the personality of the new Pope who would become beloved as 'the good Pope John' for what was perceived as his charming 'peasant' ways. He was in total contrast to his predecessor. If Pius XII was a regal figure, John XXIII was a jester who teased children and asked them to think why God had made him so ugly. Yet the Pope was no fool: with steely determination he pushed through plans for an ecumenical council that would be witnessed by other faiths and would be, most importantly, pastoral – every attempt was to be made to express the essence of the Catholic faith in new, more accessible ways. The key word was to become *aggiornamento*, Italian for 'updating'.

The preparations for the Council began almost immediately with ideas for the main agenda sought from every bishop, the head of each religious order, each member of the Roman Curia and staff at Catholic universities. Over nine thousand three hundred proposals were gathered, sorted, and repetitions removed and distributed to the preparatory commissions who were appointed by John XXIII and charged with the responsibility of producing over seventy documents. These documents were reduced to twenty texts and reduced again by 1962 to seven documents to be circulated among the world's bishops for the opening in October. The topics of discussion were sources of revelation, the moral order, the deposit of faith, the family and chastity, liturgy, media and unity. As they had been unable to prevent the council taking place, the curial officials took heart in at least being able to restrict the topics of debate.

When Pope John XXIII finally climbed out of his chair and sat on the papal throne, he addressed the gathering and explained that a path lay ahead along which the bishops must walk. In his heart he knew he would be unable to join them beyond the first leg as he had been diagnosed as suffering from inoperable stomach cancer. Yet in a thirty-seven-minute speech in Latin he urged the council to work towards the unity of mankind. 'The earthly city may be brought to the resemblance of that heavenly city where truth reigns and charity is the law.' He vocally rejected those who he said 'can see nothing but prevarication and ruin', were 'always forecasting disaster' and were 'prophets of doom'. It was a speech that left many a curial cardinal skewered to his seat. Worse was to come.

Two days later, during the first session, the rails on which the curia had designed the council to run buckled. Power at the council lay in the hands of the leaders of the ten commissions who would draft and regulate the decrees and constitutions. The curia had provided each bishop with a list of names of cardinals and bishops, drawn from their ranks for the job. The gathered bishops were expected to vote for them, a simple rubber-stamping of their authority. Cardinal Lienart of Lille in France spoke out: 'We do not know the men proposed as candidates and for membership of the commissions. The Episcopal conferences must be given time to consider their suitability and make their own suggestions.' The Cardinal's intervention was seconded by Cardinal Frings of Cologne, and instead of voting immediately, the bishops broke into regional groups to decide the best-qualified candidates. The applause that broke out around St Peter's was more than a warning shot; it was a burst of gunfire.

*   *   *

So where were the Scottish bishops during what would become the greatest turning point of the Catholic Church since the Reformation? In truth they were present in body but not in mind. Their contribution to the Vatican Council was minimal and illustrated not only a lack of interest but also the timidity of their native land. They lacked confidence and were content to nod along in the back row. When Archbishop Gordon Gray first heard the announcement of plans for the Vatican Council on the car radio, he thought to himself: 'How nice, a month's holiday in Rome.'³

Divisions within the Episcopal Conferences led to a lack of rigorous preparation. While Archbishop Campbell of Glasgow attended the preparatory commission as president of the Bishops' Conference, incredibly he did not seek the views of his brother bishops or even report on what had been discussed. Even more bizarrely, when invited along with every other bishop in the world to contribute suggestions for the agenda, Campbell never replied. Out of Scotland's eight bishops, only Archbishop Gray and Bishop Walsh of Aberdeen made any suggestions. While Karol Wojtyla, the Archbishop of Krakow and future John Paul II, contributed a seven-page essay on the need for the Church to tackle the distinctive spirituality of the human person, the two Scottish bishops, like so many others around the world, dealt with housekeeping. Among Gray's ideas was a six-year limit on parish priest postings, after which time priests would return to the role of curate and could be easily moved around.

When the time came to fly to Rome in October 1962, the bishops, like the Royal Family, flew separately, in case an instrument failure robbed Scotland of their spiritual leadership. While Bishop Scanlan, Bishop Hart and Bishop McGee flew with Aer Lingus from Renfrew to Rome, Archbishop Gray and Bishop Stephen McGill of Argyll and the Isles flew in a few days earlier. They were innocents abroad, unable to speak Italian or (except McGill) Latin, and were severely hamstrung from the early days. Gray and McGill were at least anxious to sample the international flavour of the council and booked into a small hotel, the Globe Palace, suggested by the Vatican and popular with the Latin Americans. Despite its proximity to the railway station, it was clean and comfortable and eventually the envy of their fellow Scots bishops. Scanlan, a man lost without his chauffeur, had booked the grand Columbus Hotel, but was forced to move out after a few weeks as the Scots party was unable to afford the cost of bed and board for the three-month stay. Instead they were forced to move to a smaller pensione, which Scanlan derided for serving 'horse flesh for lunch and dinner on meat days'.[4] Bishop James Black of Paisley, who was admitted to hospital in Rome, personified the lame-duck image of the hierarchy. He was diagnosed with a fractured shoulder, the legacy of an injury collected on an earlier trip to Lourdes. The lack of ambition or indeed preparation was demonstrated by the fact that the Scots were, along with South Korea, one of only two countries not to bring an official peritus or theological expert. Gray had invited Father John Barry, a professor of moral theology and the rector of Edinburgh's seminary at Drygrange, to accompany him to Rome. Yet as he was not designated as a peritus, he was unable to enter St Peter's and left after ten days.

The Scottish bishops could only watch as the Catholic Church swung on its great axis. The Vatican had already rejected Cardinal Richard Cushing of Boston's offer to fund the installation of a simultaneous translation system as used at the United Nations. From their seats among the rafters, the Scots bishops could only look down at the great debates whose repercussions would rip through their dioceses in the years to come. It was in the two cafés set up at the back of St Peter's and dubbed Bar Jonah and Bar Mitzvah that the bishops could glean what was going on.

On 22 October, as the outside world held its breath and watched as America and the USSR nudged each other to the brink of nuclear war over the Cuban missile crisis, a battle began inside the Vatican over the language of the liturgy. A great movement of Churches from Western Europe such as France, Belgium, West Germany and Holland wished to see the Mass celebrated in the vernacular. History lay on their side: in the early days of the Church the liturgy was celebrated in Greek with Latin adopted as the language of the people when the Roman Empire embraced Christianity as their official religion in the third century AD. The traditionalists were of the view that the Latin Mass continued to unite the global Church and that any change would lead to a fracturing of that unity. The Scottish bishops listened, for the liturgy was the one area in which their Latin was almost passable, as a great defence of the old tongue was raised by Cardinal Alfredo Ottaviani, Secretary of the Supreme Congregation of the Holy Office. Wielding Latin like a rapier, he attempted to slice through the argument of those who advocated change, but while he was sharp he lacked brevity and drastically overran the ten-minute time limit set for all 'interventions'. After repeated warnings from Cardinal Alfrink, the Dutchman who was presiding over the session, were ignored by Ottaviani, the presiding officer disconnected the microphone. The assembly burst into applause as Ottaviani, enraged at such discourtesy, stormed from the floor and refused to return for a number of days. The Holy Spirit, it seemed, had directed Latin towards the exit signs. The debate ran for over three weeks but the conclusion was that part of the liturgy could be converted into the language of each nation.

On three occasions during the course of the Council's four years, Cardinal Gray steeled himself to speak. His Latin was polished by a couple of students at the Scots College including John Fitz-simmons. Then Gray dosed himself with Phenobarbitone, a relaxant drug, before heading to St Peter's. Yet still he was unable to rise to the occasion. Relating the occasion to his biographer, Michael Turnbull, Gordon Gray said:

On the first occasion, my name was called at the beginning of the Assembly [for me] to speak. I went over my text. Each time I read it, I was more ashamed of my classroom Latin. I got cold feet and told Cardinal John Krol, who was a member of the Secretariat, that I would hand in my script, but would not speak. He was annoyed and twice came back to me in that aula (hall) to insist that I should. I still refused. Lately, I read my three prepared interventions in the acta (proceedings) of Vatican II and regret that I did not voice them publicly.

In his undelivered speeches, he had made valid points about the problems that the topic for debate would give rise to in Protestant Scotland. The only other member of the Scottish hierarchy to involve himself in the proceedings was Francis Walsh, a priest of the order of White Fathers who was made Bishop of Aberdeen. He contributed what was regarded as a fine paper on the topic of indulgences, the Catholic belief that certain prayers and good works while on earth can assuage punishment for sins in the afterlife.

Unfortunately, Bishop Francis Walsh would not return to the Second Vatican Council after the first year. In 1963, the Bishop became a source of scandal that would be echoed thirty years later in the case of Bishop Roderick Wright, when the wife of a Church of Scotland minister, Mrs Ruby MacKenzie, moved into the presbytery with him. Walsh insisted the arrangement was innocent and that it was one born of necessity, as her husband had evicted her because of her decision to convert to Catholicism. When his housekeeper left, Walsh compounded his error by taking MacKenzie on drives when he visited various parishes across the diocese. The situation was untenable and members of the diocese reported the case to the Apostolic Delegate, Archbishop O'Hara, in London.

In an attempt to broker a peace deal and convince Walsh of the damage he was doing to the Church, a meeting was set up between the errant bishop and O'Hara at St Bennet's, the home of Archbishop Gray. The meeting began badly as both men tried to convince Walsh to get rid of Mrs MacKenzie, with Gray even offering to make financial provision for her. When Walsh and O'Hara continued the meeting in private, the estrangement grew until the point when Walsh stormed out and O'Hara demanded that Gray call the Vatican that night and explain that Walsh should be 'retired'. Gray pleaded for more time to convince Walsh, and the bishop was given until July to remove Mrs MacKenzie from the house. Walsh refused and on 22 July he 'resigned'. On this day Scotland lost two bishops as the Archbishop of Glasgow, Donald Campbell, died the same day while leading a pilgrimage in Lourdes.

The news of Bishop Walsh's resignation however was not released until September. Walsh, now reduced to the Bishop of the titular see of Birta, a long-lost location on the river Euphrates, had moved out of Aberdeen to Banffshire. In spite of the embarrassment felt by the Catholics in the diocese, the press was surprisingly supportive of the rogue bishop. An editorial in the Aberdeen *Press and Journal* echoed the words of Archbishop Gray and insisted his integrity was never in doubt. 'A cleric of a different and perhaps coarser fibre, with a politician's ear to the ground, would not have allowed the situation to develop.' In a line that truly echoes a gentler era they wrote: 'Where matters of personal conscience are concerned, in which no man can be the judge of his neighbour, it behoves all Christians to pause before they perhaps unwittingly give the rein to scandal – that scourge which can begin with a whisper and end in a holocaust.' Walsh was to depart Aberdeen before the appointment of his successor, Fr Michael Foylan, on 8 December 1964. He went to live in Dublin, before moving to Grantham, outside Cambridge, where he lived until his death in October 1974 in a caravan in the corner of a farmyard.

When Winning was asked what his life's goal was, he said without hesitation that it was the implementation of the Second Vatican Council. As bishop, archbishop and then cardinal, he was to spend thirty years overseeing the fundamental changes in the Church that followed those four years in Rome. That he was present in the city at the time was both fortunate and frustrating. Fortunate for the spectacle he witnessed and the sense he derived of a Church in revolution, but also frustrating, for although he was considered eligible (for his fluency in Latin and doctorate in canon law) to attend with the bishops as a peritus, he was never invited to do so. While bishops throughout the world broke their vow of secrecy to brief colleagues and even newspaper reporters on the events within St Peter's, the Scots bishops stuck rigidly to the code of omerta. Winning felt lonely during what was his third period in Rome in less than twenty years and wrote monthly to Susan McCormack venting his frustration about the bishops' behaviour. McCormack considered the letters so incendiary that when Winning was made auxiliary bishop eight years later, she burned them.

Yet upon his arrival on 7 November 1961, his first concern was his health. The stomach ulcer that repeatedly flared up during times of great stress had left him incapacitated. Upon arrival he spent two weeks in bed at the college until he could be admitted for surgery to the Calvary Hospital, run by the Little Company of Mary, nicknamed the Blue Nuns on account of their distinctive habits. It was here he met Sister Elizabeth, a nurse who tended to him following his surgery and whom he would visit regularly over the next four decades. He was impressed by her humour. Upon his recovery from the anaesthetic she told him she had popped into the theatre during the operation and when he asked what part the surgeons were at she said: 'I'm not sure, but your entrails were still on the table.' At the college, Mgr Flanagan was adamant that Winning should not rush his recovery and it was arranged that he spend five weeks convalescing at a clinic in Fiesole, a small hill town to the north-east of Florence. The mild winter, fresh air and long empty hours rejuvenated his body, beaten after eight years of eighteen-hour days, but doubt continued to chew at his mind.

He genuinely felt the task of spiritual director was beyond him and that his slim reserve of 'holiness' would not stretch to the counselling and guidance of student priests. The regular visits of Fr Dominic Conway, the spiritual director of the Irish College, who took Winning on car trips to the coast, were a soothing balm. Conway broke down the job to its component parts and advised him that a friendly ear and heartfelt advice was all that was required. The task of spiritual director was fluid, for there was no set agenda; the director was not involved with discipline, but was instead concerned with each student's spiritual formation. It was only when Winning began to look back at his student days and his own poor relations with the spiritual directors that he knew how to tackle the job. He would be friendly instead of distant, he would visit students instead of waiting for them to visit him, and he would use his own past problems and experience to discuss theirs.

I felt that you really needed to start from scratch with these fellows. Nobody had ever bothered to build the foundations of what the spiritual director was for and how he should be used. I felt my task was to be available to them if they wanted to discuss anything about their spiritual life. I wanted to teach them the importance of spiritual qualities in their life, of prayer, of the sacraments, of the scriptures. I wanted to teach them how to mould themselves towards the priestly life of chastity and celibacy. I wanted to teach them how to look at their relationship with others.

Winning finally gave his first talk as spiritual director on 20 February 1962, four months after his arrival in Italy. The subject was the danger of popularity and how, though it may appear desirable, it was of little concern to the role of priest, which was to speak out clearly and strongly on what was right. The response of his students was mixed. While some, such as the biblical scholar, John Fitzsimmons, who would become one of Winning's staunchest critics, felt he was inconsequential, others such as John McIntyre, who would later become the rector of the college, found him both accessible and understanding. The departure of students after a crisis of their vocation was to be expected, but Winning ensured that each student talked through his concerns over a period of weeks before making an informed choice. 'I can't remember ever having tried to talk someone out of going, because what they told me was quite sufficient.'

In the autumn of 1962, Winning was invited by Mgr Clapperton, the retired rector, to meet Padre Pio, the Franciscan friar renowned for his mystical powers and the marks of the stigmata, the wounds of Christ, that scarred his hands and feet. Clapperton, who was sceptical about any phenomena, had become quite convinced after he was persuaded to meet with Padre Pio by a mutual friend, John McCaffery, a former seminarian who now worked at the British Institute in Milan. During the Second World War, McCaffery had worked in Special Operations Europe based in Switzerland and emerged after the Armistice as a banker in Milan. He had been drawn to the Monastery at San Giovanni Rotondo in the south of Italy, by the stories of Padre Pio's clairvoyance and bi-location, the supernatural ability to appear in two separate places at the same time, and had subsequently become a devotee. McCaffery would go on to write a book entitled *The Friar of San Giovanni*, published in 1978, exploring the priest's powers.

Together Winning, Clapperton and McCaffery hired a small car and drove south. The best time to see Padre Pio was at the public Mass he said at five o'clock each morning. A queue was already forming when they arrived at half past four. While others were preparing to weigh his authenticity by any aura they perceived him to possess, in the back of Winning's mind was: how clean would the church be? It is a strange point that cuts to the root of his attitude to the priesthood. At any Mass Winning celebrated, all the necessary robes and vestments were spotless, the altar linen immaculate. In Italy, it was rarely so pristine. Priests were often unshaven, robes filthy and stained, and the altars dishevelled. Spittoons were not uncommon in the back sanctuary. Following his ordination, Winning had travelled to Sicily on holiday and had requested permission to say Mass while in Messina. He was asked for proof of his priesthood by, as Winning remembered, 'the dirtiest old fellow in the dirtiest old place'. In Winning's mind Pio's attitude to the altar would be a true test. The doors opened just before five o'clock and people ran forward to secure a front-row seat. 'I have never seen that take place in a Catholic church before or since.' The three men found a suitable viewing spot on the balcony and watched as Pio, a small, bearded man in white vestments, came out of the back sacristy and on to the altar. When he raised his arms, Winning saw the white mittens that protected his bleeding hands.

Everything was perfect. The altar linen was so clean and fresh. The altar was spotless and he took an hour and a half to say Mass. It passed in a flash. It was a wonderful experience. He became very contemplative as he came near the consecration and then again after the consecration. As time passed, we prayed. I felt he was genuine.

There was a sense that there was something special here, that there was a special holiness.

After the Mass had ended, Clapperton and Winning went into the back sacristy. Along the walls stood crowds of men but Pio was oblivious to them. He knelt down at a kneeler, pulled the cape over his head and prayed. 'He wanted to be alone with God,' said Winning. It was said that as a priest in Rome, the young Karol Wojtyla visited Padre Pio and was told that one day he would lie in a pool of his own blood, a reference to the attempted assassination of Pope John Paul II in May 1981. Winning too was given the opportunity to speak with Padre Pio but declined through a mixture of shyness, reticence and self-doubt. Pio was in many ways a true peasant and when hearing confessions would shout people's sins aloud if he felt they were not sufficiently contrite. Winning was taking no chances. While Clapperton went over to speak to the friar, Winning hung back.

Two days each week, Winning drove into Rome for classes at the Cancelleria, a huge stone building with iron bars on the windows which sat on the Corso Vittorio Emmanuelle, a main road less than one mile from the Vatican. Archbishop Scanlan had insisted that he take extra studies that would permit him to qualify as an 'Advocate' of the Sacred Roman Rota, a position which would allow him to plead on a client's behalf. The entire college had decamped in the spring of 1962 and students were now resident all-year round at the summer villa in Marino, while a new college was under construction in the Roman suburbs. The old college required extensive repairs and refurbishment and the Bishops' Conference had made the decision to sell the property to a bank for £390,000 and use the proceeds to construct the new building – a decision they would later regret. The college staff had pooled their resources to purchase a small car for communal use, and so Winning was at least spared the bone-jangling two-hour round trip by bus that the students endured each day while attending the Gregorian University. Joseph Devine, the future Bishop of Motherwell, was completing postgraduate studies at the university and wrote a celebrated essay for the college magazine chronicling the students' adventures en route.

The Cancelleria was the office of the Roman Rota, the most active court in the Holy See. The reason for the title is lost but rota is Latin for wheel and a wheel design is inlaid on the floor of the courtroom; one theory for this is that the judges hear each case in turn, moving round like the spokes of a wheel. During his legal studies between 1951 and 1954, Winning had concentrated on the broad strokes of canon law; now, over the next three years, he focused on the fine detail of marriage law. His class consisted of twenty students, drawn from across the globe, the majority of whom were based in Rome. However, one student, dubbed 'the flying Spaniard', flew in each week from Madrid to attend lectures. There were four hours of classes each week but on top of this, students were set a lengthy essay on a particular area of marriage law. In the early Sixties, the Rota was developing a new heading under which marriages could be annulled. While reviewing the cases that came across their desk, the judges were becoming increasingly aware that many people had no concept of what constituted a marriage, entering into what the Church viewed as a lasting sacrament on a whim. A typical essay topic was to evolve a law capable of tackling such a lack of due discretion. Winning's essays were highly regarded; graded out of twenty-five, he regularly achieved full marks.

He was less fortunate in his first summer exam, which fell on 4 June 1963, the day after the death of Pope John XXIII. Winning had prayed that a particular topic would emerge as the principal question but instead found himself faced with a paper on how the three different types of schizophrenia affected a person's consent to marriage, a subject his lecturer had scarcely touched. Three weeks later, he accompanied a party of senior students to St Peter's Square on what became the final day of the conclave to elect John XXIII's successor. The students were present to catch the first whiff of white smoke from the chimney of the Sistine Chapel, but Winning was more pleased that he had passed his exam. The day was completed with the appearance of Pope Paul VI, formerly the Archbishop of Milan, on the balcony of the papal apartments.

Winning, Sean O'Kelly and John Fitzsimmons then departed for lunch at a fine seafood restaurant in Trastevere, a meal sweetened by the decision of a Milanese banker to pick up the tab to celebrate his archbishop's election. During his studies, Winning was in regular contact with Gerry Rogers, who worked at the Rota as a judge. The final exam was an ordeal which took place on 5 July 1965 and stretched from nine o'clock in the morning until nine that night. Lunch was packed in a brown paper bag and consumed at each student's desk. The structure of the examination was to put the student in the position of a Rota judge faced with an entire marriage case, including statements and reports from both bride and groom. Written arguments had been prepared by the Defender of the Bond, a lawyer whose role is to petition against the annulment and the advocate who argues for dissolution. To complicate matters, the documents were in four languages, French, Italian, German and Latin. Winning's task was to read the material and prepare a written judgement: could the marriage be annulled or not?

The case was complicated and far from common. The marriage was between a prisoner of war in Tangiers and a girl in an Italian town. They had approached a priest to marry them in spite of the fact that the groom was in detention outside the country and so all the requests had been carried out by letter. In a traditional marriage, the priest asks both bride and groom for their consent to the marriage at the altar. Winning spent nine hours poring over the papers. At one point, Gerry Rogers, who was one of the exam invigilators, asked how he was progressing. Winning said fine, apart from the dilemma of running out of cigarettes. Rogers slipped him a few and Winning began to write at six o'clock. He was convinced a valid consent had been given and the marriage was unbreakable. 'I remember thinking I had either done a great job or failed completely.' One week later, he was called into the rector's office and congratulated on his success. To celebrate the completion of his course, Flanagan and Rogers took Winning to Rome's choicest restaurant, where the portraits of movie stars hung on the walls and the maître d' mixed spaghetti with a pair of golden tongs.

Rogers then began passing work as a notary to Winning, who went on to take evidence in the case of Lee Radziwill, the sister of

Jackie Kennedy. The annulment case had reached the Rota on account of her then husband Stanislas Radziwill, an exiled Polish prince. Any annulment case involving royalty was handled by the Rota who were expected to be resistant to the pressures that might be put on a local tribunal. The extent of Winning's involvement went no further than the collection of the occasional statement, but it was a case that Radziwill's future biographer, Diana DuBois, viewed as long and difficult. In her biography, *In Her Sister's Shadow: An Intimate Biography of Lee Radziwill* she reported that, during her marriage, Radziwill had embarked on a string of affairs which included, but were not restricted to, the Greek playboy Taki and Roy Jenkins, then British Chancellor of the Exchequer.

The new Scots College was finally completed in November 1964, two and a half years after the students had first moved to Marino. It was an ugly building positioned just off the Via Cassia, putting function ahead of form in a typical Sixties design. The architect Renato Costa had been prohibited by the Scots bishops from taking any initiative which could result in a cost overrun and while the building came in on budget, it was strictly uninspired and resembled a four-storey comprehensive. Leisure pursuits were catered for by a football pitch, tennis court and outdoor swimming pool. The rector had organized for a group of Italian nuns, the Suore de Bethania, to cook and clean for the students and for college patrons to decorate the walls with artwork.

The college's official opening was scheduled for 16 November 1964, the feast day of St Margaret, one of Scotland's patron saints, and the new Pope Paul VI had agreed to officiate. Winning, as he was deemed to have the most free time, was charged with writing a short history of the college for publication in the *Scottish Catholic Observer* and the *Scottish Catholic Herald*, both of which were giving the papal visit extensive coverage. Winning's article succeeded in being celebratory and defensive with both views couched in his familiar flourish. The Catholics of Scotland, he wrote, owed their Roman college a debt which could never be overrated. 'Its history is largely the story of a struggle for a nation's soul, with all the elements of a glorious battle: a noble cause, the enthusiasm and valour of youthful patriots, the constant threat of death, imprisonment and exile, and, above all, as we now know, victory at last.' The final point was debatable, accurate, if mere survival constituted a victory, erroneous, if this involved possessing the whip hand.

He went on to pose and then evade a profound question, especially in the light of the bishops' dismal performance during the Vatican Council. The question was why Scotland lacked even one competent theologian.

One might ask to see the fruits in Scotland of such a magnificent intellectual, spiritual and cultural formation. Has not the country failed to produce even one theologian of merit in the past three hundred years? The answer is yes, but the explanation is simple: the Scots College, like its sister colleges, was intended to produce pastoral priests; men dedicated to the service of souls in parishes.

The answer was half-baked. Other national colleges had produced both scholars and priests, and while Winning undoubtedly considered himself one of the latter, he could see the need for the former.

On the day of the opening, a large crowd gathered at the gates of the college to welcome the Pope. There were cries of '*Viva il Papa*', and the Pope raised his arms in a gesture of thanks. The first to greet Paul VI was Joseph Pizzardo, the Cardinal Protector, who represented the college in the Holy See, followed by the rector, Mgr Flanagan, who led him up the stairs and into the hall where the Scottish bishops were assembled. Winning took the opportunity to introduce himself to Bishop Thomson, the new Bishop of Motherwell, who was replacing Scanlan who had been transferred to Glasgow. Flanagan delivered a message of thanks, insisting the Pope had given pleasure not only to bishops, priests and the faithful of Scotland, 'but to many other countrymen who do not share our faith'. In his own address, the Pope said he rejoiced in the improved relations between Catholics and non-Catholics: 'We rejoice that relations between Catholics and non-Catholics in Scotland are even more cordial and friendly and we bless the closer union in charity and love between all followers of Jesus Christ.'[5]

Winning was introduced, along with other members of staff, to the Pope. Gifts were exchanged, a thistle-shaped paperweight for the Pope and a chalice for the college rector. Yet the day was to end in disappointment for Mgr Flanagan. A few days previously, a rumour had emerged that the Pope was to appoint Flanagan as the new Bishop of Aberdeen, following the departure of Bishop Walsh. When, after blessing the congregation and meeting the college's nuns, the Pope walked with Flanagan out on to the patio, it was expected that he would invite him to take over the post. The invitation was never extended and the Pope departed shortly for his next engagement. Flanagan's disappointment was tangible. Three weeks later, the vacancy was filled by Fr Michael Foylan.

The land on which the new college was built had been previously owned by Ettore Villa, a lawyer, and his wife, Gabriella. After arranging for the sale, the couple went on to became generous benefactors of the college, purchasing vestments and carpets. They also became friendly with Winning, who was invited to dine in their apartment by the rector. When Ettore became ill and housebound, it was Winning who sought permission to celebrate Mass at the couple's home, a gesture which he repeated monthly until his death and which earned him Signora Villa's adoration and the sobriquet: 'Padre Thomas'.

The opening of the new college permitted the bishops to exchange their pensiones for residence in a home from home. When they arrived in September 1965, it was for the council's final sitting and at last Winning was permitted a degree of access. His former superior, the new Archbishop of Glasgow, suggested that his old secretary once again pick up his pencil and act as minute secretary to the bishops' private meetings where they discussed their views on the Council's topics.

The final session of Vatican II ran from September to December

1965 and covered such topics as religious liberty, the missions, religious life, priestly formation, priestly life and ministry and non-Christian religions, but one document towered over all others and inspired the greatest amount of debate: this was the Pastoral Constitution on the Church in the modern world – '*Gaudium et Spes*'. The Latin title was taken from the document's opening sentence: 'The joys and the hopes, the griefs and the anxieties of the men of this age, especially those who are poor, or in any way afflicted, these too are the joys and the hopes, the griefs and the anxieties of the followers of Christ.'

The document was a genuine revelation, for it marked the end of the image of the Catholic Church as a distant fortress, in which lay the answers to every moral, philosophical and theological answer. For the first time, the Church stated that she could learn from the world. A key phrase contained in the document was 'the signs of the times'. '*Gaudium et Spes*' argued that only after the Church listened to society and attempted to read the patterns of progress, 'the signs of the times' as it were, could it decide what was its mission. Though the document caused great concern among conservative countries such as Italy, Ireland and Poland and, in the privacy of the college conference room, the Scots, Winning was to find the words truly inspirational. He began to argue during the bishops' meetings about the wisdom of the document. To the older bishops troubled by the idea of a Church lacking answers, he explained that only in a static world could the Church be so infallible.

In effect, the document was to reverse the thinking of the popes of the late nineteenth century and early twentieth century, such as Pope Pius IX (1846–78) and Pius X (1903–14), who were both seen as having turned their backs on the world. Under Paul VI, and driven by the engine of the Second Vatican Council, the Catholic Church was to re-engage with the world. 'I remember that this was a great change. It was an end to the monolithic Church,' said Winning. 'The Church was saying it had the moral principles to answer all the new questions that would come, such as bioethics, but it did not have the answers yet.'

The concept of 'reading the signs of the times' and taking the appropriate action was to become a motif that threaded throughout the bishopric of Thomas Winning. When the Vatican Council closed on 8 December 1965, the final words of Pope Paul VI were always to echo in Winning's mind: 'No one in the world is a stranger, no one is excluded, no one is alone.'

SEVEN

A Better World

'There was a feeling that the Pope had made a wise decision.'

THOMAS WINNING ON 'HUMANAE VITAE'

Thomas Winning arrived back in Scotland in the summer of 1966, to endure, like every other Scottish football fan, the jubilation that followed England's 4–2 victory over Germany in the World Cup Final at Wembley. Like many Scots cursed with an inferiority complex associated with their larger neighbour, Winning was incapable of viewing an English victory, especially one of such magnitude, as anything other than a Scottish defeat. 'They'll be insufferable now,' he commented to Hugh McLoughlin, a teenage parishioner at St Luke's, a little church at the heart of a large sink estate in Motherwell, to which Winning had been appointed parish priest at the unseasonably young age of forty-one.

Winning was on the fast track to promotion. Three times now he had served his Church in Rome, completing tasks of increasing difficulty with diligence and demonstrating an enthusiasm and obedience that had been noted by his superiors. He had been invited to carry on the work of secretary to the Bishops' Conference, following the bishops' return to Scotland after the Vatican Council, and would grow to be trusted and admired by the men who composed the list of bishops-to-be. In his own diocese he was appointed 'officialis', or judicial vicar, handling canon law cases and imbued with the authority of his new bishop, Francis Thomson, who had also chosen to make him a vicar episcopal, a new post created by the recent council for priests with special responsibility.

In his fifty-three years as a priest and later bishop, archbishop and cardinal, Winning would spend less than four years in the very job in which the majority of his peers toiled throughout their entire careers. During the turbulent changes he later introduced to the archdiocese of Glasgow in the 1980s, critics among the priesthood carped that it was his lack of experience as a parish priest which led Winning to drive them to despair. 'A year as curate at Chapelhall, a few years at St Mary's, and four years as parish priest at St Luke's – the guy couldn't keep a job,' said one critic.[1] But it was Winning's experiences as a parish priest at St Luke's which were to inspire what would become the pastoral plan, his lifetime's work. It was at St Luke's that he first encountered the Movement for a Better World, discovered the importance of animating the laity, and felt the pain of watching hard work washed away by an unsympathetic successor. It was at St Luke's where his very future formed.

The parish of St Luke's was small and grim and yet it was to prove the perfect laboratory for an ambitious priest, imbued with the spirit of the Second Vatican Council. There were scarcely eleven hundred people within the parish, all of them drawn from a housing estate to which the local council consigned the troublemakers and those tardy with their rent. The Forgewood area of Motherwell was among the poorest places in a town not known for its wealth. Vandalism, alcoholism and unemployment were endemic and any decay of the district's soul was matched by its housing, street after street of crumbling grey pebble-dashed maisonettes, as dispiriting as they were uniform. Brian Logue, a young Irish priest, had been based in the parish as a curate for the past five years and watched as parish priests came and went; Winning was to be his third.

One of the few benefits of St Luke's was its positioning in a wooded area at the heart of the estate. On Sunday mornings, parishioners would walk along an avenue lined with beech trees to reach the church, a newly built wooden structure, surrounded by flower beds and an expansive lawn; afterwards tea was taken in the parish hall, an old converted stable block. The parish house had been originally built for a local pit owner and was a vast sandstone villa with large shuttered windows and was to comprise quite the grandest accommodation Winning had yet enjoyed. As parish priest, he had a large bedroom, bathroom and sitting room on the first floor, while Logue made do with a bedsit on the ground floor, where the housekeeper, Anne Boyle, also had her quarters, but the pair's working relationship was egalitarian and cordial. Winning was anxious to adopt a partner, not a lackey, and valued Logue's prior experience in the parish.

Although the reason Winning was appointed to such a small parish was to allow him to dedicate his office hours to diocesan work both at the marriage tribunal and on the bishop's behalf in the office, he had no intention of treating his parishioners as an inconvenience. Instead he did more than previous parish priests, who lacked the excuse of other distractions, to rejuvenate the parish. Winning wished to point it in a new direction and the first thing to move was the altar. For centuries the Catholic Mass had been celebrated by the priest with his back to the people in the pews. Traditionalists insisted this format united both priest and parishioners as all faced the one direction, yet Vatican II had ordered a more inclusive service in which the priest would face the people and the Latin rites would be replaced with the vernacular. The requests of previous priests to reverse their altars had been denied by Bishop Thomson, who was a cautious man by nature and had no desire to play the pioneer. The Vatican had compounded the problem by failing to issue clear instructions about the desired changes, requiring each bishop to apply their initiative, a resource withered through lack of use. Winning felt passionately that the reversal of the altar was the cornerstone on which all other changes would be built. He arranged a meeting with Bishop Thomson, where he argued that St Luke's should lead the way. As the church was only twelve years old, the altar was wooden and any reversal could be accomplished easily in comparison to older churches, whose altars were heavy marble structures often fixed to the back wall. Thomson was brought round by Winning's persuasion and Brian Logue was given the honour of saying the first Mass, a gesture he found touching. 'It was such a nice honour for me to say Mass facing the people, and I was grateful for the opportunity. Winning was very much a man of the liturgy and he was very strong on the idea of doing things well,' said Logue.

The new style of service was matched by Winning's inclusive method of management. He organized a census of the parish and discovered there were only three people who fell into the professional classes – all teachers – two males and one female, and that only 60 per cent were attending Mass, a disappointing statistic for the Sixties. Those absent were among the poorest of the parish and those he felt would benefit most from the Church's teaching. In order to draw them back, he first targeted the children, encouraging them to attend by inviting the boys to serve on the altar and the girls to read and take part in the offertory procession. He organized groups to visit the church after the Saturday morning service and took them one by one through the service. The appearance of their sons on the altar or their daughters carrying the bread and wine helped bring the parents back into the church. An early gesture that was appreciated by the community was Winning's visit to Motherwell district council to complain about their unofficial policy of using Forgewood as a 'sin bin' for troublesome tenants. He also advocated Catholics to stand as councillors in an attempt to better influence council policy.

The parishioners were also to enjoy their own council, after Winning divided the surrounding area into wards and persuaded two people in each ward to monitor any problems and report to the parish council on how they could assist. A pair of numerate parishioners visited the poorest families to help them budget better what little income they had. A newsletter was published informing local Catholics, practising and non-practising, of the parish events. 'It was a great time to be a parish priest,' said Winning. 'There was a great sense of movement.'

*   *   *

Winning was to make a rapid impact on the laity. He was rumoured at first to be a snob on account of his insistence that tea should always be taken with a saucer. A few moments in his company quickly dispelled such a notion and Winning's 'man of the people' image began to spread, through his anxiety to spend as much time with his parishioners as his many jobs allowed. Hugh Macloughlin was a third-year pupil at Our Lady's High School when Thomas Winning arrived in the parish. His father, Joseph, a household supply salesman, was president of the St Vincent de Paul Society and Winning became a regular visitor to the house.

> My father was taken aback, as were many of the other men in the parish, because Fr Winning asked what was required of him and the church to help. Priests didn't ask people in those days, they just told. He won them over to his side. I remember the first Christmas Eve after he arrived. I was singing in the Cathedral at Midnight Mass, and when I got back my father still wasn't home. It turned out Winning had brought the men into the church hall for a dram. The people in the parish grew to love him. He was like Jeremiah, honest and rough. It was like having a favourite uncle come to visit. He would kid my sister, Morag, who was eighteen: 'Have you got yourself a boyfriend, yet?' We had been brought up to respect the parish priest, it was a respect tinged with fear, but with Winning the fear evaporated.

On a Saturday afternoon, Winning indulged in his only regular relaxation: football. A Celtic fan since childhood he was now in a position to attend matches both home and away. At Parkhead, priests gained free admission as a grateful nod towards the club's founder, the Marist Brother Walfrid, while precious away tickets were secured by Pat Connelly, a parishioner of St Luke's who was also chairman of the local Celtic supporters' club and a close friend of Jock Stein, the club's new manager. Together Winning and Logue attended almost every match in a season touched by brilliance. In the 1966/7 season Celtic were to perform superbly. Under the management of Stein the team won every competition they entered:

Scottish League, Scottish Cup, League Cup and Glasgow Cup. Yet towering above them all in worth and historical value was the European Cup which, until that year, no British team had ever held aloft. The final was set for 25 May at the Estadio Nacional in Lisbon, the Portuguese capital, against Inter Milan, the Italian champions, and, unfortunately for Winning, the match fell on a holiday of obligation. Ten thousand fans in total secured tickets for the final – for many it was to be their first trip abroad – but he would not be among them. Concerned it would send the wrong signal to the parishioners if he was to attend, Winning sent his curate in his place and so remained at the parish. He did, however, have no intention of missing the match.

Aware that almost the entire Catholic population of the parish would be watching the game which ran over the seven o'clock evening Mass, he arranged for a later Mass at nine and persuaded a colleague with little interest in football to substitute for him during the first service. While Fr Logue cheered on the terraces of the Estadio Nacional, Winning and his nephew Edward, then nine, watched in a state of nervous anxiety from the sofa in the living room of the presbytery. An unfortunate penalty in the first few minutes left Celtic trailing by one goal to nil and it was not until the second half that Tommy Gemmell managed to score an equalizer. Five minutes before the final whistle and the spectre of extra time and even a re-match, Bobby Murdoch won the ball in the Italians' penalty area, passed to Stevie Chalmers, who then shot and scored. Winning and his nephew leapt from the sofa and began dancing around the room.

After presiding over the late Mass in front of rows of beaming faces, Winning dropped Edward back home and made a sick call. Susan McCormack's mother was dying of cancer in the back room of their home in Viewpark and despite her condition, she had urged her husband to travel to Lisbon for the game. Winning walked into the living room to find a cardboard cut-out of the European Cup sitting on top of the television. Susan and her sister were ecstatic and handed him a cup of tea. Mrs McCormack was weak and pale but delighted by the result. 'Now tell me that you'll say a prayer for Rangers next week,' she chided Winning. Celtic's arch-rivals were to play in the European Cup Winners' Cup final and would lose, much to his delight. 'Indeed I'll not, they'll be fine without me,' replied Winning. Early in the morning Susan's father returned, drunk on the first champagne of his life, and a few hours later his wife died. 'The Celtic victory helped my father cope, I believe. It was a strange consolation,' said Susan McCormack. To Winning the victory was an antidote to England's victory in the World Cup. 'Let them keep the world,' he said. 'We've got Europe.'

While Winning and his work at St Luke's was to attract him the reputation of a 'liberal', Bishop Thomson remained, in his view, as conservative as ever. Thomson had been born in Edinburgh and was a pupil at George Watson's, the distinguished private school in the capital, before moving on to Edinburgh and then Cambridge University, where he studied mathematics. Like Bishop Douglas, he had also worked as a teacher, spending seven years at the seminary at Drygrange on the east coast, followed by the rectorship of Blairs. He differed in many ways from his direct predecessor, James Scanlan, whose love of pomp and ceremony was common knowledge. In comparison, Thomson was uncomfortable in the robes of office, complaining during his installation in February 1965 that he was 'dressed up like Pooh-Bah'. While Scanlan barked orders like a military man, Thomson considered every option, calculated the odds of success versus failure, and made each decision with extreme caution.

Winning, meanwhile, was growing in confidence and stature. The combined load of parish and office work meant he rarely made the golf outings planned on his day off with colleagues such as James McShane and John McQuade, who began to resent his last-minute cancellations. It was never in Winning's nature to put leisure pursuits before Church business, regardless of how trivial the work or well-earned the leisure, a view neither shared nor supported by his fellow priests who would on occasion accuse him of 'toadying'. Barbs such as these would sting but would not cause him to deviate from the implementation of new ideas. He had seen the enthusiasm with which the laity at St Luke's had embraced their increased role in the parish and he wished to see it extended throughout the diocese; an ambitious, though presumptuous, attitude for a man who remained just a parish priest, albeit an influential one.

In early 1968, Winning pushed forward the idea of launching a diocesan pastoral council. At the time, the idea of a consultative body composed of priests, religious and laity was not only novel but also controversial. It had reared up in a few dioceses in England and Wales, but no diocese in Scotland had taken the step. When he raised the issue at the local deanery meeting, he gathered support from the younger priests such as Tom Connelly, but found older priests resistant to the idea of relinquishing their grip on power. Instead Winning concentrated on obtaining key converts. John Conroy, the Vicar General, under whom he had once studied, came on board and lent the project a degree of respectability, but the bishop remained his prime target. When an opportunity for conversion arose, Winning seized it. In the spring of 1968, Winning discovered that Donny Renfrew, his friend since his early days at the Scots College, was to holiday that summer with the bishop in Spain and he decided to accompany them in the hope that two weeks in a warm climate would provide ample opportunity to convince him of the wisdom of the plan. Thomson had other ideas. Exhaustive conversations on the reform of the diocese held no interest for a man who wished only a little sun and a long siesta. Each time Winning raised the subject, his bishop swatted it away like a bothersome fly, yet circumstance ensured that their holiday did not pass without discussion of an issue that was to provoke debate for decades to come.

On 29 July, the three men joined the students of the Scots seminary in Valladolid on their annual picnic on the banks of the Duero, a river which runs through Spain and Portugal, and it was here they heard an announcement on the radio that Pope Paul VI's encyclical, 'Humanae Vitae', had finally been published. Paul VI's meditation on the subject of artificial contraception was expected to come out in support of its use as, two years previously, the

Pontifical Commission for the Study of Population, Family and Births had concluded that the acceptance of contraception could be squared with the Church's teachings and tradition. Since its creation in March 1963 by Pope John XXIII, the commission had grown from six celibate men to a panel totalling fifty-five, now including economists, sociologists, theologians and, for the first time, Catholic married couples. An extensive survey was carried out among American couples which revealed the misery of serial births – women terrified to show affection to their husbands lest it lead to love-making and an inevitable pregnancy, and the failure and tension involved in the 'rhythm method', the only form of contraception tolerated by the Catholic Church, which involved carefully tracking the times during each month when a woman was infertile. Prior to the commission's formation, the Church had emphasized the procreative aspect of sex permissible to the detriment of the mutual satisfaction of the spouses. In 1930, Pius XI described artificial contraception in the encyclical '*Casti Connubii*' as 'base', 'indecent' and 'intrinsically vicious'; however, during the commission's three years of study and debate, many senior Catholic figures were convinced the Church had been acting in error.

Once the commission's report, titled 'Responsible Parenthood', had been leaked to *The Tablet* in Britain and America's *National Catholic Reporter* many priests sensed change was imminent and advised couples that contraception would soon be permissible. As a result, couples began taking the pill and using the coil and condoms. Paul VI, however, was unconvinced and instructed a second, secret commission, one comprised of the theologians who had taken part but remained unswayed by the original commission, to re-examine the subject. Chaired by Cardinal Alfredo Ottaviani, an arch-conservative and head of the Holy Office, the new commission rejected the previous findings and urged the Pope to hold the existing line. The commission then went on to draft the bulk of '*Humanae Vitae*', in which Paul VI was to describe contraception, to the surprise, anger and disappointment of millions of Catholics, as 'intrinsically evil'. Translating the announcement from a Spanish newspaper on the river bank, Winning, along with Thomson and

Renfrew, nodded in agreement. Winning had been sceptical of those who assumed change was inevitable and believed it unlikely that Paul VI could overthrow the teachings of previous popes. Paul VI had concluded he could not and would later become so demoralized by the reaction to his decision that during the final nine years of his papacy he never again published an encyclical.

The publication of '*Humanae Vitae*' was to spark a crisis in the Church throughout the Western world. Priests who could not in good conscience endorse the decision left, married couples who had become accustomed to the liberty of contraception stayed and ignored the teaching. This gave birth to 'canteen Catholicism', where individuals picked up teachings with which they agreed and discarded those which they found unappetizing. In England, the publication prompted a retaliation in the letters pages of *The Times* when, on 20 October 1968, fifty-five priests wrote in protest at the Pope's decision. In Scotland, the response was far less muted: a group of lay Catholics began to agitate, but the vast majority of Scots Catholics continued to believe that the Pope knew best. Winning himself was convinced by what he described as Paul VI's 'brave wisdom'.

> Back in the college that evening there was a feeling that the Pope had made a wise decision. We did not seriously think there would be a change and we were relieved that there was not. I could not see how the Pope was going to change the attitude that previously contraception was wrong and now it's right. I know some people found it difficult to continue to say that contraception was against the teaching of the Church. I wasn't one of them.

In September 1968, Brian Logue was moved to a parish in Shotts to serve as curate to a Canon Barry White and was replaced by a second Irishman, Neal Carlin, from Derry in Northern Ireland. If Logue was quiet and deferential, Carlin was argumentative to the point of arrogance. A star athlete who ran the four hundred yards in forty-nine seconds and was feared on the Gaelic football field, he was just as deeply devoted to his calling as to his sports, and was to willingly embrace new spiritual experiences. He may have been read 'the riot act', as Winning described it, on more than one occasion for tardiness, but he respected his new parish priest. 'There was a real humanity there, a great freedom from tradition,' said Carlin. At St Luke's he reinvigorated the youth club, organizing skiing and pony-trekking trips and he encouraged the young to work for the old and infirm. In the diocese he became part of Winning's campaign to update the liturgy and toured parishes saying the Mass facing the people while Winning explained the liturgical ideas behind the changes to the older parish priests. Yet his greatest contribution, both to the parish and his parish priest's own spiritual formation, was to introduce Winning to the Movement for a Better World.

At the time, Winning had no knowledge of the spiritual group other than a vague memory of a sign he once saw in Italy while travelling to the Villa Scozzese in Marino. The sign read: 'To a Better World', and led to the headquarters of the organization founded in 1952 by Padre Ricardo Lombardi, an Italian priest who wished to inspire the laity. The MBW, as it was known, had recently expanded into Britain and Carlin had taken part in an introductory retreat in Kilmarnock. Winning was intrigued enough by his curate's response to arrange for the group to run a series of retreats at St Luke's throughout the summer of 1969. The courses, designed to encourage lay responsibility, ran over a weekend and were led by Fr Tucker, an American Jesuit, Ellen Gielty (who would later rise to become Superior General of the Sisters of Notre Dame) and a former sea captain and his wife. During the retreat the parishioners were encouraged to imagine the perfect parish: for example, a priest who cared, strong Mass attendance, a warm social life and regular charity work. They were then asked to imagine what was required of each of them in order to achieve such a parish. 'The people were very interested and enthusiastic. For the first time they were conscious of the parish and conscious of their own gifts and abilities,' said Winning.

Carlin was delighted that his suggestion had proved popular, but he was particularly pleased by Winning's method of making decisions. A topic would be discussed and disagreements aired. Winning would inevitably get his way, but the curate felt he was open to God's call. 'Whatever decision-making process we were involved in, whether it was resolved or not, was put in the context of the Blessed Sacrament. We would go over to the chapel and pray in silence. The idea was to find what the Lord was saying.'

In later life, Winning would vehemently deny any ambitions beyond that of a simple parish priest, but according to Carlin he already had the manner of a man looking towards a bigger future. 'I got the feeling that he was very clear and open about the possibility. He never said to me he would be the Archbishop of Glasgow, but you got the sense that there was an expectation within himself that promotion would follow.'

An indication of the level of confidence in which Winning was held by the Bishops' Conference was that when he argued for the creation of a national marriage tribunal, the bishops listened and eventually agreed. The current system in which each of Scotland's eight dioceses had their own individual tribunal made little sense. Instead of each diocese struggling to cope with part-time staff and a rapidly rising workload, it was better to create a dedicated office of full-time canon lawyers, supported by full-time staff. The idea was unconventional and would require the approval of Rome, but after digesting Winning's briefing paper in which he argued that a centralized service would provide a speedier, more efficient service, the Bishops' Conference was convinced. They were also convinced that Winning was the correct man to run it and so in January 1969, he was appointed President of the new Scottish Regional Tribunal.

Among Winning's recommendations was that the tribunal should be located on a neutral site, one not already used by any of the dioceses, but as the bishops were keen for it to be based in Glasgow, he began to search for premises. His housekeeper Anne Boyle alerted him to a large detached villa in Pollokshields, Glasgow's garden suburb, which had been placed on the market by the parish priest of Our Lady and St Margaret's in Govan, who had used the property while renovations were taking place on the local parish house. Winning was taken by the high ceilings, wide rooms and ornate pillars and agreed to the asking price. In spring 1969, the tribunal was launched.

Leaving St Luke's was a wrench. The parish had begun to thrive and the parishioners relished their new involvement. Mass attendance had risen and parishioners were anxious to expand on the insights into Christian living revealed by the Movement for a Better World. The tender shoots of Vatican II had no sooner begun to pierce through the soil of the parish than they were abandoned. There was little Winning could do. When a parish priest is replaced, it is similar to a change of government; all plans or policies are ejected and his successor, Fr Jim Keegan, made it clear that he had no interest in taking up the slack. During his first sermon he declared, according to Hugh McLoughlin, that 'There will be people here who are not happy that they've got a thick Irish priest. Tough.' No events were cancelled, but under his direction no new ones were organized. 'He starved it. He killed it. He just let it die,' said Neal Carlin, who left six months after Winning's departure to study in London. Hugh McLoughlin said: 'There was a feeling of great loss when Winning left. I had a feeling that all we had we were going to lose.'

The decline of St Luke's was a source of pain and disappointment to Winning. 'I was furious that no effort was made to keep the ideas going, but there was nothing you could do, it would have been improper to speak to the priest or complain. It was no longer any of my business.' It was a pain he would not forget and one which would result in a controversial decision twenty years later in which Winning forced each parish in the archdiocese of Glasgow to adopt the same plan and thus harness new parish priests to the work of their predecessors.

In Glasgow, Winning had problems of his own. The city's own respected and successful marriage tribunal were not best pleased at the creation of a national office and were unimpressed by their new boss. 'I found that the greatest opposition was from the Glasgow tribunal who felt that I was a whippersnapper. There was a bit of petty mindedness, but I gathered them together and told them straight what they were going to be doing.' One monsignor refused to even work with Winning or attend the national office and so the new president felt pushed to speak with Archbishop Scanlan about his behaviour. Scanlan, conscious of keeping his own priests contented, assured Winning that no snub was intended and that the priest was completing private work on his behalf. Winning knew this to be a lie, but one he would have to accept.

At this time, Winning met the woman with whom he was to spend the rest of his life: she was Isobel McInnes, his new house-keeper. Anne Boyle was in poor health and decided to return to her native Ireland, prior to Winning's move to the tribunal, and suggested Mrs McInnes, a forty-seven-year-old widow from Kilmarnock who was five years Winning's senior. Her husband, an auto-trader, had recently died of lung cancer and McInnes, who had no children, was considering training as a nurse in order to support herself. When Boyle approached her with the suggestion, she was initially hesitant. McInnes was a Protestant convert to Catholicism who became a devout believer but she was concerned about what the job entailed, telling Boyle: 'The only person I have looked after was my husband.' A meeting with Winning put her at ease as he explained that all he wished was basic cooking and cleaning. When she insisted she could not work in a parish with the extra workload involved in serving curates, he said it would be highly unlikely he would be moved, explaining: 'I'll be here for life.'

For the next thirty-two years 'Mrs Mac', as he called her, served Winning, whom she referred to as 'Father' regardless of the titles that followed. It was a relationship built on respect that developed into a rich, platonic love. The relationship between a priest and his housekeeper has often been the subject of satire and scorn, from the madness of Mrs Doyle in the TV comedy series *Father Ted*, to the depiction of illicit sexual relations in films such as *Priest*, written by Jimmy McGovern. There is a truth in both perceptions. As an archbishop, Winning was forced on more than one occasion to instruct a priest to get rid of his housekeeper after she had become too possessive, erratic or rude to parishioners, and sexual relations between a priest and his housekeeper did occur on rare occasions. Yet the relationship between Winning and Isobel McInnes was a portrait of decorum that hinged on McInnes' instinctive understanding of her place. She quickly adapted to his strict diet: a warm roll and butter and cup of tea for breakfast; soup, a roll and a piece of fruit for lunch, with the main meal of the day served promptly at six o'clock. Winning never tired of roasts, beef, lamb or chicken, and would eat almost any pasta served, but disliked fried food which irritated his stomach. During the next three decades, Isobel McInnes would grow to be considered a member of his family and would join him on family holidays, travelling with his sister or niece and nephew, but she remained first and foremost his servant.

For the next two years, Winning dedicated his time to co-ordinating the tribunal and helping in the diocese of Motherwell, where he remained a vicar episcopal. At the tribunal he became known for his disorganized nature. The desk in his office overflowed with paperwork and on a number of occasions two members of staff discovered they had both been given the same task to complete. The most significant event of those two years was the Ibrox disaster on 2 January 1971 in which 66 Rangers fans were killed and 145 injured when a stairway collapsed during the Old Firm game between Celtic and Rangers. In spite of the fact Winning was in his office less than two miles from the stadium, from where the roar of the crowd was distinctly audible, he remained unaware of the incident until hours later when his niece Agnes called to inform him. In any other city the reaction of the Catholic Church would be inconsequential but in Glasgow, where religion was polarized between Catholic and Protestant, the action of Archbishop Scanlan was little short of miraculous. Three days after the disaster, the players and management of both teams united at St Andrew's Cathedral for a requiem Mass. As Scanlan said from the altar, 'In offering this Mass today, we of the Catholic community are paying the highest tribute in our power to the victims of Saturday's appalling disaster which in the words of the Pope "has plunged Glasgow into mourning"'. The presence of Rangers Football Club, a team who would refuse to sign a Catholic player until 1988, inside a Catholic cathedral offered a glimmer of hope at a time of tragedy, but a glimmer was all it turned out to be, for once the service was over both communities returned to their trenches.

In the early months of 1971, Winning's national profile began to rise. He regularly appeared in the Catholic press to comment on marriage and on 1 February he took part in *No Easy Answers*, a Sunday-night talk show on Scottish Television. The topic of debate was mixed marriages and Winning ruffled feathers among a panel that included the Moderator of the Church of Scotland with his robust defence of the Catholic Church's position that other denominations offered 'less than basic Christianity'. Two months later he was chosen to represent the Scottish hierarchy at a European conference in Geneva to discuss the role of the priest in the modern world. He had almost taken on the mantle of a bishop-in-waiting.

In the autumn of 1971, Scanlan announced that he was in search of a successor. He had less than three years until he was expected to tender his resignation, upon his seventy-fifth birthday, and was anxious to ensure a smooth transition. He already had the support of an existing auxiliary bishop, James Ward, but after being passed over for promotion on two occasions during his long years of service in the diocese, Ward was viewed as a capable administrator whose career had already reached its peak. Across the diocese priests were now in discussion about Scanlan's unusual request for the appointment of a coadjutor bishop and just who the likely candidates would be. In canon law a coadjutor is distinguished from an ordinary auxiliary bishop by his automatic succession upon the archbishop's retirement and the strict control he exerts on policy immediately following his appointment. The problem with such a position was that an inexperienced coadjutor who demonstrated himself incapable was exceedingly difficult to remove without great embarrassment. In comparison, the appointment of a second auxiliary bishop would allow Rome two years or more to monitor his success before deciding if further promotion was warranted.

When Winning arrived at the tribunal office on the afternoon of 19 October he was told by his secretary that Archbishop Enrici, the Apostolic Delegate of Great Britain, had called and wished him to call back immediately upon his return. Years later, Winning said that he believed the Archbishop was calling to complain about the tribunal's non-payment of bills for marriage cases. After dialling the number and speaking briefly to Mgr Carson, the Delegate's secretary, Winning was put through to the Archbishop who was characteristically direct and informed him that the Holy Father would like him to accept the role of Auxiliary Bishop to the Archbishop of Glasgow.

Exactly how Winning came to be chosen remains unclear. Correspondence within the Scottish Catholic archives currently remains sealed to historians and biographers, but in all probability he would have appeared as the top name on a terna (a list) of three names passed by Archbishop Scanlan to the Apostolic Delegate, who would then have forwarded it to Rome and the Congregation of Bishops. After the appointment, the terna is destroyed. Officially, the Pope appoints every bishop, but in reality only a tiny percentage in the world's largest dioceses receive his immediate attention, and in the remainder of cases he will take the advice of the Congregation who, in turn, nine times out of ten, are in agreement with the Apostolic Delegate and the country's Bishops' Conference.

In retrospect, Winning was an exemplary candidate. His education in Rome would have impressed the Congregation of Bishops who, as far back as 1880, were said to believe 'a Roman education was seen as guaranteeing loyalty to Rome'. Service at a seminary was common among Scots bishops and Winning had served as spiritual director in Rome, while his work as secretary to the Bishops' Conference had brought him closer to the hierarchy, particularly Gordon Gray, now Cardinal Archbishop of St Andrews and Edinburgh. Another influence on the decision was Cardinal William Heard, of whom it was said that no bishop was appointed between 1950 and 1974 without his opinion being sought, and Heard thought highly of the polite young man who had driven him around the countryside of Lanarkshire on his summer vacation. The most outlandish suggestion was the influence of an affluent Italian family, whom Winning had befriended while spiritual director at the Scots College. Who knows if Gabriella Villa had a quiet word in the ear of a curial official about the talented 'Padre Thomas'? It seems unlikely, but however his elevation emerged, he was to be a shrewd and successful choice.

In his office in Woodrow Road, Winning reminded Enrici that Scanlan had requested a coadjutor. The Archbishop replied that there had been no mistake and that the Holy See had instead seen fit to appoint an auxiliary bishop, and would Winning accept the invitation? Winning then asked for time to consider his position, but Enrici politely refused, and for a third time he pressed Winning for an answer. Sitting stunned in his chair the world telescoped to a single response: yes or no. No choice existed; strict obedience to the Church had informed all of Winning's actions since his ordination twenty-two years previously, and so the answer was yes. It had to be yes, always yes.

EIGHT

A Battered Mitre

'He was not happy when he first came to Glasgow. They treated him like dirt.'[1]

SUSAN MCCORMACK

'That year I did not want to see a mitre and a crosier. I felt it was all a farce. I felt totally deflated that this was the way the Church operated.'[2]

THOMAS WINNING

One hour before the eleven o'clock start of the ordination Mass, St Andrew's Cathedral on the banks of the river Clyde was packed. As yet more guests, drawn from across the United Kingdom and the Republic of Ireland, attempted to squeeze into the pews, those already seated breathed deeply and drew in their arms. For many the next few hours would not be the most comfortable ceremony they had ever attended, but for a few it would remain the most memorable. The weather had been kind to Thomas Winning on the day he was to become a bishop. The 30 November 1971, the feast day of St Andrew, Scotland's patron saint, was a cold but bright day with sharpness to air so often dulled by rain.

The surprise of the announcement one month previously had given way to delight as the bishop elect continued his work as before, giving a talk on marriage guidance to the Union of Catholic Mothers, where he was congratulated by Mgr Flanagan, his old rector, now a parish priest in Bellshill, and later a talk to the Circle of the Newman Association on the work of the regional tribunal. The announcement had not been without its problems. Winning had planned to break the news to his family at a gathering disguised as a 'Halloween party' on the morning of 25 October, the day an official announcement would be made in Rome, but the death of Alex Hamilton, his old parish priest, put paid to such ideas. Instead he and his sister attended the funeral at St Mary's in Hamilton, where he had once toiled as a curate and where Scanlan had instructed that Bishop Thomson should announce his new position from the altar. Winning found the idea unpalatable and a distraction to prayers for his old priest. He was still smarting from his decision to delay informing Hamilton, who he knew was seriously ill, and now, of course, it was too late and his 'good news' was to mar the priest's final send-off.

On the day of the ordination dozens of police officers were drafted in to co-ordinate the traffic for the arrival of guests such as Glasgow's Lord and Lady Provost, Sir Donald Liddle and his wife. As the hour approached, the first procession began with two hundred priests in black cassocks and white surplices, followed by canons and monsignori and then the Primus of the Scottish Episcopal Church and Dr Stanley Mair, Moderator of the Glasgow Presbytery of the Church of Scotland. Winning was among the last to process down the centre aisle, accompanied by fellow bishops from England, Ireland and the whole of the Scottish hierarchy. An honour guard of Scouts dressed in kilts and with flags raised high stood on the street outside.

The episcopal ordination began with the choir singing the '*Veni Creator*', the ninth-century Latin chant which calls on the Holy Spirit to bless the one who stands before him. As the last few lines died away, Archbishop Scanlan rose from his seat and was joined by the bishops of Motherwell and Paisley. Winning then walked out to the centre of the sanctuary accompanied by two priests with whom he was close friends: John Chalmers and John McQuade. Winning then stood in the centre of the altar as the apostolic mandate was read out and he was questioned before the congregation on his resolve to keep the faith and discharge his duties loyally, under the authority of the Pope. He was then presented solemnly with the symbols of office: the book of Gospels, which he was commanded to preach; the ring to mark the marriage between himself and the Church; the mitre, and finally the crosier, the sign of his pastoral role – a shepherd who must lead his sheep. In line with the new changes of the Vatican Council, a greater emphasis was placed on the laying on of hands by the Scottish bishops who, in those few seconds, completed the final piece of Winning's priesthood and bestowed upon him the power to ordain.

At the end of the ordination the principal address was given by Cardinal Gordon Gray, the Archbishop of St Andrews and Edinburgh, who used the pulpit initially to attack those theologians such as Hans Küng, Karl Rahner and Edward Schillebeeckx, who he believed had used the current time of change to undermine the Church's traditional standards under the cloak of renewal. He quoted St Paul as prophesying a time when 'people will be avid for the latest novelty and collect for themselves a whole series of teachers according to their own tastes'. Instead Gray insisted man was called to follow the truth: 'And the truth will be found in the official teaching of the bishops speaking with the Vicar of Christ.'

Once the congregation had recovered from the vent of his frustration, he turned to the hierarchy's latest recruit:

Bishop Winning's duty will be to teach, to govern and to sanctify. He will fulfil that duty of teaching with confidence for he does not speak alone. As a successor to the Apostles, as a member of the College of Bishops with the Vicar of Christ as its head, Bishop Winning will speak with the Church and with its Divine Authority – 'As the Father has sent me, I also send you'. The Church may be attacked, derided, persecuted, but it will not fail . . . Bishop Winning must govern. But the authority he will exercise is the authority not of power, but of love. Like the Good Shepherd, he will lead, not drive. He will stand out as one who serves. Like Christ himself, he will be among you as 'one who serves'. It is indeed a frightening responsibility that none would shoulder unless he were called by God as Aaron was called. But God's grace is sufficient for him.[3]

Gray closed his sermon on a cautionary note. There would be times, he explained, when Bishop Winning would know loneliness and disappointment, misunderstanding and perplexity. Sometimes he would even look back enviously on his days as a curate and parish priest. As the celebrations closed and transferred to the St Enoch's Hotel, the new Titular Bishop of Louth was unaware how quickly those words would turn to prophecy.

When Winning's appointment was announced, Bishop James Ward was admitted to Bon Secours Hospital on the south side of Glasgow and diagnosed as suffering from complete exhaustion. At the age of sixty-six, Ward had served his native diocese for forty-two years since his ordination in 1929. He could, had he chosen to, have welcomed the arrival of a younger man with a sense of gratitude and relief that a great burden was now shared. But James Ward was a bitter man. He was angry at having twice been passed over for the role of archbishop, and was disappointed that he would now never enjoy a diocese of his own. His entire clerical career had been confined to an office and it was a prison he grew to love. For eighteen years he had been Archdiocesan Secretary, then Chancellor, followed by Vicar General and Diocesan treasurer, a role he clung to even after his appointment as Auxiliary Bishop in 1960. Ward was a capable administrator and had been the choice of Glasgow's senior clergy to succeed Archbishop Campbell, a plan spoiled by the appointment of Scanlan. Yet the arrival of the new archbishop did little to disturb Ward's work. 'JD' enjoyed the role of principal player on a stage much larger than Motherwell could provide and concentrated his powers on the elevation of Catholics into the establishment, rather than the minutiae that flows from the day-to-day administration of an archdiocese. While Scanlan toured the city in a chauffeur-driven Mercedes complete with a Blaupunkt stereo system, delivered speeches to Trades House and both demanded and gained a respect previously unwarranted for a Catholic archbishop in Glasgow, Ward sought solace in his work and ensured the diocese ran smoothly.

If the relationship between Ward and Scanlan was cool, the relationship between Ward and Winning was arctic. Ward was jealous of the younger man and begrudged him his future career. Their relationship curdled from their earliest encounters. During the meetings of the Bishops' Conference at the Second Vatican Council, Winning was eligible to attend in his role as secretary, while Ward as an auxiliary was not, a ridiculous scenario which irritated Ward, who would go for long walks while the meetings wore on. This situation continued back in Scotland with Ward feeling cast as the outsider to Winning's role as a rising star. It was only a few days after Winning's ordination that the new bishop felt the point of Ward's crosier digging into his back.

At their first meeting after Winning's appointment, Scanlan had agreed with his request not to be given a position as parish priest on top of his new duties. Three years at St Luke's had taught him that the role of parish priest was a full-time commitment, one incompatible with other work. At a second meeting he was told that following separate discussions with Ward, Scanlan had changed his mind and would now be appointing Winning to a parish. 'We have reconsidered and we feel it would be much better for you to take on a parish,' explained Scanlan. The parish of St Joseph's was initially suggested, but as the church and parish house were a shambles requiring extensive renovation, Winning hesitated then suggested that perhaps Scanlan would accompany him on his inspection. This was a calculated move for he knew Scanlan would never dream of visiting such a building site and so the parish of Our Holy Redeemer in Clydebank was offered as an alternative, since the previous parish priest had recently died. Winning examined his options; if he refused, he would instantly be marked as 'trouble', scuppering further promotion and wasting what little goodwill he had with Scanlan. 'I thought, if I said "Yes", then they would owe me a favour and I would just go away and do what I liked, which was to open up the place and get to know the people.' Winning believed Ward had deliberately engineered the appointment in order to sideline him, but was determined he would not succeed and accepted the post on condition he could appoint his own assistants.

Winning's statement about his appointment to the *Scottish Catholic Observer* was terse: 'It is important that a bishop be in touch with everyday parish life.'

Winning held no grudge against either of the two curates at OHR, as the parish was called; his decision to replace them illuminates his attitude towards authority. Gerry McCallion was a contemporary with whom he had studied, while Peter Clinton was an older man and Winning felt both would be as uncomfortable receiving orders from him as he was dispensing them. At forty-six, he was the youngest bishop in the Scottish Bishops' Conference but was at times doubtful of his own authority. At a meeting to explain his position, McCallion accepted with good grace but Clinton grew antagonistic and said he had earned £100 a week before even considering the priesthood, a boast about his wider experience which Winning believed proved his very point. Both were reassigned to other parishes by Scanlan and replaced by Fr Dominic Doogan and Fr John Muldoon, two newly ordained priests about whom Winning had heard promising reports.

Like an advance guard, both men were sent on ahead to live in the parish house, while Winning continued to reside above the tribunal's offices in Woodrow Road, until the accommodation was refurbished to his satisfaction. 'The place was a shambles, the only thing we rescued was a television set and a small antique lamp. There was just a bare concrete floor in the kitchen,' said Winning. A legacy of his mother's meticulous housekeeping and presentation was Winning's desire for pathological neatness at home, on the altar, or in the office. In a strange paradox, the same rigorous standards were never applied to his own workspace, as his private study, throughout his career, was a blizzard of papers, folders and books precariously piled on top of each other. A second problem was persuading Mrs McInnes that she could cope with parish life and she agreed only after Winning had dropped a nine o'clock supper from her list of daily chores. Even then her arrival was not without mishap as her wardrobe almost fell through the rotten floorboards of her new bedroom. Winning did not take up full-time residence until March. 'It took a long time to get the place together

Thomas Winning senior: his illegitimate
birth was to inspire his son's pro-life work.

Charles Canning: Thomas Winning's
maternal grandfather, pub owner and
Baillie of the old Wishaw Parish
Council.

Agnes Canning: Thomas Winning's mother
rationed her emotions but expressed her
love not in words but in deeds.

The little prince: Winning, aged four (*right*), with his cousin Lucy Canning and his little sister Margaret.

Brother and sister: Thomas and Margaret Winning as children.

A Sunday promenade: young Thomas takes the air, complete with walking stick and accompanied by his mother and sister, Margaret.

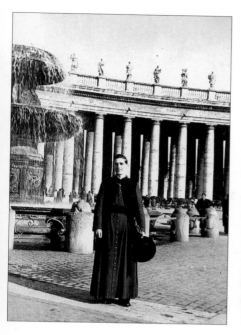

Rome at last: Thomas Winning, the seminarian, in the uniform of the Scots College, pictured in St Peter's Square, 1947.

The family gathered in Rome for Thomas Winning's ordination in December 1948. His father (*bottom centre*) sold his sweet-making equipment to pay for the trip.

Students were prohibited from walking alone, lest the temptations of Rome prove too much. Thomas Winning (*left*) with fellow students on the Spanish Steps.

'Screw your courage to the sticking place and we will not fail.' Thomas Winning as Lady Macbeth in the Scots College theatrical production.

As parish priest of St Luke's in Motherwell, Thomas Winning led the local Corpus Christi Day procession in 1969.

Winning is ordained a bishop on St Andrew's Day, 1971: (*left to right*) Bishop Stephen McGill, Thomas Winning, Archbishop James Scanlan, Cardinal Gordon Gray, and Bishop Francis Thomson.

The new archbishop: a formal portrait of Thomas Winning following his appointment as Archbishop of Glasgow in April 1974.

Passing the crook: Thomas Winning with Archbishop James Donald Scanlan.
Winning was wounded by the older man's discourtesy over his appointment.

Brothers reunited: Thomas Winning as archbishop becomes the first Catholic to address the General Assembly of the Church of Scotland in 1976.

When Andrew met Peter: Thomas Winning greets Pope John Paul II after the Pope lands in Scotland in 1982 as part of the British visit that Winning helped rescue from cancellation.

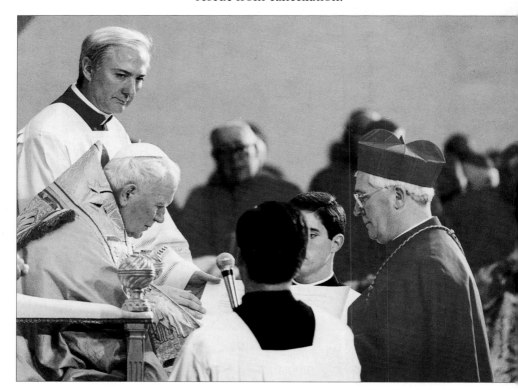

The red hat at last: in November 1994, Winning receives the cardinal's hat he thought would pass him by from Pope John Paul II.

and I was damned if I was going to do it.' Winning's early reticence about his post in Clydebank softened only slightly during the next three years, despite his eventual accrual of the title 'Bankie of the Year'. He spent little time there and when at work in his study would complain to the teachers in the neighbouring school about the noise of the children in the playground. As his residence was so close to the heart of Scottish shipbuilding, this led him to give his tacit support to the celebrated fourteen-month work-in by employees at the Upper Clyde shipyard that began in 1971 and was led by the shop steward Jimmy Reid. Yet this support did not extend to Reid himself, for when he stood in February 1974 for election as a member of parliament for the Communist Party, he was condemned by Winning from the pulpit. The fate of democracy may not have swung in the balance as it had done in Italy in 1947, but as a follower and fan of Pius XII, Winning could not allow his Catholic flock to vote for a Communist, despite his status as a local hero, without a strong word of warning.

Winning was anxious for a rematch against Bishop Ward. He had lost the battle over becoming a parish priest and so was anxious to flex his authority and muscle in another manner. The education of Catholic schoolchildren was his chosen arena. Since the close of the Vatican Council children's education had become increasingly problematic as the penny catechism, the little booklet of questions and answers on matters of faith, once learned by rote, had been rendered obsolete with little to replace it. Schoolteachers were crying out for guidance and the archdiocese was dragging its heels. In June 1970, a prominent Jesuit, Fr Gerald O'Mahony, had quit as the first director of the archdiocese's catechetical centre after branding his working terms unacceptable. O'Mahony had pushed for changes such as a pilot scheme to introduce school chaplains but had left frustrated by the Bishop and Archbishop's intransigence. Winning, however, was an early advocate of school chaplains, having seen their success in the Motherwell diocese.

In the spring of 1972, Scanlan, Ward and Winning met with a

group of four Catholic headmasters who pressed the issue of chaplains. Ward was dismissive, arguing that they would have little to do, but Winning suggested they say Mass on school premises. Ward exploded: 'What do you mean, say Mass? What is wrong with the church?' Winning retaliated by reminding Ward that the Vatican Council had instructed priests to take Jesus out of the church and to travel to the people. 'I've said Mass in schools in Motherwell many times,' he explained, 'it's a wonderful experience for the children.' Scanlan stepped in and closed the meeting by explaining to the headmasters that the diocese was too short on priests. Winning, however, was undeterred:

I was determined to push this through. The teachers felt it was important. It was 1972 and there had been a catechetical desert since the Vatican Council. No one knew what to do. The catechism had been dropped and replaced with a few pieces of paper. The diocese had set up religious advisers and they were searching for new ways of educating the children in their faith. The old catechisms were very scholastic and arbitrary. You were producing theologians, not committed, ordinary Catholics.

Winning decided to put his idea to the Senate of Priests, a consulting body of senior priests, at their next meeting. Ward had traditionally been the prime mover at these events and was disturbed when Winning's suggestion of a working party that would visit schools and discuss with staff their religious requirements was enthusiastically embraced. Outside the meeting, Ward approached Winning and asked him what time weekday Mass took place at Our Holy Redeemer. Winning replied by asking Ward if he wanted to know if children could attend Mass before school if they wished. Ward said yes and Winning explained that Mass was available each morning at 8.30 a.m. 'But you seem to question the Catholic school, my lord. What do you have against the Catholic school?' asked Ward. Winning replied: 'I've nothing against the Catholic school – I want the Catholic school worth having.'

As Winning had thought, the working party discovered that

teachers were anxious to secure school chaplains. The current system operated by Ward and Scanlan in which twenty-five priests spent a couple of days each week 'inspecting' schools and their Catholic teaching was considered a farce by staff who argued they provided little or no support. Armed with new evidence, Winning arranged a private meeting with Scanlan and took the liberty of compiling a list of twenty-four names of priests willing to work as chaplains in a pilot scheme. At the meeting he urged Scanlan to appoint them, explaining they would work in the schools between nine o'clock and four o'clock, then return to their parish. The Archbishop respected a well-formed argument and relented, but Winning was painfully aware of how an agreement could change and pushed the letters of appointment across the desk. 'Will you sign them?' Again Scanlan agreed, but said he would do so later in the day.

On this occasion, the Archbishop performed the task as agreed, but he was not above playing politics. As he was putting the last flourish to his final signature, Ward arrived at his office and Scanlan handed him the letters with an instruction to 'drop these off with Dr Winning'. Presented with a fait accompli, Ward had no choice but to carry out Scanlan's request and a couple of minutes later Winning received a curt call from Ward asking him to come to his office. No sooner had Winning arrived than Ward attacked. Brandishing the sheaf of papers, he demanded to know what they were about. 'The Archbishop is in charge. He's made the decision. It's settled,' said Winning who then took the opportunity to unload the tensions that had built up over the previous few months.

Since his appointment, Winning had received no access to the decisions affecting the archdiocese. He had been appointed to no committee and was in receipt of no briefing papers on finance or future plans. He had a small room on the second floor of the diocesan offices for which he was forced to purchase his own desk and he had little work to do at it, except that which he generated himself. All his complaints were fired at Ward who seemed visibly startled. He finished by stating: 'I don't know anything that is going on in here. Nobody says anything to me.' As a sop, Ward agreed to his appointment on the fabric and finance committee but the conversation, coupled with Ward's defeat over the issue of school chaplains, marked the complete disintegration of their strained working relationship. Winning left the meeting in the knowledge that he was entirely on his own and had attracted a formidable enemy. The next morning, he arrived at the offices early, found the mail bag, and proceeded to slit it open and read the contents of every letter, regardless of to whom it was addressed. If he was to familiarize himself with the workings of the diocese, these were the lengths to which he must now go. No one ever questioned the open envelopes and Winning's clandestine practice was to continue for the next two years. 'That year I did not want to see a mitre and a crosier. I felt it was all a farce. I felt totally deflated that this was the way the Church operated.'

There were others whose disappointment in the administration of the Church was as strong as Winning's, but whose loyalty was not bound by ordination. The growth of a group of educated middle-class Catholics, who rose up as the turbulence of Vatican II pulled down the 'Church' of the Council of Trent, led to the formation of the strongest reform group in the history of Scottish Catholicism. Since his arrival in Glasgow three years previously, Winning had been aware of the pioneering work of the Scottish Lay Action Movement (SLAM) founded in 1968 by James Armstrong, a Glasgow solicitor and a man regarded by Winning as a snob. The group had formed in December during a public meeting at the Glasgow North British Hotel called in response to the Bishops' pronouncements on 'Humanae Vitae'.

Since the end of the Second World War and the founding of the Newman Association, where Catholic graduates met at each of Scotland's four universities to discuss their faith, a new, questioning breed of Catholic was on the rise. In the past, the need to present a united front in the face of prejudice, hostility and bigotry from the Protestant majority had led to a moratorium on internal criticism of the Church. But as prejudice waned after a war in which, as never before, Catholic and Protestants fought side by side, the new breed of Catholics began to flex their intellect.

Initially, the authorities in the Catholic Church had paid little attention to the quiet revolution taking place, not in the pews, but in discussion groups at universities, over a pint in the pub, and, in Glasgow, most popularly on a Saturday morning in the back room of the Catholic Truth Society shop on Renfield Street. Subscriptions to *The Tablet* and the *Catholic Herald* rose and Dr Thomas Taylor held a discussion group where the latest theological views of Karl Rahner, Hans Küng and Edward Schillebeeckx were hotly debated. The changes of Vatican II were legitimate areas of debate but the hierarchy were uncomfortable with a laity who asked too many questions, particularly if they were stumped for an appropriate answer. In particular, Bishop Ward and Archbishop Scanlan believed in attempting to limit the supply of information. The most famous example of this was when the *Scottish Catholic Observer* bought the serialization rights to Xavier Rynne's *Letters From the Vatican*. Written under a pseudonym by a prominent Redemptorist, Fr Francis Xavier Murphy, the letters were originally published in *The New Yorker* and provided a gossipy and riveting ringside seat to the secret discussions of the Vatican Council. Bishops across Scotland were happy for the laity to read Rynne's account in the *Scottish Catholic Observer*, except in the archdiocese of Glasgow, where Ward applied pressure on the publishers, who dropped the extract for the city's edition.

When 'Humanae Vitae' was published, the response in England and Wales was much stronger than north of the border, yet the Scottish hierarchy were still anxious enough over the low grumbling of discontent emanating from the Catholic populace to issue a pastoral letter that provided the strongest backing to the Pope of any country outside Italy. While the liberals argued that Pope Paul VI's statement was neither dogma nor infallible and should be left to the conscience of married couples, the bishops argued the statement was clear and simple. 'In the encyclical he has not stated a new doctrine on birth control, but he has reaffirmed the traditional teaching of the Church and this teaching is not in doubt,' read their statement.[4] In December 1968, SLAM wrote two letters, one to the Apostolic Delegate in London and a second to Archbishop Scanlan. In the letter to Scanlan they argued: 'The failure to recognize the honesty and sincerity of those who cannot give full assent to the Encyclical's view of marriage was particularly distressing. We earnestly request that you broaden and intensify dialogue with the laity on this important subject.'[5]

Four months later, SLAM changed their name to SCRM, the Scottish Catholic Renewal Movement, and promoted the motto: Renewal, Consultation and Co-responsibility. One of their earliest moves was to issue a demand for greater collegiality between the laity, who provided all the financial resources, and the hierarchy, who spent it, over the running of the Church. They also criticized the slow nature of the changes, stating that there were 'considerable discrepancies which exist from parish to parish and especially diocese to diocese, each a source of confusion and scandal'. Their request was never going to be granted. The Scottish Church viewed SCRM as a wooden horse, anxious to penetrate the Church and then destroy the institution for the 'good, simple people' who were happy to pray and pay.

For a small, embattled organization, SCRM succeeded in attracting a stellar list of the world's theologians, names more familiar with streets such as the Via Appia than Sauchiehall Street in Glasgow. Hans Küng, Karl Rahner, Edward Schillebeeckx and John L. McKenzie all delivered lectures to packed halls in Glasgow. It was a brief spring after a long dark winter for Scotland's thinking Catholics. Perhaps the most successful event was a debate between the MPs David Steel and Norman St John-Stevas which attracted an audience of over one thousand two hundred people. Many of the meetings were ecumenical, attended by senior Protestant scholars such as Professor William Barclay and William Frend.

In 1971, Archbishop Scanlan hardened his line. When Hans Küng was awarded an honorary degree by the Protestant theological faculty at Glasgow University in June 1971, Scanlan, who had attended the service at the university's chapel, left prior to Küng's presentation in a calculated snub. In October, he issued a letter to all parish priests stating that: the 'so-called Catholic Renewal Movement'[6] had not received approbation from the Scottish hierarchy nor the local Ordinary (Scanlan), and therefore had no authority to use the title 'Catholic'. Scanlan asked that this note be brought to the attention of all the priests and head teachers. In a weak response the group acquiesced to the Archbishop's demand and once again changed their name to the Renewal Movement.

Against such a bitter backdrop, Winning was drawn into play. The Catholic chaplain at Glasgow University was Fr Gerard Hughes, a Jesuit popular among students and laity alike for his hard work and progressive views. Appointed in 1967, Hughes was dismissed then almost instantly reprieved in August 1968 for debating *Humanae Vitae* in the *Scottish Catholic Observer* and expressing doubts on Paul VI's judgement. Three years later, on Sunday 21 May 1972, he announced during Mass at the university's Catholic chaplaincy that, once again, he was to be dismissed by the Archbishop. His 'crime' was a paper prepared for a conference of Catholic chaplains in which he expressed his practice of giving communion to non-Catholics, an action forbidden under canon law. He wrote: 'Having explained the ruling, if non-Catholics then come to communion, I never refuse, because I think the harm done by refusal would far outweigh any possible advantages.'[7] The paper, which also argued for chaplains to be granted permission to marry students in the chaplaincy and celebrate Mass in student flats and halls of residence, was forwarded to Scanlan who called Hughes to a meeting on 21 April to explain himself. The meeting was a clash of progressive versus conservative and Hughes emerged with his requests denied. Three weeks later, he was told by Fr Bernard Hall, the Jesuit Provincial of Great Britain, that the Archbishop, against Hall's protests, wished Hughes to be dismissed.

The row expanded when Fr Hughes spoke to the press and appeared on the front page of the *Sunday Mail*, one of Scotland's largest-selling tabloids. In an interview with George McKechnie, who would later edit the *Glasgow Herald*, Hughes expressed his anger at the decision. In contrast, Scanlan, who considered the matter private and one of internal discipline, refused to make any public comment. The row then proceeded to rumble across the pages of the *Glasgow Herald* through a series of incisive and revealing reports by John Cooney, a young Catholic journalist. At the university, students collected three thousand signatures for a petition in support of their chaplain and in an attempt to find a solution to the matter, Winning was asked to negotiate a satisfactory settlement.

The story received so much attention that when Winning went to Glasgow Airport to collect Fr Bernard Hall, he worried that both of them would be recognized and harassed by the press. In many ways, Winning was the perfect candidate to carry out any negotiations; a devout advocate of the changes of Vatican II, where Scanlan remained slightly distant, he nevertheless was a firm advocate of Catholic doctrine, in particular obedience to one's bishop. The discussions took place at the diocesan offices in Park Circus, and over the course of two days, a settlement began to take shape. Hall's view was that Hughes had to be reinstated, not only to appease the students, but also to save the face of the Jesuits. Winning was agreeable but insisted that any reinstatement was for a strictly limited period. One year was agreed and the position of chaplain would now be 'supported' by a committee chaired by Winning himself.

Winning managed to sell the compromise to Scanlan, arguing that it was far nobler to reassess a situation and then to change one's mind, a position that would be more in keeping with the new discursive Church than the old dogmatic and implacable one of pre-Vatican II. It was a hard sell made harder by the publication on 26 May of a front-page editorial in the *Scottish Catholic Observer* which argued: 'When authority is publicly challenged, it must be exercised or abandoned ... The Archbishop has a responsibility and he must act according to his judgement and in light of his conscience. The challenge to his authority has tied his hands – robbed him of the facility of compromise. But Fr Hughes remains a free agent.' The following week, a joint statement was released signed by both Scanlan and Hall in which they said they were 'happy to clear up some misunderstandings'. In the statement Hughes was rebuked for making the issue public, however: 'It has been agreed that Fr Hughes should continue his work as university chaplain for a year, at the end of which time the situation will again be considered.' Hughes was quoted as regretting any damage caused to the Archbishop: 'I have assured him of my obedience and loyalty.'

Locked out of the running of the diocese and on difficult terms with Bishop Ward, there was little for Winning to do. He had originally been told that his responsibility was for Dumbarton, but the area was already the personal fiefdom and birthplace of Ward, and Winning had little appetite for fighting over the scraps. When appointed, he had nurtured the idea of getting out amongst the people, and a visit to Susan McCormack and her sister back in Motherwell helped to galvanize his thoughts. Susan McCormack remembered:

> One evening, he was in the house and he was low. He was really despondent. I think if it had not been a scandal and against his grain, he would have told Scanlan how he felt and taken the step back into parish work. I think he was as low as that. Kathleen was in the house and she said: 'You know what you should do? Go round every parish on a Sunday, meet the people and visit the sick. If you get the sick on your side, you will make it.'

Winning was already heading in the direction, but the nudge was welcome. He made it a plan to visit a different parish every weekend. While his curates looked after the parish of Our Holy Redeemer, Winning roamed the diocese. He would arrive on a Saturday, visit the sick, enjoy a dinner with the priests of the parish, and preach at each Mass on the Sunday. After Mass, he would stand at the back of the church complimenting the ladies on their hats, the men on Celtic's latest performance, and the children on their outfits. He did everything an astute politician could, except collect votes, but support was certainly canvassed. To parishioners familiar with the austerity of Bishop Ward and the snobbery of Archbishop Scanlan, a young, good-looking bishop with a quick wit and a ready supply of compliments was a refreshing change.

A number of priests, suspicious of a Lanarkshire man in a Glasgow post and hostile to a bishop visiting for any longer than the length of a Mass, explained to Winning that there was no room in the chapel-house. But Winning was insistent. 'Send the curate home to his mother and I'll have his bed,' was his frequent reply. He began his new career as a tough-talking bishop who was unafraid to express his views around the dinner table with the priests, but his blunt comments had consequences and Winning's opinions and offhand remarks were quickly swept round the archdiocese. 'He had to learn how to be more circumspect. He did learn it for a while till he reached the position where he did not give a damn,' said Susan McCormack.

Winning's outspokenness led to a chastisement from the Vatican after he chaired a discussion on new catechetics. At one point during a question-and-answer session, a woman asked Winning if the decree *Quam Singulari* had been abrogated. This was an arcane point about a piece of legalese issued by Pius X which technically was required to be read out on a particular date each year. The practice had fallen away much to the woman's disappointment. Winning explained that when he had been a canon law student, his lecturer had said that reading it each year was nonsense as the publication of the new code of canon law in 1917 had assimilated all those decrees. Despite his explanation, she said that she must disagree with him. The discussion became confused and Cardinal Gray, who was sitting in the audience, stepped in to rescue Winning.

Three months later, Winning was called at home by a bishop in Ireland, with whom he was friendly, who wanted to let him know that he had been listed in a pamphlet in circulation by an ultra-conservative group as campaigning that the decree was no longer in force. He then received a copy of a letter addressed to his female questioner but written by Cardinal John Wright, Prefect of the Sacred Congregation for the Clergy. The Vatican department had responsibility for catechisms and Wright had written that he did not know of any 'responsible person in the Church' who would say that *Quam* had been abrogated. An indication of the ripple-effect and how susceptible the Curia was to a well-orchestrated letter-writing campaign was that, two months later, an official letter was sent out from the Holy See stating that the decree was still in effect. Winning was so concerned about the possible damage to his reputation that he asked Cardinal Gray to speak with Wright during his next visit to the Vatican. In spite of an invitation to dinner with Wright, Gray (predictably) refused to broach the subject for fear of offending his host.

If 1972 was to prove a miserable year for Thomas Winning, the people of Northern Ireland fared considerably worse. The Troubles which began four years previously with peaceful demonstrations by Catholic civil rights marchers protesting against poor housing and prejudice in employment had escalated, after a vicious crackdown, into virtual civil war. The British troops who arrived in 1969 to protect the Catholic minority from Protestant retaliation were greeted at first with flowers and cups of tea but were now viewed as the enemy of a united Ireland by the resurrected Irish Republican Army. On 30 January 1972, thirteen Catholic marchers were shot dead by British soldiers during a march in Derry, a day that became known as 'Bloody Sunday'. In 1972, one year after the IRA began their bombing campaign, 321 civilians and 146 soldiers and policemen had been murdered.

In Glasgow, there was legitimate concern that the Troubles, just twenty-six miles across the Irish Sea, might leap the gap and ignite the tinderbox of tensions that already existed between the two religions. Prior to 1968, battles between Catholics and Protestants took place on the streets of Glasgow, not Belfast. They may have been restricted to Old Firm fans, supporters of Celtic and Rangers football clubs, or the routes of Protestant marches but there was no guarantee that sectarian violence would not spread. The increasing number of mixed marriages, combined with the complete absence of religious ghettos, areas dominated by either Catholics or Protestants common in Northern Ireland, were viewed as a firewall against any explosion of sectarian violence. Nevertheless, the outbreak of civil unrest in Northern Ireland was to have consequences for the West of Scotland.

A bombing campaign by the IRA was unlikely, as Scots were viewed as Celts who harboured a similar, though less physical, hostility towards the English, but both sides of the conflict had their supporters in Glasgow. The outbreak of hostilities helped to swell the ranks of the Orange Order who, prior to 1968, had been in steady decline as the latest generation of the sons and daughters of Ulster showed more interest in dancing and social pursuits than in studying the history of the Battle of the Boyne. In comparison, the majority of Glasgow Catholics were only a few generations removed from Irish immigrants and supported a united Ireland, though not at the cost of human lives. Other IRA sympathizers were less discerning and gave active support by arranging safe houses, organizing demonstrations, and storing explosives. A Catholic priest was not exempt from such behaviour.

On the evening of 22 March 1973, the deputy chief constable of Glasgow police knocked on the door of the presbytery of Our Holy Redeemer and asked to speak with Bishop Winning. The curates fetched Winning who led the deputy chief constable into his study so they could speak in private. Archbishop Scanlan had been stricken by a bout of pneumonia and was indisposed, Ward was unavailable, and so Winning was to be the recipient of disturbing news: an arrest warrant had been issued for a priest of the Glasgow diocese, Fr Bartholomew Burns, a curate at St Teresa's Church in Saracen Street in Possilpark, one of the city's poorest areas. Over 150 lb. of gelignite, 150 electrical detonators and documents relating to IRA intelligence services and recruitment had been found in the church premises. Three people, two brothers from Donegal and a twenty-two-year-old Glasgow girl, Caroline Renehan, the daughter of Sinn Fein's Scottish secretary, Persia Renehan, had been arrested, but Burns had fled, driven away and then dropped off in the city centre by the parish priest, Fr John Martin.

Winning was stunned. Like many Catholic priests, he saw little reason for a divided Ireland, but union was not worth bloodshed and he had regularly preached against the bombers who were beginning to terrorize cities across England. But how, if they successfully arrested three others, did they miss Fr Burns? This was a source of embarrassment to the Special Branch who, during the subsequent trial of the three, admitted procedural errors had taken place. A surveillance team had tracked Caroline Renehan in a white Morris car and James and John Sweeney in a black and yellow Capri to the chapel-house at St Teresa's where they were met at the door by Fr Burns. A few minutes after they entered, Renehan came back out, collected a brown case from the boot of her car, and went back inside. Later all four re-emerged and walked to the Capri. The Sweeney brothers were each carrying a white carton, Burns carried a brown carton, and Renehan had a dark coloured case. Burns then went back into the house while the others drove off.

The driveway was then blocked by plain-clothes police officers, and all three were arrested. While Burns witnessed the arrest from the windows of the chapel-house, at no point was he questioned. Concerned that they lacked a search warrant for the house, the Special Branch officers went back to Central Police Station, leaving two officers on a watching brief. They were told not to take action unless something suspicious took place or anything was removed. Unfortunately, the police officers were not briefed on Burns's appearance, and so, thirty minutes later, when Fr Martin drove off with Burns, no one intervened.

Winning was asked to inform the police if Fr Burns should contact the archdiocese and he agreed. In his opinion, Burns had a public duty to face these allegations. Bishop Ward did not share his concerns. When Winning spoke to Ward, he was disturbed to discover the bishop's emotions verging on jubilation at Burns's successful escape. 'Ward just seemed to pat me on the head and told me not to worry about it,' said Winning.

The Catholic Church's attitude towards alternative authorities such as the police had always been distant. The ghetto mentality from which the Church was just beginning to emerge meant it viewed both police and, particularly, the media as sectarian and virulently anti-Catholic; any cooperation was minimal and reluctant. In Ward's view, Burns's escape was a blessing to the Church which had been spared the embarrassment of a trial. Two days later, Rennie McOwan, press officer for the Catholic Church in Scotland, who was entirely unaware of the events, received a phone call from Jim McQuire, a Catholic journalist on the *Scottish Daily Express*. McQuire had heard rumours that a Fr Burns was wanted by the police and was seeking confirmation. McOwan agreed to check and was disturbed when Winning confirmed the story. He was more disturbed that Winning had chosen not to inform him straight away and dismissed the bishop's reply that he had been told by CID to tell no one, by replying, 'The police give orders to CID, not the Catholic Church.'

An emergency meeting was called between McOwan, Winning and Ward to discuss how to handle the resultant press inquiries. McOwan remembered:

> Bishop Ward began to run the meeting in an autocratic tone, saying: 'Who are the media to question us? This is none of their business.' I was tired and got angry with both of them. At one point I turned round and said that I had received no help from the archdiocese at all. TJ [Thomas Joseph] went white and Ward got extremely angry and said he was extremely willing to handle the matter himself. I then threatened to resign.

It took a ruling by Scanlan from his sick bed to resolve the matter. Ward went upstairs to the Archbishop's private quarters to discuss the situation and returned to explain that Scanlan agreed with McOwan that a brief statement should be issued stating that Fr Burns was suspended for having deserted his diocese and that his whereabouts were unknown. McOwan's next concern was whether Fr Martin would be arrested and charged with aiding a suspected criminal, but Ward, once again, could see nothing wrong with his actions. 'He was living in cloud-cuckoo-land,' said McOwan. 'They had got their man away.'

The incident culminated with a two-day trial at the High Court in Glasgow, where both James Sweeney and Caroline Renehan lodged a defence blaming Fr Burns – who remained in hiding in Ireland – for the crime, though both were subsequently sentenced to seven and five years respectively. Sweeney's brother John was found 'not proven', a judgement exclusive to Scots law that occupies a no man's land between 'guilty' and 'not guilty', and so was released and he vowed to return to Ireland in search of the missing cleric. An attempt by police to extradite Burns was dismissed by a Dublin court, but the most disturbing insight into the hierarchy's view of the case came a few months later. One afternoon Winning visited Scanlan in his office to discover him writing a letter of approval to allow Burns to operate as a Catholic priest in Ireland following a request by an Irish bishop. 'Give him a job? The guy should be in jail,' was Winning's response. Scanlan was taken aback by the strength of Winning's feelings and listened as he argued that it was unacceptable for Burns to operate as a priest until he had returned to face the charges. Scanlan was convinced and the transfer was dropped.

I feel very sympathetic towards Ireland as a nation completely independent from England. I could never find a good argument for Britain to be there at all. But the end does not justify the means and you cannot justify terrorism. A man of God and a man of peace who takes up cudgels and is accused of storing arms and giving financial help to a terrorist organization has no place in the Church.

On Sunday 21 October 1973, Winning was preparing, with a light heart, to say Mass at Our Holy Redeemer. In a few hours time he would be enjoying a rare break. Donny Renfrew, now rector of Langbank seminary, had a small weaver's cottage in Kinross and that afternoon the two friends were to drive up for a couple of days of hill walking. It was not to be. Instead, Winning received a call from a curate at Holy Cross parish telling him that Bishop Ward had had a heart attack and had refused to settle in bed until a replacement was found to perform confirmations scheduled that afternoon. Winning immediately agreed to attend to them and said he would pray for Ward's recovery. An hour later he was informed that the bishop, after receiving the last rites and briefly joining in the prayers of the dying, had passed away. Winning's reaction was divided between public piety and private relief. His statement to the *Scottish Catholic Observer* was virtuous: 'His loss will be keenly felt. He was a man of indefatigable zeal. He was a tireless worker for the welfare of the Church. He never lost his apostolic fervour.' In private his attitude was quite different. On the afternoon following Ward's death, Winning looked up to heaven and muttered: 'Well, James – you're off my back now.'

The death of Bishop Ward was an obvious advantage to Winning, for with Ward out of the way and the archbishop in increasingly poor health, greater responsibility fell on his shoulders. In spite of what he said in public, Winning had had little regard for Ward and considered his intensely administrative role a 'waste of a bishop'. Three weeks after Ward's death, Winning had persuaded Scanlan to appoint Frank Cullen, a successful accountant and former seminarian, as Ward's administrative successor, a deal he struck with Cullen at the late bishop's funeral. Winning's popularity was rising on the back of two years spent visiting every parish in the diocese. He was viewed as a bridge between the fossilized conservatism of Scanlan and the loose liberalism of those who pushed for greater change.

Scanlan had already written in his public diary on 23 April 1974, '*dies fatali*' – the 'fatal day' on which he was due to retire and on which Winning wished to succeed him. Two years spent as Ward's whipping boy had been a painful lesson on the problems of a poor boss and during this time Winning had compiled a range of ideas on how the archdiocese could be developed. Father Tom Connelly, a friend from Motherwell, visited Winning at Our Holy Redeemer at a time when false rumours had circulated that a new diocese would be created to cover Stirling. As an auxiliary bishop, Winning would be considered a front runner, but when Connelly commented that he suspected his friend of having his eye on Stirling, Winning replied: 'No. I'm after something bigger.'

*   *   *

The process of choosing a successor to Scanlan began in January 1974, four months before his official retirement date and was co-ordinated by Archbishop Bruno Heim, the new Apostolic Delegate to Great Britain who had been appointed only three months earlier. As yet unfamiliar with the personalities of the candidates, Heim relied heavily on the consultation process, which was among the widest ever carried out. Both priests and members of the laity were sent private letters asking them to recommend a suitable candidate and both Scanlan and Winning were asked to send a tertiary list of three names. When Scanlan asked Winning whom he would like to see succeed him, Winning said Mgr Gerry Rogers, a reply that pleased the archbishop who retorted that in his view Winning was still too young to fulfil the role. In a briefing to Heim, he elaborated that Winning lacked authority.

Winning would have been delighted at the appointment of his old mentor, who headed the list he sent to Heim, but he still took extra steps to ensure his own success. In March he spent two weeks compiling a report which analysed the weaknesses of the diocese as it stood and recommended a range of solutions. Winning insisted the document was a guide for the new appointment: 'I don't think I would be accused of being ambitious, in that I was hell bent on getting that job.' A more detached view was that it was a job application, designed to convince Heim of his suitability, but no such evidence was required as the consultation had already identified Winning as the most suitable and popular candidate, a combination rarely found. In little more than two years he had gained the trust and respect of the clergy, negotiated a successful settlement with Fr Gerard Hughes, demonstrated moral leadership over Bartholomew Burns, and reanimated the laity. 'There was really no contest,' said Joseph Devine, Bishop of Motherwell, who had previously worked as secretary to Archbishop Scanlan before taking over Gerard Hughes's role as chaplain at Glasgow University. 'There was overwhelming support.'

In April, Winning was invited to London to speak with Heim at his office in a large detached villa in Wimbledon. When he arrived, Fr Bernard Kenny, an English priest who had studied in Rome and to whom Winning had once given a retreat, took his coat and explained that he would be with the Archbishop for no longer than thirty minutes. Winning did not conceal his irritation. Heim was to visit Glasgow in three weeks and he had brought details of the programme as well as more notes on what could be done with the diocese after Scanlan's departure. Thirty minutes was too short an allotment for a thousand-mile round trip.

Heim was a gracious man of average build and height who in his spare time had published a study on friendship according to the works of St Thomas Aquinas, and after welcoming Winning into his study, just as the younger man began to pull out his latest report, he explained the reason for inviting him to London: the Pope wished to appoint him Archbishop of Glasgow. Winning did not need to ask for time to think. 'If it is for the good of the Church, I accept' was his reply. 'Good,' said Heim. 'Now, a drink.' Heim had a considerable flair for cocktails and while he set to work with a silver shaker, Winning sat and began to consider the implications of his appointment. The rest of his brief visit was spent discussing Heim's forthcoming visit over a couple of strawberry daiquiris. The Archbishop explained that he wished to inform Scanlan in person of Winning's appointment when he arrived in Glasgow on 13 May.

Scanlan was to remain a mystery to Winning, who had served him as secretary and now auxiliary bishop for almost seven years, but who had failed to gain the measure of the man. Scanlan had given Winning no reason to suspect he was unwelcome as auxiliary bishop, but neither was he convinced he had been his first choice. The Archbishop's response to his succession was characteristically cold. Heim had arrived two days early on the evening of Saturday 11 May and Winning had driven his own car to the airport and arranged for Scanlan's secretary and part-time chauffeur, Fr Desmond Broderick, to drive it back accompanied by Heim's own secretary. Winning would then drive Scanlan and Heim to Park Circus, allowing the three men a degree of privacy to discuss the new appointment. After putting the cases in the car boot, Winning climbed behind the wheel of the black Mercedes. Both archbishops were already seated in the back, and Heim said, 'I have just told His Grace that you are his successor.'

> Scanlan just looked at me, then turned back to Heim and said: 'As I was saying . . .' He did not say a word. I was bowled over. It was years later that I began to reflect on it. It was hurtful, all right. He could not bring himself to say anything. I thought: 'Why is he so cutting?'

One way to read Scanlan's response is that it was an appropriate curtain call to Winning's auxiliary years, a final curt gesture to file away with the others he had so long endured, and yet this is to ignore the archbishop's own anguish. A long career had come to a close and what lay ahead was retirement and death. Personal emotions are poorly expressed by priests and Scanlan may have been unable to welcome the younger man on to his chair. In a private letter to Otto Hershan, the publisher of the *Scottish Catholic Observer*, written shortly after Scanlan retired to London, he described Winning as an 'excellent successor'. Winning himself was unaware of Scanlan's judgement until a few months prior to his own death when Hershan sent him a copy of the twenty-seven-year-old letter.

The response of the other Scottish bishops to the news was more enthusiastic. A dinner had been organized for the following evening, Sunday 12 May, at which Bishop Thomson was the first to congratulate Winning, but the warmest display came from Cardinal Gordon Gray who clasped his hand in both of his and shook it long and hard. Winning's sister Margaret burst into tears when she heard of his promotion and expressed the hope that his health would be unable to withstand the pressure. The response of the clergy, however, was the most gratifying: all the priests of the archdiocese were gathered in Notre Dame College on 13 May and as Heim introduced Winning as 'your choice' each man in black jacket and white dog collar rose to his feet. The applause became thunderous. Winning said: 'It took your breath away.'

The Archbishop Years

NINE

The New Archbishop

'Pope Paul has entrusted me with the Church of Glasgow. One day
God will ask me what I have made of it. But I am not alone. There
is a spirit, the spirit of God, guiding me as Christ promised.'
ARCHBISHOP THOMAS WINNING'S INSTALLATION ADDRESS,
3 SEPTEMBER 1974

On an August evening in 1974, before an audience of Rotary Club
members, Thomas Winning described the type of archbishop he
had no wish to be: 'He has no time for ordinary people. He is a
comet who speeds through a diocese leaving a trail of ordained
clergy and confirmed adults. People tend to shrivel up when they
meet him.'[1] Instead, Winning wished to clamber down from the
pedestal and bring a new earthiness and approachability to his
position. He explained that autocracy would be replaced by team-
work and that his Roman formation belied a Glaswegian soul. 'The
suit and shoes I am wearing were bought the last time I was in
Rome,' he said, concluding his short speech. 'The rest come from
Marks & Spencer.'

After decades under the spiritual leadership of a series of distant,
authoritarian men, Glaswegian Catholics were very taken by their
new Archbishop, a reaction reflected by the press. 'He is concerned
that people will be able to look on him as an ordinary man,'
commented the *Glasgow Herald*, while the *Scottish Daily Express*
concluded that he 'was a cheerfully disposed man of the people'.
In the early days of the Church, the appointment of a bishop was

a right of the laity who conferred the status on a man of sound judgement and holy disposition and the arrival of Thomas Winning as Archbishop had the welcome feel of olden times.

In the Catholic Church the Archbishop of a large diocese resembles the branch manager of a colossal, global company whose role is to keep the operation in his own patch ticking over before passing the key to the executive bathroom to the next incumbent. Winning's new responsibility stretched over 300 priests, 105 parishes, 42 religious communities, 311,500 baptized Catholics, and, later, two auxiliary bishops. His headquarters was a five-storey Victorian town house in the West End of the city and his appointment was for life, with mandatory retirement at seventy-five, almost three decades in the distance. On paper, his job was divided into three sections: teaching, leading and sanctifying, of which teaching – or preaching, to be more precise – the gospel was considered pre-eminent. He now had the sanctifying power to ordain priests as well as offer the sacrament of confirmation and while some archbishops were content to limit their public appearances to just such an occasion before scuffling back to their paperwork, his ambition was on a far grander scale.

He wanted to build the City of God. He wanted the Holy Spirit to sweep through the avenues, lanes and streets, tenements, bungalows and homes, and to penetrate the hearts of every man, woman and child. The Vatican Council had stated that holiness was no longer the preserve of priests and religious, but was a requirement to which everyone should aspire. Winning wanted God's 'universal call to holiness' to be adopted by teachers and plumbers, painters and engineers, secretaries and journalists, by both the young and the old. He wanted the teaching of Jesus Christ not to be confined to a solitary hour on Sunday but to sink deep into people's lives until it suffused each action.

Winning had touched lightly on the issue in February, prior to his appointment, when he had urged the Catholic Transport Guild to 'put forward, in your walk of life, the Christian ideal', and he developed the theme for the conclusion of his installation address, delivered at St Andrew's Cathedral on 3 September. The ceremony was conducted by Stephen McGill, his old spiritual director, now Bishop of Paisley. Winning told the packed congregation and thousands listening to the radio transmission that through baptism and confirmation they had been invited to be 'ambassadors of Christ' and that they were needed, now more than ever.

The year 1974 was a disastrous one. The dithering of Prime Minister Edward Heath over an early date for the polls had cost him the General Election and Harold Wilson, the Labour leader, had entered 10 Downing Street shackled to the unions. Inflation was rife, oil was in short supply, unemployment was climbing and society seemed to have gone off the rails. Films such as *The Exorcist, Straw Dogs* and *A Clockwork Orange* were being blamed for crimes of violence rising to almost one hundred thousand per year by the end of 1975, while the Women's Liberation Movement, sparked by Germaine Greer's book, *The Female Eunuch*, was attacking the twin pillars of marriage and motherhood. Referring to these dark elements, Winning said:

> We live in a world where man has acquired a new arrogance, a false independence: he senses a victory over the forces of nature and has pushed the true God into the background of his life and fashioned new gods to worship ... How are we to penetrate this darkness? That is the task of the Church today. It has never had to tread quite the same depth of darkness. But it has to pierce it.[2]

His solution was the mobilization of the laity who, like stormtroopers, would infiltrate a corrupt and nihilistic society and bring redemption through their loving example. Closing, he explained: 'Serving the Church today means, more than ever, that the Christian has to be the best wife, the most loving husband in the home, a holy priest ... in his job, the best worker, in society, the best citizen.'

The blueprint for Winning's early years as Archbishop of Glasgow was a document published as part of the Vatican Council entitled the *Decree on Bishops' Pastoral Office in the Church*, a wordy tract

revising the role of bishop with the emphasis on service. 'Their
ultimate goal as bishops is that all men may walk in all goodness
and justice and truth,' explained the document. Over the past ten
years, Winning had made thorough studies of the Council's sixteen
documents and was determined that they should shape his every
act. The decree called on bishops to regard their priests as 'sons
and friends', to nurture their spiritual life and to treat failings with
'active mercy', a command that Winning, who had been sickened
by the previous harsh treatment of priests who succumbed to drink
or women, or 'punch and Judy' as it was described within the
Church, was only too glad to embrace. Compassion was to be
balanced by a strong command as the priests discovered when they
gathered at St Andrew's College in Bearsden, two weeks after his
installation. Winning had firm ideas about the behaviour of priests.
Constructive criticism would be welcome, but pernicious gossip
and cynical comments were unworthy of men of the cloth. Smart
attire was compulsory. As he explained: 'We do not subscribe to
the cult of the scruffy.'[3] A midnight curfew was strongly recommended and he insisted priests should earn their one day off per
week through hard work and diligence.

Winning was aware that priests perceived themselves to be among
the biggest losers from the Vatican Council. The priest's elevated
position was being eroded by a strengthened laity who were now
encouraged to be as spiritual as their parish leaders. The changes
in the liturgy had brought confusion and depression as older priests
struggled daily with the unfamiliar style of the new Mass and in
private mourned the loss of mystery that followed the departure of
the Latin rite. The Council's document on the priesthood had been
overshadowed, and remained unread by many priests in the diocese.
Throughout the world, priests were suffering frustration, anguish
and a lack of identity. Winning said: 'They felt: "We are ordained
and we can say Mass and forgive sins and celebrate the sacraments
but if the laity are going to assume such a great position in the
Church, we must be diminishing."' To tackle his priests' malaise,
Winning announced the introduction of a one-month refresher
course where groups of thirty would study the Council documents,

contemplate the Church's new direction and reignite their enthusiasm. At first, the courses were held in Scotland, but when priests began to miss lectures, citing a funeral or other appointment, Winning switched them to Rome. A programme was developed by the professors at the Gregorian University and the idea developed over a number of years into a successful sabbatical. A second idea, introduced more swiftly, was, as Winning explained, that 'the priests as a group with the bishop had to assume responsibility for running the diocese'.

Winning introduced a cabinet style of diocesan government, inconceivable to his predecessors. So that he could be free to spend time with the laity, he announced the appointment of Vicars Episcopal, priests who would have responsibility for specific areas and would in turn be assisted by a committee comprised of both laity and religious such as brothers and nuns. The areas now covered by such 'cabinet ministers' included: religious orders and congregations, communications, ecumenism, fabric and planning, justice and peace, vocations, youth councils, the lay apostolate, the liturgy, marriage advisory councils, missionary awareness, religious education, and schools and education. As his new chief of staff, Winning appointed Mgr Charles 'Donny' Renfrew, then rector of St Vincent's College in Langbank as a third Vicar General, to complement the two priests who remained from Scanlan's era. After explaining to the clergy the direction in which they would now march, Winning turned his attention to the laity.

On 20 October 1974, he wrote the first of what would become a blizzard of personal letters to his public over the next twenty-seven years. The letter, sent to every Catholic family in the diocese, described himself as a 'pastoral bishop'. 'This means that I will try to spend the greatest part of my time amongst the clergy and people, meeting you and getting to know you, understanding your problems and trying to solve them.' An early intervention was the removal of Jack McGavigan, the chairman of the archdiocese's lay apostolate, on the grounds that he had made little constructive progress and, in Winning's opinion, spent his time berating the priests. Winning's goal was the reanimation of the parish, to recreate the dedicated and loving society he had experienced as a boy. While it would be another eight years before he began the introduction of his Pastoral Plan, his great challenge to the priests and laity, introduced in the early Eighties, which would dominate the final twenty years of his life, glimpses of his agenda are to be found in an essay he wrote on the tenth anniversary of Council's conclusion:

> I do not see the end of the parish as basic structure; rather I should hope to see its renewal in a very obvious way. The parish community is composed of a variety of smaller communities which are now more closely knit and already possess a lively spirit: families, friends and relations, lay associations, youth, schools, neighbours, while other such as family discussion groups or circles already exist or can be formed without much difficulty. We should turn to them and build them up, paying particular attention to the occasional celebration of the Eucharist for them. They are not to become exclusive or elite groups, for the parish community needs them, and they need the parish.

The media was the final group to discover that the new Archbishop of Glasgow was cut from a brighter cloth than his predecessors. While Scanlan and Ward viewed the media as a menace, untrustworthy and invasive and best ignored, Winning perceived it as a megaphone through which he could both disseminate his beliefs and raise the Catholic Church's profile. In early November, he spoke at a lunch organized by the Glasgow Publicity Club, an association of journalists and publicists, where he said he had no intention of becoming a 'no comment' personality. A point he then illustrated by stating that football was in danger of becoming the nation's new religion and that excommunicating the IRA would be of little practical significance; comments which appeared as prominent news stories the following day. Two weeks later, he leapt into the headlines of the *Glasgow Herald* and *Glasgow Evening Times* with a speech delivered at the jubilee dinner of the Glasgow Catholic Nurses' Guild at the city's Ingram Hotel. At the rostrum, he drew parallels between the recent IRA bombing of two Birmingham pubs and the innocent lives lost through abortion, stating, 'Nothing, absolutely nothing, can justify the killing or maiming of innocent people', before adding, 'How strange it is that a society which so rightly denounces bomb-killings should complacently approve of the killing of thousands of unborn children', a speech that attracted the headline ' "Destroyers of Life" condemned by Archbishop of Glasgow' in the *Glasgow Herald*. The issue of abortion had also taken on a more immediate quality when, shortly after his appointment as Archbishop, Winning discovered that his father had been illegitimate. The secret had been uncovered by Mgr David MacRoberts, a true ecclesiastical polymath who had been charged with researching the new Archbishop's family for inspiration in the design of his bishopric coat of arms, and the revelation hit Winning like a hammer blow. His father had always been vague when questioned about his background and now he knew why. Winning's reaction to the news was to conceal the findings. He told no one, not even his sister, who ironically was already aware of the fact and had also chosen not to tell him, both sides fearful of upsetting the other. Margaret had discovered the news when her father was required to produce his birth certificate for application for a passport to allow him to travel to Rome for his son's ordination, a fact that only emerged after her brother's death. The undesired, fragile start to his own father's life and the near certain knowledge that, had he been born in the new permissive society growing around him, he would likely have been a victim of abortion, steeled Winning's fervour on the issue, but it was to be almost twenty years before he was able to make a dent in the issue.

Winning's relationship with Scanlan had cooled dramatically after the older man's unenthusiastic response to his auxiliary's appointment and so when the retired archbishop showed no intention of leaving his flat above the archdiocesan office, Winning began the search for alternative accommodation. 'He invited me to share the flat, but I had no intention of accepting; I put him off by explaining that I wanted a garden.' Winning may have abandoned Scanlan's chauffeur-driven Mercedes in favour of a more nondescript vehicle but in those early years he still preferred to be driven than to drive and so would often enlist the 'unofficial' services of Tony Docherty, a funeral director with whom he had become friendly while resident in Clydebank, though within a year he was driving himself. While his choice of vehicle may not have rivalled Scanlan's, his choice of accommodation would far exceed the old Archbishop's residence. Accompanied by the diocesan lawyer, Winning toured Glasgow's more salubrious suburbs of Pollokshields and Giffnock before settling on a detached villa in Newlands.

The Oaks was a beautiful Arts and Crafts-style villa with ten rooms spread over three floors and complemented by an acre of gardens. The archdiocese paid £35,000 for the property and after four weeks of preparatory work by Willie Robertson, a builder and friend of Winning, the Archbishop moved in, accompanied by Mrs McInnes. The top floor accommodated Winning's bedroom and study, his housekeeper's quarters were on the ground floor along with the oratory and two large living rooms, while the dinning room and kitchen were in the basement. The Oaks was to become Winning's beloved retreat, a private space he furnished with photographs of his parents and his sister's family, where he would retire to work in solitude or relax by listening to the concertos of Mozart and Bach, sometimes through the prism of James Last's orchestra.

In May 1974, just as Winning's appointment was generating applause in the west, the Church of Scotland made a decision at its annual General Assembly that triggered murmurs of discontent. On the recommendation of the Inter-Church Relations Committee, an overwhelming majority of commissioners voted to invite a senior Roman Catholic to address the following year's General Assembly, a first in their four-hundred-year history and one that unsettled a powerful minority. The Reverend Dr Roderick Smith, Convenor of the Inter-Church Relations Committee, insisted a 'wind of change' was blowing through the Roman Catholic Church and praised the late John XXIII, 'that great Apostle of Christian Unity', for its inspiration. The fact that a minister could describe the Pope, a traditional figure of hate among generations of Protestants, in conciliatory language was evidence of a deep fissure in the icy relations that existed between the two Churches. That many miles of frozen tundra remained was pointed out by the Revd Sutherland of Killearn and Kilkenzie, who said he spoke for a body of moderate opinion concerned that such an invitation would imply that vast theological differences between the two Churches did not exist.

The theological differences remained. The Pope is the Vicar of Christ to Catholics but to Protestants he was once viewed as the Anti-Christ. While Catholics believe God has revealed himself in two forms, through the Bible and through the various traditions of the Catholic Church, which stretch back to the Apostles, Protestants believe the Bible to be the sole source of revelation. In the Protestant faith there exist two holy sacraments, baptism and the Eucharist. Catholics enjoy another five: reconciliation, confirmation, matrimony, holy orders and the sacrament of the sick. The crucial distinction concerns the Eucharist; Holy Communion to Catholics is the body of Christ, the miracle of transubstantiation performed by the priest during Mass, but to Protestants it remains only a potent symbol, little more than a slim slice of bread. For four centuries, the Catholic Church had treated the reformed faiths with an open contempt, which was in turn reciprocated. Actual bloodshed between either side gave way to an ingrained bigotry and a caustic ill will. In 1964, as part of the Vatican Council, the Catholic Church stepped out of its trench with the publication of a decree on ecumenism, *Unitatis Redintegratio*, which tore down some of the barriers between the Churches. In the past any official involvement by the Catholic Church with other Christian Churches was prohibited on the grounds that, as the one true Church, such involvement would lower its stature. The same vast differences remained and would be non-negotiable, but at least Church leaders were in a position to discuss them. A second crucial concession by the Catholic Church concerned the redemptive nature of the reformed faiths, as well as a plethora of other religions such as Judaism. Formerly, the only access to heaven was through the Catholic Church, or so the Church believed; all other faiths were merely a cunning ruse depositing their unwitting adherents into hell. The belief that heaven was a garden surrounded by the walls of the Catholic Church had given way to the more enlightened belief that the garden was, in truth, so much bigger than the Church and that while the Church remained God's official route, other faiths, beliefs and denominations provided a far more circuitous, though no less successful, pathway. A drawbridge had been lowered from the fortress of Catholicism and dialogue was now possible.

In March 1975, the Church of Scotland announced that Thomas Winning had accepted their invitation to speak at the next General Assembly in May. Winning was conscious of the magnitude of the opportunity presented to him and turned for guidance to two men notable for their experience in ecumenical matters. The first was James Quinn, a Jesuit priest from Edinburgh who had wide experience in the field of inter-Church relations, while the second was a Catholic priest with an unusual background. Ronnie Walls had previously been a Protestant minister before converting to Catholicism, and after his wife's death in a car crash he trained and was subsequently ordained as a Catholic priest. Winning's chosen theme was two brothers who had not spoken for four hundred years and various drafts bounced across the country between Quinn, Walls and Cardinal Gray. Winning said: 'It was a stressful event as well as a momentous occasion.'

On 21 May, Winning arrived on the Mound, the Church of Scotland's meeting rooms in central Edinburgh which overlook Princes Street, in muted dress. The mitre, crook and robes of a metropolitan archbishop would be out of place and deliberately provocative at a meeting of Presbyterian ministers. Instead, the occasion marked the final outing of his black tonsure suit, an austere black coat that fastened at the throat but was open across the chest. He even went so far as to remove his pectoral cross. In return, officials removed troublesome elements from the hall. The most vociferous critic of Winning's appearance was Pastor Jack Glass, the leader of the Twentieth-Century Reformation Movement, a small Protestant sect that harboured extremely hostile views towards Catholicism. Prior to mounting the podium, Winning's concern was that Glass would hector him. Church officials had already prevented Glass from entering but no one had informed Winning, who spent the first few minutes of his speech awaiting the pastor's first cantankerous outburst. 'I began my speech, and all the time there was this part of me that was expecting a howling match to start. It was right at the front of my mind. The longer that went on, however, the more I realised that it was not going to happen.'

Winning began his speech:

My dearly beloved brothers in Jesus Christ, 'This is the day that the Lord hath made; we will rejoice and be glad in it.' These are the most appropriate words I can find to describe this event. For me and the Church to which I belong it is a unique and happy occasion, the memory of which, one knows instinctively, will last as long as life itself.[4]

Explaining that he brought greetings from the entire Roman Catholic community, he also told his listeners how the Apostolic Delegate had just that morning sent a telegram of prayers and good wishes on what was undoubtedly a historic occasion. In a gracious nod to the protesters, he acknowledged their right to show dissent before calling blessings down on both Churches. It was then that his theme began to unfurl: 'What do brothers say to one another after years, and, in our cases, centuries of estranged silence? Surely they ask forgiveness.' He then repeated the words spoken by Pope Paul VI, explaining how the pontiff had turned to all the observers from different faiths and spoken of the deep sadness he felt at their estrangement.

If we are in any way to blame for the long years of separation, we humbly beg God's forgiveness. And we ask pardon too, for our brethren, who feel themselves to have been injured by us. For our part we willingly forgive the injuries which the Catholic Church has suffered and forget the grief endured during the long series of dissensions and separation.

Winning then went on to talk of ecumenism, stating that the Catholic Church was 'utterly' committed to the unity of the Christian Churches, but that this was ultimately the work of the Holy Spirit. 'Hence the union of Christian Churches will not be achieved by one Church taking over, nor by the clever adjustments of churchmen, but by the power of the Spirit bringing the whole body into a living unity.'

He accepted that the Catholic Church was a stumbling block:

We, for example, in the Roman Catholic Church, realize that we are a stumbling block to other Churches because of our convictions regarding the nature of the Church and her authority. Nonetheless, we are fully committed to working with you and the other Christian Churches towards unity, for we are confident that the Holy Spirit will guide all of us to an ultimate solution.

At the conclusion of his speech, the floor began to shake as the ministers stamped their feet in support. The Moderator, Revd James Matheson, quoted John Wesley in his response: 'I don't say come to my side nor draw me to thine. But if my heart is now thy heart in the love of Christ, then give me thy hand.'[5] Winning gave his hand to strong applause. He was approached by one Church of Scotland minister who confessed he now felt closer to the Catholic Church than the Episcopalian Church, and a few moments later an Episcopalian made a similar remark. 'I thought it was a very successful attempt at reconciliation,' said Winning. The Vatican, however, did not agree. A speech of such historical significance would expect to make a prominent story in *L'Osservatore Romano*, the official newspaper of the Holy See, or the Pope's *Pravda*, as it was sometimes described. The following week's edition made no mention of the speech or Winning's appearance. It was not until two years later that Winning discovered the reason why. Bruno Heim had dutifully despatched a copy of the speech to Rome, but Cardinal Benelli, head of the Secretariat of State, the foreign office of the Holy See and the department responsible for external relations, was unimpressed by the contents and questioned Winning's suitability to have made such a speech. The news story was subsequently blocked and it was left to the chief of the Secretariat for Christian Unity, Archbishop Willebrands, to write to Benelli justifying Winning's credentials. The correspondence had flown above Winning's head and it was not until he met the editor of *L'Osservatore Romano* in Rome two years later that he discovered the truth. 'My reaction to Benelli would have been: "I'm as good a Catholic as you are and I'm as well educated a priest."'

Ecumenism in Scotland during this time displayed all the motion of a drunken man, lurching one step forward only to stagger two steps back. After Winning's triumph, the Church of Scotland invited Edward Daly, the Bishop of Derry, to speak in St Giles's Cathedral in Edinburgh at an ecumenical conference on Christianity and the violence in Northern Ireland. Daly managed to speak just three words, 'I consider it . . .', before being shouted down by Protestant demonstrators, to the intense embarrassment of the Moderator. The Moderator himself endured the protesters' wrath on 24 February 1976, when Winning returned the invitation and asked James Matheson to speak to the Glasgow senate of priests and lay council. Dozens of demonstrators led by Pastor Jack Glass gathered outside the hall to brandish banners that declared: 'Winning: Bigot of the Year' and 'Mass Mongerer Matheson'. The invited audience may have squirmed in their seats as Matheson argued for the integration of Catholic schools – 'If we are to have one Christian people instead of two then we must bring up our children together, not apart'[6] – but they still ensured their guest a cordial reception.

Winning had taken an instant liking to Matheson, whom he regarded as straight-talking and sincere. It was for this reason, combined with Winning's first flush of enthusiasm for his new role, that ecumenism rose up the list of priorities to a position far beyond the importance he attached to the matter in private.

Behind closed doors Winning could be scathing of 'the Prods', as he often referred to them. Years later, when Cardinal, he politely ushered a group of Protestant visitors out of his Clyde Street offices and as soon as the door was closed mimed the flute players of the Orange bands to indicate to a Church employee who the group were. The indignities of his childhood and his father's long unemployment meant that there forever existed an 'us' and 'them' barrier between the faiths, one he was both reluctant and unwilling to climb over. In his mind, Glasgow Cathedral, the Church of Scotland's granite monument, remained 'stolen property', booty from the Reformation. Although he was unable to reclaim the bricks and mortar that once belonged to his Church, his ambition extended to restoring the Catholic Church as the genuine voice of Christianity in Scotland, and this could only come at a cost to the Church of Scotland. Winning was a pragmatist, aware that his loyalty to Rome and belief in the superiority of the Catholic faith precluded any movement on issues such as inter-faith communion. A reunion would only occur when Protestants returned, head bowed, to Rome, and in the meantime the best that could be achieved was to replace antagonism with pleasantries. Throughout his career he would diligently take part in inter-faith conferences and ecumenical meetings on the small island of Iona, but his attendance was more from duty than active choice, as he would often vigorously disagree with the Revd George MacLeod, founder of the Iona Community.

Pleasantries, however, did produce results. On two Sundays in 1975, 26 October and 2 November, a joint pastoral letter signed by Winning, Matheson and Richard Wimbush, the Primus of the Scottish Episcopal Church, was read out to the congregations of each church, asking them to dwell on the current disintegration of society. The letter explained that rising unemployment, alarming rates of inflation and increasing violence were fracturing society and that drinking, gambling, pornography and promiscuity now threatened a moral collapse. Christians of each denomination were called upon to promote their values at home, at work and in society. 'Christians who take an active part in the fight for justice and charity ... make a great contribution to the welfare of mankind and to the peace of the world.'[7]

Monsignor Gerry Rogers died on 10 August 1975, having 'drank to the dregs a cup of suffering', as Winning was to describe his last few months in a homily at his mentor's funeral. Rogers had been among the first people Winning contacted with the news of his appointment but elation soon sank into concern as he listened to Rogers' slurred and stuttered attempt to offer his congratulations. While Italian doctors had been unable to detect the cause of his speech impediments, a diagnosis of a brain tumour was made by medical staff at the Middlesex Hospital after he collapsed during a visit to his aunts. For a few weeks his two elderly relatives attempted to care for him in their home, at which point Winning discovered his condition and brought him home to Glasgow and the Bon Secour Hospital. It was here that he visited Rogers as often as his position would permit. He recollected the visits during his homily in Motherwell Cathedral during Rogers' requiem Mass, three days after his death. For Winning, who so often restrained his emotions and for whom friendships were firm, but went unspoken, it was an opportunity for release.

> Gerry Rogers accepted this one final cross. He drank to the dregs a cup of human suffering which tasted of almost all the humiliations the human frame can support. There were times, he said, when all he could do was to cling to God in dark faith. But if he was gentle in health, he became gentler in sickness. He never wallowed in self-pity; rather he was alert to the needs and concerns of those who visited him, and nursed him. In his brightest moment he radiated joy, in his dark days his silence spoke eloquently of his deep faith and humility.[8]

Winning was to lose a mentor, but the following year he glimpsed a successor – one who would also go to Rome, but in a far more powerful position. The man whom Winning would describe twenty-five years later as having made him 'a better priest, a better bishop and a better man' was Karol Wojtyla, the Cardinal Archbishop of Krakow and the man who, in 1978, would be elected Pope John Paul II.

Winning's relationship with the Pope was to remain one of deep respect, tinged with the knowledge that John Paul II existed on a far higher mental plane. He would read each of his encyclicals upon publication and grew in the belief that the Church remained in secure hands, but his relationship with John Paul II was not close. When he later became Cardinal he did not visit the Pope when in Rome or utilize his access as others did. He later explained that he did not wish to 'bother him'. John Paul II was a mystic who saw within the world an eternal battle between good and evil. Winning, in comparison, was more pragmatic and was almost uncomfortable with such a view. As President of the Bishops' Conference, he would prepare meticulously for the Ad Limina visits, which took place once every five years, and he enjoyed the opportunity that the visits provided the bishops – saying Mass with the successor to St Peter – but he was just as relieved to leave. The relationship between Winning and the Pope would become akin to teacher and student, although Winning would choose what to hear. The Pope might have said, for example, that the tridentine mass should be available to those who wish it, but Winning disagreed and felt this would only confuse his flock.

The location of the first meeting between Wojtyla and Winning was the pilgrim city of Philadelphia during the forty-first Eucharistic Congress in August 1976. The occasion was the opening Mass in the cathedral and Winning was among the celebrants in the back sanctuary. 'I spotted this guy with lovely white, curly hair, with a strong face and high cheekbones. I remember at the time thinking he looked like a medieval pope.' Cardinal Wojtyla had been brought over to Philadelphia by Anna-Teresa Tymieniecka, a Polish philos-

opher with whom Wojtyla was collaborating on a book on phenom-
enology, the study of how the material world is the bearer of the
sacred. An early advocate of Wojtyla's philosophical writings, she
arranged for the Polish cardinal to speak at Harvard University
during his visit, an event covered by *The New York Times*. During
one Mass at the Eucharistic Congress, however, Wojtyla preached
for forty minutes in his heavily accented English and while others
were enraptured by his erudition, Winning was not yet impressed.
'He was just a bore,' he remembered.

While Wojtyla followed the Eucharistic Congress by spending
time with Tymieniecka and her husband at their home in Vermont,
continuing their work on the book, Winning took a short holiday.
In one parish where he stayed an elderly woman phoned after
reading in the local paper that the Archbishop of Edinburgh was
in town. When Winning explained the error, Clara Manning, an
eighty-one-year-old who had left Glasgow in 1911 and had not
spoken to a Glaswegian since, was delighted – even more so when
he paid her a visit and spent the afternoon updating her on the
changes her native city had endured over the past sixty-five years.

Winning was a 'people person', and two years into his new role he
still wished closer contact with the parishioners of the archdiocese.
The Decree on the Bishops' Pastoral Office in the Church encouraged the use of 'various means at hand' to make Catholic doctrine
known. In early 1976, Winning consolidated his reputation as a
pioneer when he took the Decrees' suggestion to heart and launched
a monthly diocesan newspaper entitled *Flourish*. The Council had
encouraged each diocese to develop a newsletter, a suggestion many
ignored and few embraced, but none did so with the vigour of
Winning who unveiled one of the largest and most elaborate publications of its type in Europe. Like many of his early decisions,
it was against conventional wisdom. Critics insisted it would destroy sales of the *Scottish Catholic Observer*, the national weekly,
whose largest readership centred around Glasgow. Winning was
unconcerned, for he believed direct contact with Glasgow Catholics,

uninhibited by an independent editorial team, was crucial to the success of his new agenda. An early idea was to give each vicar episcopal a half-page in which to update the public on his different departments, but this was scrapped as a result of poor communication skills and concerns over the appropriateness of discussing sensitive issues, such as education negotiations, in public. Instead, under the editorship of Vincent Donnelly and backed by the generosity of Catholic newspapermen who lent their services, *Flourish* mixed Catholic news and comment with a monthly column by the Archbishop, snappily titled 'Let's Talk'. The doomsayers who predicted that a miracle was required for it ever to succeed were astounded when one emerged as the publication's first front-page story.

TEN

Glasgow's Miracle

'You are bold to say your Mass in a reformed city.'[1]
EPISCOPAL ARCHBISHOP JOHN SPOTTISWOODE

At four o'clock on the afternoon of 10 March 1615, a noose was strung around the neck of Father John Ogilvie as he stood on the wooden gallows at Glasgow Cross. A crowd of several thousand had gathered to witness the execution of the Catholic priest who, for the past five months, had resisted the attempts of Court and Crown to persuade him, through trickery and torture, to deny the primacy of the Pope and acknowledge King James VI and I's supremacy in matters spiritual as well as temporal. Three hours earlier he had been found guilty of 'most hainous, detestable and unpardonable treason' by a jury of fifteen and while his accusers, among them John Spottiswoode, the Episcopal Archbishop of Glasgow, and Provost James Hamilton, retired to lunch, Ogilvie spent his last hours on his knees in prayer. When Robert Scott, a Protestant minister, who had attempted to change Ogilvie's mind and save his life, informed the crowd from the scaffold that his death was for treason not religion, the priest protested, a response that triggered John Abercrombie, a Catholic supporter, to reassure him: 'The more wrongs you suffer, the better.' John Ogilvie would have his martyr's death. After he had thrown his rosary beads into the crowd and had begun to chant the Litany of Saints, the executioner pushed him from the ladder and pulled on his legs, breaking his neck and sparing him from the suffering of a slow strangulation.

Born in 1579, John Ogilvie was the son of Walter Ogilvie of Drum, then a rural area of Banffshire in the north of Scotland. His parentage has been loosely tied by historians to Sir Walter Ogilvie, an affluent landowner in the area, whose own father, James Ogilvie of Findlater, was once treasurer to Mary Queen of Scots. Unfortunately, no such mention was made in the contemporary records, an oversight that has since caused doubt that a captive Catholic priest was heir to such a prominent Protestant family. What is known of Ogilvie is that after matriculating at the Protestant university of Helmstedt in Germany in 1592, he transferred four years later to the Catholic Scots College of Douai in Flanders and later spent time at the Scottish Benedictine abbey at Regensburg in Bavaria before entering the Jesuit noviciate at Brunn in Slovakia. During his long years of training he taught across central Europe before being ordained a priest in Paris in 1610. This decade of wandering had left him longing to return to Scotland and for the work of a missionary priest, bringing comfort, the Mass and sacraments to the country's few remaining Catholics. In November 1613, he received his instructions, '*ut dedocerem haeresim*', to unteach heresy, and arrived on the east coast, disguised as John Watson, an ex-soldier seeking work as a horse-dealer.

Ogilvie spent the winter of 1613 attending to Catholics in both the Highlands and in Edinburgh, saying Mass in the homes of supporters, baptizing children and administering the sacrament of confession, before returning to Paris via London, a decision that displeased his superior, James Gordon of Huntly, who promptly sent him back. Ogilvie's second visit began in the summer of 1614 and would end with his arrest in October. For those few months he worked out of Glasgow where he resided at the home of Marion Walker, the daughter of the chamberlain of David Beaton, the last Catholic Archbishop prior to the Reformation. Ogilvie was betrayed to the authorities on 14 October by Adam Boyd, who had earlier approached the priest with a desire to convert. When John Spottiswoode heard of his arrest, he visited him in prison, slapped him on the face and said: 'You are bold to say your Mass in a reformed city.' Ogilvie's response was to predict

Spottiswoode's plan for him: 'You act like a hangman and not like a bishop.'[2]

Since the departure a decade earlier of James VI of Scotland to London where he was crowned James I of England and Wales, John Spottiswoode had loyally carried out the King's Church policy to elevate the Episcopal Church above the Kirk, which earned him his appointment as Archbishop of Glasgow. The death of Ogilvie would see him rewarded with the position of Archbishop of St Andrews and Primate of Scotland, but for the five months of Ogilvie's interrogation Spottiswoode was reduced from bishop to pawn in a battle between King and Pope. James VI took his position as Defender of the Faith with great seriousness, a belief he buttressed by the careful study of theology and politics. The Gunpowder Plot that had threatened to tumble parliament down on his head in the early years of his reign in England had toughened his resolve against Catholic agent provocateurs and his was the guiding hand behind Ogilvie's relentless interrogation and eventual torture. By comparison, Ogilvie was fortified by his own faith and was determined to walk a narrow line. He would neither deny his beliefs nor incriminate himself, nor endanger his secret parishioners. When asked if he had ever said Mass, he declined to answer. When quizzed: 'Is it treason to assert that the Pope has spiritual jurisdiction in the King's dominions?'[3] he denied that treason was possible on the grounds that no man-made law could deny the Pope his God-given responsibility. Spottiswoode's request to use torture on the recalcitrant cleric in order to obtain the names of his accomplices was granted by the King three months later, by which point Ogilvie had been moved to and from Edinburgh. The rack, the seventeenth century's traditional implement of torture, was set aside in favour of a more insidious system of sleep deprivation. For seven days and eight nights Ogilvie was kept awake by incessant questioning and enforced marches. When asked for the names of accomplices, he replied that an answer was possible only 'by damning my soul, offending my God and ruining my neighbours'.[4] The torture was abandoned, having revealed nothing, after physicians examined him and decided he was only hours from death.

The King, frustrated by the priest's silence, was determined to conclude the overdrawn interrogation and personally composed a series of questions that would place the noose around Ogilvie's neck. The questions concentrated on the claims of the papacy. First, Ogilvie was asked if the Pope had spiritual powers over the King's subjects, to which he said yes, a reply he repeated when asked if the pontiff could excommunicate the King. Yet when the questions moved on to confirm whether or not the Pope had the power to depose or kill the King, Ogilvie insisted that he could not speak on the issue until the Pope himself had spoken. By refusing to deny the questions, he was viewed to have confirmed them and therefore be guilty of treason, a charge that the jury, assembled in Glasgow a few days later, were quick to find proven. In comparison with the hundreds hanged or burnt at the stake in England and Wales, the death of John Ogilvie was to provide Scottish Catholics with the only martyred priest of the Reformation.

At four o'clock on the afternoon of 7 March 1976, 361 years later, Archbishop Thomas Winning stood before a crowd of several hundred marchers and announced that Scotland was to be blessed by a new saint. Winning had kept the news as the culmination of the fifty-third Ogilvie Walk, an annual activity initiated in 1923 to commemorate the priest's heroism by marching from the scene of his death to St Mungo's Church at Townhead while saying the rosary for his canonization. A final decade of the rosary was said each year for the conversion of Scotland's Protestants to Catholicism and the completion of the martyred priest's work.

In order to raise a figure to the realm of a saint, the Catholic Church requires proof of that person's intercession from heaven on earth in the form of a miracle, an act unascribable to either human or natural circumstance. By announcing the canonization of Ogilvie, the Vatican had agreed that a miracle had taken place through the intercession of the long-dead Jesuit priest. The miracle was in the shape of a man, and the man was called John Fagan.

Nine years previously, on the morning of 6 March 1967, a large cancerous tumour in the stomach of Mr Fagan, a checker at Glasgow's Princes dock, began to recede. Until that point he had been on the brink of death after eighteen months of weight loss, violent vomiting and excruciating pain. A quiet, diligent man who worked hard to support his wife Mary and to feed and clothe his six children, John Fagan was in many ways the epitome of the Catholic working class. The family lived in a small council house in Easterhouse, a housing scheme two miles from the city centre that, by the 1980s, had become synonymous with drug abuse and poverty. At first Fagan began to suffer dramatic weight loss and a feeling of nausea at the sight of food; this was followed by his vomiting blood, a symptom which led to a barium meal examination and the tumour's eventual diagnosis. An operation in the autumn of 1965 relieved the pain temporarily, but by Christmas 1966 he was drifting in and out of consciousness and tackling the pain with twice-daily injections of morphine. As their local parish church was entitled Blessed John Ogilvie, the family were advised to direct their prayers to the dead priest by Fr Thomas Reilly, the parish priest and the postulator of the cause for canonization of John Ogilvie.

Attempts to reward Ogilvie's suffering with canonization had begun scarcely a decade after his death. The Jesuit order had appointed a priest, Fr Virgilio Cepari, who was charged with the task of promoting the canonization of all the priests of the order who suffered martyrdom. Interviews were carried out with two Scots who had encountered the priest during his brief Scottish ministry. John Mayne had been a prisoner beside the priest in Glasgow, while James Haygate had run errands for him and caught the rosary beads the priest had thrown from the gallows. Both men went on to become Benedictine monks at the Scots Abbey in Würzburg in Germany and, unsurprisingly, testified to his bravery, charity and strength of character. The further steps towards sainthood required evidence of public devotion – visible displays not of worship, as in Catholic theology only God is suitable for such an expression, but veneration – however, in Protestant Scotland such demonstrations were not feasible until the early 1920s when the Ogilvie Walk was launched. After seven years the marchers received an extra impetus when Pope Pius XI announced that Ogilvie would be addressed as 'Blessed John Ogilvie', a notch below saint.

John Fagan was clearly dying. The doctors at Glasgow Royal Infirmary insisted his condition was terminal and had advised his wife to leave him in the care of a hospice. Mary Fagan had refused and insisted she would care for her husband at home. When news of John Fagan's condition reached Fr Thomas Reilly and his curate, Fr John Fitzgibbon, the pair encouraged the couple, their family and friends to pray to Ogilvie that he would intercede with God on the dying man's behalf. A medal of John Ogilvie was pinned to the patient's pyjamas and prayers were offered by parishioners for his cure. On Saturday 4 March 1967, Fagan was near death; he had lost four stone, was unable to raise his head from the pillow, and when conscious could barely speak above a croaked whisper. John MacDonald, the family's doctor, visited that evening and explained death was hours away and that there was little more he could do but return to sign the death certificate.

Mary Fagan held a vigil beside her husband's bed through Saturday and Sunday night and when at six o'clock on Monday morning, after dozing lightly in her chair, she noticed her husband was without breath or pulse, she assumed he had passed away. Grief and exhaustion resulted in her falling asleep while waiting the return of Dr MacDonald. Three hours later, at nine o'clock, she was stirred by her husband's voice. The thin, chesty wheeze which had been his only means of communication during the past few months had been replaced by a clearer, stronger voice, and his standard lament at the pain was replaced by a request for food. 'Mary, I'm hungry,' he said. She boiled him an egg and watched trembling as he sat up and ate. Dr MacDonald was even more disturbed to discover not a corpse, but his patient, pale but alive, taking tea. He told Mary Fagan that as a non-Catholic he was unacquainted with miracles, but if her husband had recently been dipped in the waters of Lourdes this would be his conclusion. Father Fitzgibbon was equally startled and declared: 'I believe God is in this house.'

Nine years would pass before the Vatican agreed, and only after extensive research and analysis of what became known within weeks of Fagan's recovery as 'the miracle in Easterhouse'. Winning's involvement in the case began in November 1972 when, as auxiliary bishop, he was asked to take on the role of Judge Delegate to aid a sickly Scanlan in the Apostolic Process, the Vatican's official inquiry into the alleged miracle. This took the form of a tribunal, headed by Scanlan but run by Winning, which quizzed the participants on the exact sequence of events using questions scripted in Rome by the Congregation for the Cause of Saints, the department that processes petitions for canonization.

Winning entered the process as an arch sceptic who believed a miracle on the streets of Glasgow was almost inconceivable. It was an attitude he sustained after his examination of Fr Reilly, whom he found unconvincing and guilty of dissembling. When Winning pressed him to state if Mr Fagan, his family and the parishioners of Blessed John Ogilvie were aware that the Catholic Church was praying to God through the intercession of John Ogilvie for the man's recovery, the priest was uncertain. In Winning's opinion, he gave the impression of being unaware that prayers were even being said for Fagan's recovery. At one point, Scanlan slipped him a note that read: 'Did John Ogilvie know?', suggesting that if the parish priest was unsure whether or not prayers were said, the saint-to-be must also have been in a similar state of bemusement. Winning managed not to laugh out loud. There was a degree of condescension from Winning and Scanlan to the parish priest and his curate, whom Winning described as 'one of the dumbest priests I've ever met', but the heads of both bishops were turned by the comprehensive nature of the medical investigation.

At first a panel of three Glasgow doctors – Andrew Curran, a senior general practioner, Aloysius Dunn, a consultant, and John Fitzsimons, a senior lecturer at Glasgow University – was formed by Fr Reilly, on the recommendation of Fr Paul Molinari, a Jesuit in Turin who had taken over the role of postulator for John Ogilvie's canonization. Their task was to uncover a natural explanation for Fagan's rapid recovery. All medical records, biopsy reports and x-rays were put at their disposal while each person involved in the patient's treatment was thoroughly interviewed. One possible answer to the recovery was that a spontaneous regression of the cancer had taken place, that Fagan's body had successfully overcome the malignant cells; unfortunately, this scenario was dismissed since none of the recognizable features of spontaneous regression was present. The next possibility was that the cancer was not cancer but a misdiagnosis of a non-lethal alternative; once again the available evidence failed to fuse. Over the years, Fagan's charts and medical records were passed like a baton to a relay of doctors, consultants and specialists on the insistence of Livio Capocaccia, the professor of gastroenterology at Rome University and the secretary of the Vatican Medical Tribunal. Capocaccia travelled to Scotland to examine the evidence himself and failed to find a natural reason why John Fagan should not otherwise be dead.

As no natural explanation could be found, the medical establishment cleared the way for the Church to apply a supernatural one. The sheer ordinariness of John Fagan's life helped to convince Winning that a divine intervention had taken place. 'He was not a man who was famous or whom society wished to stay alive, yet I felt the hand of God was there,' recalled Winning who decided the inspiring story of Fagan's recovery and the Vatican's final agreement that a miracle had taken place should be the cover story for the debut issue of his new monthly diocesan newsletter *Flourish*.

The canonization of a new Scottish saint, the first since St Margaret, who died in the ninth century, and the only native Scot, was a cause of concern among a pocket of prominent Protestants. Veneration of saints was a practice abandoned by the Protestant reformers in the sixteenth century on the grounds that it detracted from devotion to Christ, and Robert Kernohan, editor of the Church of Scotland's magazine *Life and Work*, argued in an article in his publication that canonization was a threat to ecumenism. Kernohan was supported by Professor William Barclay, a lecturer, author, and Kirk theologian who said: 'I do not think this will set back the cause of unity, but I do not see that shutting your eyes to these things will do ecumenism any good.'[5] It was left to the Moderator, Dr James Matheson, to distance the body of the Church from their comments when he argued: 'That way of thinking is alien to us Protestants, but if Catholics believe so, why all the fuss?'[6] Kernohan's article attracted a brief flurry of correspondence in the *Glasgow Herald* but died away and Winning refused to be drawn into the fray. Instead he cautioned: 'Patient, friendly and enlightened discussion has been the hallmark of joint conversations between the Catholic Church and the Church of Scotland in recent years and I trust it will continue. I certainly do not want to be drawn into this kind of controversy, because resolution does not come that way.'[7]

When, on 17 October 1977, Paul VI made the solemn declaration of Ogilvie's sainthood from beneath Bernini's baldacchino, the huge twisting bronze canopy that sits over the site of St Peter's tomb, he did not dwell on the catholicity for which he died. Before an audience of five thousand Scots, including Winning and John and Mary Fagan, he highlighted Ogilvie's defence of the universal belief that religion remain independent of political authority. 'The saint that we venerate, far from being a symbol of civil or spiritual discord, will soothe the unhappy memory of violence or the abuse of authority for religion's sake.'[8] In a subtle irony the man who was so close to death would go on to outlive his wife, his family doctor, parish priest and Paul VI. John Fagan died seventeen years later on 29 September 1993 and although he had moved from Easterhouse to West Lothian, on the outskirts of Edinburgh, he was buried at his old parish, renamed through the 'miracle' of his recovery Saint John Ogilvie.

At the beginning of 1977, Winning received a letter from a Scots doctor, Ian Jackson. A plastic surgeon of considerable skill and charity, he had recently spent time teaching and operating in Lima, the Peruvian capital, where, with his wife Marjorie, he had encountered a pitiful little boy. David Lopez was a two-year-old Campa Indian who had no face. Under a mop of black hair and deep brown eyes was a hole where a nose, upper jaw, gums and teeth should have been. A few months after his birth, the bite of a sandfly had left a legacy of leishmaniasis, a virulent disease that gnawed through the soft tissue and bones of his face. His parents were primitive people and, disturbed by his horrific appearance, they passed him on to Catholic missionaries for treatment. Doctor Jackson had been introduced to David by a Swiss aid worker, Martine Schopfer, who had discovered him alone and untreatable in the cot of a children's hospital, and he agreed to treat the child at Canniesburn hospital in Bearsden, the specialist centre for plastic surgery where he presently worked.

It was a promise that was proving difficult to keep. The extent of the child's disfigurement would require numerous operations and while he was prepared to work for free, the National Health Service were unwilling to set a precedent and declined to make a similar offer. Letters requesting funding from Save the Children and UNICEF were either unsuccessful or went unanswered, and the couple were growing desperate when Marjorie Jackson made the suggestion that as David was a resident of a Catholic country, perhaps the Catholic Church in Glasgow could offer assistance. Winning was moved by the letter and was quick to agree and sent a prompt reply explaining that he did not yet have the £2,000 necessary to commence the child's treatment but would find it and gave his assurance that the Church would not let David down.

A fund-raising campaign began in primary schools throughout the archdiocese after Winning visited them to tell them of the plight of the child the world would come to know, through the powerful BBC documentaries of Desmond Wilcox, as 'The Boy David'.

Within a few weeks, the funds were in place as the archidocesan offices were inundated with the contents of smashed piggy banks. In February, Dr Jackson telephoned Winning at the diocesan offices to inform him that David had arrived from Peru. Winning then sent Fr Tom Gibbons, the priest in charge of Catholic Child Welfare, to act as his envoy and assess what the Church could do to help. Initially, the Jacksons were adamant that David's face should never be photographed in full, for fear that he be branded a freak, and a book or comic was always strategically placed to conceal his true condition. An exception was made for Winning who argued that shock was sometimes a necessary tactic to educate people on the suffering of others and so with the Jacksons' consent a photograph was taken at Canniesburn hospital of Winning beside the little boy, so ordinary in his cord dungarees, polo neck jumper and Paddington Bear badge, but grotesquely unique in the condition of his face. The picture appeared on the front page of *Flourish* under the headline: 'If this picture shocks you we're sorry, but . . . it's David's plight.' The picture broke the city's heart. The *Glasgow Evening Times*, under the editorship of Charles Wilson, who would go on to edit *The Times* in London, followed the Church's lead and launched an appeal for funds which, combined with the Church's, totalled £46,000. As Marjorie Jackson wrote in her memoir *The Boy David*: 'We believed Archbishop Winning's motives were right and this was certainly proved to be so. The effect of that pitiful little face staring out from the newspaper was devastating; there was an overwhelming response to the plea for help.'

The story of David Lopez would go on to move people throughout the world. If Winning's generosity and compassion were illustrated by the aid and assistance he offered David and the Jackson family, his intransigence and unbending commitment to Catholic teaching were demonstrated five years later when the family adopted the child and chose to raise him as a Protestant. It was a decision with which Winning bitterly disagreed and that led to the collapse of the relationship both parties had previously enjoyed. As David had been baptized at the Catholic mission of Puerto Ocopa on the 29 July 1975, seven months after his birth, he was entitled, in the eyes of the Church, to a Catholic upbringing. Any adoption should be by Catholic parents or those willing to raise him in the faith into which he was born. Yet while many Catholics had aided the Jacksons in their pursuit of a legal adoption without asking in which faith the child would be raised – most prominently the Primate of Peru, Cardinal Juan Landazuri Ricketts, who put his diocesan lawyer at the family's disposal and sent a telex to the judge considering the case, urging him to proceed with all possible haste – only Winning took such a restrictive view.

When he was informed by Marjorie Jackson that the child would be raised as a Protestant, he argued that the family had a responsibility to the Catholic Church.

> The last conversation I had with her was when she said, 'We are bringing him up a Presbyterian.' I said, 'The kid's parents had him baptized as a Catholic.' She said, 'Well, our next-door neighbours are Catholics and they said that would probably be all right.' I thought: 'To hell with you. That's me finished with you.'

Winning said he was 'sickened' by the situation, but had little say in the family's decision.

To Winning's mind, the Jacksons had displayed disloyalty to the Church into which their son had been born and baptized and to which they themselves had turned in their hour of need. Their duty to David extended beyond his physical requirements to his spiritual needs, which, compared to the great emotional and financial changes they had already embraced, were minor; a Catholic school and access to the sacraments of confession, Holy Communion and confirmation. Their decision to raise him in the same faith as their own four children so as not to further isolate a child so obviously dogged as different was entirely understandable, but in his view it was incorrect and one he refused to condone.

> God will see to his salvation, of course, but I did feel they could have brought him up a Catholic. But that was their decision and so be it. I expected it, but I took a dim view of it. They could have given him a Catholic education. All I said was that the kid was baptized a Catholic and comes from a Catholic family and I would have thought you would have followed that through. We never would have allowed a child to be adopted if we knew it was going to be brought up Presbyterian. We would have found Catholic parents.

On paper, Winning's comments are harsh and uncharitable. It is a relief that he did not express himself so brutally to the Jacksons; instead, he allowed their relationship to dwindle and die. In private, he wished David well, remembered him in his prayers, and believed that God would ensure his salvation. Winning was simply unwilling to compromise the teaching of the Church, or to allow sentiment or circumstance to permit an action of which he disapproved.

ELEVEN

Tough Talking

'The Catholic Church did not count. The conscience of the country
rested with the Church of Scotland. We kept our heads down below
the parapet. I felt there was something not right about that. I wanted
the Church to be able to speak out in a prophetic way in society.'

THOMAS WINNING

'My mother always used to say to me: "I like our new archbishop,
because he is a fighter." There was something very true about that.'

JOSEPH DEVINE

The two boys were only visible for a couple of seconds, but their
pitiful clothes and long, tired faces had an impact that stretched
far beyond the brevity of their appearance. Winning was driving
back to his office in Park Circus, Glasgow's West End, in October
1977 after an appointment in the east end of the city, when he
pulled up at traffic lights. Two schoolboys under the age of ten
walked across the road in the rain, wearing clothes ill-equipped for
the season and with faces that reflected the poverty of their parents.
'I only saw them for a few seconds. I don't know if they saw me.
But it remained one of the saddest sights I had seen,' said Winning.
In the time it took for the lights to switch from red to green,
the Archbishop had changed his mind. A planned £1.6 million-
expansion programme to renovate St Andrew's Cathedral would be
postponed until wealthier days and the funds diverted into poverty
relief. His conscience would no longer countenance such expendi-

ture at a time when poverty and unemployment remained a persistent problem throughout his city. It was a decision which was applauded in the press, and the *Glasgow Herald* reported: 'Few acts in recent years can have done more to restore confidence in organized Christianity than that of the Roman Catholic Archbishop of Glasgow.'

Winning enjoyed the attentions of the press in a manner unknown by either his predecessors or his contemporaries. The president of the Scottish Bishops' Conference was Cardinal Gordon Gray, Archbishop of St Andrews and Edinburgh, a man with a deep distrust of the media and who feared saying anything that might upset what he described as 'the good Catholic people'. Gray was content to restrict his comments to the largely toothless Catholic press and actively avoided their mainstream secular cousins. Winning, in comparison, believed in actively courting the media as a means of trumpeting Catholic values and raising the profile of a Church he felt had spent too long with its head down and its eyes lowered. Winning wanted to give the Catholic Church in Scotland back her backbone. In order to achieve this, he made a decision to deliver provocative speeches, equipped with phrases polished for the press.

The first occasion backfired badly. On 2 February 1978, Winning was invited, as a successful former pupil, to rededicate the war memorial at his old school, Our Lady's High, which had been closed for a massive refurbishment programme. The memory of former teachers such as Patrick O'Brien, killed whilst serving in the RAF, or Harry McQuire, who had taught him German, inspired Winning to launch an attack on the erosion of the values both men had given their lives to defend. What were prenatal screening and the subsequent abortion of handicapped children, Winning argued, but an extension of the Nazis' sterilization programme? The analogy was classic Winning: simplistic, controversial and memorable. He would refer to the Second World War time and again during his career, when illustrating how the noble forces of Christian truth and justice were perpetually being attacked by a liberal, secular, sex-mad society. When Albert Naismith, the national Catholic press officer, read an early draft of the speech, he warned Winning that it would hit the headlines.

At the memorial, surrounded by dozens of staff and over a thousand pupils, Winning said the following:

> We fought a war to defeat a totalitarian regime whose atrocities still shock us, but in the intervening time, since the bells of victory rang out, we have almost imperceptibly come to espouse not a few of the tenets of such a regime, but under pseudonyms. True, we would defend with our lives the dignity of the human person and his basic freedoms, but what if we reach the stage of eliminating the unfit from the possibility of a life in our society? The Nazis sterilized those who were not able to contribute to pure, healthy, Aryan stock. Is the screening of the unborn to detect deformity and eliminate it merely a more refined, more euphemistic way of achieving the same end? We wage war against deprivation and want and disease, not by showing care and love to those who are victims but by a subtle process of elimination before they become victims. We are becoming a nation of spiritual dwarfs.[1]

The 'spiritual dwarfs' line was picked up by the *Evening Times*, but the *Glasgow Herald* proved more cautious, reporting: 'Archbishop hits out at "Nazi-style Britain".' While Winning was content to chuck brickbats, he was always surprised when they were returned with equal force. Among a battery of critics who took him to task was Professor Malcolm MacNaughton, head of obstetrics and gynaecology at Glasgow University, who insisted the analogy between his colleagues' work and the Nazis was 'ridiculous' and 'completely wrong', a view shared by the *Herald* whose editorial accused him of 'shock tactics' and 'intemperate language'. The editorial continued: 'Many will take the strongest exception to such terms; and many will be dismayed to hear them from a man known beyond his own archdiocese for humanity and moderation.'

Winning's reaction to the response was interesting: he neither regretted the speech nor its contents, but was instead anxious to avoid further argument for fear of losing his credibility. For some time he had been considering appointing a communications officer for his exclusive use. Albert Naismith was an admirable hard-working professional, but his services were divided between the seven bishops of Scotland and Winning desired a closer, more intimate working relationship. He had always highly rated Rennie McOwan – Naismith's predecessor – despite their differences, and it was to him that he now turned. McOwan was a convert from the Church of Scotland who had spent the Sixties and early Seventies pin-balling between mainstream journalism and religious posts, first as editor of the *Scottish Catholic Observer*, and then as national communications officer for the Scottish Bishops' Conference. He had left the former position five years previously, having been unable to accept the Church's teaching on contraception. Winning invited McOwan to tea and found that his attitude towards '*Humanae Vitae*' was unchanged but that his desire to work for the Church had been reignited. Winning pushed his concerns over the issue of contraception to one side. 'His attitude was: "Don't worry about it. You're not as clever as the ordained clergy is, or else you would not be saying what you are saying",' said McOwan, who accepted the new post on three conditions: automatic access to Winning at all times, an acceptable pension and an adequate salary. 'All of which, I'm sorry to tell you, he broke.'

The appointment of Rennie McOwan surprised Winning's fellow bishops, who began to suspect a new empire was under construction in the west. Bishop Thomson of Motherwell approached McOwan in private to ask if he would consider working instead for all the bishops. He was not the only uninvited guest to approach with advice; a number of priests warned McOwan that the chalice on offer was poisoned. Agnes, his wife, was convinced the job would be disastrous. The return of his predecessor, albeit in a separate role, was to cause concern for Albert Naismith, who was entirely unaware of Thomson's offer. In a statement to the *Scottish Catholic Observer*, Winning attempted to reassure Naismith by stating: 'I know that both offices will benefit from the friendship and co-operation which already exists between these two men.' Regardless of their friendship, Naismith resigned nine months later, weary of his employer's reticence towards the media. Winning remembers the national Church failing to react to a story: 'I gave Albert a hell of a doing for it over the phone and I think that finished him.' (Winning could be easily provoked. A harshness would enter his tone if his authority was questioned. Even parishioners contributing to a debate could be startled by his manner. Priests who embarked on a fully fledged row would watch as his face contorted and his nostrils flared, and his finger would jab his points home. He talked about giving people 'verbal doings', a practice about which he would later feel guilty and include among his sins during his monthly confession.) McOwan's first task as communications officer for the archdiocese of Glasgow was to curb Winning's willingness to talk to the press. As a newspaper reporter, he had admired the Archbishop's accessibility and his habit of answering the phone while at home and engaging in off-the-cuff conversations that would invariably lead to news stories. But as a press officer, he wished Winning to be inaccessible and his comments carefully controlled. McOwan said: 'He was a news desk's dream and a media officer's nightmare.'

Four months after taking the job, it was McOwan who embroiled Winning in his largest battle to date, one that involved the heir to the nation's throne, the ancient Act of Settlement and the Catholic Church's laws on marriage. The genesis of what would become a public row between Prince Charles and the Archbishop of Glasgow was a love affair between Prince Michael of Kent and Baroness Marie Christine von Reibnitz. The baroness was a Catholic who had received an annulment of her previous marriage to Tom Troubridge, an English merchant banker, and who wished a dispensation from the Church in order to wed the Prince, who was an Anglican.

While dispensations for a mixed marriage were a routine occurrence and the prerogative of the local diocesan bishop, all matters concerning Catholic royalty were handled by the Vatican to prevent any undue pressure on the local diocese. A condition of all dispensations was that any children resulting from the marriage would be raised in the Catholic faith but as the Prince was an heir (though distant) to the throne of England, he was under pressure to confirm that the children would instead be raised as Anglicans.

The Vatican promptly announced the baroness's application was unsuccessful and as the Anglican Church prohibited divorcees from remarrying on Church-owned property, the couple had no choice but to forego the splendour of a royal church wedding for the indignity of a civil ceremony at the Viennese town hall. The matter disappointed Prince Charles who, on the day of the couple's wedding, addressed the Salvation Army Congress at the Empire Pool in Wembley and launched what was regarded by many as a thinly veiled attack on the doctrine of the Catholic Church. In his speech the Prince said:

> When people are uncertain about what is right and wrong and anxious about being considered old-fashioned, it seems worse than folly that Christians are still arguing about doctrinal matters, which can only bring needless distress to a number of people. Surely what we should worry about is whether they know what is right and wrong or whether they are going to be given an awareness of the things of the Spirit and of the infinite beauty of nature; these are the things that matter.[2]

Winning believed the Prince's speech smacked of ignorance and hypocrisy. While railing against the rules governing other Churches, he seemed patently unaware of the Salvation Army's own criteria that required members who marry non-members to leave the congregation; the reference to 'the infinite beauty of nature' was the type of pantheistic drivel Winning despised and the very idea of an heir to a throne which specifically precludes Catholics, a prohibition enshrined in law through the Act of Settlement, lecturing on the folly of Catholic doctrine he felt was arrogant and absurd. Rennie McOwan was equally irritated, but where his employer was only capable of outrage he spotted an opportunity for Winning to defend Mother Church. The Prince's speech was delivered on a Friday and the following day McOwan was contacted by the *Sunday Express* for comment, which he and Winning drafted together. McOwan assured Winning that his statement, though necessary, was unlikely to receive much prominence outside Glasgow as Cardinal Basil Hume, the new Primate of the Catholic Church in England and Wales, appointed in 1976, would monopolize the national media with his retort. Winning's response, issued by McOwan in a press release, stated:

> Prince Charles's statement presumably applied to the Pope's refusal to grant a dispensation in relation to the marriage of Prince Michael of Kent and Baroness Marie Christine von Reibnitz. His remarks will cause annoyance and anger to millions of the Queen's loyal subjects who care deeply about doctrine and principle and who also care deeply about relationships with fellow Christians in other Churches. Perhaps he might care to enlarge his remarks to cover other aspects of the case, such as the law of the land, which prohibits Roman Catholics from becoming monarch. We all want to see relationships between Christian Churches further improve, but it will not be achieved by papering over the cracks and pretending that major differences of belief and practice do not exist.

Winning's comments led the next day's newspapers and he expanded on them in an interview on BBC Radio's *World at One*, where he accused the Prince of advocating 'a woolly type of Christianity' and called for the repeal of the Act of Settlement:

> I feel that the law these days is rather an anachronism. We are all campaigning for equal rights and justice and this law is allowed to remain on the statute books as if there were a fundamental danger to the British Isles or the Commonwealth. That is a terrible slight on Catholics.

To judge by the reaction from his fellow Catholic bishops, Winning languished in a minority of one. Far from an eruption of complaint and comment about the Prince's statement, the bishops of Scotland, England and Wales were united in silence. When Cardinal Gray did contact Winning, it was not with praise for his position, but to question his judgement in speaking out. The only message of support was a telegram from a Labour MP Winning had never met. On the following Monday, the issue had moved from Prince Charles's comments to Winning's, with the Revd John Gray, a former Moderator of the Church of Scotland, describing them as 'astonishing, mean and unbecoming behaviour for a leading churchman',[3] while in England the Bishop of Worcester, the Rt Revd Robert Woods, formerly chaplain to the Queen, said: 'I think it is a pity that the Archbishop of Glasgow introduced this element into what is such a difficult issue of matrimonial doctrine and law.'[4]

The controversy inspired a leader in *The Times*, headlined 'The Prince and The Pope' in which the paper went out of its way to explain that the Pope could not be criticized for upholding the tenets of his faith, but that the Prince's reaction was perhaps understandable. Winning was not mentioned by name, but the paper agreed that the Act of Settlement was an absurd anachronism.

The final few days of the controversy coincided with the arrival at The Oaks of houseguests from America, and so Winning was able to escape with them into the Highlands and nurse his feelings of abandonment by his brother bishops. 'Nobody said anything. Not a flaming word. I felt let down. In those days there was a great fear of putting your head above the parapet. I appreciate that it was in the middle of summer and some of them were away, but for none of them to say anything was pretty awful.' The experience cultivated in Winning a compassion for those whose conscience drove them to speak out against a powerful opposition. A few years later when Cardinal O'Fiaich, the Archbishop of Armagh, criticized the policy of internment in Northern Ireland and was lambasted by the Home Office, Winning wrote O'Fiaich a letter of support, a gesture the Cardinal never forgot.

Rennie McOwan, whom Winning presented with a desk knife and scissors set as a thank-you for his support, believed the Archbishop emerged a 'hero' with a reputation for 'plain-speaking'. Certainly, once the dust had settled, his fellow bishops emerged from the shadows and congratulated him on having the courage of his convictions. The Apostolic Delegate phoned Winning to express the Vatican's satisfaction at his performance and a few months later he bumped into Mgr Justin Rigali, rector of the Pontifical Ecclesiastical Academy, the training centre for Vatican diplomats, who assured him Paul VI had been delighted by his defence. The Royal Family held little interest for Winning. In the years to come, Cardinal Basil Hume evolved into a member of the Establishment – so much so that upon his death the Queen described him as 'My Cardinal'.

Winning, distanced by hundreds of miles, by his class and by his attitude, wished only for the repeal of the Act of Settlement. By the time of his death there was universal support for constitutional change but little political will. Following the 'Prince Charles affair', Winning was tagged as a Republican and at the next Press Fund Lunch a rumour swept the hall that he had refused to stand for the loyal toast. McOwan fielded a number of calls after the lunch from journalists enquiring about the distance from the Archbishop's derrière to the seat. Five years later, following the birth of Prince and Princess Michael of Kent's children, Winning suggested to the Papal Nuncio that their marriage had become eligible for convalidation and official recognition by the Catholic Church. The ceremony took place in 1983 and was led by Cardinal Hume at Archbishop's House in Victoria, next to Westminster Cathedral.

The Mediterranean sun was Winning's antidote to the stress of the previous few months. Accompanied by his nephew Edward, now twenty-one and a graduate of Stirling University, he retreated in August to a hilltop convent in Malta, run by the Blue Nuns, the same order of sisters who had nursed him back to health after the removal of his stomach ulcer in Rome. The first few days were idyllic; while Edward swam, his uncle wandered the local villages each morning, sat in the shade during noon and retired in the afternoon to the solitude of his room to say his Office. Winning invested tremendous faith in the power of the Divine Office to sustain his spirit. While other priests on holiday might take an illicit break from the practice, Winning would take more time over the prayers, a luxury denied him during the work-crammed hours in the remainder of the year. A radio broadcast was to ruin the pair's rural retreat. On 6 August 1978, four days after their arrival, the BBC World Service announced the death of Pope Paul VI. The papacy had been a heavy cross for Paul VI – the controversy over *'Humanae Vitae'*, combined with the implementation of the Second Vatican Council, had drained him until barely a flicker of a smile remained. Winning decided to fly from Malta to Rome to attend the funeral, leaving Edward in the care of a Salesian priest.

The funeral was scheduled for Saturday 12 August but Winning arrived early to pay his respects, along with hundreds of thousands of mourners who gathered at St Peter's to file past the wedge-shaped casket, illuminated by a single candle and watched over by four Swiss Guards, one at each corner. At the Scots College, where Winning was staying, he met Gordon Gray. The Scots Cardinal was depressed and worried about the approaching conclave, where he and the world's cardinals would gather to elect a successor. He had arrived in Rome, minus his luggage, after what he described as his 'worse flight in decades' and felt burdened by the daily round of meetings he was expected to attend as a member of the Congregation of Cardinals who, under the guidance of the Camerlengo, Cardinal Jean Villot, maintained the running of the Vatican during the vacuum. More than a hundred thousand mourners gathered in St Peter's Square to watch the open-air funeral of Pope Paul VI, while a further hundred million watched on television. The Pope's request for a funeral 'pious and simple' was observed by the use of an unadorned pale yellow coffin made of cypress wood. An open book of the Gospels was placed on top. Winning was among the two thousand prelates and delegates in the giant apse on the steps of the basilica and he listened as the seventy-strong choir of the Sistine Chapel sang *'Requiem Aeternam'*. The funeral closed with the coffin being carried towards the huge doors of St Peter's, where a spontaneous burst of applause broke out. Winning commented that Paul VI was carried to the crypt under an ovation the likes of which he had never heard during his lifetime. After the funeral, Winning joined Cardinal Gray and Bishop Thomson of Motherwell for dinner at the home of the British Ambassador to the Holy See. They were joined at the elegant town house that served as the ambassador's official residence by the Duke of Norfolk, Mervyn Rees of the Home Office, Lord Ramsay, former Archbishop of Canterbury, Cardinal Basil Hume, and the Archbishops of Birmingham and Liverpool. The dinner drifted on until after midnight, before Gray and Winning departed for the Scots College, one to prepare for the rigours of the conclave and the other to return to Malta to collect his nephew.

Winning spent the thirty-three-day pontificate of Pope John Paul I fighting a losing battle to save a sewing machine factory. The Singer factory in Clydebank was more than an ordinary manufacturing plant. It was a brand name as universal in its day as Nike was to become, but unfortunately the day of the Singer sewing machine had passed. At its height, the factory employed a labour force of over 16,000, but by 1978, this figure had dropped to 4,800 and management were anxious to make further cuts, reducing staff levels to 2,800. Just as the threatened closure of the Upper Clyde shipyard in 1971 had led to the Right to Work campaign and the sit-in organized by Jimmy Reid, so the fate of Singers galvanized both the workforce and the local community. Church leaders, including Fr James McShane, who had studied with Winning in Rome, united to protest the plans and Winning cancelled a visit to Rome to attend the investiture of the new Pope, sending his auxiliary bishops Joseph Devine and Charles Renfrew in his place. Instead, the Archbishop attended a day of prayer at his old parish of Our Holy Redeemer. There he told a packed hall:

We are here today to pray as a community, to ask God's help, because we feel threatened. Not by men but by an economic system. We are not here in a spirit of confrontation or hate, but because we cherish the dignity and the total vocation of the human person, whatever condition in life he has.

In spite of private meetings between Winning and the shop stewards and a letter of appeal signed by the local clergy to Mr J.B. Flavin, the company's chief executive in America, the campaign was unsuccessful. The redundancies began around the date of the death of Pope John Paul I. As Cardinal Hume said at the time: 'What is the Holy Spirit trying to tell us?' For over a decade, the pontiff's sudden death would fuel rumours of assassination and nefarious activities in the Vatican. The rumours were silenced only by the publication of *A Thief in The Night* by John Cornwell with its portrayal of the Pope as an ill man, improperly treated by his curial staff, who was killed, in effect, by the stress and strain of his position. Winning, like the rest of the world, was unaware of this when he awoke at 7 a.m. on the morning of 29 September 1978 and turned on the radio:

> I'd recently taken to lying in bed for half an hour, listening to the radio. I heard the news that the Pope had died and I thought it was a review of the month and then it dawned on me. It was real. The thing about John Paul I was that he gave everybody a boost as he came on the television, smiling. We had not had a smiling Pope for a few years because Paul had kind of lost it. He was depressed. With John Paul I, we felt 'here we are in a new era'. He made the way for John Paul II.

On 10 November 1978, an announcement was made that Winning had been appointed a member of the Sacred Congregation for the Doctrine of the Faith (CDF), the successors to the Holy Inquisition and the guardians of Catholic teaching and dogma. What appeared on the surface to be a swift reward for shielding the Pope against the arrows of princely criticism was a coincidence. Winning had been appointed to the CDF by Paul VI over a year before, but had yet to attend a meeting. On the death of a pope all positions are rescinded and the reappointment is made by the new Pope. On the eve of his attendance at his first meeting in Rome in November 1978, the news was made public. Why Winning? Why now? The CDF was initially founded in 1542 by Pope Paul II as the

Sacred Congregation of the Universal Inquisition with the role of rooting out heretics with the use of smouldering pokers and then rewarding them with immolation. This, their victims were assured, was only a taste of what lay beyond should they fail to kiss the cross and repent before their demise. As times change, so do titles and tasks and in the nineteenth century, the Inquisition was replaced with the Holy Office, custodians of the Index of Forbidden Books, a list of titles such as *Lady Chatterley's Lover* deemed unsuitable for consumption by Catholics. University students were encouraged to seek permission from their parish priests if their literature course dictated they read titles on the list. Among the books damned by the Church was Graham Greene's *The Power and The Glory*, his powerful tale of the whisky priest martyred during Mexico's anti-clerical crusade. When the author pointed this out to Paul VI after he had praised the novel as a personal favourite, the Pope replied that while he may offend some Catholics, they should pay no attention. Paul VI was to abolish the Holy Office and the Index as impractical in an age when more books poured from automated presses, the majority of a prurient nature, than any Church censor could read. He wished the new body to extinguish the memory of the Inquisition and instead the CDF was to be a gentle guide, shepherding theologians and academics away from thorny issues and encouraging them to adopt a more positive pursuit. Where the Holy Office was censorious and condemnatory, the CDF would be inspiring and international in outlook.

The internationalization of the Curia was a principal concern during Vatican II, when delegates argued that the departments were clogged by Roman clerical civil servants. When asked why he had been chosen, Winning replied that it was the work of a blindfolded altar boy armed with a list of names and a pin. He was more than likely chosen for two reasons: first, as a representative of a small country he would demonstrate the Curia's new international outlook, and second, his loyalty and orthodoxy were without question and thus he would be sympathetic to the work of the congregation. An example of Winning's orthodoxy was his recent

attack on 'renegades' who wished to wind the clock back fifteen
years.

In May 1978, a new Catholic church opened its doors in Glasgow
in direct defiance of Winning as Archbishop and of the Pope. The
Catholic Church of the Holy Ghost inhabited an old Church of
Scotland property on John Street, in the heart of the city centre,
and offered disgruntled worshippers upset at the vernacular Mass
a return to the Tridentine rite. The rogue church was the latest
outpost in the continuing campaign by Archbishop Marcel Lefebvre
against what he believed were the diabolical changes instructed by
the Second Vatican Council. Lefebvre was a former Vatican diplomat, the Apostolic Delegate for French-speaking Africa, who had
attended the early Council meetings, but had refused to recognize
the Council's decisions. In 1970, he opened a traditionalist seminary
in Switzerland and in defiance of Rome began to ordain priests
loyal to his ideas. Six years later, after all attempts at reconciliation
had failed, Lefebvre's priestly and episcopal powers were suspended.
Pockets of resistance to Vatican II had popped up in countries such
as France, Holland and Switzerland. Scottish Catholics had prided
themselves on their loyalty to the Pope, yet still there existed a
substantial number of traditionalists reluctant to move with the
times. Although the Tridentine Mass was never banned, priests were
uncomfortable permitting it, in case they were labelled troublemakers. In an early 'Let's Talk' column, Winning held out a sop
to the traditionalists suggesting that in future 'a sung Mass in Latin
will be a regular feature of parish life in this archdiocese'. He
permitted one Tridentine Mass per month in a small church in the
Gorbals. He dispensed with his earlier suggestion on the grounds
that to permit a two-tier structure of worship would be impractical
and potentially divisive.

Winning would not stand for confrontation and defiance. As
soon as the opening of the Catholic Church of the Holy Ghost was
brought to his attention, he sought to close it down and starve the
pews of parishioners. As Fr Thomas Fouhy, a seventy-year-old priest

from Wellington in New Zealand, had neither asked nor received permission from Winning to operate in his diocese as was required under canon law, Winning chose to exercise his authority. He composed a pastoral letter to be read out at all parishes in which he condemned those involved as 'misguided' and insisted they were striking at 'the unity of the body of Christ which is the Church'. Parishioners drawn to the new parish were warned that they were 'gravely misguided', bore a 'heavy responsibility', and what they were doing was 'wrong'. Two hundred people attended the church's inaugural service where Fr Fouhy dismissed Winning's condemnation as a 'con trick' that displayed 'satanic influences'.[5]

The dilemma facing the Church of the Holy Ghost was securing a regular priest. No Scots priest, however sympathetic to the old ways, would risk his collar or Winning's fury and so the congregation was forced to utilize any renegade available. At one point, Glasgow's arch conservatives were ministered to by a priest who, unknown to them, had been dispensed with by the Church and had married a member of his congregation. A married priest saying Mass would be an answered prayer to many liberals, but embarrassing and detrimental to those who considered themselves the last outpost of the one true Church. Winning called the priest to his office and threatened to unveil his background unless he left the city immediately, which, reluctantly, he did. The Church of the Holy Ghost struggled on for a few more months before attendance dwindled to nothing. Winning described the Tridentine movement within the city as a 'blip' over which he lost no sleep. He explained: 'The Church was not going to progress or improve its spiritual life if people continued to look back.' The more people called for a return to the rhythms of the Tridentine rite, the more aggressive became Winning's hostility towards them.

Winning's initial visit to the CDF in November 1978 was characterized by confusion and disappointment. The Congregation consisted of eleven cardinals, seven bishops and twenty-eight consultors or officials, and any spirit of cooperation evaporated within a few minutes of his arrival. It quickly became apparent to Winning that international members such as himself, Cardinal Baum from America and others were principally decorative – figureheads lending the Congregation an international image while allowing it to remain distinctly Roman. The visitors had almost no opportunity to influence policy or promote new ideas; instead they were rubber stamps pressed into service. The reason for this was that cardinals and archbishops, whose principal role was working for the Congregation, carried out the bulk of the CDF's work in weekly meetings. The plenary sessions, as the annual or even bi-annual gatherings of the full membership were called, were little more than talking shops where the report at the beginning of the meeting was identical to that presented at its conclusion.

There were other problems. Winning and his fellow visitors had been given a résumé of the CDF's work for the past two years only a few weeks prior to the meeting. With little opportunity to review the document, verify its accuracy and prepare subsequent ideas, there seemed little point in their appearance. A second problem centred around language difficulties. All discussion took place in Italian and while Winning spoke the language fluently, others did not. During his first visit he spent most of his time providing a translation service for Cardinal Baum. Winning left the first session disheartened, but an opportunity to speak his mind arose two years later following the CDF's treatment of Hans Küng.

Küng was the Swiss Catholic theologian on whom the CDF had a burgeoning file. A trusted peritus chosen by Pope John XXIII and an architect of Vatican II, Küng was to become the subject of a CDF investigation as early as 1967 when the Congregation withheld approval of the translation of his book *The Church*. Three years later, Küng published *Infallible? An Inquiry*, in which he challenged the declaration of papal infallibility in 1870 at Vatican I. He argued there was a lack of historical evidence to support the idea, there was no basis in the writings of St Paul, and the very concept had rendered terrible damage to ecumenism.

Infallible? led to a further investigation and a series of critical essays by figures such as Karl Rahner and Joseph Ratzinger. *On*

Being a Christian, Küng's book published in 1977, was also criticized, and in September 1979, he wrote a highly critical essay on the first year of the pontificate of Pope John Paul II. Despite the many years of whispered rumours that he was under investigation, coupled with warnings from the Bishops' Conference of Germany, the first hint that disciplinary action would be taken against him came in an interview with Joseph Ratzinger, Archbishop of Munich, in October 1979. Two months later, on 18 December 1979, the German bishops held a press conference to announce that the Congregation for the Doctrine of the Faith had made a decision concerning Hans Küng. The *missio canonica*, a licence every Catholic theologian required to teach at an institution recognized by the Vatican, was to be stripped from Küng. The decision was confirmed a few weeks later during a private meeting with the German bishops and the Pope and a letter was then sent to Küng revoking his *missio canonica* just before the new year.

Winning next attended a meeting of the CDF in 1980 and during the tour de table he was able to exert a degree of pressure that would in turn lead to change. He criticized the CDF for their timing in announcing the withdrawal of Küng's teaching licence just one week prior to Christmas. It should be noted that Winning did not disagree with the act, merely its timing. Winning had little interest in Küng, as he had most contemporary theologians – there was part of him that resented their intellect and sided with Ratzinger's attitude that 'The Christian believer is a simple person: bishops should protect the faith against the power of intellectuals.'[6] However, as a lawyer familiar with the cut and thrust of debate, he was disturbed that the CDF was all attack and no defence. Pointing out that in the marriage tribunal, when one lawyer examines methods in which a marriage may be dissolved, another, the defender of the bond, will argue for its maintenance and it is only through the tension between the pair that the truth is revealed. At the CDF, there was no one to defend Küng or his fellow theologians against attack, no sympathetic ear to argue their case. Cardinal Franjo Seper, the head of the CDF, was startled by Winning's complaint and turned to Pericle Felici, the Congregation's canon lawyer, for his opinion. Felici explained that under previous rules an advocate was available but that Seper had altered the process and dispensed with the advocate. Winning believed that it was as a result of his suggestion, that when Leonardo Boff, the Brazilian Franciscan who was a pioneer of Liberation Theology, was later called before the CDF, he was offered an advocate to help prepare his case.

In 1980, the bishops of the world were given their first opportunity to comment on *'Humanae Vitae'* when Pope John Paul II called a synod to discuss 'the role of the Christian family in the modern world'. Synods were created by Paul VI in 1967 in an attempt to foster greater collegiality – democratic discussion – within the Church, but the previous five had already begun to calcify their public image as echo chambers where the most interesting ideas failed to reach the outside world. During the synod, which took place in Rome over two weeks in September, Winning was to display the credentials that had earned his appointment to the most conservative department in the Vatican by his personal reaction to Basil Hume's famous 'I have a dream' speech made at the synod. In subsequent years, the short speech by the Cardinal Archbishop of Westminster became celebrated by his supporters for its gentle criticism, lyrical nature and, most crucially, its call for greater compassion towards those alienated by the Church's teaching on contraception. The comparison with Martin Luther King derives from the structure in which Hume talked of falling asleep and dreaming of two types of Catholic Church, the old pre-Vatican II fortress and its successor, the Church as a pilgrim walking through life. The problem, he related in a subtle reference to *'Humanae Vitae'*, was that the signposts of the Church had faded and the wrong paint had been reapplied, confusing the poor pilgrim so 'the last state was worse than the first'.[7] Although the Pope took copious notes throughout the speech, as he did during all the bishops' contributions, Hume's plea that 'I hope and I pray that as a result of this synod, I shall be better able to give guidance to those married people who are looking to the Church for help' was unsuccessful as the Apostolic Exhortation, or teaching document, issued by the Pope in the synod's aftermath reiterated the contradictory nature of contraception when used in an act where 'one gives oneself totally to the other'. Winning disliked Hume's speech, which he believed 'played to the gallery' and was an attempt to 'please the liberals at home'. Prior to the synod, a National Pastoral Conference had taken place in Liverpool, attended by over two thousand delegates from across England and Wales who had made their concerns about contraception felt.

> It was not enough for somebody to come from their background and say how about doing away with the disapproval of contraception. That is what they were doing and I had a funny feeling that they were playing to the gallery. If you want to get something done, that is not how you do it . . . I felt there was no great theological depth underpinning that kind of attitude. It is possible that they came to Rome with some kind of vague mandate from the clergy or national conference and it would please the liberals at home.

Winning's own contribution to the synod was restricted to small group discussions and arguing with Derek Worlock, the Archbishop of Liverpool, over his suggestion that bishops should be permitted to decide if marriages were valid or invalid, a concept Winning rejected on the grounds that this was the type of decision canon lawyers struggled with and that if left to bishops, wild inconsistencies would appear. The idea was rejected by the group, as Winning remembered with evident delight: 'Eighteen to two. It was worse than a Rangers match.' Winning later described the synod as being divided between those who put compassion first and those who believed the laws of the Church had superiority. He fell into the latter category, but felt compassionate towards the compassionate.

Upon Winning's return from the synod, he discovered that Rennie McOwan had resigned his post. In a statement to the *Scottish Catholic Observer*, the communications officer explained: 'It has not been possible to reach a mutually acceptable professional and personal working formula.' McOwan had grown weary of what he viewed as obstructionism by other senior priests on Winning's staff who resented the presence of an opinionated layman. Documents would become unavailable, and meetings relevant to the media would take place without his knowledge or attendance. The final straw was when he received a memo from Bishop Charles Renfrew insisting his access to Winning be restricted to a single weekly meeting at 3 p.m. on a Friday afternoon. McOwan felt irritated that while he was among the first to be called when a priest had got a girl pregnant or had developed an alcohol problem, his dream of collaborating with the Archbishop on evangelizing the public had come to nothing:

> I had never worked with him on a day-to-day process, and I was taken aback at how shambolic the administration was. Files would build up on his desk unread, at times two people would be working on the same project, unbeknown to each other. There was also a degree of tension between Winning and his clergy. He was seen as interfering to a much greater degree in the running of the parishes.

McOwan also believed that Winning's temper, ignited by those who challenged or criticized the Church, clouded his judgement. On two occasions, McOwan said he acted in an irresponsible and ungodly manner. The first was Winning's reaction to a story in the *News of the World* that involved a priest from the diocese of Middlesbrough who had indulged in a number of affairs, both with nuns and parishioners, one of whom had borne a son. The priest had left the Church and given a salacious interview with the paper. The Monday following the article's appearance, Winning arrived in McOwan's office, brandishing the paper and shouting: 'How did this guy get through seminary?' Before McOwan was able to reply, Winning instructed him to travel to Middlesbrough, track the priest down and gather enough information to 'destroy him'. McOwan realized the task was a logistical nightmare. How long would it take to find the former priest? What material was he looking for?

Where exactly would the material be published? Was *Flourish*, an archdiocesan newspaper, the appropriate vehicle for the character assassination of an unknown priest from a distant diocese? The furthest he got was a call to the diocese of Middlesbrough, where he explained with some trepidation the Archbishop of Glasgow's interest in the case. 'In a very polite and, in my view, correct manner, they asked what business was it of his?' Reverting to his journalistic background, McOwan chose to 'kick it up a close', ignore it until Winning had calmed down and forgotten about it, which he eventually did. The second incident was more disturbing. McOwan said he was shown a damaging file on a Catholic individual who was criticizing the Church. In what McOwan describes as 'a simple character assassination', Winning invited him into his office and produced a file detailing a number of personal problems the man had suffered, including what McOwan described as 'a marital problem, a sexual problem'. He described the Archbishop's motivation in revealing the material as an attempt to undermine the man's credibility, saying in effect, 'Don't pay too much attention to this guy, he is clearly an untrustworthy character.' The incident stunned McOwan:

> I was shocked for two reasons. First, I felt it came very near to confessional issues. I imagine he found it [his information] via the marriage tribunal. This was shown to me. I thought it highly improper, because from that day to this, if ever I see this guy my mind sets back. I should never have been shown that. I'm only saying this because his zeal clouded his judgement.

Winning had been aware of McOwan's unhappiness. The previous year he had arranged to loan him to the Irish bishops' conference to assist in the preparation for the Pope's visit to the country in 1979, in the hope that a change of scene would improve his attitude. Unfortunately, McOwan's attitude was determined by his working environment and as this declined so did his spirits. Winning said there was 'no great bust-up', which was correct, and that 'Rennie just decided to leave', which fudged the issue. Either way, McOwan chose to resign just at the point when his skills would have been most valuable. After his triumphant visit to Ireland, the new Pope was coming to Britain. Peter was about to embrace Andrew.

TWELVE

When Peter Met Andrew

'Let Scotland flourish by the teaching of the word.'[1]

POPE JOHN PAUL II

'The Holy Spirit was there. That joy and happiness that invades a crowd is the presence of God.'

THOMAS WINNING

Standing on the back of a Leyland truck on a scorching afternoon in June, Thomas Winning looked out at a sight that had almost slipped away. Where once there had been acres of green grass there now stood people, hundreds of thousands of people. Bellahouston Park, on the south side of Glasgow, had been transformed into a church packed with three hundred thousand parishioners all crying out for their priest. And there, standing behind the bulletproof glass of the specially converted truck, the 'Popemobile', Pope John Paul II returned their waves, clasped his hands in a display of unity, and smiled at the chants of: 'John Paul Two. We love you.'

The Pope's visit to Scotland, as a part of his British tour in the summer of 1982, was a triumph of hope over adversity that belonged in no small way to the indefatigable zeal of Thomas Winning, working in close collaboration with Derek Worlock, the Archbishop of Liverpool. While the Archbishop of Glasgow may not have extended the invitation himself, and resented its handling (the visit to Scotland was an afterthought, hurriedly tacked on after Basil

Hume forgot to brief the Scottish bishops of his plans), it was he who fought to ensure that the invitation was honoured when others were prepared to let their guest cancel. It was Winning who believed the outbreak of war between Britain and Argentina over the Falkland Islands was not enough to prevent a visit by the representative of the Prince of Peace.

For eighteen months, from the announcement of the papal visit in August 1980 to 2 April 1982 when Argentine forces landed on the distant islands, the only threat to the Scottish visit was disruption by a rump of Protestantism who viewed the Pope's arrival as the beachhead of a Catholic revival.

Religious tensions in Glagow had been exacerbated in 1981 by Republican marches in sympathy with the H-block protests in Northern Ireland led by Bobby Sands. These were then followed by counter-demonstrations organized by the Scottish Loyalists, a breakaway group from the Grand Orange Lodge of Scotland, who had formed an alliance with the Ulster Volunteer Force. A coalition of Protestant groups planned direct action against the visit. Ian Paisley, as chairman of the British Council of Protestant Christian Churches, under the invitation of Revd David Cassells, a relative by marriage and the group's Scottish representative, announced that he would tour Scotland for the duration of the Pope's stay.

Cassells was the minister of the Jock Troup Memorial Church in Glasgow and himself chairman of the Scottish Constitutional Defence Committee, a militant loyalist organization. The final leg of the tripod was Pastor Jack Glass, minister of the Sovereign Grace Baptist Church who stood as the candidate for the Crusade Against the Papal Visit in the Glasgow Hillhead by-election on 25 March 1982 which returned Roy Jenkins for the SDP. Glass won 388 votes and lost his deposit. Together they planned to organize flying pickets at each papal event in Scotland as well as travel to Liverpool to exploit the religious divide that existed there. The largest protest was planned for Bellahouston Park where they wished to rally 1,500 men at the gates during the Pope's celebration of Mass and threaten violence should they be stopped. 'I am very much for non-violent protest, but loyalists are not going to be happy if the police position them five or six miles away from the Pope,'[2] said Revd Cassells. Pastor Glass was more forthcoming: 'I am sure there will be violence. The streets are not a church and I have no right to dictate who shall come out on them.'[3] Protests against the visit emerged from unlikely quarters. William Wolf, President of the Scottish National Party, insisted the Pope was unwelcome on the grounds that Scotland remained a Protestant country, a statement for which he was later forced to resign. Meanwhile, the Church of Scotland, whose Moderator had agreed to meet the Pope, appealed for tolerance. The Kirk's inter-Church relations committee advised followers to uphold their tradition of hospitality to such a distinguished guest and for those unable to hold out their hand in friendship then silence was an adequate protest: 'What must be urged, if not a welcome or a dialogue, is rejection of all aggravation. Silence on such an occasion is not surrender. It is the quiet assertion of our tradition of generosity and tolerance towards the stranger.'[4] The view of the Free Church of Scotland was less favourable. A fifteen-strong committee dismissed the visit as a 'propaganda exercise' designed to ignite a revival of Catholicism in Scotland.

The invasion of the Falkland Islands was to throw the papal visit to Britain into serious jeopardy. Under the leadership of Margaret Thatcher, the British government had no interest in a negotiated settlement and prepared to take back the islands by force. Two days after the invasion, the Pope, in his Easter Sunday address, appealed for a peaceful settlement between what he carefully described as 'two countries of Christian tradition', yet six days later, the British task force set sail. The careful word play was not enough to disguise the obvious dilemma facing the Pope, for Argentina was a traditional Catholic country and Britain was not; the fact that the Argentines were the aggressors served only to complicate an already delicate diplomatic situation. While preparations continued with Archbishop Paul Marcinkus, head of the Pope's security, arriving in Britain on 12 April to iron out details with Cardinals Gray and Hume, a consensus began to build that a visit would be impossible in the event of war breaking out. The great distance the task force was required to travel, some eight thousand miles, meant an armed invasion would coincide directly with the Pope's arrival.

Both continuation and cancellation posed problems. To continue regardless while a nation was immersed in a war, albeit a distant one, could be considered tactless, and an unnecessary distraction at a time of national mourning. Yet to cancel a visit to a country legitimately defending itself against attack could be viewed as condemnatory and sympathetic to an aggressive Catholic country. For the first few weeks of the crisis, a policy of wait-and-see was adopted while the task force steamed south. It was Cardinal Hume who was the first to speculate that the visit was in jeopardy. During a press conference to announce details of the papal Mass at Westminster Cathedral, he admitted that in his opinion the Pope would be unable to attend if war broke out between Argentina and Britain, in spite of the fact that his visit was a pastoral one as opposed to a State visit. 'The Pope can't arrive at Heathrow and ride on the underground, there has to be a level of welcome that does not turn it into a State visit,' explained Hume.[5] The conflict was also to highlight the differences between the two British cardinals. While Hume adopted a hawkish stance supporting armed retaliation on the principle that it fitted the criteria of a just war, Gray condemned the British government for ignoring the option of a peaceful negotiation. After another visit to the Vatican in mid May, both were united in agreement that a visit was impossible without the complete cessation of hostilities. The sinking of the Argentine battleship *General Belgrano* on 2 May with the loss of 360 sailors had hardened the line of the Vatican's Secretariat of State, and with a negotiated settlement unlikely the visit would not go ahead. As Hume explained on 15 May: 'The sinking of the *Belgrano* has done a tremendous amount of harm. I am not justifying whether it was right or wrong. I think it was a turning point in world opinion which has made a lot of people in the diplomatic world say: "You can't go to England if that is the way things are."'[6]

*   *   *

If Gray and Hume were prepared to accept that the visit was sunk, the sentiment was not shared by either Winning or Worlock. The Archbishop of Liverpool considered himself a Vatican player and although he had worked closely with Hume throughout his career, he had never quite recovered from Rome's decision to choose the Benedictine monk for the diocese of Westminster over the man he considered the superior candidate: himself. Worlock revealed in a journal kept during this time and published in *The Worlock Archive* by Clifford Longley that he considered Hume's behaviour during the crisis as too 'hawkish'. He criticized an article Hume had written for *The Times* about the prospective visit of the Pope as having: 'for ever branded GBH (George Basil Hume) as a warmonger in the eyes of the Latin Americans'.

As Hume and Gray began the difficult task of deflating expectations and preparing for the imminent abandonment of the plans, Worlock decided to make one last attempt to persuade the Pope to push ahead. In Scotland, Winning too was rebelling against the defeatist attitude of his cardinal and had begun to marshal his troops independent of Gray. He had been informed of the trip's forthcoming cancellation by the cardinal while he was in Guernsey, attending a meeting with the insurance company used by the Catholic Church in Scotland, and had returned to Glasgow on Friday 15 May in a mood he described as 'flaming mad'.

His immediate task was to rally the laity, and so he spent the morning on the phone to every Catholic lay organization in Scotland to ask them to send a telegram to the Pope asking him to accept their invitation to visit. His second tactic was to contact the other Scottish bishops and suggest that they too send a communal telegram urging the Holy Father to visit his children.

Winning deliberately kept the telegram from Gray until each of the six bishops had agreed, at which point he presented him with a fait accompli, to the cardinal's considerable irritation. Gray asked why Winning wished to send a telegram as the Pope was patently aware of the bishops' desire that he visit Scotland, but the younger man argued that while Gray had spoken to the Pope, the others had not. 'You were out there. We weren't,' said Winning. 'We've got to try and reinforce what you were saying.' The cardinal then relented, but before permitting the telegram to be despatched, he insisted that Winning make clear in the text that the final decision remained with the Pope. Winning believed this to be rather stating the obvious, but agreed, as it brought comfort to the cardinal who was already concerned that the Scots were bullying the Pope – a mildly ridiculous idea, but understandable in one so deferential.

The telegram was despatched and the following morning, as Winning waited, the telephone rang. It was Derek Worlock suggesting that he and Winning travel to Rome to 'salvage' the visit. Winning had mixed feelings about the Archbishop of Liverpool, whom he found brash and over-confident, exactly the adjectives others would use to describe himself, but as Worlock saw everything as a competition, divided strictly between winners and losers, he took on the appearance of an attractive ally. Worlock explained that he had already discussed the idea with Hume who approved. Winning wanted to know why Worlock had asked him. In many respects it made perfect sense; both Winning and Worlock could represent their respective nations, but without the baggage that comes with a cardinal's hat, allowing them more room to manoeuvre.

Winning agreed to the visit on condition that Gray did too. The cardinal gave his blessing and invited Winning to spend the night prior to departure at St Bennet's, his Edinburgh home, but as Winning had confirmations to attend to on the Sunday it was after midnight before he arrived and 3 a.m. before he went to bed. The next morning he awoke to the news that a 'go slow' strike by Italian air traffic control had started.

Winning arrived at Heathrow Airport early on the morning of Monday 17 May after flying from Turnhouse Airport in Edinburgh, and met Worlock at the check-in desk of Alitalia in Terminal 2, already surrounded by journalists and television crews, alerted to the fact that a rescue mission was now in motion. Worlock took the lead and explained their plans: 'To quote a phrase used in another area, we are still in business. A decision must be made by Wednesday, and it will be made by the Holy See. We have an open-ended ticket and are not sure when we will be back.'[7] Under the present circumstances they were not even sure when they would be able to depart. The strike was scheduled to last all day, ruining the pair's plans for a working lunch with the Pope and Secretariat of State. Instead of pasta in the papal apartments they snacked on complimentary sandwiches and coffee in the airport's VIP lounge until they themselves were rescued by a stroke of good fortune. An Italian air force plane had arrived from America to refuel before heading on to Rome, and the embassy had granted permission for it to carry the two archbishops. Just after 5 p.m., Winning and Worlock took their seats among the empty rows of the deserted jet.

Winning had bought a spiral-bound reporter's notebook decorated with tulips and as the plane took off for the two and a half hour flight, he began to formulate his arguments for the continuation of the Pope's visit. He began by listing the initial reactions of the nation's Catholics to his abandonment of the visit, such as disbelief and disappointment, and wrote that to cancel would have a 'worse effect on public opinion of Church and Papacy, than the decision to come would have'. This was followed up by an extensive list that detailed the effects of cancellation, including the financial cost of £1 million. Although true, this was effectively the responsibility of the Catholic Church in Scotland who had failed to arrange the appropriate insurance policy. A principal part of Winning's argument, however, was concerned with how the Protestants would view the Church. The opportunity to meet with leaders of the Church of Scotland on their own ground would not return for at least a generation, and the subsequent loss of ecumenical momentum by cancellation would tar the Catholic Church in their eyes as partisan to the Argentinians. He also argued that this would resurrect the Protestant 'belief that the pennies of the poor' are 'abused by the Church', and confirm their belief that 'Rome decides everything and we must all obey like children'. In number nine of sixteen arguments Winning wrote:

Catholics in our country have suffered a great deal over the past years from those hostile to the Pope and Catholicism. They have borne these taunts and hurts with dignity and have not returned in kind. Now all their hopes are being dashed. Their courage in the face of this kind of persecution has gone for nothing, humanly speaking.

It was after nine o'clock in the evening when the military plane touched down at Ciampino, the smaller of Rome's two airports, about twenty miles from the centre. Bishop Agnellus Andrew, who handled communication matters for the Holy See, and Kate Adie, the BBC correspondent, were there to meet the party off the plane. While Bishop Andrew explained that the lunch had been rescheduled for the following day, Kate Adie was anxious to secure an interview but there was little to add to what had already been said at Heathrow. Instead of making the trek out to the Via Cassia and the Scots College, Winning agreed to accept the hospitality of the English College, which was in the city centre, a short taxi ride to the Vatican. As Winning and Worlock rested after an exhausting day, the man they initially considered their central opponent was at that moment flying over the Atlantic on a red-eye flight from JFK to Rome.

Alfonso Lopez Trujillo was the Archbishop of Medellin in Colombia and president of CELAM (*Consejo Episcopal Latinoamericano*), the South American Bishops' Conference. The Archbishop was one of the most powerful men in the South American Church. A dark, brooding character with an appearance more comparable to a Mafia don than a servant of Christ, Lopez Trujillo was a fierce opponent of Liberation Theology. Shortly after the election of Pope John Paul II, he wrote to Archbishop Luciano Cabral Duarte, a Brazilian critic of the theological movement, about the upcoming battle over the ideology. 'Prepare your bomber planes. You must start training the way boxers do before going into the ring for a world championship. May your blows be evangelical and sure.'[8]

Trujillo was a hard man who did not take lightly to phone calls in the early hours of the morning. The previous day he had been woken at 5 a.m. by a call instructing him to return to Rome 'as soon as possible'. The reason for his immediate return was not given; he was told only that should he require further verification he should contact a number at the Secretariat of State, where he found that the message was the same: return 'as soon as possible'.

When Trujillo broke the news the following morning to the Primate of Colombia, he was furious and insisted that such a return was impossible under such secret circumstances. Trujillo later discovered that the reason he was left in the dark was the fear among members of the Secretariat of State that should the South American bishops become aware of his mission they might attempt to prevent his return. In the end the Archbishop knew he had no choice but to fly from Buffalo to New York and from there to Rome, where he arrived unshaven and irritable on the morning of Tuesday 18 May. At the airport, he was met by a private secretary and told to leave his luggage on the carousel to be collected later and to go immediately to the Vatican. 'I had no time to shave, tidy up or even change my clothes,' remembered Trujillo. 'I had to go again "as soon as possible".'

Winning and Worlock spent the morning prior to their rearranged lunch in discussions with Archbishop Achille Silvestrini, Secretary of the Council for the Public Affairs of the Church, in reality, a 'foreign minister' for the Secretariat of State. Silvestrini's advice was to promote the idea of reconciliation between the bishops of Great Britain and Argentina. He emphasized the hostility among many South Americans to the visit and the difficulties that lay ahead. Winning then met Tom Connelly, the press spokesman for the Scottish Catholic Church, and collected the latest issue of *Flourish*, which trumpeted the visit, and which he planned to use as an extra emotional charge. However, he was also informed of the leader that appeared in that morning's edition of the *Glasgow Herald* in which the paper called for a cancellation. 'The historic papal visit to this country looks like being a casualty of the Falklands dispute. It is hard to see the mission of Archbishop Winning and his colleague changing the minds of the Pope's advisers . . . Prudence may compel cancellation before the exhaustion is certain; and prudence should prevail.'

The lunch took place in the dining room of the Pope's private apartments on the third floor of the building overlooking St Peter's Square and coincided with the Pope's sixty-second birthday. Among the guests round the table were Trujillo, Cardinal Agostino Casaroli, the Secretary of State, and Marinez Somalo, the Under-secretary of State. Winning knew Trujillo vaguely from meetings they had both attended as members of the Congregation for the Doctrine of the Faith, and Somalo was a former classmate at the Gregorian University, but circumstances left little opportunity to catch up. Before the first dish was served the Pope asked in which language the discussions should be conducted. Italian was deemed the most common and Winning agreed to translate for Worlock who was unable to speak fluently. A second problem for Worlock was the meal itself; as a coeliac he was unable to consume bread or pasta and had brought his own lunch in a couple of Tupperware boxes, a necessity that only served to exaggerate the 'us' versus 'them' nature of the discussions. Winning, meanwhile, decided to pick sparingly and pass on the birthday cake lest he find himself with his mouth full when an important point required expression.

Archbishop Trujillo opened the discussions by stating that, as president of CELAM, he felt a papal visit to Britain in the current circumstances would cause considerable offence to Argentinian Catholics. He accepted that the situation was the result of aggression by Argentina but that this was not reflected in the mood of the people who actively supported their government's actions. Winning began by counterarguing the greater offence to Britain, the victims of Argentinian aggression, and the terrible loss of face among British Catholics should the visit fail to take place. Weaving all the points composed at 32,000 ft into his argument, he pointed out the pedestal on which the Pope was placed, and the long drop should he cancel his visit. He then passed the Pope a telegram from Professor John McIntyre, the Moderator of the Church of Scotland, in which he explained how the pontiff was viewed as a prophetic figure among

Church of Scotland members but would not be afforded the honour in future if the visit was cancelled. The telegram had a sobering effect. Throughout the lunch, which lasted two and half hours, Winning became increasingly confident that the Pope would come to Britain, in spite of the conflict, if only the tensions between the Catholic Church in Britain and Argentina could be eased. While the Vatican officials present repeatedly referred to the islands as 'Las Malvinas', the Argentinian term, the Pope himself spoke of 'The Falklands', an indication of where his sympathies lay. It was Winning who suggested the possibility of an early visit to Argentina by the Pope as a means of bringing balance to the situation, an idea with which the Pope agreed, and one strongly supported by Trujillo. In Winning's notes of the meeting, which he composed that evening, he wrote: 'We have to try to explain to the Argentinian cardinals that it would be a great disaster for the Ch[urch] in Britain if this visit did not go ahead as planned. Therefore the purpose of this collegial initiative, argued the H.F. [Holy Father], is an attempt to create the kind of climate in which it could be possible for him to continue the visit without offending Arg[entina].'

Trujillo believed such a climate could be created but that it was necessary for the Argentine cardinals to come to Rome. Curiously, Casaroli argued that this would not be possible. There was so little time and any meeting would require giving them proper notice. As Trujillo had been dragged out of bed and flown across the Atlantic with scarcely an opportunity to change his clothes, the point attracted no sympathy. 'I was told "as soon as possible" and I'm here,' he said, reasoning that if he could do it, then so could they. The Pope concurred and instructed that both the British and Argentine cardinals were to travel to Rome 'as soon as possible.'

Following the negotiations, Worlock stated in his diary that it was he who had suggested a Mass of reconciliation between the cardinals of Britain and Argentina. However, Winning insisted it was Lopez Trujillo who raised the idea, a point confirmed in an interview with the Colombian. The idea of the Mass was to unite the two countries and to reiterate that the British visit was purely pastoral and in no way political. During the discussions it was agreed that Archbishop Worlock would ask the British government to take a step back and accept that a planned meeting with the Prime Minister would be inappropriate under the circumstances. The discussions then moved on to clarify which events would need to be cancelled. Among the 'limits' discussed was the death of Prince Andrew, serving in the battlefield as a naval helicopter pilot, and the eventual retaking of the Falkland Islands. The meeting was concluded on the note that the visit would go ahead, but further talks were required to convince the Argentinian people.

After lunch, Winning and Worlock returned to the English College to inform their respective cardinals on their successful mission and reiterate the need to travel to Rome. Winning's conversation with Cardinal Gray demonstrated the Scot's unquestioning loyalty to the Holy Father: 'Sure, Tom. You know I'd stand on my head if the Pope wanted me to.' Worlock, meanwhile, was forced to wrestle with an irritable Basil Hume, who was not only reluctant to return to Rome, but, according to Worlock, considered the conditions, such as the cancellation of a meeting with Mrs Thatcher, as entirely unacceptable. In his biography, *Cardinal Hume and the Changing Face of English Catholicism*, Peter Stanford wrote: 'That the Pope still came to Britain was a tribute to Cardinal Hume's delicate diplomacy and his international standing among his fellow churchmen ... It was Basil Hume who in the end persuaded the Pope to override the objections of the Latin American bishops. The nature of that achievement should not be underestimated.' In reality, however, it was Winning and Worlock who were principally responsible for the visit's resurrection. According to Worlock, who, it must be said, made a habit of spinning situations to reflect himself in the best possible light, Hume's response to their negotiations took him completely by surprise. He wrote:

I have to say that far from reflecting the enthusiastic hope I felt at a breakthrough, GBH expressed anger and horror. He had no wish to go to Rome, no wish to meet the Argies, and these conditions would give grave offence in Britain. I tried to explain that these were not conditions but points for consideration if the planning of the visit was to continue. He said his reaction was against what was being proposed but he would put the points to the bishops and someone would phone back.[9]

It was after 6 p.m. when George Leonard, Hume's secretary, called Worlock then passed the phone to Hume who was in a 'great fury', feeling cornered into accepting conditions which he feared the Foreign Office would view as 'near treason'. The Bishops' Conference, which had been called at Westminster House to await Worlock's report, had narrowly voted eleven to eight that Hume should return to Rome. Hume himself had abstained from this vote, but was still considering ignoring the vote as the Bishop of Arundel and Brighton, Cormac Murphy-O'Connor, had regretted his initial decision, as one of the eleven, and now sided with Hume, reducing the vote to ten to nine. If Hume had chosen to use his own vote, this would have then brought the decision to a deadlock. Worlock was left to return to the Vatican, to be told that both Gray and the two Argentinian cardinals were en route. 'I said merely that as a race we were always more cautious . . .' In the event, it took the silver tongue of the Vatican's Secretary of State, Cardinal Casaroli, and the reassurance of the British minister to the Holy See, Sir Mark Heath, to convince Hume to attend. Casaroli said: 'We are not asking him to come here to prove Britain's case, nor to negotiate a settlement. We ask his help in explaining to our Latin American brothers, why the visit must go ahead.'[7] Heath, meanwhile, insisted that Hume's fears were misplaced and that the government was only too glad to step aside if it would help facilitate the visit, for the Prime Minister was anxious to avoid the perception of papal condemnation of their retaliatory actions, which the cancellation would undoubtedly trigger. The following day, Winning and Worlock met again with Lopez Trujillo and Cardinal Casaroli and the Scottish archbishop suggested the following: 'God will act in and through this dialogue. The Church cannot allow the spectacle of her children being at war with one another. The Church has to set an example of dialogue leading to better human relationships and therefore to better understanding and peace and harmony.'

A second lunch with the Pope was organized for Friday 21 May. The table was crowded with the arrival of both Gray and Hume and the two Argentinian cardinals Raul Primatesta of Cordoba and Juan Carlos de Aramburu of Buenos Aires. As Hume and Gray waited in the ante room next to the papal apartment, Cardinal Aramburu, who had last met Gray during the Vatican Council, came up and embraced him exclaiming, *'Bene, bene, Gordon.'* It was a propitious start to what would become a positive meeting. During the working lunch the Pope led the discussions and pressed home the importance of the trip to Britain. At one point he attempted to reassure the Argentinian cardinals about a proposed meeting with the Queen by explaining it was in her capacity as the head of the Church of England. As he said this, he turned his head and winked at Archbishop Worlock. The Argentinian cardinals began to realize the weight of the argument was drifting away from them and wearily agreed to whatever the Pope wished, graciously accepting a papal visit to their own country nine days after the Pope was to depart Britain. That evening, Winning and Worlock were left with the unenviable task of drafting a joint statement with the Argentinians, in the knowledge that, seven thousand miles away, British troops had landed at San Carlos on East Falkland Island.

At seven o'clock the following morning, 22 May, the Pope presided over Mass in the nave altar in St Peter's Basilica. As a public symbol of reconciliation, the hierarchy of Britain and Argentina were joined by each country's seminarians, drawn from their Roman colleges. Outside the basilica before Mass began, Winning said he was approached by Cardinal Juan Carlos de Aramburu who asked the Archbishop of Glasgow: 'Are you Winning?' 'Right now,' replied Winning, 'I'm not entirely sure.' The humour was entirely lost on the cardinal and in reality Winning had already won. During the service he began to think of the violence and bloodshed taking place at the bottom of the world. 'The irrationality of the war came home to me as I looked around St Peter's at the young men from South America and Britain. It was just possible that their blood brothers were killing one another in the Falklands at that moment.'

The words of the Pope echoed around the basilica: 'Kill war with words of negotiation rather than kill men with the sword.'

The visit was still on; in fact, it had never officially been off, but there is little doubt that without the steady pressure of both Winning and Worlock the papal visit would have been cancelled, another victim of the Falklands war. On Winning's final afternoon in Rome, he was once again called to the Vatican to meet Cardinal Casaroli. In front of Gray and Winning, Worlock and Hume, Casaroli made a public gesture of washing his hands of the situation. Having persuaded the Pope to press on against the early advice of the Secretariat of State, it was now the duty of the British bishops to inform the Vatican if the political climate in Britain changed. If within the next few days, Prince Andrew was killed, the QE2 was sunk, or huge casualties were inflicted, then the responsibility for cancelling the visit remained with the British bishops. Winning returned the following day, 24 May, accompanied by Basil Hume, while Worlock stayed behind to tie up the loose ends. At Heathrow Airport, Winning announced: 'I would say to all the people who have worked so hard and prepared themselves for this trip to Scotland to look forward to it just as they have before. It is a very delicate situation, but as I speak tonight I would quote odds at sixty to forty in favour of the trip going ahead.'

On the morning of Friday 28 May 1982, Winning rose from his bed at St Bennet's in Edinburgh, where he had stayed the previous night, with an air of intense satisfaction. History was being made today with the first visit of a pope to British soil and Winning had played an important part in bringing it about. The previous day's edition of The Times had carried the headline: 'How Glasgow May Have Saved the Pope's Visit', and praised the Archbishop's negotiations. In public, he insisted that Archbishop Worlock and both cardinals shared the success, while in private he was delighted to be singled out. Although the first leg of the papal visit was to England and Wales, and would include the Pope's historic embrace of the Archbishop of Canterbury, Winning and Gray had arranged to greet their guest upon his arrival at Gatwick. Tom Farmer, the millionaire businessman behind the Kwik Fit chain, had arranged a private jet and accompanied them on the journey from Edinburgh Airport to Longhorn, an air force base near Gatwick. As they disembarked and walked to the car which Farmer had organized to take them on to their destination, Winning was saluted by an RAF sergeant who said: 'Morning, sir. Thank you for bringing the Holy Father to Great Britain.' Winning was tickled by his greeting, which was warmer than the one he received from the Pope. After moving along the line of dignitaries, the Pope reached Winning and asked: 'What are you doing here?' Winning laughed and said: 'I'm here to greet you. What do you think?' It was Father Stanislav, the Pope's secretary, who captured the relief of their arrival when he shook Winning's hand and said: 'We're here.'

Four days later, on the evening of Tuesday 1 June, the papal entourage touched down at RAF Turnhouse outside Edinburgh, where a crowd of eight thousand had gathered and cheered when Pope John Paul II kneeled and kissed the grass in recognition of Scotland's nationhood. The next thirty-six hours were to be among the proudest of Winning's life as for two days the Catholic Church and its charismatic leader dominated the media and captured the country's heart. For centuries the Pope had been a figure of hate, an emotion which had slowly dissolved into distrust, but over the next few hours he would be revealed as a man of peace. His first appointment was with the nation's young Catholics, fifty thousand of whom had gathered at Murrayfield Stadium, where the atmosphere was more comparable to a rock concert than a religious event. Banners of yellow, white and gold, the papal colours, swayed with their holders and the cheers of 'We want the Pope, we want the Pope' had become deafening. Shortly after six o'clock, thirty minutes later than scheduled, Gordon Gray took to the stage and said: 'Dear Holy Father, I give you the young Catholics of Scotland.' For five minutes the Pope could only stand, arms outstretched, as he bathed in the warmth of an extraordinary welcome.

Winning stood at the side of the stage and watched as the Pope delivered his message with the spirit of a natural orator. To the young, he explained, the world might appear grey, cast in the shadows of unemployment, uncertainty and the nuclear mushroom cloud, but faith in Jesus Christ was the answer.

> Left alone to face the difficult challenges of life today, you feel conscious of your own inadequacy and afraid of what the future may hold for you. But what I have to say to you is this: place your lives in the hands of Jesus. He will accept you, and bless you, and he will make such use of your lives as will be beyond your greatest expectations.

In an irony that probably had as much to do with the intoxicating atmosphere as ready agreement the loudest cheers and longest interruption were reserved for after the Pope had quoted from St Paul and advised his audience on the consequences of ignoring the Holy Spirit:

> When self-indulgence is at work the results are obvious: fornication, gross indecency and sexual irresponsibility ... feuds and wrangling, jealousy, bad temper and quarrels, disagreements, factions, envy, drunkenness, orgies and similar things. I warn you now, as I warned you before: those who behave like this will not inherit the kingdom of God.[11]

The exact location of the Pope's next appointment had been the subject of fierce debate. Where should the Moderator of the Church of Scotland meet the Pope? Officials of the Church of Scotland had been reluctant to welcome the Pope into the Moderator's residence on George Street, while their suggestion of the pavement outside the General Assembly building was rejected by the Catholic Church as inhospitable and rude. A compromise was struck with the Pope agreeing to meet the Moderator in the courtyard of the Assembly Hall, where their historic handshake would take place under the gaze of a towering statue of John Knox. The Falklands crisis had overshadowed the threat posed by Protestant protesters, two hundred of whom had gathered, led by the Revd Ian Paisley, to hurl abuse as well as a solitary egg at the Pope. And in spite of their banners stating: 'We Don't Want You' and 'Jesus Saves, Rome Enslaves', the disruption of a minority of Protestant extremists was to be drowned in a sea of goodwill. Professor John McIntyre, that year's Moderator, extended a cordial greeting to the Pope, stating that they shared 'one Lord, one Faith, one Baptism'. He went on to praise the Pope as a 'man of peace' and pointed out that Scotland was a country scarred with religious conflict and controversy. 'And so from this spirit of reconciliation which informs our meeting today, we, for our part, would look forward to further dialogue with your Church, not just on the subjects of disagreement, but also on the joint themes on which we agree in the face of a hostile world.'[12] The Moderator then presented the Pope with an address prepared by the Inter-Church Relations Committee of the General Assembly, included in which was an explanation of the Kirk's unease over Catholic schools. The Pope responded briefly: 'I am profoundly grateful for your words and for the contents expressed in your words. They are very near to my heart and also to my attention, my activity and my programme: but my first programme is to be the servant of God.'[13] Over dinner that evening, Winning asked the Pope if he did not find the Protestants cold people. 'No,' replied John Paul II. 'Not cold, but serious people.'

The Pope followed his meeting with the Moderator with an address to a gathering of clergy and religious at St Mary's Cathedral before retiring to St Bennet's, where an upstairs bedroom had been redecorated for his arrival and a picture of Our Lady of Czesto-chowa, the Polish shrine, hung to provide a hint of home. The next day involved appointments with Church leaders, a home for the handicapped and St Andrew's College, the Catholic teaching insti-tute in Bearsden. The highlight of the entire Scottish visit was the papal Mass at Bellahouston.

Winning had wanted the Pope to be driven through the streets of his city but was prevented by the police who feared an attack and insisted he arrive by helicopter. Any disappointment he might have had dissolved upon his arrival when he found what seemed like the entire city crammed into the park. The experience of standing beside the Pope as the truck wound its way through the lanes dividing the worshippers was unforgettable. 'It was the most joyous occasion. The Holy Spirit was there. That joy and happiness that invades a crowd is the presence of God,' said Winning. The weather was also read as a presence of the divine: the 'June Monsoons' that so often drench outdoor events were replaced by bright sunshine and a temperature of 72°C – 'Pope weather', as it would become known. The cheering became so intense during the Pope's homily that he had to pause for several minutes until the crowds allowed him to continue:

> Today marks another significant moment in the history of our sal-
> vation: the successor of Peter comes to visit the spiritual children of
> Andrew. We are bound one to another by a supernatural brother-
> hood stronger than that of blood. Here and now we testify that we
> profess that identical faith in Jesus, and we finally hope that we too
> can lead others to him.[14]

In his speech, the Pope touched on the Reformation and commented on how far Scots Catholics had come, but instead of praising
the past he wished to urge the country's Catholics into the future:

> You originate in a glorious past, but you do not live in the past.
> You belong in the present and your generation must not be content
> simply to rest on the laurels won by your grandparents and great-
> grandparents. You must give your response to Christ's call to follow
> him and enter with him as co-heirs into his Father's heavenly king-
> dom. But we find it harder to follow Christ today than appears to
> have been the case. Witnessing to him in modern life means a daily
> contest, not so quickly and decisively resolved as the martyrs of the
> past.

These words would echo through Winning's future plans but at
the time he, like the audience, sat and listened. As the Pope left
the park the crowd began to sing 'Will ye no came back again', a
song in tribute to Bonnie Prince Charlie. When Winning began to

explain the background to the song and the identity of the Young Pretender, the Pope interrupted and said: 'Yes. I had tea with him and his mother in London.' Winning remembered: 'At the time I thought: "So much for Papal infallibility."'

The Pope flew home the next day. His final words before climbing the steps of the plane at RAF Turnhouse were: 'Thank you for your hospitality. It was wonderful. I love your country.' The visit that came so close to cancellation had passed without a hitch and with a tremendous degree of success. In Glasgow Winning wanted to achieve a lasting memorial and in a letter to Glasgow District Council he suggested renaming a significant street or area after an aspect of the visit such as 'unity'. 'If a city like Cardiff can mark the Holy Father's visit by granting him the freedom of the city, surely the least Glasgow can do is to make some significant gesture that will recall to future generations this historic event,' wrote Winning. At the council's general purposes committee one area suggested was in the vicinity of Ibrox, the location of Rangers Football Club, but the idea progressed no further. If the Pope failed to receive a permanent memorial, Winning was more fortunate. The *Glasgow Herald* named him Scot of the Year in recognition of his work in securing the visit, Glasgow University presented him with an honorary degree, and in his home town of Wishaw, 'Winning Quadrant' was unveiled in June 1983, though not without protest from the Orange lodge. Winning, meanwhile, had other plans. He had decided that the papal visit would be remembered not by plaques or renamed streets, but in the actions of the city's Catholics. He would use the exhilaration of the recent visit as a springboard to launch the people into a closer relationship with God. He was planning little short of a revolution.

THIRTEEN

The City of God

'The Pastoral Plan was our Cuba, and Winning was our Fidel.'[1]

FR PHILIP TARTAGLIA

'The guy was a prophet, his greatest strength, in my view, was that he followed his intuition.'[2]

DR ANNA MURPHY

The greatest passion of Thomas Winning and the task to which he devoted the last twenty years of his life is entirely unknown outside the archdiocese of Glasgow and even within those boundaries it has been woefully misunderstood. In March 1983, the Archbishop launched what became known as his Pastoral Plan, an innocuous title for what was a revolutionary concept that went on to divide his priests, confuse his laity, and, at the same time, redeem Winning and bring him closer to a God he had privately feared. Winning's ambition was as simple as it was expansive: he wished nothing more than to build the City of God on the streets of Glasgow.

His search for a suitable vehicle to renew the diocese had started in April 1979 with the publication of an extensive survey of Scotland's six hundred thousand Catholics by Gallup that revealed only 54 per cent attended weekly Mass while just under half (46 per cent) favoured birth control and over half (58 per cent) approved of divorce. The poll was described by Gallup as 'the most sophisticated Catholic study in the world' and had been funded by Winning and the Bishop of Motherwell, Francis Thomson, in order to strip away decades of assumptions and discover the true depth of the religion's malaise in Scotland. While a number of the survey's findings were disappointing, others inspired hope such as the overwhelming support for Christian unity (89 per cent) and Catholic schools (73 per cent), but no one point galvanized Winning more than the revelation that among Scottish Catholics active concern for others ranked higher in importance than Mass, communal prayer and even obedience to Church teachings. It was this belief in the importance of Christian charity that Winning wished to tap.

The Movement for a Better World (MBW), the organization with which Winning had worked in 1968 as parish priest in St Luke's, Motherwell, had made a reappearance into his life in the form of two people – Anna Murphy, a Catholic doctor, and Bob Bradley, a parish priest. Winning had met Dr Murphy during a visit to the Yorkhill Sick Children's Hospital in 1979 where she was the consultant in charge of the renal unit and was impressed by her enthusiasm and readiness to discuss her faith, an ability she put down to her decade-long involvement with the MBW, which she had first encountered as a young registrar. Winning believed her to be charismatic and decided to stay in touch, while Murphy agreed to keep the Archbishop informed of developments within the movement. Father Bob Bradley, meanwhile, had already experimented with the movement's basic retreat in a previous parish, St Stephen's in Sighthill. In October 1980, he was moved to Our Lady and St George in Pennilee, a parish in one of Glasgow's solid working-class areas, where he once again introduced the movement to his parishioners with a degree of success.

Winning's interest in the theology of MBW had been rekindled by both encounters. He had recently sent six priests whom he considered sympathetic to the ethos, including one of his auxiliary bishops, Joseph Devine, on a short retreat run by the MBW. So when both Bradley and Murphy told him of a three-week retreat to take place in September 1981, tied to the movement's plan to expand from individual parishes to dioceses, Winning agreed to attend. He had been anxious to secure a spiritual system that would help break the repetitive cycle of Advent, Lent and Easter and move the diocese towards the type of Church envisioned at Vatican II. What he did not expect was to embark on a spiritual autopsy.

The retreat took place at the House of the Sacred Heart, a retreat-home buried in the English countryside a few miles from the little town of Malpass, on the Welsh border. Winning was driven there by Fr Bob Bradley in the company of Dr Anna Murphy and Fr Willie Donnelly, one of the few interested Glasgow priests, and spent the journey in a Stygian gloom. The appointment five years previously of Abbot Basil Hume as the Archbishop of Westminster had introduced a new phenomenon into British religious life: a genuinely holy man. Winning believed that the Ready-Brek glow of goodness that emanated from England's cardinal left him pale and spiritually anaemic by comparison. He would often say to Dr Murphy, with whom he developed a close friendship, 'I can't ever compete with Basil' or 'How can I be a Basil?' On the eve of a retreat the doubts about his spirituality that had dogged him since seminary would grip his attention. A fortnight with the MBW held out the added anxiety of isolation and a degree of passive hostility, for he was to be the only bishop in attendance at a group that prided itself on egalitarianism and collapsing the existing hierarchy.

Shortly after their arrival on Sunday evening, Winning was sitting in the lecture room beside a stout Irishwoman who confided in him that she was keeping an eye out 'for this big-shot bishop'. When he explained who he was, she was immediately apologetic, but quickly changed seats. A second problem was Winning's reluctance to be addressed as 'Tom' or 'Thomas'. In Church etiquette, the correct form of address for an archbishop was 'Your Grace', but in deference to his surroundings he compromised and suggested 'Father'. It was still not enough for Sister Mary Cross, one of the retreat's directors, who could not hide her dissatisfaction. Winning, meanwhile, was unhappy at what he viewed as the 'shirt-tail liturgy' on display; many of the priests insisted on saying Mass without a stole or alb and with hand gestures so casual and loose that they infuriated him. After the first evening's Mass, Winning insisted to

Bob Bradley that the Dominican priest who had presided would never return to Glasgow again.

Winning was to find the next few days exceedingly difficult. He was uncomfortable with the spontaneous prayers uttered by lay guests, the casual dress of the priests, and what he viewed as the pugnacious attitude of the nuns – in particular, Sr Mary Cross. In the morning, there was a series of talks that began with an examination of how each baptized person, working in partnership with the Holy Spirit, can take on a prophetic role in society. He agreed with this, but when Mary Cross argued against his supposition that the Catholic Church and the Kingdom of God were synonymous, he reacted with anger. 'I had made the decision to wring Mary Cross's neck,' said Winning. In time, he became aware of the difference between the two and the richer nature of the Kingdom. Meanwhile, in small group discussions, he had to contend with Bob Bradley dismissing the Church in Glasgow as 'rubbish'. It was left to Dr Murphy to provide a stabilizing influence. 'He was a churchman, that was part of his identity. If you told him the Church is not the most important thing, that it is the Kingdom, what did that do to him?'

There was one fellow retreatant who refused to call Winning 'Father' and against whom Winning had no defence. The youngest participant in the retreat was a thirteen-year-old girl, Jenny, who each morning and at every meeting said, 'Hello, Thomas.' What at first proved irritating became, with time, endearing, and as his name was picked up by others his resistance collapsed. For the first time in over a decade, he was no longer viewed as a bishop, and for the first time in over thirty years, he was no longer viewed as a priest. He was just a man, a fellow pilgrim. The layers of loneliness that accumulate from the long-term exposure to an isolated position began to strip away and the warmth of the environment and the dynamism of the ideas seeped into his soul. 'It was all part of a big opening up for me. It was a turning point in my philosophy of pastoral work. I thought that I was open, but during that retreat it was as if you had taken a tin opener and opened yourself up. It was as painful as that.'

The retreat moved from an analysis of Church and its meaning to people on to what kind of Church is relevant today, and Winning was becoming a willing convert. 'When it got to that part, the guy couldn't admit it, but he had had a personal conversion. As the days went on the guy was bulldozed with the message,' said Dr Murphy. The message of the MBW was to highlight the theology of Vatican II, which states that each baptized person shares in the role of Christ and is called to be a priest, a prophet and a servant. Individuals were called to read the signs of the times and to allow themselves to be steered by the Holy Spirit and act for the greater good. A principal strand of the group's idea was the restructuring of the Church – philosophically, if not physically – which was seen as a triangle with the laity strung along the bottom and standing on their shoulders, in ever-decreasing rows, the priests, canons, monsignors, bishops, archbishops and cardinals, with the Pope, like the fairy on the Christmas tree, at the top. Instead, the goal was to create a circle of laity with the priests in the centre. While discussing the type of Church required and how to achieve the goal, Winning became convinced he had found his Pastoral Plan. The concept of reading the signs of the times and putting thoughts into vigorous action appealed to the workmanlike aspect of Winning's spirituality. He was acutely aware that he would never enjoy the tangible aura of holiness that drew people to Christ, like moths to a flame, but the retreat allowed him to open himself to the Holy Spirit, to be guided by God, and to realize that he could achieve his work through speaking out loudly, not just by praying in silence. Winning reflected:

The prophet has to be able to stand up and promote the values of the Kingdom of God – truth, justice, peace – and to denounce the evil that is against those values. The prophetic element of charism in the Church was apt to be forgotten because people found it difficult to promote the values of the Kingdom and to denounce evil. It is not a question of getting up and condemning the world; you have to put something in place of those evil wicked things. This is what clinched it for me. I felt this sense that the Church had to have a prophetic voice in the world and that has made me pay great attention to having that voice, promoting the Kingdom of God, denouncing evil – whether it is abortion or cloning or euthanasia or sexual permissiveness or not enough pensions or too much poverty. That is the thing that overtook me.

At the end of the first week after a rest-day spent on a picnic, Bob Bradley suggested that Winning say Mass. 'He went on to do much worse than the poor guy he slated the week before. He had loosened up tremendously. He was dealing with people on equal terms,' said Bradley. Winning was to leave one week early to attend a conference in America, but before he departed he gave a gift of a stole to one particularly scruffy priest with the message: 'It's a keepsake and for God's sake, use it.' The keepsake Winning received was a change of heart, the basis of a pastoral plan, and a sense that once again God was guiding him.

What Winning wanted to tackle was the old rhetorical question: if Christianity were illegal, would there be enough evidence to convict? The answer he wanted the archdiocese of Glasgow to be able to give was 'yes'. In 1981, 52 per cent of the Catholic population attended Mass; Winning wanted this to rise, the lapsed to return and the regulars to deepen their faith. Catholicism was not only about Mass attendance, regular communion and a personal relationship with God, what Karl Rahner described as 'the cultivation of a beautiful soul'. It concerned social action, togetherness and charity. The last fifty years had witnessed the integration of the Catholic community into mainstream society, but also the collapse of the sense of unity that flourished in the ghetto. In a reaction to the cult of the self currently being propagated by Thatcherism, Winning wished to create a thriving Christian community which not only believed there was such a concept as society, but that it was to society that it owed a debt. Using the current parish as a starting point, he wished to build basic Christian communities. These would be a second family, bound in groups of about fifteen, who would meet together, pray together, and assist one another with the deepest problems of their lives, whether financial or spiritual, drugs or drink, divorce or depression. They would live out their faith during their daily lives, at work and on the streets. In time, if the communities grew and thrived, they would begin to assist the destitute, the elderly, the addicted – all by living out the teachings of Christ. Instead of the archdiocese of Glasgow consisting of 110 parishes, it would consist of thousands of Basic Christian Communities (BCCs), clustered around parishes, utilizing the abilities of the priest, but independent. The ambition was staggering and his commitment total. Winning would single-handedly push against the grain of society at a time when the individual was all; he would attempt to lasso men and women into a new Catholic corral. The twin problems would be the priests and Winning's impatience.

The reason for Winning's early departure from the MBW retreat was to meet Fr Vincent Dwyer, an American Trappist monk and founder of the Ministry for Priests Program based at the Center for Human Development in Washington, DC. Father Dwyer used behavioural sciences to give an accurate insight into a priest's character with the goal of revitalizing a generation of men weary with the incessant demands of the job. Winning had always taken a keen interest in the mental, physical and spiritual well-being of his priests, and believed the Ministry for Priests Program would be of invaluable assistance. When launched in Glasgow in early 1982, the programme had two distinct phases. In the first, the priests were profiled using a detailed questionnaire which revealed that the body of priests fell into three distinct and equal categories: one third enjoyed a positive 'can do' attitude, one third were uninspired but obedient, while the final category, a total of a hundred priests, were obstinate and openly hostile to any form of change. In the second phase, to help alter their attitudes, each priest was given a personal growth plan and encouraged to take part in a new 'peer ministry' where priests assisted each other with problems and relaxed together one weekend a month in groups themed around a common hobby such as golf, hill-walking or badminton. Those who embraced the concept were able to find a support system in which their work and well-being flourished.

Winning had been unimpressed with the spiritual preparations in place prior to the papal visit, but had had no choice but to keep his own counsel and his new plans quiet until the autumn of 1982 when he invited Fr Max Taggi, an Italian Jesuit who was a long-standing member of the MBW and a renowned expert in religious planning, to speak to both his auxiliary bishops and episcopal vicars. He had been developing ideas since the spring with a 'cabinet' comprised of Anna Murphy, Bob Bradley, his auxiliary bishop Joseph Devine, and Fr Hugh McEwan. Among the six priests sent on the MBW retreat, McEwan had been the most passionate and emerged an ardent advocate of renewal.

During his week-long visit, Taggi, who with his pens lined neatly along his breast pocket had the air of a weary maths teacher, explained that the plan's first aim was to establish better communications between parish priests and their parishioners, as only then could they promote partnership, spiritual growth and a greater understanding of the Church's mission. Communicating this to the priests took place two months later in November, one month before the plan's announcement in Advent 1982, which was to be spent praying for the plan's success when it was officially launched the following spring. Over three nights, Winning spoke to different groups of priests about what Christ would want from the Church in Glasgow and while they agreed on the answer (a greater involvement in the life of the people), they were far from unanimous about the method.

Winning described his priests in *Flourish* as 'a zealous band of servants . . . looking for a deeper commitment to the Church they love'. Yet in retrospect he regretted not dedicating far greater efforts to their conversion to the idea of renewal.

The Pastoral Plan was launched during Lent 1983, and, for a nerve centre, Winning purchased a large villa in the grounds of the Sisters of Nazareth convent in Cardonald in Glasgow which he named *Sal Terrae*, Latin for 'Salt of the Earth', in reflection of his views on the people of Glasgow. As director of the new pastoral centre and coordinator of the plan, he appointed Fr Hugh McEwan, who possessed an astute intelligence but would lack the aggressive quality necessary to fend off the project's many critics. McEwan's role, working closely with Dr Murphy, was to train dozens of resource teams, a band of five people drawn from among the priests, religious and laity, whose purpose was to visit the thirty-six parishes chosen to pilot the Renewal Programme. Guiding the archdiocese from Heaven was an angel, Gauden, who wrote a monthly column in *Flourish* and who foresaw the plan evolving from the people and the religious upwards, though this did not happen in practice.

One of the eight targets of the first year was to inform the whole diocese of the idea of Renewal, and so twelve teams were assembled to visit each parish and hold a short retreat designed to inspire parishioners about their role in their church. To a percentage of the diocesan population, those weary of the years of 'pray, pay and obey', as the Catholic Church was previously characterized, Winning's plan was an answered prayer. The ideas drawn from '*Lumen Gentium*' and '*Gaudium et Spes*', two prominent documents from the Second Vatican Council which encouraged action, were particularly potent. As one parishioner said: 'I now understand that as an ordinary Catholic my vocation was as much a vocation as the ordained and religious. That I should be implementing the Kingdom of God here and now and not just looking inward to save my soul.' The parish meetings were to produce a flood of ideas concerning what was missing from the Church: dynamism, charity, youth and a greater spirituality.

In March 1984, Fr Noel Barry, a curate at St Ninian's in Knightswood, was appointed communications officer for the Pastoral Plan. A young Irishman from County Cork, his writing skills had been recognized by Fr Tom Connelly, the Church's media spokesman who encouraged Winning in his appointment. Within a year, Barry had taken over as editor of *Flourish* from Vincent Donnelly, with whom he clashed in his first few days after the editor took exception to a line in Barry's copy that ran: 'There are eight sacraments and the eighth is the Christian himself – the only one the vast majority of people will ever receive.' Donnelly had argued the Church only recognized seven sacraments. Barry, quoting Pope John XXIII as his source, insisted the line ran as written. As a loyal supporter of the Pastoral Plan, Barry went on to become one of Winning's closest aides.

The second year of the Pastoral Plan began confidently, but ended in disappointment. In June, Taggi returned to the city and encouraged the diocese to concentrate on the prophetic nature of a Catholic and praised their determination. 'It is a privilege to share in this project because there are so few like it in the Church today.' A second theme was the construction of a community spirit, which Winning dubbed 'close harmony' after the tenement spirit once found in the Gorbals 'when every door was open to neighbour and no one suffered in secret'. By September 1984, eighteen months after the plan's launch, 104 people had been trained for resource teams and had visited 80 out of the diocese's 110 parishes. But the plan received a body blow in December 1984 when the Jesuit order withdrew Taggi from the MBW and reassigned him to the Far East. His successor as religious planner for the movement was Fr Juan Baptista Cappellaro, a former member of the Argentinian Episcopal Commission for Renewal. In his opinion, Taggi had pointed the archdiocese in the wrong direction. Instead of encouraging a few pilot projects, the entire diocese was to move as one. The resource teams carefully trained were to be scrapped in favour of a Deanery Animating Team or 'DAT', with far fewer numbers, resulting in dozens of disgruntled laity who felt they had been discarded. Before unveiling his suggestions, Cappellaro asked for a detailed analysis of the diocese to be prepared ahead of his arrival in September 1985. The report, which ran to ninety pages, reached the brittle bones of the diocese, recounting the effects of poverty, long-term unemployment and a drug problem in its infancy. The priests were revealed to suffer 'burnout', to lack trust in the laity, and to have 'psychological needs' which were not being met. The religious suffered similar problems while the resource teams were 'overworked', lacked an adequate formation, and were baffled by increased use of jargon.

Winning was to remain undaunted in spite of the problems. The retirement in November 1984 of Cardinal Gordon Gray had been followed in April by Winning's election as president of the Bishops' Conference, and he enjoyed the prestige of being Scotland's most senior Catholic churchman. It was in this capacity that he attended the Extraordinary Synod of Bishops in Rome in late November and early December 1985. The Pope had called the synod to reflect on the twenty years since the close of Vatican II and in a move crucial to his conservative agenda, he wished to draw a line under those changes and extinguish any further attempts to push the envelope with liberal views being presented as in 'the spirit of Vatican II'. Winning travelled to Rome with the results of a nationwide consultation that showed the Scottish laity were overwhelmingly supportive of the changes following the Second Vatican Council, but still advocated a greater role for women. He spoke on the first morning about the Pastoral Plan and called on the synod to encourage spiritual renewal programmes. In a reference to his current dilemma, he argued that 'only with consensus can the whole diocese move forward as it should . . . in unity and without polarization'.[3] The speech was low-key but effective; his idea to encourage pastoral plans was included in the synod's final report and was praised by Basil Hume – to Winning's delight. The Pope was absent on the morning of Winning's speech, but when he dined with the English-speaking bishops on the final night, John Paul II presented him with a 700-page book, in Polish, on the renewal plans of his old diocese in Krakow. A sign which Winning read as God encouraging his work.

Winning's deepening friendship with Dr Anna Murphy was as much a source of guilt to Winning as it was of pleasure. So involved had she become in the coordination and running of the Pastoral Plan, that she was dubbed the 'deputy archbishop'. Winning was attracted by her charisma and intense spirituality and invited her to give retreats to both priests and seminarians, but his priestly formation was initially resistant to a warm, platonic friendship for, in his belief, within the personal forum lay sin. For all the entirely erroneous rumours or nudge, nudge, wink, wink remarks which surround the life of a celibate man – and Winning was faithful to his vows till the day he died – he did suffer guilt at the idea of a personal friendship with a woman. As a handsome young priest he was wary of any female who made frequent visits to the chapelhouse without any particular reason, and as a spiritual director he had urged his students to maintain a rigorous prayer life as it would be 'insulation to guard them from a mistake'. In spite of the fact that his friendship with Anna Murphy was above reproach, he still attempted to keep a certain distance and so always addressed her as 'Dr Murphy' in public, though he would refer to her as Anna when meeting her privately at The Oaks. Murphy believed the principal reason for their strong relationship was their shared values and her medical experience, on which Winning would often draw for reassurance. It was she who encouraged him to take more exercise and to watch his intake of wine and whisky, she who pushed him to spiritually develop 'Thomas' the man, not just 'Winning' the archbishop, and she who would fight back against his tendency to bully.

'It was denial and guilt that prevented him from being open with female friends,' explained Dr Murphy. 'For him it was not appropriate for a churchman to have friends. His friends were priests, he had his family, he had his housekeeper, but if you introduced another relationship, the result was guilt, guilt and guilt! Denial, denial, denial. He had a tremendous heart with sharp edges. The sharp edges were from his Church background. He was soft and could be very loving.'

When, in the winter of 1985, Murphy approached Winning with concerns that the plan was in danger of derailing through a lack of tangible spirituality, it was merely to confirm a conclusion he had already reached. The clergy had so far failed to take on a leadership role as Cappellaro had requested and the laity were weary of meetings, forms, clipboards, flow-chart diagrams and endless acronyms. Cappellaro, McEwan and priests such as Bob Bradley, argued for Winning to be patient and persevere; instead, he flew to Newark, New Jersey, to explore an alternative, called – confusingly – Renew. This was a spiritual programme developed by Mgr Tom Kleisser, which had been adopted by eighty dioceses across America and in countries such as New Zealand, Australia and India with promising results. Parishes where as little as 13 per cent attended Mass reported a rise to 20 per cent after one year and 40 per cent after the third and final year. Renew lasted three years, to reflect the period Jesus spent moulding his apostles, and was based on drawing parishioners into a closer, more personal relationship with Christ through Sunday Mass, take-home material, group activities and small faith-sharing groups through which the Holy Spirit could more readily act.

Winning was accompanied on the trip, funded by the Catholic trust behind the C&A chain of department stores, by Bishop Cormac Murphy-O'Connor, and while Murphy-O'Connor would wait four years to introduce Renew into his diocese of Brighton and Arundel, Winning took just six months.

His decision to change horses in mid-stream was in the face of heated protest. Cappellaro believed Winning was mistaken, McEwan argued the system would be problematic, and Bob Bradley refused flat out to take any part in what he regarded as pure folly. The MBW was firmly established in the parish of Our Lady and St George, the roots having bedded down three years earlier, and the priest was unwilling to exchange their progress for Winning's diversion. 'He brought it in because he did not understand the length of time that was required,' said Bradley. 'He was impatient.' Bradley's behaviour irritated Winning, who privately dismissed his parish as a bunch of spiritual snobs. 'I always had the feeling when I visited that they looked down their noses at you.'

In May 1986, Renew's founder, Mgr Tom Kleisser, accompanied Sr Donna Ciangio, a Dominican sister with eight years experience in the project, on a visit to Glasgow. The pair met a majority of diocesan priests over two days at St Peter's Pastoral Centre and pushed on them the importance of their role if Renew was to succeed. 'Priests need to stop being the experts and start being the listeners. Instead of behaving as if we have arrived, we need to act as pilgrims,'[4] explained Kleisser. Hugh McEwan was once again charged with training the parishioners, and spent four weeks in Newark in preparation, accompanied by Fr David Brown, a young curate. In their absence, Winning had Renew T-shirts printed up depicting the St Andrew's flag with a vine tree and the slogan 'Together into the Future', which they first spotted being worn by a particularly buxom young woman.

Launched on 12 October with a large Mass attended by a thousand representatives from every parish and concelebrated by sixty priests, Renew was to become a debatable success. For the next three years during each autumn and spring, 15,000 people from 104 parishes took part in small group prayer meetings, set up a messenger system to contact the lapsed, and slowly became conscious of their duty to evangelize. While a proportion of priests embraced the idea, the gulf between Winning and his clergy had increased. Donny Renfrew, his auxiliary bishop, had often cautioned patience while John Mone had attempted to counsel priests angry at what they viewed as the Archbishop's dismissive treatment. 'I remember speaking to one elderly priest at a funeral who was literally shaking with rage,' he said. Mone had succeeded Joseph Devine to become Winning's second auxiliary bishop in April 1984 after Devine's promotion to become Bishop of Motherwell. Mone was to serve for four years until he too was promoted to bishop of the diocese of Paisley in March 1988.

In retrospect, Winning believed part of the problem was a historical lack of leadership in the Catholic Church. 'There was never any time when the bishop said "I want you to do this". There was no tradition of the bishop as a leader. Diocesan policy in the past was visit the sick, visit families, and the celebration of Mass. You did what your predecessor did twenty years before. But Vatican II had happened and my conviction was that you could no longer just keep the engine ticking over. We were at a crucial stage in our history.' His conclusion was that the clergy were 'the biggest gurners on the face of the earth' but that he had to fight for their conversion.

In 1987, he arranged to meet them all in groups of fifteen and spend a day of intense bridge-building, a process that was concluded with a concelebrated Mass.

The Pastoral Plan was to take a toll on Winning's prayer life. By the time he took part in a five-day retreat at Craighead, between 20 and 25 July 1987, he was weary, distracted and increasingly resentful at his priests' lack of support. Doubts about his ability, ideas and even health began to emerge into the vacuum of those empty days. The theme of the retreat, led by Father Philip Walshe, was 'Deep Confidence and Trust in God's Fatherly Care' and for the first few days Winning struggled to settle into meditative prayer, distracted as he was by the warm weather and his own internal dilemmas. Trusting God was an idea Winning found easy to preach but difficult to practise, and to correct this he spent time meditating on the person of Mary, whom he asked: 'What is it like to trust as you did?' While Mary viewed God as loving her, Winning viewed God as judging him, a concept that had dogged him since childhood. He was conscious of his faults: his impatience with people, his cynicism directed at Church leaders; the humour he extracted at another's expense, and his increasingly domineering attitude, and as a result he feared that God's judgement would be harsh.

In an attempt to reconcile the two sides of his character, the theological convert to the concept of a loving God and the doubting Thomas who viewed God as a harsh judge, he utilized the Ignatian method of prayer in which one imagines oneself present within a scene from the New Testament. He picked a passage from St Matthew's Gospel where a crowd of people are begging Jesus to heal them. Sitting in the quiet of his room he imagined the heat and dust, the din of the crowd and the figure of Jesus. In his meditation he attempted to guide two young disabled children to Christ who cured them before turning to Winning himself. In his imagination, Jesus placed a hand on his head and told him: 'My Father is a loving God and you should see Him as such.' Before he departed, Jesus spoke again, telling him: 'You have not chosen me. I have chosen you.'[5] At the end of the retreat, Winning commented to Fr Walshe that he had embarked less on spiritual exercises than a spiritual exorcism. 'I think I have laid a few ghosts, and expelled some demons,' he explained.

The conclusion of Renew meant the reanimation of Renewal, and Winning wanted a new director of the Pastoral Plan. In the summer of 1988, he appointed Fr Angus MacDonald, a tall, diffident man of Highland stock, who carried a constant air of concern. MacDonald was a priest at St Stephen's, a parish in Dalmuir, and was a leading member of the deanery coordinating team. He had opposed the introduction of Renew, but afterwards worked hard for its success.

The posting was confused from the start. While MacDonald was officially the new director, his predecessor remained on the board, lived in the building and remained the man to whom many people turned.

'As often happens in these situations, a person's qualities become a curse. The Archbishop's quality of fidelity to his friends, appreciation for work done, did not allow the Archbishop to say: "Hugh, away you go, leave it to this guy." Some of the lay folk considered I was the usurper and so there were always going to be difficulties.'

An early and unpopular decision made by MacDonald was to disband the small faith-sharing groups that had blossomed during Renew. The logic was correct but unappreciated. The distant goal of Basic Christian Communities meant that to retain the current groups would lead to confusion further down the line. By 1989, 80 per cent of all parishes had a coordinating team, but, without the unqualified support of the priests, progress on the plan was slothful. After three years MacDonald was asked to step down, to be replaced by Fr John King, then director of diocesan social services. 'I don't think we succeeded at all,' said MacDonald. 'I would characterize my experience as a failure.' After almost ten years, Winning's attention to the plan began to drift.

*　　*　　*

Winning loved to travel, but a purpose was as mandatory as a suitcase. He was incapable of sedentary relaxation and so combined holidays with invitations to visit far-off dioceses in continents such as South East Asia, North and South America and Australia, where each day was spent visiting parishes, offices and projects, which he would record in mundane detail in a travel journal he started (though rarely finished) with each trip. A trip to South America in the mid-Eighties to visit projects supported by the Scottish Catholic International Aid Fund inspired him to write a two-part series in *Flourish*. The pitiful poverty of his hosts, who built homes from reclaimed rubbish, struck him to the core, but he was inspired by the joy they were able to derive from their faith and their stoic acceptance of their hardships – qualities entirely absent among those in the relative comfort of the affluent West. His globetrotting was never risk-free. In 1992 he was hospitalized with malaria upon his return from a three-week trip to visit missionaries in Nigeria and Kenya.

The collapse of the Berlin Wall and the end of the Cold War was a source of celebration for Winning who had for decades prayed for such an eventuality, even celebrating Mass in a hotel room overlooking Red Square during a visit to Moscow, to heighten his petition. But the expected period of global stability and peace he hoped would follow collapsed a year later with the Iraqi invasion of Kuwait on 2 August 1990. Winning was quick to condemn the actions of the dictator Saddam Hussein in the leader column in *Flourish* as an 'act of aggression unprecedented in modern times', but he was equally swift to apply the brakes on the West's war wagon. Oil, he argued, appeared to be the principal concern of the coalition, not human life – or the West would have taken sterner action three years previously when Saddam had gassed five thousand Kurds. Basil Hume and Robert Runcie, the Archbishop of Canterbury, advocated negotiation but felt the scenario fell within the bounds of a 'Just War', using the criteria developed centuries before by St Thomas Aquinas. Winning did not.

The Archbishop of Glasgow's stance on war was characteristic of Scottish Catholicism, which over the past twenty years had become among the most outspoken and pacifist in the world. In March 1982, three months before the papal visit to Britain and only weeks before the outbreak of the Falklands campaign, the Scottish hierarchy had published a statement condemning as 'immoral' not only the use of nuclear weapons, but also their possession and threatened use. The statement was stronger than any made by the Pope, who had given his reluctant and unenthusiastic backing to the devices as a deterrent. The reason for their hostility was apparent. Britain's nuclear response was centred at the Faslane submarine base, fifteen miles from Glasgow, which placed Scotland in the front line and four minutes from annihilation. Yet self-interest was not the only motivating factor. As a small nation with no tie to the government or the Establishment, the bishops felt able to take a pioneering approach.

In November, as troop movements built up in the Middle East, Winning announced that a war in the Gulf would be 'morally indefensible', arguing that the Just War criteria could not be met. 'The Christian Just War tradition demands that it should be undertaken as a last resort, it must not be waged in a way which would involve non-combatants and its consequences must be less harmful than not engaging in war.'[6] As the deadline for Iraqi withdrawal approached, Winning switched his focus on to the arms trade and insisted that the current crisis was its 'poisoned fruit' and that any future peace should involve a ban on such 'criminal business'. Winning's policy was not to promote pragmatism but to uphold Christian ideals, and in so doing he roped the words of previous popes into his rhetoric, including Paul VI's exhortation to the United Nations: 'War never again! Never Again!', and John XXIII's, in his encyclical letter '*Pacem in Terris*', when he wrote: 'In this age, which boasts of its atomic power, it no longer makes sense to maintain that war is a fit instrument with which to repair the violation of justice.'

On Christmas Day, Pope John Paul II added another weapon to Winning's armoury when he said: 'War is an adventure with no return.' Yet while the Pope eventually came round to the necessity of the Gulf War, phoning President Bush on the eve of the attack to wish him a swift victory, Winning did not, in spite of the huge contingency of Scots troops, 13,500 of whom took part in Operation Desert Storm, and the increasing unpopularity of his stance.

In January 1991, he organized a series of Masses for peace and wrote to each parish priest instructing them to contact the family and friends of troops on active service to offer the churches support and prayers. When war broke out, he began to urge a just peace, in which the plight of the Palestinians, an issue raised by Saddam and so dismissed by the Allies, be properly addressed. At the time, Winning was ignored as an impractical churchman demanding utopian solutions, but, a decade later, the legacy of the Gulf War would remain a burning issue. His stance was welcomed by Glasgow's Moslem community with whom he would later unite on the issue of Section 28, the battle to prevent the abolition of legislation that prevented the promotion of homosexuality in Scottish schools. The Young Moslem Movement invited him to the city's central mosque to discuss the crisis and it was with one eye on the sensibilities of non-Christians that he refused to read a specific prayer during the Gulf War Memorial Service on 4 May. In tribute to the huge contribution of Scottish soldiers, the national ecumenical service was held in Glasgow Cathedral, but when Winning received a copy of the prayer Dr William Morris, the cathedral minister, wished him to read out, he insisted that, in good conscience, he could not utter the words: 'Turn the hearts of all who have been our enemies to the truth, as you have revealed it in Jesus, that they may know and do your will.' Winning believed the prayer bordered on triumphalism and implied that the Iraqi nation should convert from Islam to Christianity and, despite the fact that the order of service containing the prayer was already printed, he wrote and read his own prayer in which he called God's grace upon those afflicted by the 'bitter harvest of injury and death, illness and pain, homelessness and hunger'. The press coverage of the dispute with Morris was to be the final twist in Winning's controversial war.

Winning's stance, though consistent, was flawed. The Just War theory, as the Pope himself came to realize, was applicable in the crisis and negotiation against a despot such as Saddam, if unsupported by military action, was unlikely to succeed. Kuwait was a sovereign country invaded by an aggressive neighbour, however, and Winning's insistence that oil was a principal concern was correct. The consequence of the Allies' failure to implement a 'just peace' as he pleaded begat a repetition twelve years later. The Gulf War and Winning's aggressive promotion of peace would mark his arrival as a truly national figure to which the media would increasingly turn.

Winning was to spend the next eleven years in a struggle to implement his beloved Pastoral Plan. The day before he died, he was given an update by Cappellaro. Yet for eleven years his priests continued to resist. Asked to explain their reticence, Cappellaro shook his head, rolled his hand into a fist, and slammed it into his palm. 'He was too hard. They did not want to know.' Asked if the plan had succeeded, Winning replied: 'I have no doubt.' He believed those who embraced his ideas had enjoyed a richer spiritual life and a swell in confidence. A number of Basic Christian Communities had formed, but many of these were photocopies of a brilliant dream. Angus MacDonald spoke for many frustrated advocates when he said: 'I think the plan badly needed a boost by the Holy Spirit but it has been a blessing for Glasgow.' Critics describe the entire project as Winning's folly, at best a Pyrrhic victory, and at worst a labour-intensive, result-shy failure; a misadventure encapsulated best in Latin, the language of the Church, as '*paturinte montes et nascitur ridiculus mous*' – 'The mountains have given birth to a ridiculous mouse.'

FOURTEEN

The Collection Plate

'You can't run the Church on Hail Marys.'
ARCHBISHOP PAUL MARCINKUS

'We could easily have been bankrupted.'
THOMAS WINNING

Thomas Winning was never very good at mathematics or handling money, for he had little interest in either. As a pupil, he would hand his maths or arithmetic homework to his father to complete; when he was archbishop, the assistance of a paternal figure was replaced by an accountant to whom he passed the books, then paid little heed. His will was never published, which led journalists to conclude that it contained less than £20,000, a figure neither confirmed nor denied by his executors, who privately insisted that his beneficiaries would not become rich. Yet this did not stop Church figures and religious commentators from tripping over themselves to applaud his relative penury as the symbol of a life that ranked poverty of equal importance to chastity and obedience. In reality, Winning had no need of personal wealth when every aspect of his life, from food and drink to travel and accommodation, was paid by the archdiocese to whom he passed bills unopened. The very lack of abstinence and a life of considerable personal comfort actually caused him concern during religious retreats, where he would berate his plenteous lifestyle and vow to be more disciplined. An archbishop has no business being his own accountant, it is souls he must save, not pounds, but nor should he ignore his cash flow, as Winning did – with the result that the archdiocese of Glasgow ran up a public debt of almost £9 million, three times that of the archdiocese of Rome and twice that of the archdiocese of Westminster. In the early Nineties, Winning was engulfed in a catastrophe that drove the Church to the brink of bankruptcy and threatened his position.

Before going on to explore what was undoubtedly Winning's darkest hour, it is important first to grasp the complexities and at times absurdities of Church finance. The relationship between the Catholic Church and mammon has often been a source of discontent down through the centuries from when the building of St Peter's was paid for by the sale of indulgences and a few thousand ducats in the right hands secured a red hat and a papal vote. Even today the Church is not immune from financial scandals such as that which swamped Archbishop Paul Marcinkus, Winning's former classmate and head of the Institute for the Work of Religious – or the Vatican Bank, as it is known – in the mid-1980s. While the uninformed layman may believe each diocese is funded by the Vatican from its 'limitless' supplies of wealth, the cash flow in fact runs in the opposite direction. Glasgow, like every other diocese in the world, is entirely self-sufficient, and each year holds a collection known as 'Peter's pence' (a practice that began in the eleventh century and has been renamed, at least in Britain, 'Peter's pound' to take inflation into account) to fund the work of the Vatican. Only the very poorest dioceses in the world receive direct financial assistance. Pope John Paul II has made a practice of giving envelopes stuffed with thousands of dollars to the bishops of the Third World during their *ad limina* visits, to the consternation of his officials.

In Glasgow the archdiocese relied for finance almost entirely on the generosity of parishioners, their legacies and, most importantly, their contributions to the weekly collection. Unfortunately, as this fell far short of their annual expenditure and dropped each year with Church numbers, the diocese turned to high street banks to borrow funds for the building of churches and for the redevelopment of dilapidated properties. Banks, in turn, looked favourably on the diocese with its untapped assets in the form of property and land. A third source of income was what was known as the levy, a flat tax on income that every parish was expected to pay towards the diocesan expenses such as seminary provision, social work and the care of elderly priests. The levy took little account of ability to pay, demanding the same percentage of income from every parish, severely hampering those churches cursed with low incomes and high expenditures. At the time, the diocese ran a diocesan bank that allowed parishes to borrow money to build and repair churches. Parishes with a surplus could hand over their money and received 2.5 per cent interest, while those which borrowed money were charged 3 per cent. On paper this should have led to a 0.5 per cent profit, but in actual fact the money lent by the diocese was borrowed from the high street banks as the Church in Glasgow existed on an ever-increasing overdraft for which it was charged as much as 16 per cent. For decades, the Church had made a practice of robbing St Peter to pay St Paul with the net result that it staggered deeper into debt.

When Winning was appointed auxiliary bishop in 1971, the diocesan debt stood at £484,000. Fourteen years later the figure had risen to £1.3 million and would climb year by year to £2.9 million in 1987 and £4 million by 1988. As the debt rose, so Winning's plea for parishioners to dig deeper each Sunday grew increasingly shrill. The average donation at the time was 64 pence and as he pointed out, 'What can you get for 64p? Ten cigarettes.'[1] He had recently given up smoking after a habit dating back over forty years and now encouraged the laity to contribute a week's tobacco or £2.50 for every £100 earned: a quarter of the Christian concept of a 10 per cent tithe, but still almost five times what they were currently prepared to part with. In a personal letter to each parishioner written in March 1988, Winning encouraged the take-up of a covenant scheme that allowed parishes to claim back tax on donations. In the text he praised their generosity to the Third World but reminded them that 'charity begins at home'. The personal plea produced a rise in covenants and a cash boost of £175,000 in two months. A whole list of reasons were given for the diocese's current financial woes: eight new churches had been built, ten presbyteries and four parish halls; essential repairs had been carried out on forty-five buildings and interest rates had risen dramatically, but no single item was a bigger cause than that which was absent from the list – the £3.8 million spent on converting the new archdiocesan offices.

Since 1982, the archdiocese had been involved in centralizing its services, which were scattered among three disparate buildings, into a newly refurbished office block which sat beside St Andrew's Cathedral on the banks of the river Clyde. The former Cremola Foam factory had been spotted as being for sale by Donny Renfrew, who persuaded Winning, then on holiday in South East Asia, to approve its purchase rather than see it slip into the hands of a night-club proprietor. In a fit of exuberant optimism, Renfrew announced that the sale of their existing properties would cover the cost of conversion, but instead the properties in Park Circus, Carlton Place and Newton Place netted just £462,000 against the final bill of £3.8 million, three times the original estimate. The conversion of 196 Clyde Street took six years and stumbled each step of the way into pitfalls and down dead ends. An early source of unhappiness was Winning's decision to overrule the planning committee who wished to put the job out to tender; instead it was handed to his choice of developer. A series of problems was finally solved when the city council's planning department approved a glass-fronted design in 1986, two years after they had first rejected it as unacceptable. When the centre was finally opened in May 1988, instead of being praised as the visionary move it undoubtedly was, placing the Church once again at the heart of the city, and equipping it for the twenty-first century, it was dismissed as an expensive folly and dubbed 'Marcinkus Mansions'. The reason the five-storey structure almost became a tombstone to Winning's career was his reluctance to reveal its true cost, in keeping with his ostrich-like attitude to fiscal responsibility. The leader in the May 1988 issue of *Flourish* read:

No churchman relishes the prospect of asking for money. It is a humbling experience, but proof that the financial worries of too many people today are shared and experienced even by archbishops! Any inhibitions there may have been in asking for more money have clearly been diminished by the immediate support forthcoming from all sections of the community. This is not to say that appeal will be made with a monotonous regularity. There should now be no need for that, if a new realism takes root.

The root would wither before enjoying the chance to grow. Only the persistence of Frank Cullen, the diocesan accountant, led to the root being planted in the first place. The former seminary student who had studied with Winning was appointed in 1973, following the death of James Ward, and spent eighteen years guarding the Archbishop from his more generous nature. 'I was often at my wits' end trying to discuss money affairs with Tom Winning. He was just not interested. He said to me one day: "That is a long, long way down my list of priorities." I can understand that attitude, but it [money] was important.' Stories of Frank Cullen holding Winning against a wall and beseeching him not to sign another cheque are entirely apocryphal, but capture the frustration of a man who was both penny and pound wise in his dealings with a superior who was neither.

The withering of the 'new realism' was tied to Winning's decision to sideline Cullen and take counsel instead from his protégée, Frances Watson, the book-keeper for the neighbouring diocese of Motherwell. Winning first met Watson when, at the suggestion of Frank Cullen (one he would later regret), she attended a meeting of the Bishops' Conference to brief them on the creation of a national fund for retired priests. The meeting at Chester's College in 1989 was followed by supper, where she sat on Winning's right. 'She was a glamorous lady and the boss noted her glamour,' remembered Dr Anna Murphy. He was also attracted by her diagnosis of his financial woes which she laid at the feet of the levy, insisting this was killing the priests' loyalty, an argument Cullen had made on a variety of occasions, but without the support of Watson's feminine charm and radical solution. Watson's idea was to separate the bank interest – running at around £500,000 a year

– when calculating the levy and to compensate for this by developing property deals which would liquidate a portion of the Church's assets. This would in time lead to the levy dropping from £1.2 million to under £800,000, with a similar drop-off in complaints from priests.

She had secured her job in Motherwell on Cullen's recommendation, despite what he claimed was a striking omission from her CV: she was not a fully qualified accountant, having left her previous position to start a family. Yet after Watson's presentation to the Bishops' Conference, it was Cullen who felt ill-educated as she began to take over the ear of the Archbishop. For almost twenty years, the archdiocese held its central account with the Bank of Scotland, with whose senior staff Cullen had developed close ties. One morning, he called the bank to discover the account had been transferred by Winning, on Watson's recommendation, to the Clydesdale Bank, in order to take advantage of a 1 per cent cut in interest rates. Cullen was deeply embarrassed by the loss of face and angered by Winning's discourtesy in not informing him. On his behalf two colleagues confronted Winning about his treatment and, though he agreed to speak to Cullen, he instead buried his mistake in silence. Urged by friends to resign, Cullen chose to complete his final year before retirement. 'The last few months were very difficult,' he said. He found he wasn't being kept in the picture. On the day of his retirement, he was visited in his office by Frances Watson. She began to speak, but he cut her short: 'Frances, I'm leaving today. The trouble is all yours.'

Father John Patrick King, who was to leave the priesthood as a result of this episode, was a man who existed on a high wire strung between the sacrifice implicit in his spiritual vocation and the reward his intelligence and business acumen would reap in everyday life. As a young curate in Glasgow, he worked as a school chaplain in Winning's pioneering scheme and served as an assistant priest to St Bernard's in Nitshill under Fr Matt Carney, parish priest and noted maverick. Carney had once run a pub from the church hall and when asked to close it down by Winning, who was concerned that the Church was seen to be encouraging alcoholism, sent the archbishop a case of champagne, surplus stock, by way of an apology.

Prior to 1974, King sought a lengthy sabbatical at Scanlan's discretion to complete a law degree in England, where he qualified as a barrister. In 1985, he reappeared, as Winning commented, 'like Melchisedech', and asked to serve once again as a diocesan priest. Winning, weary of watching priests depart, was gladdened by his return, but insisted it be without ties. As King had accepted a position as the manager of a housing association, it was a further six months before he was able to take over the management of Glengowan House, an establishment run by the diocese for homeless boys.

In 1987, King was promoted by Winning to director of social services, a department the Archbishop had founded in 1976 as a means of alleviating poverty and assisting, irrespective of religion, the city's poor and needy. Under King's dynamic leadership, the Church stepped in to fill the vacuum left by government cutbacks in the field of social care, and as a consequence his department exploded in size. King was inspired by the recent papal encyclical 'Sollicitudo Rei Socialis' – 'On the Social Concern [of the Church]', which argued that wealth and private property were on a social mortgage that required each to aid their neighbour. His concern was not only for the rehabilitation of drug addicts, the care of the elderly and handicapped but also for the creation of employment, and to this aim he launched four companies whose philosophy was to put people squarely before profit: a business plan decidedly at odds with the golden years of Thatcherism. The idea behind the firms was to teach individual skills that would later allow them to find outside employment.

A charismatic speaker who drove a nice car and owned a mobile phone a decade before they became de rigueur, King was disliked by some as a 'Flash Harry' but supported by Winning who delighted in his confidence and achievement. As a public symbol of his appreciation and good companionship, Winning invited King to accompany him on a tour of Nigeria, Kenya and South Africa in 1989.

In November 1991, Winning launched what he described as 'one of the most visionary ventures ever undertaken by the archdiocese'. On the eve of the five hundredth anniversary of the founding in 1492 of the diocese of Glasgow, he wished to make a grand gesture. He had already paid £250,000 to Glasgow University to establish the St Kentigern's chair in child welfare, and now planned a more magnanimous gift: £8 million to the citizens of his beloved city. He was, of course, entirely unaware that in thirteen months' time the Catholic population would begin raising a similar sum to bail out their archbishop.

The Pastoral Care Trust was set up to raise the figure by the year 2000 so that the sum could be invested to supply annual income for a variety of care projects. The chairman was Brian Dempsey, a leading Catholic businessman and millionaire, whose late father James Dempsey, a Labour MP for Airdrie and Coatbridge, had been a friend of Winning. As the MP was blind, his son would come and collect him from late-night conversations with Winning at St Luke's Parish House. 'They would discuss the morality of trade unionism and if they weren't finished when I arrived I would sit on and listen,' said Dempsey. Service to the Church ran in the family; it was said at his father's funeral that no church was built in the diocese without his advice being sought first while his son's cousin, Mary Pat Cooper, was a principal fundraiser in the archdiocese of Los Angeles. The Trust's formation was officially announced at a Mass at St Andrew's Cathedral on 12 January 1992, and while other members of the trust committee planned charity events Dempsey wished to put the squeeze on the city's most affluent Catholics, requesting annual donations of £10,000, £5,000 or £1,000 according to their income bracket.

At first Dempsey found Frances Watson charming and attentive, but as the weeks progressed he became suspicious of what he thought were evasive responses to detailed questions about the current state of the diocesan finances. In March he invited her to lunch at the city's Holiday Inn in an attempt to put some of his doubts at rest, but this, together with other earlier concerns, raised more questions in his mind than credible answers and he resolved to take the matter to Winning. But, distracted by his own business affairs, it was a Friday evening in early June 1992 before he met the Archbishop at The Oaks and opened the discussion with a quotation from *Hamlet*. Referring to the finances of the archdiocese, Dempsey said he believed 'something was rotten in the state of Denmark' but confessed he was unaware of the exact nature of his concerns and urged Winning to undertake a comprehensive audit by an independent firm. Winning said he would take the matter into consideration and the discussion moved on to the appointment of a professional fundraiser but, as he rose to leave, Dempsey repeated his warning and said: 'Your Grace, I'm told that you listen to the last person you speak to. Between now and the time you get back, don't speak to anybody.'

Dempsey was not the first to approach Winning with concerns about the financial health of the archdiocese. Archie McLullich, the assistant director of social work at Strathclyde Region, had raised issues that he believed meant the department was developing far too quickly. But Winning's natural loyalty stayed his hand. There was another reason. One year before, Winning had appointed King as director of the Pastoral Plan in the hope that his management skills and popularity with the priests would breathe new life into fading embers. Yet it was King's concept of the Pastoral Plan, which he unveiled at a meeting in July, that cracked open the door to doubt. King announced that the diocese should close a whole series of parishes that were, in his opinion, financially and physically unsustainable.

He proposed, using projected population trends to support his argument, to cut excess fat and reduce the diocese to raw muscle. In many ways it was a bold and arguably necessary step. The rise of secularism, the drop in the city's population and the growing shortage of priests had left dozens of churches populated by a sprinkling of elderly women and a handful of young children. Painful surgery was required and King was proposing that the patient slip on to the table under the anaesthetic of the plan. Resources could be better spent on more, smaller churches and sharing churches rather than on the upkeep of older, expensive buildings with diminishing congregations. In an uncharacteristic oversight, King did not soften the ground by discussing his ideas in depth with Winning; instead he decided on the surprise approach. If King misjudged his presentation, he also misunderstood his boss. Closing a church, regardless of how untenable its state, was anathema to Winning's community values. If he viewed King's plans as owing more to mammon than to God, Anna Murphy detected the quiet swish of the Devil's tail. The suggestion that the Devil was working to destroy the church was patently absurd, but gives an insight into the strong emotions John King's radical development evoked. From another, more progressive, archbishop, one who was prepared to grasp the nettle and tackle a difficult issue, he may even have received applause.

In spite of colleagues' concerns and his own increasing disappointment in John King, Winning did not act for a further five months. He was reluctant to start asking questions and was fearful of what he might find. Grief still afflicted him during this period. The death on 27 February of Charles Renfrew had come as a terrible blow, in spite of his steady decline. Renfrew had been suffering from a debilitating kidney disease for a number of years that was later compounded by the loss of his sight. John Mone, his second auxiliary bishop, had been promoted to Bishop of Paisley and the death of his closest friend had left Winning both emotionally and physically isolated. Charged with writing the eulogy, he had attempted to raise his spirits and pay homage to his friend by focusing on the triggers that led Renfrew to break into song, but the darkness had closed around him after the funeral Mass when he accompanied the body into the cathedral's crypt and watched as it was sealed in the tomb. 'I couldn't help but brood upon the fact that the next time the crypt would be open would be for me.'

As Frank Cullen's recommendation of Frances Watson eventually led to his departure from the Church, so Frances Watson's support of John Rafferty as director of development would lead directly to her own departure. A graduate of Stirling University and member of the British Institute of Management, Rafferty was also a talented church organist, who had met Watson through a mutual friend at the Allied Irish Bank. Watson was concerned that collection money was failing to rise and that instead of it being handed over, parish priests, sickened by the levy and what they viewed as the taunting gleam of 'Marcinkus Mansions', were opening secret bank accounts, to secure the money for their parishes' own requirements. Rafferty examined a number of ideas in America before settling on a planned giving programme, whereby a parish highlighted the gap between income and expenditure and parishioners signed pledge cards agreeing to provide a weekly sum which collectively would make up the difference, an idea successfully used in the archdiocese of Westminster.

Shortly after his arrival, Rafferty began to receive disturbing tip-offs that all was not well in the finance department, with rumours of lax financial practice, car loans, and signed cheques left in the safe. He became aware of severe financial difficulties when the bank balked at transferring wages into staff accounts as a result of the department's drastic shortage of funds. On a couple of occasions notes were left on Rafferty's desk by members of staff, and one of these related to King's salary, which was exorbitant when compared to a priest's small stipend. A letter from the Allied Irish Bank advised that penalty payments were now being applied as the diocese had failed to manage down its debt. The atmosphere in the finance department was tense and depressed with staff troubled by their involvement in affairs they felt were 'unchurchlike'. For months Winning had felt that he was being prevented from seeing the whole picture of the diocesan finances and that Frances Watson was reluctant to put everything down on paper. In December, after a particularly uncomfortable finance meeting, where Winning had grown suspicious about the true state of the account figures, Watson is said by one of the partners, who later conducted a review of the situation, to have returned to her department and instructed a member of staff to destroy the management payroll records and delete all files from the computer system. Winning later claimed she used the phrase 'as if they never existed'. She is also said to have instructed staff to check if the diocesan chancellor, Fr Peter Smith, had examined the management payroll records using his own personal password. Although Watson may have thought her instructions had been carried out, the member of staff had only removed Fr King's salary record, while still keeping a manual record of the December payment to him. Watson has taken issue with this version of events.

Rafferty's belief that the archdiocese was in serious trouble led him to contact one of its most loyal supporters. Frank McCormick had spent many years as diocesan lawyer and was aware of the current rumours, as he explained when the pair arranged to meet in the upstairs restaurant of the Glasgow Central Hotel. The transitory nature of the hotel's clientele made a comfortable setting for a couple of secret meetings where Rafferty and McCormick attempted to piece together the gossip. On 21 December, Rafferty decided to approach Winning. It was late afternoon before Rafferty was shown into his corner office. Rafferty explained in a grave tone his concerns that the archdiocese was on the brink of bankruptcy. He had given up a stable job and now found himself on a sinking ship faced with the unpleasant task of informing the captain. Winning was shaken as his closest fears took substance, but visibly calmed when told Frank McCormick was aware of the situation, and he agreed to Rafferty's suggestion that all three meet the following day at The Oaks. On the afternoon of 22 December, Winning told both men that he had been aware of stories circulating for some time and had been considering bringing in an independent auditor to re-establish his authority. Rafferty and McCormick concurred but Rafferty pushed for both Watson and King to remain absent until all the facts had been established. Winning agreed to McCormick's suggestion that Grant Thornton, the archdiocese's former accountants, handle the investigation, and Tom O'Connell, a senior partner, sensing the urgency in the Archbishop's voice, agreed to come over that afternoon. After being briefed by Winning and Rafferty, O'Connell phoned the practice's managing partners and began assembling a team that under the circumstances included an insolvency accountant.

The 23 December 1992 was dubbed 'Black Wednesday' among diocesan staff. When Winning had previously discussed the possibility of an independent audit, Fr Peter Smith had strongly supported the idea and was delighted when informed that one was scheduled to take place that morning. Winning called Watson to his office at 9.45 a.m. where she was told that until the auditors' work was complete she was to remain at home. As she departed, she turned to Peter Smith and said, 'They won't find anything wrong, you know.' Smith replied that he did not expect them to, that this was about putting everything down on paper as she had been persistently asked to do. Neither party wished the other a Merry Christmas, but Winning had to be persuaded that his idea of sending Watson a bouquet of flowers to keep her spirits up was inappropriate.

The audit team arrived in the finance department shortly after Watson's departure and instructed staff not to touch anything. When Peter Smith came downstairs to assist in the retrieval of files from the computer's hard drive, he was surprised to hear one member of staff exclaim: 'This is wonderful.' Relief was the principal emotion among employees, not embarrassment or discomfort; they were delighted that the burden of trying to handle the difficult financial situation the Church had found itself in was over. By the time Winning celebrated Midnight Mass in St Martin's parish in Renton the following evening, he was aware of the auditors' initial report that his diocese was in debt of upwards of £10 million. He said nothing to his family when he arrived at Margaret's house in Wishaw for Christmas lunch and, while the antics of his grand-nephew Thomas were a brief and pleasant distraction, the turkey and pudding turned to ash in his mouth and he excused himself in the early evening. On Boxing Day he phoned Tom Connelly, spokesman for the Catholic Church in Scotland, who described Winning as 'ash white' and 'trembling' when he arrived at The Oaks. 'He looked as if someone had shot the person standing next to him,' recalled Connelly. Winning explained that the diocese was in a very serious financial situation, and when Connelly asked how much he replied: 'Millions and millions and millions.'

The first few days of January 1993 brought a disturbing portrait of the diocese's financial health. The new accountants revealed that the diocese was £12.8 million in debt. As £4.2 million was owed to parishes within the diocese, and balanced by £4 million owed by other parishes, the largest cause of concern was a variety of overdrafts, divided among four high street banks, which totalled £8,663,000. The largest debt of £6.6 million was owed to the Clydesdale Bank, with the remainder spread between the Bank of Scotland (£669,000), Royal Bank of Scotland (£174,000), and Allied Irish Bank (£1,160,000). The main cause of debt was the almost £4 million spent on new diocesan offices. This was the core around which the debt grew as it rolled from year to year with the diocese borrowing from banks to make interest payments that by 1991 came close to £1 million per year.

The area that caused Winning greatest concern was the approximately £1.5 million of debt associated with the social services department under the former management of John King. King's aim was to adapt and improve a programme of buildings to provide care in the community to meet the needs of special groups targeted by the Church. In order to fund these projects King used the same overdraft facility as the Church; however, this was clearly not the most cost-effective arrangement available. Now, instead of covering the cost of running nursing homes or day-care centres the social services' income was outweighed by their expenses. A debt of nearly £1 million was directly related to four companies within social services: Gorbal Industries Ltd, Clyde Street Services Ltd, Braehead Builders Ltd and Exquisite Furnishings Ltd. The companies had been launched to provide employment and training to the disabled and disadvantaged, a noble idea, but unfortunately they had since become highly uneconomical. Almost their entire income was derived from an overdraft at the Allied Irish Bank which Winning insisted had been arranged without the permission of the trustees. However, Winning's version of events is contradicted by the existence of a letter to the Bank dated 17 May 1990 in which he, one of the trustees, specifically requested an overdraft facility. King pointed out that this overdraft facility was provided by the Bank on more favourable terms than normal. Furthermore, King stated that he was responsible for the acquisition of two major assets (a building in Howard Street, Glasgow, and a building in Helensburgh called 'Red Towers') purchased by a grant and through private benefactors. He maintained that the combined value of these buildings was easily enough to underpin the overdraft that developed.

While Watson and King's intention was to develop a dynamic social services programme, they ended up with a department that was too ambitious and slackly managed. Watson, who was still officially paid by Motherwell diocese which then in turn billed Glasgow archdiocese, had had her salary upped by £22,000 per year, a rise she believed was justified on account of her new responsibilities, but for which permission was neither sought nor received from either diocese. On top of her salary Watson was also the recipient of two cheques from social services, one for £1,900 and a second for £5,600, which were described in the cash book as professional fees although no income tax or national insurance was deducted from the amounts. The sum of £5,600 was used to repay part of a £10,000 loan she had received with permission from the diocese of Motherwell. Watson insists she behaved entirely properly throughout her period with the archdiocese, that she kept the Archbishop informed constantly, that she 'only ever did my best for him and the Church' and that she 'worked night and day for them'. She said the accounts were prepared at arms' length from her and appeared solvent on account of money outstanding.

While Watson's salary was upped by £22,000 per year, it was King's behaviour as an ordained priest, blessed with a higher calling, that infuriated Winning. A diocesan priest is expected to operate on a basic stipend of £2,200 per year, a form of pocket money for men whose bed and board is provided by their parish. While director of social services, King was paid a salary of between £30,000 and £50,000 and ran up credit-card expenses of £24,790.59 in one year between 1991 and 1992, which he insisted covered the legitimate expenses of a large number of staff. When transferred to direct the Pastoral Plan, he was awarded a 'redundancy' payment of £25,000 and a consultant's salary of £45,000, which was paid in place of his previous salary. King insisted the 'redundancy' payment had been with the full authority of the directors of social services and was to sustain him during the first seven months that he was in charge of the Pastoral Plan. He pointed out that the consultancy fee was paid at an identical rate to his previous salary, was paid monthly on a 'pro rata' basis, and benefited the social services department as they did not have to take him on as an employee. An audit of the department would later state: 'Although the amounts paid to Fr King are comparable with other lay people employed at a similar level in social services, we understand that it is unusual for a priest to receive such payments for carrying out his duties.' Winning felt a sharp stab of indignation upon discovering that a few days before King accompanied him to Africa his salary had increased by £10,000.

Before the auditors arrived on 23 December, John King had been instructed to take over the running of St Leo's, a parish on the south side of the city, whose own parish priest had recently suffered a heart attack. In January, Winning and King had two meetings, one alone and one in the company of Peter Smith, which were described by Smith as particularly tense. At one point, according to John King, Winning wished to know whom he would support, Watson or the Church, if the situation arose, and insisted he would be a 'dead duck'[3] if he supported 'Frances against the Church'.

During one meeting on 15 January, King, according to Winning, stated that the redundancy payment 'should never have happened', a statement King denied making. Winning was also insistent that he sign a statement agreeing that at no point was he given permission to create a legal entity, outside of the diocese, known as the Archdiocese of Glasgow Social Services Centre. King refused on the grounds that a legal document signed by Bishop Renfrew had already made this change (a point the archdiocese denied was possible since there were four trustees, none of whom, including Winning, could sign such a document on their own) and that he had acted at all times within his lawful authority. King would later defend his salary payments as an entitlement for a professional doing a professional job, and had he not factored in a lucrative salary his position would be difficult to fill with a lay person. John King's argument was that his salary was paid for by external agencies and never by the Church, and that the level of his pay was budgeted for and approved by the Strathclyde Regional Council and the Greater Glasgow Health Board. As Smith remembered, 'John had ambitions for the Church that maybe the Church did not have for itself.'

Winning was keen that King depart as quickly as possible to his family home in Ireland, before moving into a retreat house in Dublin for a period of reflection: a concern that was heightened by the news that a senior business reporter on *Scotland on Sunday* was pursuing the story of the diocesan debt, which had so far remained under wraps. After hearing rumours that the Catholic Church in Glasgow had debts comparable to Celtic Football Club, then standing at £7 million, Bob Wylie trawled Companies House, the repository of Scotland's business accounts, and located the companies set up by Watson and King to support the disabled and disadvantaged. When Wylie called Tom Connelly to request an interview and a set of accounts for the year ending 31 December 1991, he was informed by the press spokesman that as he was not a member of the Catholic Church he was ineligible to receive such information. This was a lie, as was Connelly's denial of any cash crisis, and after meeting briefly with Wylie, he passed the reporter on to Fr Noel Barry, who acted as Winning's personal press spokesman.

On Friday 15 January, Wylie met Barry in the offices of *Flourish*, on the second floor of Clyde Street. The pair were joined by John Rafferty whose presence, it was agreed by the reporter, would be 'off the record'. Wylie was told that an investigation was ongoing and no details were available as yet, but after he departed, Rafferty turned to Barry and said: 'He knows far too much.' The pair decided to approach Harry Conroy, a Catholic business journalist on the *Glasgow Herald*, and feed him the same story Wylie had uncovered, but spun in the Church's favour. Winning agreed and met Conroy on the morning of Saturday 16 January. Although they felt it was too late to avoid what they believed would be a ruinous front-page splash in *Scotland on Sunday*, Conroy's story, scheduled to appear on Monday 18 January, would provide balance. Fortunately Wylie's story was held back for further investigation and did not appear until the following Sunday. This was a lucky break as Sunday 17 January marked the official closure of the five hundredth anniversary celebrations of the diocese's founding with a Mass at St Andrew's Cathedral attended by a host of dignitaries including Luigi Barbarito, the Papal Nuncio. Winning was deeply embarrassed that the Church was foundering under his watch, and as he entertained the Nuncio that evening Noel Barry visited John King in an attempt to reason with him and ensure a quiet departure. King had said he would not discuss his future with Barry, only Winning. He thought Winning should have been aware of the difficulties he faced building up the social services.

John King finally agreed to resign all directorships on 20 January 1993, and vacated his ecclesiastical offices two days later on 22 January. In an attempt to redirect the blame from Winning, Peter Samson, a reporter on the *Sunday Mail*, was briefed on elements of King's role in the current crisis, which appeared under the headline 'Father King's Cash Muddle' on 24 January. So furious was King at his portrayal that he visited the newspaper's offices to remonstrate and sent a lawyer's letter to Winning threatening civil action if the accusations in the *Sunday Mail* were not retracted. On 26 January, an interesting letter appeared in the *Herald* newspaper which accused the archdiocese of being disingenuous by highlighting the problems with social services while ignoring the expenditure on the new curial offices, the final cost of which had never been revealed. 'Those of us who will be called upon to give yet more to the archdiocese must be reassured that we have a complete and accurate account of the financial position and that the archdiocese has got its priorities right.' On Sunday 31 January, a pastoral letter written by Winning and addressed to the people and priests was read out at every service, but it was neither reassuring nor entirely accurate. When explaining the reasons behind the debt, Winning once again ignored the offices and concentrated instead on the repayment costs of the Church building programme, repairs, care of sick and retired priests and the central administration costs of elements such as the pastoral plan and marriage tribunal. Social services was dispensed with in a few lines: 'More than any other area of activity the development of Church-delivered social services, caring for numerous people in need, including young homeless, the elderly, people with learning disabilities, and those suffering from drug-related problems, has proved to be a serious burden on archdiocesan finances.' Five years after he promised that fiscal responsibility would take root, he was forced, once again, to ask for an increase in donations.

If the public were disappointed, the clergy were irritated at the letter's tone which contained not a hint of apology or contrition. A number of priests told their parishioners that they would rather preach the gospel than read the letter and that afterwards they would make no comment, leaving them in no doubt as to their true feelings on the matter. That evening at around 11 p.m., one of them received a phone call from one of Winning's advisers, explaining that people were concerned by his attitude and that he would be advised to change it. The individual then abruptly hung up.

The following day, a brief press release was issued by the Catholic Press and Media Office announcing the resignations of Fr John King and Frances Watson:

MRS FRANCES WATSON

Following the recent financial and management review of the archdiocese of Glasgow, it has been decided that the post of administrator within the archdiocese is no longer required. This has resulted in Mrs Frances Watson leaving the service of both the diocese of Motherwell and the archdiocese of Glasgow.

FATHER JOHN KING

Following the review of administrative functions within the archdiocese of Glasgow, Father John King has resigned from his post as Vicar Episcopal for Pastoral Action.

Archbishop Winning has given Father King permission to take sabbatical leave. Archbishop Winning said: 'Father King brought tremendous vision and energy to the social services department of the archdiocese. In addition, during the past two years, he has been to the fore of the pastoral renewal programme. I wish to acknowledge this.'

On Wednesday 3 February, Winning tried once again to force King to return to Ireland. Monsignor James Clancy, the Vicar General, called him at St Leo's, with the message that if he did not travel home by the weekend the Archbishop would be obliged to make a 'clean breast of the whole thing'.[4] Clancy said he did not know what he meant by such a statement but that perhaps King would. King said he might choose to visit his mother, who was ill. In the event he moved in with a friend in Carmunnock, a Glasgow suburb, where he remained for three months before moving to London.

The most painful meetings in a schedule crammed with appointments with accountants and bank managers were two afternoons in late February, Monday 22nd and Tuesday 23rd, when Winning met with his priests. To clerical critics of Winning's Pastoral Plan, the current crisis was the end result of a turbulent decade, a Church broke, laity demoralized and a priest embarrassed. Prior to the meeting, Winning had asked Frank Cullen, the man he had marginalized and embarrassed, to accompany him and explain the debt's history. When Cullen agreed and asked how much he should reveal, Winning said: 'Everything. Tell them everything.' Accompanied by Tom O'Connell of Grant Thornton, Cullen talked through the growth of the debt. Winning was adamant that King was not responsible for the vast majority of the debt or that he was being presented as a scapegoat, but that there were questions over his behaviour.

When Winning came to speak he said:

Right from the very start of the year I have felt the need for you to hear something about the recent goings-on. Not out of curiosity but for the simple and yet most important reason that we are presbyterium, a community having given ourselves to the Church and the service of the people of God. In other words, I was feeling the possible loss of a brother priest – your brother too – and if you are feeling as I am there is a need to share something of this.

He then broke the talk down into facts and the reaction. When talking about the facts he claimed that there had been 'a deliberate policy of keeping from [him] knowledge of certain things', that it took an audit to uncover the truth, that there had been gross mismanagement by senior management. He then discussed the reaction of gossip, press reports and his own feelings of anger and sadness, but insisted he had taken steps to ensure that compassion tempered his reactions.

The money is one problem. The personalities involved are an even greater one. I feel greatly and deeply the loss of one of our presbyterium. I would feel the same about any of you. But I feel for you too and for the Church, that our family has been involved. I have done all that I can to cushion a period of distancing until this blows over. John King has great qualities that could be and were used by the Church. I think he needs our prayers and our compassion now. I have made available some ways of doing this.

He described feelings of 'anger, pain, hurt, helplessness, bewilderment, worthlessness, failure, depression, frustration'.

It was a testament to the nobility of the gathered priests that none of this speech was leaked to the press and that instead of rebelling against their archbishop, who had led them, through a combination of ignorance and generosity of trust, into the current predicament, they displayed a remarkable degree of solidarity. Had a majority or even a powerful minority displayed a lack of confidence in Winning and written to the Papal Nuncio or the Congregation of Bishops expressing such sentiments, he may have been removed. He certainly had no intention of resigning. While John Rafferty believed he was devastated by the debt and may have considered resignation,

Winning himself denied any such thoughts and Peter Smith insisted 'he would no more have resigned over this than flown in the air'. This was not to say he was not deeply depressed, but when cornered he preferred to fight, and so threw himself into the process of debt reduction.

As director of development, John Rafferty became unofficial 'director of debt'. The most senior figure in the archdiocese with a financial and management background, he worked, in cooperation with Grant Thornton, to develop a five-year plan of debt eradication. An early rule he set was that the diocese would not borrow another pound. The annual budget of £2.4 million was slashed by £700,000 to £1.7 million with the resulting loss of seventeen staff jobs. After a decade of condemning the Conservative government for rising unemployment, Winning was forced to add to the figure, but delegated the task to Peter Smith, who explained the situation to each person, while Winning sat in his office and stared into space. He later admitted he would have been unable to do the task himself. A second Sunday collection specifically for debt clearance was introduced in the hope of generating an extra £1 million per year, which would be used to tackle the current interest payments. Property sales were crucial to punching a sizeable hole in the debt, and on this occasion Frances Watson's behaviour was beneficial. In an attempt to reassure the banks she had revalued all the Church's property and entered into a development deal with the Walker Group that granted them rights to build homes on land sold. The four prime sites had the potential to accrue over £4 million. Winning was at first reluctant to authorize the sales, telling Brian Dempsey, who was also offering financial advice, that he was selling the family silver. Dempsey's approach was more pragmatic, telling him to sell the silver while he still had a family. There was, however, one property he would not countenance on the open market: The Oaks. John Rafferty argued that the sale of his luxury Arts and Crafts villa would be both a wonderful gesture and a further £200,000 wiped off the slate, but Winning had no desire to don sackcloth and ashes or to render himself homeless. He was unimpressed by Rafferty's alternative accommodation which included a lavish flat in St Theresa's in Possilpark, perhaps one of Glasgow's grimmest areas, or a penthouse on the fifth floor of the Clyde Street building.

If Winning was unwilling to endure personal hardship in order to reduce the debt, the ordinary people, or 'little people' as he would sometimes refer to them, were not above such endeavours. There is little doubt the Church in Glasgow and Winning's reputation were saved by the generosity of its Catholic citizens. There were individual incidents that broke his heart: an elderly woman arrived at the front office of Clyde Street with £743 in loose notes, her life savings; children brought in their piggy banks and a Clydebank woman posted a cheque for £27,982 and 38 pence, the proceeds of her house sale. The second collection averaged £110,000 per month and exceeded £500,000 by June, when Winning issued a second pastoral letter in which he admitted to being 'humbled' by the response, but urged them 'not to weaken in their efforts'. A stronger diocesan finance committee was set up to rigorously police the new era of prudence, while a sub-committee led by Professor A. L. Brown monitored each department's spending on a week-by-week basis.

A portrait of Thomas Winning in the autumn of 1993 would reveal a man tortured by opportunities lost. The Pastoral Plan, a decade on, had failed to take root, the diocese was deeply in debt, and his archbishopric was teetering on the edge of disgrace. In September a rumour swept through parish houses that he was to be punished for the crisis with the appointment of Clarence Gallagher, a Glasgow Jesuit, then rector of the Oriental University in Rome, as coadjutor archbishop. Though the rumour proved to be false, the *Herald* diary took the opportunity to suggest Winning's redeployment to the Vatican as Keeper of the Sacred Penitentiaries or, as they wrote, 'the chap whose job is to raise cash through the sale of indulgences'. A sense of entropy had entered his career, a perception exacerbated by the death in July of Cardinal Gordon Gray. On a personal level Winning was greatly saddened, for he had been increasingly fond of the old man, often visiting him in Edinburgh for advice or to rest in his garden and think. A few days after his death, Winning released a statement that in retrospect was more applicable to himself than his subject:

> When the history of the Scottish Catholic community in the second half of the twentieth century comes to be written, Cardinal Gordon Gray will shine out as a giant of the Christian faith. A Scot to the very core of his being, his pride in the people of this country was mirrored by his fidelity to the gospel and by his keen loyalty to the Holy Father. Despite the high office he achieved he never lost the common touch. He was a much-loved father figure, a pastor graced with enormous sensitivity, and widely appreciated for his humanity, humility and prudence. Gordon Joseph Gray was a man of faith and therefore a man of the people.

On a professional level, the demise of Scotland's cardinal triggered a fresh bout of 'scarlet fever' and where once Winning had been the only reasonable candidate in 1985 when Gray retired, the new Archbishop of St Andrews and Edinburgh, Keith O'Brien, now offered stiff opposition. The resident senior cleric of Scotland's capital, O'Brien had kept the diocese on an even keel while Winning believed his current problems would count against him.

In March 1993, John Patrick King had his faculties as a priest of the archdiocese of Glasgow withdrawn by Winning, preventing him from publicly celebrating Mass. He left shortly afterwards to pursue a new career in London, where he currently works as a barrister. No further action was taken against either King or Frances Watson, as Winning was anxious to avoid the appearance of public scandal. A decade after the debt, Winning still insisted, rather incredibly and arrogantly, that he bore no responsibility for the fiasco. 'I trusted these people. If there was something wrong they should have come to see me. I don't blame myself.' Yet in the final analysis he must shoulder a heavy proportion of the blame. He blithely transferred the trust earned by Frank Cullen through twenty years of diligent service over to Frances Watson, a woman he scarcely knew, and he ignored concerns about John King. Aware of a debt of £4 million, he ignored it, only giving it his attention when the figure had doubled. Winning deserves praise for the assured manner in which he doggedly tackled the debt, which was finally wiped clean in five years, but the legacy was another wedge between his priests and the added disappointment of his people. A bond of trust had snapped, one which would prove difficult to retie. A decade later, Frances Watson said she was made a scapegoat to protect Winning's chances of securing a red hat. 'Tom Winning was truly a man with feet of clay. Don't put your trust in Kings and Princes, especially not Princes of the Church.'

The names of Frances Watson and John King would become linked, within the archdiocesan offices, to the diocesan debt. This was as much through Winning's slight of hand as by their own unfortunate behaviour. By focusing so much attention on his staff's shortcomings, the archbishop directed warranted attention from his own. In the final judgement, Thomas Winning had been blind to his responsibilities and would survive only through overdrawing copiously from his parishioners' bank of generosity and goodwill.

The Cardinal Years

FIFTEEN

The Red Hat

'I would say that Archbishop Winning's instinct is to look at a glass and see it as half empty, while I would see it as half full.'

BISHOP JOSEPH DEVINE

The red hat of a cardinal held a powerful allure for Thomas Winning. So strong were his ambitions that in the wake of the diocesan debt, when the current that previously seemed destined to wash it to within his grasp began to ebb away, he took to praying each night for the strength to cope with such a disappointment. Ever since Gordon Gray had retired in 1984, stories had circulated that his appointment was imminent, and on more than one occasion a fellow bishop called for his elevation. In 1985, Mario Conti, the Bishop of Aberdeen, while addressing a public meeting of SCIAF (the Scottish Catholic International Aid Fund), said in reference to the red hat: 'It's about time that something was happening to Archbishop Winning.'[1] But the aftermath of Gray's death saw Winning doubt his credibility for such a role and prepare instead for the indignity of being overlooked. His preparation for what he feared would be a public embarrassment began with a deliberate attempt to block thoughts of promotion, a practice he combined with frequent prayers for the grace to accept whatever the Pope's choice might be.

'At the time of the debt, there was a voice amongst others that said "Winning has made a hell of a mess of this, and therefore he is no good at administration and that will leave him out of the running for a red hat. On the other hand, he *is* the senior bishop in Scotland, and if he doesn't get it, it would be a slap in the face to him." I said: "What am I going to do? Am I going to worry day in and day out? Why the hell should I?" So I put it on this level: I am totally indifferent as to whether it comes or doesn't – if it comes, I will welcome it, but if it doesn't, please God, don't make me feel insulted or let down.'

In search of distraction, he turned his focus on the Conservative government of John Major, whose policies he had watched unveiled at the 1993 party conference with an increasing degree of incredulity. From Peter Lilley's proclamation of having a list of girls who got pregnant to secure a council flat, to Michael Portillo's hijacking of the SAS motto 'Who Dares Wins', each new announcement against the unemployed, the single parent and the disadvantaged served to stoke up his anger. The only respite was reading extracts from Margaret Thatcher's memoir *The Downing Street Years*, published that autumn, in which the former Prime Minister admitted that criticism by Catholic and Protestant Churches in Scotland had caused her considerable damage; a comment which inspired a fresh round of Winning's invective. An invitation to address a service of thanksgiving to celebrate the tenth anniversary of the founding of Shelter, the homeless charity, at St Giles's Cathedral in Edinburgh provided Winning with the opportunity to climb into the pulpit and tackle the government head on. He was to call for the creation of a Royal Commission to investigate poverty in Scotland which he believed had intensified after fourteen years of Tory 'misrule', but for Winning to ask politely was anathema to his character and a lesson he would never learn. Prior to his address, he gave an interview to the political editor of *Scotland on Sunday*, Kenny Farquharson, in which he hinted that to vote for the Conservatives was incompatible with the possession of a Christian conscience. 'Jesus Christ came to bring good news to the poor, but the Tory party has come to bring bad news to the poor.'[2] In a partisan statement he said Scotland had 'chickened out' by not voting overwhelmingly against the Conservative Party in the 1992 General Election. He asked the government to 'attack poverty and not the poor', and pointed out how multinational companies escaped adequate Inland Revenue payments while those who fiddled their social security benefits to survive were prosecuted. 'The Home and Health department, as far as I'm concerned, is riddled with ideas and values that are totally against the Christian values.'

In his speech, Winning criticized what he saw as a new selfishness that had infected society, a 'hardness of heart' which he felt was unworthy of the Scottish nation. He asked for the launch of a Royal Commission, focusing his attention on Lord James Douglas Hamilton, the Housing minister, who was representing the government in the front pews. After the service, Winning and Hamilton shook hands but there was little actual agreement. One Conservative MP accused Winning of causing offence to Roman Catholic Conservatives, but the Archbishop was praised by the *Herald*, which insisted: 'Churchmen cannot be expected to give anodyne weasel-worded sermons for fear of causing offence to politicians.' 'Amen to that,' trumpeted the *Daily Record*. In the opinion of Sir Nicholas Fairbairn, Winning was a 'left-wing socialist', but was he successful? On this occasion, he was not. Five days after his request for a Royal Commission, Winning received a reply from Lord James Douglas Hamilton in which he insisted such an investigation would be both impractical and time-consuming.

In private, the Conservative Party in Scotland were both weary and wary of Winning. For the entire duration of their government, the Archbishop had been a formidable foe, criticizing senior ministers and drubbing their public policy. Now the party wished to move past his hulking form and promote a more empathetic voice in Scottish Catholicism, that of Bishop Joseph Devine. The current battleground was the reorganization of the Local Government (Scotland) Bill, which would see twenty-nine single-tier councils replacing fifty-three district and nine regional councils. The Catholic Church was concerned that reorganization would affect Catholic schools, in particular pupils who fell outside their old catchment area who could lose their automatic right to a school place. What

Winning wanted was a guarantee protecting the catchment areas of Catholic schools and the provision of free transport across the redrawn boundaries, and to achieve his goal, he marshalled his favourite tactics, a voice of concern followed by one of stern condemnation. In order to track the progress of the bill and lobby on the Church's behalf Noel Barry was despatched to London to attend the select committee meetings and to speak with Labour MPs. The second approach was to motivate the Catholic population of Scotland to man the barricades in defence of their schools. A pastoral letter from the Bishops' Conference was issued to be read at every Mass on 6 February 1994, in which the bill was described as 'ill-considered' and the laity were urged to write to their MP to express their concern. Ten days later, on 16 February, Winning attended an hour-long meeting at Whitehall with Lord James Douglas Hamilton, who was also the education minister, to discuss the Church's concern. To avoid any potential grandstanding or media bullying, the government requested that any press comment be restricted to an agreed statement and the meeting closed with just the hint of progress.

In fact, the government had every intention of acquiescing to the Church's concerns, but no intention of providing Winning with the triumph. Instead, they were grooming a more congenial recipient of their largesse. As Ian Lang (Secretary of State for Scotland) explained, it was a matter of choosing an appropriate partner:

> Cardinal Winning had a lot of misperceptions about the Conservative Party and he said a lot of critical things that were ill-founded because he was not fully aware of the political facts. Bishop Devine, by contrast, had an inclination to give us the benefit of the doubt. We were not picking sides, nor were we choosing a route that was congenial to us; we simply saw an open door and therefore were prepared to go through it.

Bishop Devine, however, argued that the Conservative Party constructed the door. He was visited by Gerry O'Brien, a former director of communications for the Scottish Conservative and Unionist

Party, who was now head of public relations for Scottish Enterprise, the government's development agency. During their meeting, O'Brien hinted that the Church could benefit by scratching the Tories' back during a forthcoming visit by John Major. 'He said: "You're going to do yourself a favour if you write something that is kind of favourable",' said Devine. The Bishop, who held Conservative sympathies, agreed to write an article, pegged to the Prime Minister's visit to Motherwell, which praised the government's regeneration of the town since the closure in 1992 of the Ravenscraig steel works. After passing the completed article to O'Brien, he was called up and told that the Prime Minister's visit was to remain confidential for security purposes and if the article were published the visit would be cancelled. O'Brien made an alternative proposition: could Devine give an interview favourable to the government? Again Devine agreed, and O'Brien arranged for William Clark, a political correspondent with the *Herald*, to meet the bishop in Motherwell. The auspicious day was Ash Wednesday, and while Winning was in London speaking with Lord James Douglas Hamilton, his former auxiliary bishop was praising Major's Back-to-Basics policy as having 'a lot going for it' and 'a lot more right with it than is ever wrong'. Clark then began to probe the difference between Winning and his former auxiliary bishop, to which Devine responded:

'I would say that Archbishop Winning's instinct is to look at a glass and see it as half empty, while I would see it as half full. It has a lot to do with the characteristics of each of us. I am not saying that the Archbishop preaches a different message; it is just that we have a different way of presenting it. My instinct is a gentler approach, and maybe not an unfair approach. I look at reality and judge it according to conscience.'[3]

Devine was later told by O'Brien that the newspaper was to hold the interview to run on Friday, the day of Major's Scottish visit, when the Prime Minister would attend a large dinner at the Hilton Hotel in Glasgow. The Bishop had also agreed to attend on the grounds that 'there would be a lot of Catholics there and they had never seen one of us there'. On Friday morning, as Winning was raging at his comments, now splashed on the front page of the *Herald*, Devine travelled to the Scottish Office in Edinburgh for a long-scheduled meeting with Lord Peter Fraser, the minister for Home Affairs. The reason for the meeting was never disclosed, and, as a result, led to the belief shared by Mgr Tom Connelly and Fr Noel Barry and, through them, the Scottish press, that Devine had launched a covert mission to lobby for Catholic schools.

The reality was that Devine was lobbying on an entirely different matter. For the past year, the hierarchy had been attempting to have a senior Scottish Catholic appointed to the House of Lords to fulfil a function similar to that of the Duke of Norfolk, who for decades had represented the interests of the Bishops' Conference of England and Wales. While the Duke was always willing to assist the Scots, he had recently suffered a stroke which threatened his capabilities. Meanwhile, Winning had grown weary of playing second fiddle to the English bishops and wished to see his own man in the House. The issue had first been raised with Chris Patten, then Chairman of the Conservative Party, during a private lunch arranged by Gerry O'Brien with the bishops at Scotus College, and although he warmed to the idea and agreed to support their suggestion in Westminster, he directed them first to the Scottish Office.

Devine's meeting on Friday 18 February was to discuss a potential candidate, nominated by the Bishops' Conference, but deemed too old by the government. 'You'll only have to start the whole thing again in a few years' time,' explained a civil servant to Devine. The issue of the Local Government (Scotland) Bill was raised only in the last few minutes of the meeting, when Devine asked if, having had their candidate rejected, the Church might fare better with their proposed amendments. Lord Fraser then explained that he could guarantee that he would have them the following week. When Devine said it was unnecessary to send them to him, but proper to pass them to Archbishop Winning, he was told: 'I think we prefer to do it this way.' Devine was aware that the government was attempting to implement a policy of 'divide and conquer' but that what mattered most was the end result. At dinner that evening, Devine sat to the left of John Major, who thanked him for his comments in the *Herald* and said, 'You have been very helpful and I think we can be helpful in return.'

Winning was less than grateful for Devine's assistance to the government and had smarted at the bishop's description of him, which he viewed as a break in the ranks. 'I wasn't angry,' recalled Winning, though both Connelly and Barry insisted he was furious. 'I was sad that Joe had suggested that we were all that different and I thought going to the dinner was bad, but I didn't say anything. He was being manipulated by the Tory party.' When Devine told him over the weekend that the Church was likely to secure their goal, Winning was unconvinced. Despite Devine's repeated requests that any communication with the government be copied to Winning, a faxed letter agreeing to the amendments and signed by Lord James Douglas Hamilton arrived at Devine's office in Motherwell at 3.30 p.m. on the following Wednesday. Devine immediately faxed it on to Tom Connelly with instructions that it be forwarded to Hugh Farmer, editor of the *Scottish Catholic Observer*, who, having been tipped off by the bishop that good news was imminent, had literally held the front page. Devine then left his office to chair a meeting of BBC Scotland's religious advisory board and returned at 10 p.m. to the news that the statement had not been released.

A collective decision had been taken by Winning, Connelly and Barry to suppress the statement on the grounds that it contained errors. Their true concern was that Devine would receive the unearned credit, to which goal the government's spin doctors were already working. The Church might have refused to release the statement, but the government had no such compunction and with it came a series of off-the-record briefings that the amendments were secured not by Winning's 'shouting and bawling' but by Devine's 'constructive remarks'. As Connelly and Barry were both unaware of the nature of Devine's visit to Edinburgh the previous Friday, they concluded, just as the bishop said later, that he 'had gone through to Edinburgh behind the Archbishop's back to negotiate about education'.

Winning did not enjoy the theft of his thunder and so called a meeting with Devine on Saturday 26 February. Tom Connelly, who attended along with Noel Barry, said that for the first few minutes Winning was furious with Devine and began to accuse him of being uncharitable towards him in the press and meddling in politics. Devine denied this account and only when, after Barry and Connelly had been asked to leave the room he explained to Winning that the reason for his visit to the Scottish Office was to further their clandestine attempts to promote a Scottish Catholic Lord, did the Archbishop calm down.

As Winning battled to secure his due credit, it was left to Hugh Farmer, deprived of his front page on account of the Church's internal wrangling, to point out the identity of the true heroes. On the front page of the *Scottish Catholic Observer*, he strung the headline: 'Media Office Denies Readers Information' and pointed out that: 'It is the people, who responded to the appeal of their bishops and wrote to their MPs over the school issue, who must now feel aggrieved.' Winning treated what was a valid article with disdain and fired back a response so wildly over the top as to be humorous were it not for its seriousness. In a letter marked 'not for publication' he wrote: 'I wish you to know that, in more than forty-five years as a priest and a bishop, I have never seen such a profound disservice to the Catholic Church in Scotland as that on the front page of the *Scottish Catholic Observer* today.'

According to Winning, Gerry O'Brien arrived at The Oaks a few weeks later to apologize and explain how the government had attempted to blackball him. O'Brien, however, insisted that he had nothing for which to apologize and had arrived simply to defend Bishop Devine's conduct and point out that he was the victim of a smear campaign by Barry and Connelly. There is little doubt that the government made a deliberate attempt to sideline Winning and promote Devine as a credible alternative, but it was a scheme doomed to failure. As an archbishop, Winning already outranked Devine, a distance in status that would only increase.

*　　*　　*

The Red Hat

In the autumn of 1994, Pope John Paul II was of a mind to create a new Scottish cardinal. As an independent nation, though one bound within the British union, Scotland might deserve its own red hat, but history tends to disappoint such expectations. Unlike the archdiocese of Westminster, neither Glasgow nor Edinburgh had been designated as a diocese that automatically entitled the incumbent to elevation to the College of Cardinals. Edinburgh may have been the last recipient and the country's capital, but many within the Church put the promotion of Gordon Gray down to his personal friendship with Paul VI rather than a bestowal of a badge of superiority to the city's dwindling number of Catholics. The first to know of the Pope's intentions was not Thomas Winning or Keith O'Brien, but a priest a great deal lower down the pecking order. A Glasgow priest who was in Rome that autumn was asked to contact a senior official at a prominent Vatican department. After he was escorted past the Swiss Guard into the Vatican City and walked to the offices of the department, he exchanged pleasantries before the official explained the reason for his invitation. 'The Pope is minded to introduce a new Scottish cardinal, but he can't make up his mind between Keith O'Brien and Tom Winning.'

The retirement of Gordon Gray in 1985 was followed by the appointment of Keith O'Brien, then rector of St Mary's College, Blairs, to the archbishopric of St Andrews and Edinburgh. Born in Ballycastle, County Antrim, O'Brien moved to Scotland as a child and was ordained a priest for the archdiocese of Edinburgh in 1965, after first attending the city's university. As Archbishop, one of his earliest victories over Winning was to maintain a seminary on the east coast in the face of the Glasgow archbishop's desire to consolidate a national seminary in the west following the closure of Blairs. Gillis College in Edinburgh was founded in September 1986 but lasted just seven years before closing with the inevitable transfer of students to Scotus College, outside Glasgow.

The Vatican was in a dilemma and, anxious to secure the right man for the post, had embarked on a series of secret soundings. 'Personally, I have lots of reasons not to speak too highly of Tom Winning, but he is able,' the priest told a Vatican official. 'It would be a terrible upset if it went to O'Brien.' Back on the streets, the priest was under no illusion that he had secured the title for Glasgow. He had said no more than any reasonable, astute observer of Scottish Catholic affairs, but within the next few weeks, as Winning celebrated his appointment, he would reflect on how close the pendulum had swung towards the nation's capital.

Winning was never to discover if his fervent prayers had accumulated the necessary grace to cope with disappointment. On the morning of Wednesday 26 October, he had wandered down from his study in The Oaks to the basement kitchen to fetch a cup of tea. Mrs McInnes had departed the previous day to South Africa for a holiday, and as he stood waiting for the kettle to boil, the phone rang. When he picked it up, he recognized the accent and heavy wheeze of Archbishop Barbarito.

'Can I speak to the Archbishop of Glasgow?'

'It's me, the housekeeper is away.'

'Are you alone?'

'Sure – I'm just making a cup of tea.'

'The Pope has decided to make you a cardinal.'

The brevity and directness of the exchange winded Winning so much that he sat down, and barely listened as the nuncio offered his congratulations then explained that his advice to the Vatican had been that Glasgow and Edinburgh should take turns in hosting the red hat. The official announcement would be made by the Pope in four days' time and, although sworn to secrecy, Winning was permitted two exceptions, Frs Peter Smith and Tom Connelly, who would help with the preparations. Winning's emotions were both proud and poignant.

'I felt stunned, not emotional, I didn't cry. My main emotion was for the Church, for the diocese and for Scotland. I began to think of how proud my mother and father would be if they were alive. How proud my family would be now.'

Winning was to spend the remainder of the day alone and in silence, sitting in a chair in his oratory, as he allowed waves of relief and gratitude to break over him. The doubts that had niggled and rubbed like a grain of sand in an oyster had produced a pearl. After so much recent disappointment and distress he was now to join the elite of the Church, a body of one hundred and twenty men, whose number made kings and queens ordinary by their ubiquity. The son of an illegitimate miner was to become a prince of the Church.

The following day, Winning broke the news to Peter Smith, his chancellor, in a manner that diminished his own accomplishment: 'The red hat is coming to Glasgow.' As Smith recalled, 'I always remember that it was the city that was being rewarded as much as it was the man.' The two men then embraced. The planning for Sunday's announcement got underway once Tom Connelly was also inside the circle of trust. A notable absentee from Winning's confidence over the matter was Fr Noel Barry, his press secretary. Despite the fact that as editor of *Flourish* he would benefit most by being informed as soon as possible, Winning believed that if news of his appointment leaked, Barry would be the source. There is no evidence that Barry, if sworn to secrecy by Winning, would not have maintained the confidence, particularly as any leak would be readily traceable to himself. However, Winning's decision not to take him into his confidence is interesting in the light of the later collapse of their working relationship.

Instead, Barry and members of Winning's family were left to wonder what possessed Winning to invite them for Sunday lunch on the strict understanding that they arrive before eleven o'clock, a time at which breakfast was barely digested. When Barry arrived on Sunday 30 October and cornered Winning to ask him what the hell was going on, he was told with a poker face that the Archbishop was to announce his retirement. As the Pope announced from the balcony overlooking St Peter's Square his plans to create thirty new cardinals, Winning, standing in front of the fireplace, said he would be one of them.

Among the first to know was the Lord Provost of Glasgow. Winning, conscious of the city's new honour, had instructed a messenger to deliver a sealed envelope on the dot of eleven o'clock. In the press office, Tom Connelly began to fax the nation's media. Their response was as exhilarating as the blizzard of congratulatory faxes that began to pour into the archdiocesan offices. James Shield, the Lord Provost, urged him not to lose his 'common touch'; Ian Lang, Secretary of State for Scotland, received the news with 'great pleasure'; Basil Hume declared himself 'very pleased' and Cardinal Cahal Daly, the Archbishop of Armagh, praised him as a 'very good friend of Ireland'. Yet the message which most closely mirrored Winning's own interpretation of his honour was extended by Cardinal Eduardo Marinez Somalo who said it was 'the ultimate proof of confidence which the Holy Father has given you'.

The College of Cardinals is often described as the 'most exclusive club in the world' on the grounds that for centuries there were rarely more than fifty recipients of the title. The position arose through the growth of the Catholic Church in Rome, where the term 'cardinal' was used to describe a cleric 'incardinated' to a new position: these were men chosen as the brightest and best to run the city's social services, and on the grounds of their intelligence, were quickly drawn upon as advisers to the Pope. A second tier of cardinal priests were charged with running the diocese and churches of Rome and as the Church grew, so inevitably did their power. In Latin 'cardo' means 'hinge', and it was upon these men that the Church swung. Only a cardinal could vote in a papal election, and while technically any Catholic male could be picked as pope, in reality he was always drawn from their own scarlet pool. For centuries, the position of cardinal existed only within Rome and it was not until the papacy of Leo XI in the eleventh century that senior prelates in foreign lands were afforded the title. The Scots had to wait four hundred years before the Vatican got round to bestowing the title upon one of their own: David Beaton, the Archbishop of St Andrews and Edinburgh, who would later be murdered by Protestant reformers, was the recipient in the sixteenth century. 'From Beaton to Winning', the new cardinal would joke, but others lay in between. In the eighteenth century, the younger brother of Bonnie Prince Charlie, Henry Benedict Maria Clement Stuart, was appointed Cardinal Duke of York, although he spent his entire career in Rome as the Cardinal Bishop of Frascati. In the post-Reformation era, both Cardinals Gray and Heard were Scots-born, with the latter spending his entire career in the curia. It was not to these men to whom Winning turned his thoughts in search of guidance and inspiration, but to characters such as Charles Borromeo, the Cardinal Archbishop of Milan, an ardent reformer during what Winning described as an 'age of mediocrity and turbulence', John Henry Newman, former Cardinal Archbishop of Westminster, and Henry de Lubac, who, as a progressive theologian in the Fifties, fell out of favour with Pius XII. As Winning wrote in a private note: 'You can walk tall in such company.'

The consistory took place on 26 November and for a few days under the warm winter sun the Eternal City fell into the possession of the Scots. Of the thirty cardinals drawn from around the globe to receive their red hats, no country delivered as many pilgrims as did Scotland. Over 1,500 flew to Rome from across Scotland, Ireland and even Canada, from where one émigré from Motherwell travelled in support of her former parish priest. At the gate to greet each incoming flight of followers was Winning himself, cracking jokes, dispensing hugs and handshakes, and even hoisting luggage from the carousel. Brian Dempsey, the prominent Catholic businessman, had paid for twenty-two return flights for members of Winning's family and other invited guests, but had declined to attend himself. A second supporter had agreed to pay for Winning's new robes, purchased a few days before the ceremony at Gammarelli, the finest clerical outfitters in Rome.

For the duration of Winning's stay, he was ensconced, together with Smith, Barry and Connelly, in a suite at the Regina Hotel. On the evening prior to the ceremony, Winning returned, footsore and weary after a day acting as tour guide for his family, and chose to soak in the room's sunken whirlpool bath. In a scene reminiscent of the bumptious Bishop Brenan in the television series *Father Ted*, he decided to add an exceedingly generous dose of bubble bath, which combined with the vigour of the whirlpool proceeded to fill the entire room in soapy bubbles to the extent that he was unable to find his slippers.

At 10.37 a.m. the following morning in the Vatican's audience hall, the opening words of the ceremony were sung by the Sistine choir: '*Exsultate iusti in Domino*' . . . Rejoice ye just in the Lord. In a central chair sat the Pope, bowed down by the crippling effects of Parkinson's disease and wrapped in a gold and silk cape. He pronounced in Latin: 'With the authority of God Almighty, of the Holy Apostles Peter and Paul, and our own authority, we create and solemnly proclaim to be cardinals of the Holy Roman Church, the following brothers of ours . . .' In a list of thirty names, drawn from twenty-four different countries and including a former window cleaner, the name of 'Thomam Iosephum Winning, Archiepiscopus Glasguensis' was the eighth name called and the one greeted by the loudest of cheers. As Winning approached, wearing a white surplice with a red mozetta, he kissed the Pope before bowing as the red biretta was placed on his head and the Holy Father spoke:

> To the glory of God Almighty and for the good of the Apostolic See, receive the red biretta as a sign of the dignity of a cardinal, as a reminder that you must be ready to act with renewed vigour, up to the point of shedding your own blood, for the Christian faith, for the peace and tranquillity of the people of God and the spread of the Holy Roman Catholic Church.

Winning kept any display of emotion for the final Mass of a long and memorable pilgrimage. On Wednesday 30 November, the feast of St Andrew, the new cardinal took charge of his titular Church, a tradition stretching back centuries in which each cardinal is given his own church in Rome. To Winning the venue was charged with history. The gift of the Basilica of Sant' Andrea delle Fratte saw the restoration of a link to Scotland that started in the holy year of 1450 when the church began setting aside beds for visiting Scottish pilgrims. It is rumoured that Bishop Turnbull, the founder of Glasgow University, lies buried in the grounds. As he processed through the church to kiss a wooden cross offered to him by the parish priest, Winning was struck by the splendour of the church's golden baroque basilica, decorated by marble angels designed by Bernini and complemented by a marvellous vision of Our Lady. After the Mass, he was close to tears when he spoke to the gathered pilgrims:

> To all of you, and all those who have had to go home already, this has been a great event. It has been an experience of faith which has given us greater depth in our commitment to Jesus Christ, and allowed us to catch glimpses of the real origins of Christ's words, Christ's gospel. Your encouragement and support, and your great welcome here, has been overwhelming.[4]

Turning to the priests who had accompanied him, he said: 'I cannot find the words to say what I feel', and gesturing to his new cardinal's ring, he added: 'This will not make a difference to me, and I hope it does not make one to you in our relationships.' The event closed with a presentation by his grand-niece and -nephew of an Italian cut-glass fish reflecting the legend of St Mungo, Glasgow's patron saint. Outside, as everyone prepared to leave, a lone piper played 'Auld Lang Syne'.

The sexual abuse of children and young teenagers by priests, a stain that has spread throughout the world over the last fifteen years, came to dominate the first two years of Winning's cardinalate, rearing its monstrous head before he had time to don his red hat. Winning had personal experience of the problem, which a decade or so ago would have been considered unbelievable and which was now reaching the public consciousness with a string of gruesome cases documented in Australia, America and Ireland. Like a row of dominoes, one tipping over the other, the crimes in Scotland were uncovered after Ireland's own sins were revealed. In the middle of November 1994, just as Winning was preparing to depart for Rome, Albert Reynolds, the Irish Prime Minister, resigned and his coalition government collapsed over revelations that they had dragged their feet in the extradition to Northern Ireland of a priest accused of sexual abuse. Father Brendan Smyth, who had been sent home from Scotland in the 1950s 'in disgrace', had spent thirty-five years sexually abusing a string of young children, crimes for which he was eventually sentenced to four years' imprisonment. The focus on Ireland and the subject of 'paedophile priests', as they were becoming known, made Brian Groom, the editor of *Scotland on Sunday*, re-evaluate the newsworthiness of a recent interview Winning had given to Victoria Streatfield, a freelance journalist hired by the paper to investigate Church finances. In a long interview on 9 November, principally on the subject of finance, Streatfield had touched on the issue of abusive priests and had asked Winning if he would report such a man to the police. Winning said he would not. 'I would pursue him as we have done in the past until he agreed to look for help . . . Yes, it's a criminal offence, yes, but I'm not going to inform the police about that man. Let someone else do it.' When contacted by the paper to clarify his position he stated:

I would investigate the situation and I would remove the person from that situation so that they would not have any more opportunities. I'm not going to go and start dealing with the police. It's the people who are connected with the victim who do that. But I would talk to the parents. I would get some therapy for the child. There is no way I would countenance injustice. There is no way I would be allowing it to take place without doing something about it. There is no way I would be trying to cover up or keep anybody from justice.

On 20 November, *Scotland on Sunday* ran a small front-page story, linked to a larger feature on the Irish crisis, which used Winning's comments and was headlined: 'I Wouldn't Shop Paedophile Priest, Says Winning', a story to which he reacted with apoplexy and the uncharacteristic threat of both legal action and a formal complaint to the Press Complaints Commission. It was a curious response, as at no point did he retract his view or argue that it had been maliciously manipulated, only that it had been lifted out of the context of an interview on finance. In an unguarded moment he had expressed his honest opinion and, at the time, that of the Church. While Winning would be sympathetic to the victim, the responsibility to inform the authorities remained theirs and their family's; his was to support and seek assistance for his priest as he had quietly done in the past. In 1980, Winning had arranged for a priest, Fr Alan Love, to relocate – first to America for treatment, and then, eventually, to the English archdiocese of Arundel and Brighton – after he admitted the 'sexual' and 'inappropriate touching' of two young boys while a priest in two Glasgow parishes. Although charged with 'lewd and libidinous behaviour' by Strathclyde police, the case was not pursued by the procurator fiscal, and after appropriate treatment in America, he took up a new position in an English parish under the supervision of Cormac Murphy-O'Connor, then Bishop of Arundel and Brighton, now the Cardinal Archbishop of Westminster. Love left the priesthood in 1995. (Six years later, Cardinal Murphy-O'Connor would be heavily criticized over an incident involving a different priest who had been found to be abusive but whom he had allowed to operate as chaplain to Gatwick Airport, where he had abused again.) In 1994, Winning's attitude to the sexual abuse of children by priests was one of both horror and disgust but tinged with compassion for the perpetrator, whom he viewed as being in the grip of a destructive malady. Lacking today's universal understanding of paedophiles as incorrigible serial offenders, he believed, wrongly, in offering priests a second chance under a veil of secrecy but nevertheless under strict supervision. Even Winning's claim to a lack of knowledge of the condition is deeply questionable, considering the slowly increasing profile of child-abusers in the media during the 1980s. It is a disturbing and regrettable stance that Winning, like so many Church leaders before and since, would put protection of the Church before that of a child. In a long letter which *Scotland on Sunday* agreed to publish to avoid legal action, Winning clarified his position and pointed out the Church's role:

Whatever the specific circumstances of any case which may arise, and however it may have to be tackled, this much is true: paedophilia is always wrong but it also always involves broken people, innocent as well as guilty, and the specific task of the Church when faced with such brokenness is always to assist in the lengthy process of healing.

Honesty is a crucial ingredient in healing and one in short supply when concerning the Church and abusive priests. In the original article the Catholic Church, through Tom Connelly, had stated that there was no evidence of a priest being involved in abuse – a statement Winning knew to be false, as also did one infuriated reader, Michael X, a married father of two: as a student at Blairs junior seminary, he had repeatedly been abused by two priests between 1973 and 1975, incidents which he had brought to the attention of the hierarchy. On three occasions over the past twenty years he had contacted the Church with concerns that his abuser, Fr Desmond Lynagh (a second priest accused of abuse, Fr Frank Kennedy, had since died), still had access to young children. A few days after the article appeared, he approached Mgr James Clancy, now Vicar General of Glasgow archdiocese, who had been the priest at Blairs to whom he had turned initially. Unsatisfied by Clancy's explanation of how such a statement could be made, he approached both the police and the press to reveal the full extent of the Church's cover-up. At the age of fourteen, Michael had spoken to Clancy and Fr John McIntyre, the college's master of discipline, about the abuse. Under a 'gentleman's agreement' Lynagh was removed from the college and the student continued his studies, but three years later, while at St Peter's College in Glasgow, he abandoned his training and informed his parents and college rector of his abuse. While the victim and his parents wanted Lynagh removed from his then current position as chaplain at Stirling University, and also from the priesthood, they were told that Cardinal Gray would take appropriate action when he returned from the conclaves of 1978. Gray, however, did nothing. Twelve years later, when Michael discovered that Lynagh was still operating as a parish priest in Stirling, he contacted his superior, Archbishop Keith O'Brien, who in an extraordinary turn of events paid him £42,000 in compensation for his abuse, but refused to remove Lynagh from the priesthood. Instead, the priest was despatched for a course of therapy at the Gracewell Clinic in Birmingham, run by Ray Wyre, a counsellor who specialized in the treatment of sex offenders. Upon his return, he was given an administrative job within the archdiocese and asked to sign a document declaring that he would never work with children again. Following the publicity Lynagh was charged, and in June 1996 sentenced to three years' imprisonment.

The revelation of Michael's treatment and increased media attention on the issue prompted the Bishops' Conference to fast-track plans to re-examine their approach to child safety and, in January 1995, a Working Party on child safety was set up to develop new guidelines and restore public confidence. The chairman of the Working Party was Alan Draper, the retired deputy director of Stockport's social work department who was joined on the eight-strong party by John Mone, Bishop of Paisley, Des Browne, who would later become Labour MP for Kilmarnock, Professor Anthony Busuttil, a pathologist at Edinburgh University, Martin Henry, a social work manager in Edinburgh, and two religious sisters, Mary Ross and Sister Breda O'Sullivan, who ran a treatment unit at Solihull. Child sexual abuse, though prevalent throughout society for centuries, had always remained hidden and only in the previous few decades had such practices come to light in the caring professions. The concept of ordained 'men of God' perpetrating such acts on small children was deemed unthinkable and so they were protected under an umbrella of trust. Clusters of cases in America, Canada, Australia and now Ireland, Scotland, England and Wales had opened society's eyes to an unsightly truth. At the time of the Working Party's formation, research into abusive priests was extremely limited and exclusively American; by 1992, four hundred priests had been accused of abusive behaviour, costing the Church its reputation and over $700 million in damages. A second explosion of cases in 2002 would throw the American Church once again into crisis and lead directly to the resignation of Cardinal Bernard Law of Boston. In three academic reports, published between 1990 and 1995, the percentage of priests sexually involved with minors was gauged at between 3 and 10 per cent, with abusive priests subdivided again between paedophiles, those fixated by pre-pubescent children, and ephebophiles or pederasts, whose interest lay in adolescents, with the latter twice as common as the former.

In the spring of 1995, the only priests accused of such behaviour in Scotland were Lynagh and a Fr John Archibald, who had recently been transferred from St Paul's at Milton Campsie, near Glasgow, and would later abandon his collar after altar boys made allegations of abuse. In order to discover the depth of the problem, the Working Party asked that each diocese detail the number of allegations received against their priests since 1985. The only diocese to report no allegations was Paisley, ironically led by the only bishop on the Working Party, but together the remaining seven dioceses produced a total of twenty-two 'problem priests'. While a number of these cases would come to light over the next seven years as publicity and public understanding encouraged victims to confront their abusers, others, the perpetrators of a single incident on a victim whose parents were adamant the police should not be involved, were quietly shuffled to a different parish, their past behaviour unknown to their new parishioners.

Winning's attitude to priests accused of the sexual abuse of minors was never to strip them of their collars, a power he did not in fact possess, even if he wished to. He genuinely believed that society was safer if such priests remained within the Church, were treated for their condition, and either relocated within the archdiocese to work that did not involve children, or were placed under strict supervision, or were retired with the certain knowledge that any repetition of such actions would lead to the withdrawal of their pension. He believed that if a priest left, he could no longer control the situation and they would be a greater danger to children. It is an attitude that today is unacceptable, but it was one to which he clung.

Alan Draper was to discover an example of Winning's moving a problem priest, one entirely uninvolved in the abuse of children, during the Working Party's visit to each diocese to speak with the clergy. The archdiocese of Glasgow was among the most accommodating, while Argyll and the Isles, led by Bishop Roderick Wright, sought to postpone each suggested visit. Winning arranged three mornings in various church properties across the city which, though poorly attended, did succeed in throwing up one disturbing case. A priest 'A' approached Draper after a meeting with concerns about a female parishioner he was counselling. She claimed she had been sexually abused by a priest from when she was four years old, up until she was twelve. The woman, now in her twenties, and working as a prostitute, refused to name the priest, whom she said was now in a hospital for the mentally ill, but she said that the abuse had been repeated by a member of her family. At the time, there was no Catholic priest in a home for the mentally ill, leading priest 'A' to the conclusion that the abuse was a figment of her imagination. She had sought the priest's support twelve months previously after seeing hallucinations of penises and black hosts while attending Mass, and the relationship had gone over the boundaries and involved sexual activity. Draper believed the relationship was entirely inappropriate and could be, potentially, abusive, and so he advised the priest to no longer meet the woman on his own. Despite the priest's protests, he wrote informing the cardinal of the situation. The priest, who displayed a pattern of forming inappropriate relationships, was relocated to a different diocese.

After almost a year of research and consideration, the Working Party's primary recommendation was the establishment of an independent child protection officer to whom all reports would be passed and who would have the authority to contact the police. Winning did not favour this idea, which he believed was Draper's attempt to create a new job for himself, and he was also unwilling to relinquish such control to a layman. Instead, the Bishops' Conference accepted an alternative suggestion to appoint a lay person in each diocese as child protection officer; they, in turn, would work with a National Childcare Coordinator. The Church would still not contact the authorities themselves, but instead complainants would be encouraged to do so.

Despite his methods of handling such situations, and how we perceive them today, Winning was not without deep compassion for the victims of abuse by religious. On one occasion, he received a pitiful letter from a middle-aged woman who as a child had been separated from her parents and raised in Nazareth House, an orphanage run by the Sisters of Nazareth, a religious order with a reputation for treatment which was less than charitable. The letter lacked an address or phone number and had arrived on a Saturday morning when Winning was at a loose end. For over an hour he worked through the phone book until he tracked her down and offered to accompany her to the home, in an attempt to exorcise the demons that continued to disturb her life. As the woman had lapsed in her faith and was unable to reconcile her treatment to a caring Church, Winning encouraged her return and agreed to hear her confession. On a separate occasion, he organized the reconciliation of a mother and her daughter who had been taken from her thirty years before. Christian charity towards victims of religious abuse is the least one would expect of a cardinal. Yet Winning, like many senior officials of the Catholic Church throughout the world, was guilty of putting the protection of an institution before that of a child.

At the time of the Working Party's conclusion, Alan Draper was content that adequate protection was in place, but he would later change his position and become a vocal critic of what he believed was the Church's maintenance of a culture of secrecy. At a lunch organized in the late summer of 1996 to update the Bishops' Conference on the party's progress, he suggested widening the Working Party's remit to examine 'inappropriate relations' among the clergy, at which point Roderick Wright, the Bishop of Argyll and the Isles, stood up and left the table. Draper was startled, but Winning reassured him, explaining, 'He's a heavy smoker', and indicating that Wright was off for a fly puff. In reality, he had already lit the touch paper on what would become one of the biggest scandals in the post-Reformation Church.

SIXTEEN

The Affair of the Errant Bishop

'Crisis! What Crisis?'[1]

CARDINAL THOMAS WINNING

'Tom Winning is a religious leader, not a politician served by spin doctors. He gave us an honest shambles.'[2]

JIM SILLARS IN THE *SUN*

The flight of Bishop Roderick Wright was planned with the precision of a military exercise and propelled by prayer. In July 1996, in the kitchen of the bishop's house, a dark, comfortless room in the stone villa attached to the cathedral in Oban town, two lovers sat hunched at an old table sipping coffee from cracked mugs. During the past two years an illicit love affair had blossomed between the Bishop of Argyll and the Isles and Kathleen MacPhee, a nurse and a divorcee with three children. An early meeting at the graveside of Kathleen's dead infant in the 1970s was followed up fifteen years later, when Wright attempted to mediate between Kathleen and her husband, William, over their fractured marriage. Attempts at reconciliation faltered, the couple separated, and four years later, in 1994, Wright and MacPhee became unhappily entwined.

What began with pastoral visits to Kathleen's sick bed – she suffered regular bouts of illness from endometriosis, a gynaecological complaint – deepened with long phone calls, love letters and regular house visits, a respectable part of a bishop's role, but not when of such frequency and duration. Friends of MacPhee were

313

later to allege that the relationship quickly became sexual and at one point the geriatric nurse was panicked she might be pregnant. It was an accusation the couple would later deny as they insisted the relationship's physical aspect extended to no more than a warm hug and a chaste peck on the forehead or cheek. After two years of mental turmoil, clandestine meetings and the constant fear of discovery, the pair made a decision to run away together.

And so the biggest public scandal in the Scottish Catholic Church's history during the twentieth century was initiated over a cup of coffee. Within two months, both parties would be household names, the subject of a nationwide search, a press feeding frenzy, and the trigger for a tabloid 'reign of terror' that would strike at the very heart of Thomas Winning's administration. In America, their story would inspire Randa and Patte Starr, the authors of self-help books such as *Learning to Love With Success* and *The 21 Spiritual Secrets of Beverly Hills*, to embark on a screenplay entitled *Forced to Live a Lie*, which they planned to pitch to Liam Neeson and Meryl Streep as '*The Thorn Birds* in Scotland'.

Roderick Wright, or Roddy to his friends and the media, bore little resemblance to Richard Chamberlain, the handsome and windswept actor who portrayed Fr Adams in the television series of the best-selling novel. In fact, when the media storm broke it was commented that he more closely resembled Paul Michael Glazer, the actor who played Starsky in the 1970s TV show *Starsky & Hutch*. This led to a memorable headline in the *Daily Record*: 'I Love You, Father Starsky'. A tall man, blessed with a long face and dark hair flecked with grey, he was remembered by his fellow bishops as anxious and ill at ease. 'He looked as if he had the troubles of the world on his shoulder,' remembered Winning. 'At the time, I suppose he did.' In the late summer of 1996, however, Wright took on a new purpose. An initial plan to quietly resign, travel abroad and have Kathleen join him later was abandoned at her request and instead, like teenagers under the rule of powerful parents, they decided to elope. Familial considerations were set aside. The recent death of Wright's favourite sister, while devastating, was one less peg tying him into position; the remainder of his family, he felt sure, would understand in time. The situation for Kathleen was much more complicated. The mother of three children – Stephen, twenty-four, Donald, eighteen, and Julie-Ann, just fifteen – she believed her oldest sons could cope alone and that Julie-Ann would later join her and Wright in their new life.

In an error that would prove devastating for all parties, the couple chose to settle into a new life first, before informing their respective families or the Church authorities. In August, they hired a small three-bedroom house in Kendal, nestled in the Lake District, and began ferrying Kathleen's possessions into a spare room at Wright's official residence, in preparation for the final move. On Sunday 1 September, Kathleen drove Wright to Glasgow to collect a hire van which he then drove back to Oban, while she headed home to Fort William. The following morning, the couple met at Kathleen's home, loaded furniture and supplies and travelled back to Oban, where they quickly realized two trips south would be necessary. The first trip began on the morning of Wednesday 3 September, and they arrived at 7 Mountain View, their new home, at lunchtime and paid a couple of builders to help move their belongings. The next morning they drove north to Oban for the final time but their frantic packing and cleaning were disturbed by two female members of a Justice and Peace group who had waited hours for their bishop's signature on some crucial paperwork.

Wright and MacPhee departed Oban for the final time in the late afternoon of 4 September. A Catholic bishop turned 'white van man' en route to a new life, Wright could not help but 'bid a final farewell to Oban'. At her family home in Inverlochy, outside Fort William, MacPhee had left a note for her daughter instructing her to stay with relatives. In the bishop's house, Wright had left no note, but instead laid out his car keys, cheque book and cash cards neatly on the kitchen table, an act that, when discovered, fuelled concerns that the priest had, like Reginald Perrin, abandoned his life for the comfort of suicide. It would be a further two days before Wright wrote an explanatory note to his brother, which unfortunately, due to errors in the postal service, would on four occasions be delivered to the wrong address. It finally reached Donald John Wright ten days later, courtesy of the *Daily Record*.

It was the evening of 5 September before Wright and MacPhee, after a drive north to Glasgow to drop off the rental van, could relax in the unpacked clutter of their new home with a bottle of wine before retiring together to bed.

The disappearance of Bishop Wright was first noticed three days later when an alibi provided to excuse a long-standing invitation became unstuck. On Sunday 8 September, he had been due to officiate at a Mass at Carfin Grotto, a popular Marian shrine, and to excuse himself, he had called Joseph Devine six days before to explain a fictitious hospital appointment to correct a 'little problem'. Devine was under the impression this was a delicate matter such as haemorrhoids, and so pressed no further and decided to preach himself and not trouble the Cardinal or any other of the attending bishops. Yet when he first arrived at the grotto, the parish priest asked him to call Roddy Macdonald, the Vicar General of Argyll and the Isles, who was anxious to track down his bishop. Devine explained Wright's appointment and listened as Macdonald insisted this was wrong. 'I can't find him,' said Macdonald. 'I went to Oban. He's not there. He's gone.' Aware of the acute concern in Macdonald's voice, Devine put Winning on the phone. After a brief conversation, the Cardinal hung up, turned around to Keith O'Brien, the Archbishop of Edinburgh, who had just arrived, and said: 'Remember the old lady? Maybe she was right.'

Four years previously, in June 1992, Winning had been informed of Wright's colourful love life by the bishop's own housekeeper, Ileene McKinney, who had found a number of sexually explicit letters to her employer from four different women, as well as his draft replies, including one in which he pleaded for the correspondent not to leave him. McKinney had originally confronted Wright, who swore an oath on his mother's grave that there was no affair and allowed a year's grace, but when she discovered a recent cache, she did not hesitate to contact Archbishop O'Brien.

After visiting McKinney at home, O'Brien arranged a meeting with Winning at Clyde Street, and on 1 June 1992, McKinney, who was then sixty-two years old, took the bus from Oban towards what she later described as a 'horrendous'[3] meeting. For two hours she was grilled by Winning, admitted retrieving the correspondence from a bin, and explained that she no longer possessed the incriminating letters. When she asked for Wright's resignation, Winning replied, 'Is that not a bit harsh? What about confession?' The meeting closed with both men insisting they would look into the matter and asking Ileene McKinney to remember them in her prayers.

Wright had been confronted with the allegations by Winning and O'Brien two weeks later following a meeting of the Bishops' Conference at Mount Carmel retreat house in Glasgow, and he had made a vigorous denial, insisting the letters had been sent anonymously. Winning lacked proof and so when asked to take the word of a female housekeeper who raided bins in search of incriminating evidence over that of a brother bishop, his instinct immediately favoured Wright, but in this he was wrong. Not only was he wrong, he compounded the error by his decision to punish the whistleblower for the din in his ears. After Wright's denial, Winning told him: 'You should get rid of her. What is she doing anyway, rooting around in your basket?' Wright returned to Oban and sacked McKinney, instructing her to gather her belongings and 'get out'. There is a temptation, once one is equipped with hindsight, to judge Winning's decision harshly; certainly it points to what, at times, was a characteristic disregard of women as meddlesome troublemakers, but without definitive evidence Winning felt he had no choice but to believe a fellow bishop. Yet a wiser, more suspicious individual might have kept tabs on Wright's potential weakness. Instead, the Church's favoured response was activated and the sleeping dog lay on.

In September 1996, Roddy Macdonald was under no such illusion. An eyewitness had confirmed the bishop's clandestine flit and it was assumed he had left with a woman, though suicide had not yet been ruled out. On the evening of Tuesday 10 September, Winning was called at home by Wright's brother, Donald John, an oil worker in the Persian Gulf, and while Winning attempted to reassure him, advising him not to return home just yet, he was unsuccessful and a flight to Aberdeen was booked the following day. The disappearance of a Catholic bishop was too sensational a story to remain under wraps for long and a disappointed priest in the diocese announced from the pulpit that 'His Lord, the Bishop of Argyll and the Isles' had abandoned his post for a woman. In the Highlands, gossip is a match to dry kindling and within an hour the news was roaring south. Joseph Devine first saw confirmation while checking Ceefax for a weather report.

Under canon law, the Roddy Wright affair should have remained the sole responsibility of Keith O'Brien, the metropolitan archbishop, under whose wing the bishop's diocese fell, but he was currently abroad. As president of the Bishops' Conference and (since receiving the red hat) as the self-styled 'leader of Scotland's Catholics', Winning was to become the lightning conductor for the oncoming storm. Five days after discovering Wright's disappearance, no preparatory action had yet taken place for what quickly became a huge national news story: while Tom Connelly was inside the loop, Noel Barry was outside and, soon inundated with phone calls, he had to call Winning, Peter Smith and Connelly before he was able to establish the correct line – which was 'we know nothing'. The following day, Saturday 14 September, the story appeared in every national newspaper but it was not until mid-morning that Roddy Wright heard reports of his disappearance on the radio. Two weeks after abandoning his post, Wright still believed the story would only emerge when he chose to announce it, and in a panic called the office of Tom Connelly and listened as his answering machine insisted: 'I have no idea as to the whereabouts of Bishop Wright.' A second call to Keith O'Brien, who had returned that day, was more successful. While Wright, in his memoirs, said the Archbishop immediately asked if he was resigning, O'Brien's own recollection was of a brief conversation in which Wright asked to visit him, and he suggested The Oaks at seven o'clock the following evening.

Winning spent that afternoon in his study drafting a letter of resignation for Wright, while hoping nevertheless that it might prove unnecessary. However, that morning, the *Sunday Mail* had named Kathleen MacPhee as Wright's secret partner. Winning told Keith O'Brien, when he arrived at around 6.30 p.m., that he had booked places for both Wright and MacPhee at a private retreat house in the Republic of Ireland, should they wish to consider their future, but neither man favoured their chances. When Wright rang the doorbell thirty minutes later, he was, in Winning's words, in 'a terrible state' – shaking, red-eyed, and with the pallor of pale paint. On the long drive from Kendal he had stopped for petrol, and when he saw the front page of the *Sunday Mail*, had almost been sick in the forecourt. Winning welcomed him in and told him that Mrs Mac had prepared supper; without an appetite and having left MacPhee sitting in the car, parked around the corner, Wright, however, wished only to say his piece and go. Winning and O'Brien took the armchairs and Wright sank into the sofa, beneath a large tapestry of Christ with his arms outstretched in a gesture of comfort, and immediately he began to insist: 'I want to resign, I want to resign.' Winning's original plan was to calm Wright down and then begin to persuade him that a decision of such consequence could not be made in his fevered state. He had no illusion of immediately convincing him to change his mind; his goal was simply to buy time and to persuade the pair to attend the retreat house. 'They had to resolve their problems and I felt they could do it there quietly, maybe he could talk himself out of it,' recollected Winning.

Yet the more Winning sketched an option that involved returning to his office, the stronger grew Wright's desire to flee. Suddenly, as if to shatter any bridge back to his past life, he announced: 'There is a child, there is a boy of fifteen.' There on the sofa Wright confessed how in 1980 as a priest in Fort William, he had met a woman called Joanna Whibley, the fiancée of a Catholic, who was then looking to convert. A relationship between himself and Joanna had begun, and after he moved to South Uist, he began travelling to where Whibley had moved in southern England. Their friendship rolled into an affair and a boy, Kevin, was born. Of Wright's two superiors, O'Brien was less startled than Winning, for as a friend of Eamonn Casey, the disgraced Irish bishop, he had been in his house when the phone had rung perpetually, and Casey had admitted to being blackmailed, although he did not reveal the identity of the blackmailer. A few months later the news emerged that Casey had fathered a son by an American divorcee, Annie Murphy, and kept the pair using £70,000 embezzled from diocesan funds. Winning, meanwhile, was stunned: 'I was pretty shaken but I didn't want to show what a dreadful surprise it was. If a bishop runs away with a woman, anything else is just adding fuel to the fire.' It was obvious to both men that Wright was not for turning, but in a final attempt to change his mind, Winning employed an unfortunate analogy. After pointing out that there was no such thing as an 'unforgivable sin', he asked the bishop if he truly wished to 'throw the baby out with the bath water'. He made no attempt to browbeat or abuse a man whom he considered to be in deep distress and abject mental turmoil. Winning had a genuine fear that the bishop might be suicidal and had no wish to push him over the edge, so while O'Brien remained with the trembling man, he went upstairs ostensibly to 'draw up' the resignation letter, but instead sat in his study. 'I knew in his mind, he had to go. The woman would have slaughtered him if he went back on her.'

After signing the statement, witnessed by Keith O'Brien, Wright prepared to leave and Winning said he would accompany him across the gravel drive to the wrought-iron gates. As well as Wright's mental state, he was worried about his financial health. The bishop had insisted all payments to Joanna Whibley had been made from his own pocket (a financial audit would verify his statement), but still Winning felt a need to alleviate a little distress and so pressed an envelope containing 'a few hundred pounds' into his palm with the instruction to 'keep in touch, and not to do anything drastic'. He lingered in the driveway until Wright was around the corner and out of sight. He would never see him again.

*   *   *

The same evening, Winning made the decision to inform only the other Scottish bishops and the Vatican's Congregation of Bishops about Wright's love child. As Keith O'Brien recollected: 'He said we cannot betray this woman. It was basically his decision.' In Wright's memoirs he castigates Winning and O'Brien for their refusal to agree to his wish that the full reason for his resignation be revealed; however, both men said no such demand was ever made. Like many of Winning's judgement calls, it was entirely understandable, but woefully mishandled. There is no doubt that, had the Catholic Church announced that Wright had fathered a son, the media would have tracked him down and exposed Joanna Whibley and her son to public scrutiny, regardless of their wishes. Where Winning built a rod for his own back was by failing to contact Joanna Whibley and offer comfort, advice, or verify her financial security. He was provided with her name and address and could have tied up what was in fact to become an inflammatory loose end. Yet his unreconstructed attitude, that when trouble arrived one should always 'cherchez la femme' and that the Church should not pay for the mistakes of their priests – or, in this case, bishop – won out. Winning's attitude to Whibley and her son was that they were 'none of my blooming responsibility', and that as far as finances were concerned, she might be a 'gold-digger'.

O'Brien stayed overnight at The Oaks rather than return early the following morning for the long drive to Fort Augustus, to the ancient abbey at the head of Loch Ness where Wright's clergy would be gathered in secret to discover his fate. The meeting had been switched from Oban to throw off the press and the monks had prepared a buffet lunch. Winning and O'Brien, having been driven the two hundred miles by Peter Smith, were frank about Wright's resignation and relationship with Whibley, but made no mention of his child. Shortly after the party set off back south at around 2 p.m., Smith's mobile rang. The Secretary of the Congregation of Bishops wished to speak to Keith O'Brien and, in order to get a better reception, Smith pulled over into an old graveyard. The Archbishop was asked to take over the role of Apostolic Administrator for Wright's diocese. Glasgow was their final destination and with it the unappealing prospect of an aggressive press conference. Roadworks delayed their arrival and it was after 6 p.m. before they took their seats at a desk set up in the Eyre Hall on the first floor of Clyde Street. Noel Barry had argued that O'Brien should lead the conference, aware as he was of Winning's temper when under pressure, but it was predictable that the questions would be directed towards the Cardinal. First a short statement was read out from Bishop Wright:

> I am physically and spiritually unable to sustain the responsibilities of a diocesan bishop and ask to be released from my office as Bishop of Argyll and the Isles. I ask forgiveness and your prayers. In particular, I ask pardon of my brother priests in the diocese and of my brother bishops in Scotland. I wish to remain a committed member of the Catholic Church.[4]

While Wright's relationship with Whibley was confirmed, Winning went out of his way to wish Wright well and made a statement for which he was later castigated. 'I would send Bishop Wright every best wish, and hope he finds happiness and some peace. I would still hope he would continue some time, somewhere, his ministry as a priest.' A veteran of hundreds of press conferences, Winning found this the most difficult and at one point, seized by emotion, appeared to be on the verge of tears. A black and white photograph captured his distress, his eyes closed and his head resting on four fingers of his left hand, his traditional black shirt replaced by one of maudlin grey. As if sensing the bleakness of the Church's position, the following day's press was surprisingly sensitive, and seemed as interested in the pressures of celibacy as in the Church's public disgrace.

The annual meeting of the Catholic bishops with their Episcopalian counterparts had long sat in the diary for Tuesday 17 September at Scotus College in the suburbs of Bearsden. Yet in a nod to the Catholic's current difficulty, Bishop Richard Holloway, Primus of the Scottish Episcopal Church, had offered to cancel or at least postpone the meeting to a more favourable hour. The Catholic bishops, however, were anxious for a breath of normality and insisted the meeting went ahead, but while they were familiar with a rear entrance and arrived unnoticed, the 'Piskies' in black coats and dog collars were ambushed with the flashlights of press photographers in the mistaken belief that they were Catholics, arriving for another crisis meeting. The meeting was characterized by robust good humour, but little actual work, with the room collapsing with laughter when they heard that a prankster had called the college posing as Bishop Wright's 'wife' to explain his absence. On departure, Holloway, no stranger himself to controversial press coverage, shook Winning's hand and offered his support saying: 'Don't let the bastards grind you down, Tom.' Winning had agreed to do a little 'grinding' himself that afternoon in an interview with the BBC for *Everyman*, a documentary examining the connection between Christianity and Britain's political system. After ten days of stress and strain, it was almost a relief for Winning to take Tony Blair to task over what he viewed as his 'canteen Christianity', with the result that David Campanale, the producer, was delighted with the results which would explode seven weeks later.

By Thursday 19 September, Winning believed the Church was out of the woods and climbing back towards the high ground. Wright had officially resigned and while the tabloid press still scoured the country in search of him and his mistress, the broadsheets had moved on to reflective opinion pieces on celibacy and the Church. Winning had moved on too, and arranged a meeting with Ron Mackenna, a reporter with the *Herald*, for an off-the-record chat in an attempt to sway the paper's views on the recent sex-abuse allegations against the Church. 'It was basically a long rant against these people and how a lot of them were in it for themselves,' said Mackenna, who found his attempts to discuss Wright rebuffed. Neither Winning nor Mackenna was aware that the story was about to return with hurricane force and that the Cardinal's feeble attempts to shield himself would be torn away. On the following Monday night in the living room of her small terraced house in Poole, Dorset, Joanna Whibley and her son Kevin had watched footage of the Church's press conference for any mention of their own existence. Grievously misled by Wright, who had said that he was leaving to join her, and now finding herself erased, in her eyes, by the Church, she had contacted the BBC to tell her own (as she put it) 'pathetic story'. Peter Smith was originally contacted by the BBC, who sought Winning's reaction, but he passed the message to Tom Connelly who, since he was unaware of the story, returned ninety minutes later with confirmation of it and a prepared statement. Winning was unable or unwilling to face the press or even to issue a personal statement, and he insisted on perpetuating the illusion of business as usual by attending a deanery meeting at St Stephen's in Dalmuir.

The footage of Joanna Whibley broadcast on the BBC's *Six O'Clock News*, accompanied by shots of Kevin, looking weary and embarrassed as his mother explained how Wright had threatened to move to Peru if forced to publicly acknowledge his existence, was excruciating. As Joanna Whibley said: 'I would not want this trivialized, this pathetic story. I want it to serve some purpose. I'm quite sure there are some other women in relationships with priests who want to end their secret lives.' True to her word, she gave no other interviews, despite the offer of substantial sums, but once was enough. The Catholic Church in Scotland stood accused of perpetuating a cover-up and among the most concerned and irritated was Basil Hume who, seconds after watching the story on the news, had the Catholic Media Office release a statement saying: 'Cardinal Hume had no prior knowledge whatsoever of what has been disclosed about the bishop.' Although the statement said he would make no further comment, Hume then proceeded to invite the cameras of ITN, Channel Four News and the BBC to his private residence at Westminster Cathedral where he said: 'I am very, very shocked and saddened about these recent, latest revelations. But my heart goes out, especially to Kevin and his mother, and also to those people let down by this. I find myself very, very distressed

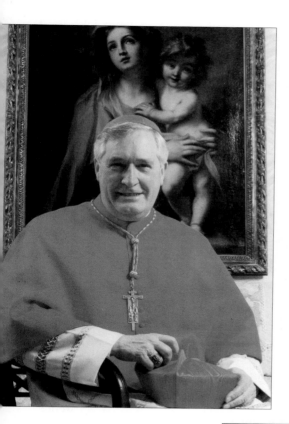

The cardinal: the clothes maketh the man, but it would be months before Winning was comfortable enough to introduce himself as 'the cardinal'.

'One of our bishops is missing': Bishop Roderick Wright congratulates Thomas Winning on his elevation to cardinal. Two years later he would elope with a divorcee.

'Father of the Nation': Donald Dewar may have earned the sobriquet for deliverin the Scottish Parliament, but Winning believed he was a 'bigot'.

The holy monk: Thomas Winning (*centre*) with cardinal Cahal Daly and cardin Basil Hume, whose tangible spirituality he coveted.

The wood of the cross: Thomas Winning in quiet contemplation as he carries the cross along the Via Dolorosa in Jerusalem during a Scottish pilgrimage.

"Up three points ... "

Promotion-seeking: critics suggested Thomas Winning's public spats with Tony Blair were designed to elevate his chances of becoming Pope. © *Steve Bright/Mirrorpix*

WHO'S LEFT HOLDING THE BABY?

Thomas Winning's Pro-Life Initiative attracted the mockery of the media (© *Steve Bright/Mirrorpix and* © *David Austin*)…

…but the thanks of hundreds of women, such as Melinda Cox, whose daughter Penelope was born after she received financial assistance through the initiative.

A portrait Thomas Winning adored: a drawing by his niece, Claire Frances, on the occasion of his being made a cardinal.

Uncle Thomas by Clare Frances

Fancy dress: each Halloween his nieces and nephew would visit in costume. On this occasion Winning dressed in an African costume, a present from a recent trip. *Left to right*: Claire Frances, Fiona Cameron, Winning, and Thomas Cameron.

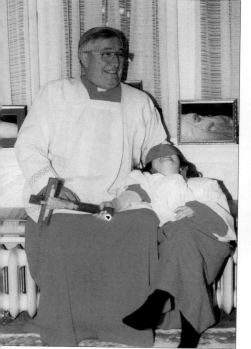

Winning had cardinal outfits made for his niece and nephew, with comical results.

Princes of the Church: Thomas Winning displays the solemn face of duty during a papal ceremony in St Peter's Square.

Out of the ghetto: Thomas Winning after introducing Henry McLeish, the First
Minister (*top left*) and John Reid, Scottish Secretary (*next to him*), at a Papal
Audience to mark the 400th anniversary of the Scots College in Rome.

Thank you: Winning expresses his gratitude to the Pope after Mass with the new cardinals.

indeed ... I am not calling for a revision of the rules. I believe fully in the rules of celibacy.'[5]

Hume's comments stood in stark contrast to Winning's silence. The driveway of The Oaks was quickly clogged with reporters, photographers and camera crews, but instead of agreeing to speak to them or issue a statement, he called the police to have them removed. When he finally reached the deanery meeting, it was a pleasure to divert his mind with talk of priests' pensions and any other competent business, but Noel Barry, who had accompanied him and was aware of Hume's comments, urged him to speak out. He was also anxious that Hume make no further comment. After tracking down the Cardinal's private number, he listened as Hume defended his right to speak out and expressed his anger at being kept in the dark on a matter that had brought shame and embarrassment on all Britain's Catholics. A compromise was reached and Hume agreed to limit his comments.

It was after ten o'clock when Winning returned to The Oaks and found Ron Mackenna standing by the gates. The reporter came forward and rapped on the car window, which Winning wound down. 'I sat in your house for two hours, you knew this was going to come out, and you never told me.' Winning replied that it was none of his business. 'It's all over the place now and you need to talk about it.' Winning knew it was time to remove his head from the sand and so agreed, but insisted on delaying their conversation until the arrival of Noel Barry. As Mrs McInnes had retired to bed exhausted and distressed by the earlier press blockade, Winning made the tea himself. At close to 11 p.m., with the *Herald*'s final deadline looming, Winning began to justify his actions. He began by expressing crocodile tears over the plight of Joanna Whibley and her son Kevin. 'I weep for the mother and child and the way in which they have been treated, but I have been so duped by the events of the last few days that I don't know what to believe any more.' He then defended his handling of the situation.

We have not been telling lies about this. It is too serious, and lies are always found out. I want people to understand that we could not say anything about the child in public. It would not have been right. We didn't know what the situation was. We were not aware whether the child knew who his father was. The mother has rights in this as well and we could not speak publicly about her situation.

The newspapers of the following day, 20 September, saw the Church crucified. The *Daily Record* used the headline 'Sins of the Father' and ran a devastating piece by Joan Burnie in which she lambasted Wright, MacPhee and the Scottish Catholic Church for what was viewed as a cover-up. 'The higher echelons of the Catholic Church cannot and must not absolve themselves. They, too, are guilty of hypocrisy.' The *Sun* was even stronger, headlining their coverage 'Scandal of the Bonking Bishop'; their editorial personalized the issue with an attack on Winning himself, writing under the headline 'Cardinal Must Pay for Sins'. 'Cardinal Winning's face should be as red as his robes this morning . . . the Cardinal, in trying to save the Church's already tarnished reputation, deliberately deceived the entire Catholic establishment. He must now stand up and be counted for his sins.' Both the *Scotsman* and the *Herald* weighed in with the Glasgow paper also accusing the Church of a cover-up in their leader: 'The first instinct of the Church in situations of this sort is to cover them up. This is a most serious misjudgement.'

A solitary interview given to the *Herald* would not be enough to deal with the continuing accusations of cover-up, and Noel Barry was unwilling to put Winning through a second press conference. His temper had been reined in tightly during Monday's press conference, but there was no guarantee of a successful repetition under a more hostile examination. The remedy was a pooled interview with Ronnie Convery, a reporter with Scottish Television who, as a member of Opus Dei, a shadowy conservative Catholic organization, as well as a regular contributor to *Flourish*, was sympathetic to the Church's plight. On Friday morning, 20 September, as Convery and his crew set up their equipment in the lounge, Barry asked Winning and Keith O'Brien if the cupboard was now bare, or whether any skeletons remained. Winning was insistent they had come clean, Barry pressed again, only to be described as a 'prophet of doom' for his troubles, but then O'Brien stepped in and raised the subject of Wright's former housekeeper. Winning attempted to dismiss her as 'nuts' but Barry was immediately concerned: had the Church not just been coruscated for hiding the truth? If the press broke the story that Winning and Keith O'Brien were aware of Wright's past and had done nothing, the perception of a cover-up would deepen. It was imperative the Church release this information, before it was uncovered. Barry then spoke to Convery and suggested that he ask Winning when he first knew there was anything wrong, allowing him to come clean about his dismissal of the housekeeper's legitimate concerns.

Following the interview, Winning chose to write a letter to the priests of Argyll and the Isles. It read:

My Dear Brothers,
In these emotionally charged days as we all experience a Gethsemane as Church, I wish to affirm my solidarity with you and your people and to assure you that each one of you is constantly in my thoughts, Masses and prayers as we go through this dark night. We can express our feelings in different ways and I think we need to be open with our people in order to allow them to talk through their hurt.
'If one part is hurt, all parts are hurt with it,' Paul says (1 Cor 12:26), and that is so true of the Church at present. Nevertheless, Paul reminds us to have hope and trust, and in that vein I, like you, need to reflect on his stirring call: 'Never give in, then, my dear brothers and sisters, never admit defeat. Keep on working at the Lord's work always, knowing that, in the Lord, you cannot be labouring in vain.' (1 Cor 15:58)
Yours devotedly in Christ,
Most Rev. Thomas J. Cardinal Winning
Archbishop

For Roddy Wright, the sale of his story to the *News of the World* was necessary, as circumstances had grown increasingly desperate. He and Kathleen MacPhee were isolated in their small rented house in Kendal, and, the couple's location having been uncovered, by Thursday 19 September they were surrounded by press and had taken to lying still on the upstairs bedroom floor, creeping down to the kitchen to cook food only under cover of darkness. The offer of £50,000 that was pushed through the letterbox offered a solution as well as a degree of financial security. When Winning was told of Wright's plans, only a few hours before publication, he took it as further evidence of the bishop's unhinged mind: how else could he betray his position in such a public manner, joining the company of good-time girls and disgraced politicians prepared to unlock their jaw for money? The analogy of Judas and the thirty pieces of silver struck him as all too accurate. Yet his fears that Wright would get drunk and disclose the privileged secrets of the Bishops' Conference proved unfounded; readers were instead treated to page after page of banality led by a headline that proclaimed how the bishop would rather watch Celtic than say Mass. A statement less than edifying, but hardly earth-shattering, and, in the light of the magnitude of his previous disclosures, a relief.

Meanwhile, the ripple effect of Wright's actions was still being felt across Scotland. A mini 'reign of terror' was unfolding as the tabloids, having discovered one 'bonking bishop', were anxious to unveil another, as well as any other priests who failed to honour their vow of celibacy. One national newspaper had spent days check-ing false rumours of an improper relationship between Bishop Joseph Devine and his housekeeper. As Wright's 'revelations' were to extend to a second Sunday, Winning was anxious to do all in his power to shut the story down, or at least minimize the fall-out, and with this aim in mind he contacted Tony Meehan, the director of TMA (Tony Meehan Associates) Communications, a public relations company from whom Winning had taken soundings in the past. Meehan joined the Cardinal that Saturday and insisted upon a full 'war council' on Tuesday 24 September to include Bishop Devine, Tom Connelly, Noel Barry and Peter Smith. Those in attendance remember Winning as angry and uptight, furious at the treatment of Joe Devine whom he viewed as an innocent victim of Wright's legacy. Meehan suggested that the Church draw a public line under the affair by issuing a letter withdrawing all cooperation with the media on the grounds that there was nothing more to say and they would no longer tolerate the invasion of innocent people's privacy. While Tom Connelly was in favour of such a suggestion, Noel Barry believed it would only provoke further investigation and perpetuate the perception of the Church as having more to hide. Winning, however, was adamant this was the correct approach and asked Meehan to prepare a draft.

Unfortunately, the excommunication of the press as news of the letter became known was to coincide with Wright's shadow falling across one of Winning's closest advisers. After the meeting, Noel Barry returned to his parish house in Milngavie at around 6.30 p.m. A few minutes later, the bell rang and on the doorstep stood Alan Muir, a senior reporter with the *Sun*, accompanied by a photographer who began to take pictures. As Barry explained that he had no further comment to make on Roddy Wright, and began to close the door, Muir shouted: 'We know all about your affair with Annie Clinton.' Behind the door, Barry was in shock. Clinton was a close personal friend, a former head teacher who now worked as a schools inspector. The allegation was entirely false, but no less distressing. When he called Clinton, he found her in tears, having received similar treatment from the newspaper at the home she shared with her elderly mother. The next morning, Clinton's mother became so distressed when a reporter returned looking for her daughter that she ran to a neighbour's house shouting: 'There's a man at my door, there's a man at my door.' The elderly woman's treatment led to Winning's criticism of the tabloid's 'Gestapo tactics'. Barry assured his boss that there was nothing to the newspaper's allegations, but feared the forthcoming letter would be read as a cover-up where none was required.

On Thursday 26 September, a two-page statement from the Bishops' Conference, signed by Winning as president, was issued by Tom Connelly's media office. The 'Open Letter to Editors'[6] began with a charitable first sentence: 'I greet you in peace and friendship', but lost no time in setting out its agenda and taking the tabloids to task over their recent behaviour. The Church defended once again its decision to withhold news of Wright's child, insisting it was 'the mother's decision to make a public statement . . . and hers alone', and after explaining that the Church 'does not speak the same language as the media', said it was time to draw the curtain on recent events.

> We respect the rights of everyone to express their view, even when they are different or opposed to those of the Church. We too, however, have the right to withhold participation in any public debate on this, or any other matter which serves no purpose other than to feed the needs of those who take pleasure in others' misfortune, or who see an opportunity for revenge. In view of the ongoing and unjustifiable attacks on priests and innocent people in the tabloid media, the Church is exercising this right.

Four days later, on 30 September, the *Sun* retorted with a front-page story on Fr Noel Barry's friendship with Annie Clinton. A statement released the following day said both parties would sue for damages. While Winning's letter infuriated members of the press, it arguably had the desired effect. The story had, in a little over three weeks, run its course, but the consequences, particularly for the people of Argyll and the Isles, had far greater resonance. In response to a letter of explanation of Wright's behaviour, Winning received a supportive reply on behalf of the Pope from Cardinal Angelo Sodano, the Secretary of State for the Holy See. In the letter faxed to Winning on 26 September, Sodano explained that the Pope 'wishes me to assure you that he is particularly close to the Church in Scotland during these days'.

'While deeply saddened by the scandal brought to the clergy, religious and laity by the events surrounding the resignation of Bishop Roderick Wright, His Holiness is confident that the Catholic community of Scotland will clearly distinguish between human failings, however serious, and the richness of our inheritance of grace.'

*   *   *

330

Beyond the boundaries of Wright's former diocese, Catholics were quick to bounce back. Unlike in Ireland, where the Church was a firm part of the Establishment and as a result the disgrace of Bishop Casey had sent Catholicism into a sharp tailspin, Scottish Catholics had been the underdogs for so long that they had no desire to devour themselves to the delight of 'the other side'. Priests across the country commented that instead of a drop in Mass attendance, the numbers actually rose as Catholics displayed a mark of solidarity during an hour of need. It did not last. Just as Roddy Wright jokes drifted from the work place, so the numbers faded from the pews, but for those few weeks their presence steadied nerves and showed all was not lost. In spite of his decision to ignore the earlier warnings of Wright's housekeeper, Winning emerged with scarcely a scratch from the misadventure, which served only to harden the reputation that his robes were coated with Teflon: nothing would stick. The media may have been less forgiving than Rome, but a few weeks later, when Winning was hauling Tony Blair over the coals, his authority and profile were undimmed by his handling of Roddy Wright's elopement. The affair, however, was enough to inspire a root-and-branch review of the Church's handling of the media.

Behind the closed doors of the Holy See, an internal review by the Secretariat of State and Congregation of Bishops was to conclude that Archbishop Luigi Barbarito had made a serious error in 1990 when he failed to speak directly to Wright upon offering him the position of bishop. Indeed, it was a full month after Wright's elopement that Barbarito, who had been on holiday, even contacted Winning. Instead, at the time of the Bishop's appointment, the Archbishop had asked Fr John McNeil, then administrator of the diocese, to approach Wright and persuade him to accept the job. Wright refused McNeil a number of times before finally relenting. Vatican officials felt that if Barbarito had asked Wright directly with the full weight and solemnity of Rome, instead of being cajoled by a friend into acceptance, the priest would have refused and spared the Church in Scotland the consequent embarrassment. Yet it was still with a sense of trepidation that Winning visited Rome a month later to speak with Cardinal Bernardin Gantin, the head of the

Congregation of Bishops. As was customary in a time of need, Winning had no wish to go alone and asked Joseph Devine to accompany him and wait outside in an ante-room. In spite of his personal concerns, Winning's instinct was not to go red cap in hand but to exert a false confidence and when Gantin expressed his concern about the consequence of Wright's actions on the faithful of Scotland, he retorted that he had received hundreds of letters of support and that the Bishop of Motherwell was at this moment outside willing to testify to the fact.

Three years would pass until Mgr Ian Murray, a former rector of the Scots College in Spain, was appointed as Wright's successor, an inordinate length of time that led many parishioners to feel they were being punished for a crime they did not commit. During this period Winning made several visits to the diocese – in particular, to visit the former bishop's ageing aunts. 'They had a terrible burden of guilt and shame and it was important to talk to them and reassure them of our support,' said Winning. In 1999, Roddy Wright and Kathleen MacPhee married. Winning's letters urging him to return to the priesthood remained unanswered.

SEVENTEEN

The Thorn on Labour's Rose

'Nobody can dismiss the criticism from a cardinal. I think they sting him more than they would because [Blair] is a Christian person. I suspect, in his heart, he is a Catholic.'[1]

GEORGE GALLOWAY MP

'My role is not to tell people for whom they should vote. Instead, I have the duty to counsel people as to how they should use their vote.'[2]

THOMAS WINNING

Given the abyss into which their relationship would later tumble, it is bittersweet that at Tony Blair's first meeting with Thomas Winning, he should have asked coyly for the new cardinal's autograph. True, the recipient of the archbishop's signature, which was gladly applied to a menu, was not the new leader of the Labour Party, but his eldest son, Euan, whose heroes must have extended past pop stars and footballers to include a 'prince of the Church', but as a symbol of the pair's first encounter the gesture could not have held more promise.

The occasion was the Scottish Press Fund lunch held at Glasgow's Marriot Hotel on 11 November 1994, six months after Blair was elected to succeed the late John Smith and a week before Winning travelled to Rome for the consistory. Both men were settling into powerful new roles and the potential for an alliance appeared unquestionable. After all, wasn't Winning described by the socialist moniker 'Red Tom' long before the colour corresponded to the hue of his new hat? The Archbishop of Glasgow was tagged as an ardent Labour supporter who had little time for Conservatives, nationalists or the moral laxity of the Liberal Democrats. And if Winning's hand was outstretched on the matter of personal politics, then surely Blair reciprocated the gesture in terms of his personal faith. He was, for instance, the most openly Christian politician since Gladstone, not only reading the Bible on a daily basis, but blessed with a wife who was a practising Catholic and three children raised in the faith. Although Blair himself was an Anglican, he still joined his family each Sunday in the pews of St Joan of Arc, a Catholic church in Highbury, and would continue to receive Holy Communion for another year, before Basil Hume requested he desist on the grounds that he had ample opportunity to receive the sacrament with his own denomination.

From the outside, a beautiful friendship was on the cards, one in which the Catholic Church could work hand-in-hand with a Labour government to achieve their mutual goals of social justice, full employment and a 180 degree turn from the individualism of the Conservatives towards the brighter lights of a more generous society. At the lunch, Blair, the guest of honour, took the first step by announcing the creation of a devolved Scottish parliament within the first year of a new Labour government, and this, coupled with a few hours' conversation on subjects as varied as football, politics and faith, led Winning to conclude that the Labour leader 'seemed a pretty decent spud'. However, he then added the same addendum the party would attach to a single European currency, namely that he would 'have to wait and see'.

Thomas Winning and Tony Blair would go on to develop a deep dislike and distrust of one another. Their fractured relationship would consist of just two more private meetings and a number of public spats. It was concluded with Blair effectively locking Winning out of 10 Downing Street and branding him in private as an untrustworthy character. When years later Cardinal Cormac Murphy-O'Connor read a letter from the Prime Minister at Winning's funeral, those aware of their turbulent relationship could only stare at the casket and strain their ears to catch the sound of him turning, if not yet in his grave, then at least in his coffin. They were lucky to have heard it at all since it only arrived, by fax, after the ceremony had begun.

The death of John Smith in May 1994 was the tremor that first opened up a fault line in the relationship between Winning and the Labour Party. For decades, Labour and the Catholic Church in Scotland had enjoyed an unofficial 'red-green' alliance, with party officials convinced the bishops could deliver hundreds of thousands of votes en bloc, for in truth, who else was there for Catholics to turn to? In the late nineteenth century, the passion of Irish Catholics for home rule led them to the door of the Liberal Party, but after Ireland's partition, their attention focused on the Labour Party, the one political organization which would not only welcome them, but which promised to improve their own lot. The Conservative and Unionist Party and the Scottish National Party were perceived as Protestant, and the latter's founding fathers were vocal in their dismissal of Catholics as expendable riff-raff. Andrew Dewar Gibb, a prominent SNP politician, said the Irish were responsible for 'most crimes committed in Scotland',[3] while his colleague George Malcolm Thomson alleged their presence in Scotland was suffocating: 'The Scots are a dying people. They are being replaced in their own country by a people alien in race, temperament and religion, at a speed that is without parallel in history outside the era of Barbarian invasions.'[4] In the early days of the Labour Party, the Church, mindful of Pope Leo XIII's encyclical '*Rerum Novarum*', published on 15 May 1891, which equated socialism with atheism, warned the laity off Labour, but then did a volte-face and began to encourage membership to prevent the party tipping towards Communism.

The reality of Winning's political views was that they were more subtle than the broad strokes in which he was so often painted. He was no longer the diehard Labour cheerleader that people presumed; instead, he had uncoupled himself from the party's bandwagon and had already begun rolling towards the Scottish National Party. There were two areas in which he held the Labour Party in deep distrust.

First, he believed them to be liberal on lifestyle issues such as gay rights, and second, the decision by Neil Kinnock prior to the 1992 General Election to elevate the party's pro-choice attitude to abortion to official party policy and out of the realm of a personal conscience had angered him greatly. He also believed the Labour Party was prejudiced against Catholics and populated by bigots. This was a rather bizarre belief given the over-subscription of Catholics within the party, but Winning was adamant that 'Donald Dewar and all those fellows were bigots'. That he should share this belief with Helen Liddell, the former general secretary of the Scottish Labour Party and a practising Catholic, after she had just endured one of the most gruelling sectarian by-elections in recent history points to a growing unhappiness with the party's positions.

The Monklands by-election in June 1994, triggered by the death of John Smith, was to become a cauldron of sectarian bile as a result of the public's belief that Catholic councillors in Coatbridge had lavished jobs and housing on their 'own kind' to the detriment of 'Protestant' Airdrie. The SNP, Liddell's principal rival in a safe Labour seat, were accused of highlighting her 'Catholic'-sounding name and school background with the result that the Labour candidate regularly suffered catcalls of 'Fenian bitch' during public appearances. Although elected, Liddell saw Labour's majority reduced from 16,000 to 1,600 and the SNP excoriated in an editorial in the *Herald*, only for the paper to be forced to apologize the next day. Within a few weeks of the by-election, Winning had personal meetings with both Helen Liddell and Alex Salmond, leader of the SNP, but any assumption that he would commiserate with the former over her experiences and chastise the latter for his party's behaviour was thrown into reverse. Instead of commenting on the bigotry Helen Liddell had just endured, he raised the issue of the problem within her own party.

I remember really annoying her by saying there was a lot of bigotry in the Labour Party. She did not like that at all. She denied it. Donald Dewar and all these fellows were bigots. I never experienced it but there was a common feeling that Donald was quite anti-Catholic. I have picked that up a lot since he died. I just think there is bigotry in the Labour Party because there are men who could have gone further, but who didn't seem to go any further because of their religion and she said no, that wasn't true.

By comparison, Winning's meeting with Salmond was the beginning of a close political friendship that would bloom over the next seven years. Since rising to lead the party in 1990, Salmond had been anxious to dispense with the party's old image as 'Tartan Tories' who preferred to restrict their membership to Protestants. He believed the large Catholic population was an untapped resource who would favour his brand of left-wing social policies. The rapid integration of Scots Catholics into every walk of public life during the past three decades had resulted in a confident outward-looking populace. He agreed with the words of John McCormick junior, the son of the party's founder. While his father had argued against the 1918 Education Act and thrown hard words on the Catholic population, his son, a convert to Catholicism, who became an SNP MP for Ayrshire between 1974 and 1979, wrote: 'Catholics could make a great contribution to the Scotland of the future were they to cast aside the "ghetto" approach to Scottish politics.' Unfortunately, the behaviour of fringe supporters in Monklands had sickened Salmond to the point of questioning his current vocation. His goal when asking for a meeting with Winning was to convince him of the changed face of Scottish Nationalism, but when he arrived the door was already ajar.

Privately, Winning had developed over the last few years into an ardent nationalist, a man who believed Scotland would thrive once the chains of the union had been cast off. While celebrating Mass in a South African township, he once declared: 'You want your freedom, we want our freedom.' But in the past he had harboured the fear that Catholics had not yet assimilated into the Scottish population enough to prevent their mistreatment at the hands of a ruling Protestant party. In 1979, he had voted against a devolved parliament for fear that it would be a shortcut to independence and the fate of Catholics would not fare well in such conditions.

He shared this with Salmond when the pair dined on spaghetti at his office. Winning explained to the SNP leader that his ambition was to see Catholics finally accepted as Scottish, their loyalty seen no longer as attached to Ireland or Rome. Salmond, meanwhile, expressed his ambition to remove all trace of anti-Catholicism from the party and to provide a natural alternative to the Labour Party, to which Winning commented: 'By your deeds you are known.'

If public actions were to speak louder than private words, Salmond lost no time in rising to the task. A few months later, he took the opportunity provided by Stirling University to make a speech calling for the repeal of the Act of Settlement as an outdated and prejudiced piece of legislation. The speech earned Salmond the ire of the usual suspects: the Conservative Party, the Orange Lodge and sections within the Church of Scotland, but it fortified Winning's respect for him as a politician with whom he could do business.

Tony Blair, it was quickly becoming apparent to Winning, did not fall into this category. The pair's first public duel took place in February 1995, two months after they broke bread at the Press Fund lunch, and centred on the decision to ban from the Scottish Labour Party Conference, for the second year running, a stall for Labour For Life. The organization consisted of Labour Party members who held a pro-life agenda and wished to provide information on alternatives to abortion and what they viewed as the creeping threat of euthanasia. The stall had been banned on the grounds that their views contradicted official party policy since the party's adoption of 'abortion on demand' three years before. Winning had protested at the initial ban but was anxious to utilize his powerful new status when the party repeated their prohibition.

There was also a second reason. Each new cardinal is appointed to a pontifical council or congregation whose work they are expected to promote as well as to develop during regular attendance at meetings in Rome. John Paul II had appointed Winning to the Pontifical Council for the Family, which was led by Cardinal Alfonso Lopez Trujillo, the Colombian with whom he had argued and finally allied during the negotiations for the papal visit to Britain in 1982.

The council was the front line in the Vatican's battle against what John Paul II had described as 'the culture of death'. The Eighties had seen the Church's might pitted against and triumph over the forces of Communism, and since the collapse of the Berlin Wall, the issues of abortion and euthanasia had been promoted to take the place of the Soviet Union. Labour's behaviour allowed Winning the opportunity to reignite the debate. The ban had also followed on from the introduction of Emily's List, a policy for increasing the number of female MPs within the party, but support was restricted to candidates who were pro-choice. A third issue of concern to Winning was the pressure he believed was placed on Labour MPs with pro-life beliefs to restrict their activities or face de-selection.

When the ban came to Winning's attention in early January, he began to work behind the scenes in an attempt to facilitate its removal. Noel Barry, who had contacts within the party, began discussions with Jim Devine, Chairman of the Scottish Labour Party, while Winning wrote a personal letter on 1 February 1995 to Tony Blair asking him, as party leader, to intervene on what he considered to be an issue of freedom of speech and the denial of democratic rights to a legitimate organization. Instead of a direct response, Blair's office insisted the matter was administrative and passed Winning's letter to Tom Sawyer, the party's general secretary. One week later, on 8 February, Winning sent a second letter reiterating his argument and asking for Blair's direct assistance but again there was no positive response and during the next two weeks Noel Barry's negotiations made little progress with the party refusing to lift the ban. Winning then began to hint that unless the matter was resolved quickly he would go public with his criticisms of the party, and as his sabre rattling was ignored, the cardinal proceeded to charge.

Winning wrote an opinion column for the *Daily Mail* in which he mixed consternation with outrage in order to argue that the ban was part of a persistent programme of discrimination against pro-lifers within the Labour Party that extended across Emily's List and now threatened to restrict the fundamental right of free speech. 'The embers of totalitarianism are not far from the surface of New

Labour. Its capacity for intimidation can be gauged by Mr Blair's shirking from uttering a word about blatantly undemocratic behaviour within his own party, lest he provoke wrath and find his leadership crippled.' Before going on to criticize Blair for his lack of courtesy in responding to his letters, he laid down a challenge to Blair's style of leadership:

> The Labour For Life ban is about more than abortion. Is it really expecting too much of Mr Blair to spot an issue of principle when it confronts him? Is it demanding too much of his leadership qualities to expect a principled response without delay, to a matter which touches the heart of fundamental democratic rights in a pluralistic society? If Mr Blair can campaign openly and vigorously to change Labour's constitution, how can it be right to stand idly by while ordinary party members are denied the right to argue for changes to policies on abortion? Why is it that proposals to change policies on everything from nationalism to nuclear weapons can be discussed – but not abortion?[5]

The ban was patently unjust and had been criticized by a number of senior Labour MPs, including Dr John Reid and George Galloway, but Blair had been anxious to distance himself from the decision. Winning's attack on Blair's leadership and the credentials of New Labour, particularly in a newspaper that epitomized the audience the Labour leader was so anxious to attract, was a heavy blow that irritated Blair. Within a few hours of first reading the article, Blair had faxed the following response to Winning. In a precursor to Blair's matey request to 'call me Tony', he dispensed with the new cardinal's official title of 'Your Eminence' in favour of 'Tom':

Dear Tom,
Thank you for your letter of 8 February.
I was astonished to read in the newspapers this morning a highly personal attack upon me regarding the stall being sought by 'Labour For Life' at Scottish Conference. I was particularly dismayed by your

references to my having stood idly by and your correspondence not even being 'acknowledged'. This is, as you must know, wholly at odds with the facts. For the past two weeks my office has been in contact with your office. There has also been contact between Fr Barry and several Scottish Labour MPs, including the Shadow Secretary of State for Scotland, George Robertson. What is more, two of these MPs have arranged to see you about this very issue next week. We have been trying our utmost to obtain a sensible solution and to do so as sensitively as possible given the very strong feelings aroused by this issue on both sides of the argument.

As I said to you in my earlier letter the question of what stalls are permitted to which organizations is a matter for the Scottish Party and the Party organization. There has been a very long-standing practice not to award stalls to either pro- or anti-abortion lobbies, in part because of feelings this arouses. However, I have always made it clear that people are perfectly entitled to put forward their views in the Labour Party; that it is an issue of conscience and irrespective of the positions in relation to stalls at a regional conference people do express pro- and anti-abortion views within the Labour Party vociferously.

The chance of this being resolved sensibly – which I believe was possible – has not been helped because of the way in which it has become a media attack before we had resolved the matter properly. I am completely committed to freedom of speech on this issue, have frequently made this clear and since I became aware of the problem on 1 February I have been trying to get it settled. I will continue to do so, despite the difficulties.

Yours sincerely,

Tony[6]

In his own handwriting, Blair had scrawled a PS: 'I really am most sorry about all this; but a very personalized attack in the *Mail* has not helped create the right atmosphere of trust.'

Winning's reply two days later was not apologetic and instead had an edge as pugilistic as his article. Formally addressed to the Rt. Hon. Tony Blair, the cardinal's response had none of the Labour leader's personal touch:

I received your letter of 20 February yesterday but was unable to reply immediately because of a meeting of the Bishops' Conference of Scotland.

I am concerned that you interpreted my article in the Scottish *Daily Mail* as a personal attack. This was not my intention. I did emphasize in my letters of 1 and 8 February that the Scottish Executive's decision about Labour For Life raised vital issues of principle of considerable public importance and that I was coming under pressure to take a public stand on the matter. I delayed doing so until 20 February.

I write again because my concerns about the issue of principle have not been addressed in any way either by you or by Mr Sawyer. As Fr Barry also emphasized to Pat McFadden, the issue centres on the freedom of the Labour Party members to put forward a legitimate point of view on what is the most crucial moral issue of the age.

Quite simply, Pat McFadden's assertion on your behalf, and your own position as stated to me – that the matter is essentially an administrative one – completely sidesteps the issue. I do not believe that the Scottish Executive should be the arbiters of principle, and I find it difficult to believe that the Leader of the Labour Party (whoever he or she may be) should have no locus in tackling what, according even to your own MPs whom you have spoken to, is a denial of democratic rights and a denial of opportunities to exercise the right of free speech.

I repeat the issue is not so much about abortion as about democratic rights and clear and consistent decisions to prohibit party members from putting forward alternatives to what is currently party policy.

I recognize only too clearly that abortion arouses strong feelings. That is precisely what it should do. You will be aware of course, that a host of other issues also raise strong feelings – Clause 4, unemployment, the Health Service, Europe, top people's salaries, and so on – but nobody in any political party in Britain has ever suggested that opportunities to air points of view should be denied because of strong feelings provoked.

As I asked of Tom Sawyer in my letter of 20 February – a copy of which I faxed to you – 'If you can decide this regarding the pro-life issue, the question in people's minds is what other issues can you exclude from dialogue in the future?' I should also point out that I have as yet received no reply from Mr Sawyer.

Apropos the specific issue of Labour For Life, Fr Barry, in his discussion with Pat McFadden, alerted him to a crucial point which might have led to a resolution: namely, Labour For Life is not a single issue campaign group and this year, in fact, sought to mount a stall on euthanasia.

Incidentally, that meeting with Pat McFadden took place at Fr Barry's request, to reinforce the point that as far as we are concerned the issues of principle simply cannot be ignored. He stressed to Mr McFadden, and to several Labour MPs, on 14 February, that your failure to reply to my 8 February letter was proving most unhelpful. Mr McFadden responded, in clear terms, that the matter was 'administrative' and not a matter for you. The assertion seems to be totally at odds with what you state in your letter of 20 February regarding your efforts to obtain 'a sensible solution and to do so as sensitively as possible'.

Having spelled out my concerns in three letters to you, one letter to Mr Sawyer and in my article in the Scottish *Daily Mail*, I believe that my primary concern – the issue of principle regarding democratic opportunities for free speech – has adequately been brought to your attention. The remedy to this matter lies in your hands, and a full response to the questions I have been posing would, hopefully, help to resolve what remains a most unsatisfactory situation.

Yours sincerely,

Thomas J. Cardinal Winning
Archbishop of Glasgow

Winning emerged quasi-triumphant. The Scottish Labour Party finally permitted Labour For Life access to the conference, but only after more pressure from inside the party and, in a show of solidarity, a group of MPs including John Reid and George Galloway covered the organization's conference fees. The tough talking had been seen as a success and in order to emphasize the Church's disappointment with New Labour, as Blair had rebranded the party, Winning attempted to turn a long-standing lunch engagement with Ian Lang, the Conservative Secretary of State for Scotland, to his own advantage. Two years after accusing Scots of 'cowardice' for failing to evict the Conservative Party in its entirety, Winning attempted to infuriate the Labour Party by moving closer to the government. Emerging from the appointment on 1 May 1995, Winning described Ian Lang as a man with whom he could do business. Before the meeting took place, Noel Barry was quoted anonymously as stating relations between the Church and Tony Blair had reached 'rock bottom' and was 'it not inconceivable that this meeting could bring the Tories and the Catholic Church much closer together'?[7]

In reality, Winning was moving closer to a political corpse and the meeting angered a number of Glasgow priests who took to grumbling with their parishioners after Mass the following Sunday about their archbishop's behaviour. 'What the hell does he think he is playing at, hanging out with the Tories?' said one priest. It was a question Ian Lang asked himself. During the lunch, which was also attended by Noel Barry and Lord Peter Fraser, the Health minister, Winning had said to Lang: 'You think I'm a socialist and a Labour supporter, but I'm not. I'm a Catholic, and that is what determines my reaction to politics.' Winning had originally heard Jacques Delors make a similar statement and liked the political philosophy so much he had borrowed it. Lang's reaction was to stay silent. 'I think I bit my tongue there because he had said some pretty outrageous things about the Conservatives, which were simply factually inaccurate and based on prejudices.' As Secretary of State, Lang had wanted to improve relations with the Church and wished to point out that on a range of issues such as denominational schools and lifestyle issues, the Conservatives were closer to the

Church's thinking than Labour. 'It is actually revealing on a Freudian level that he saw the Labour Party as the important relationship and lunch was therefore aimed at sending a message to them rather than to make contact with the Conservatives and value the links that would flow from that,' said Lang.

After the antagonism that emerged over Labour For Life and Winning's meeting with Ian Lang, the Secretary of State's shadow counterpart on the Labour Party's front bench, George Robertson, wished to redress the balance and invited the cardinal to a private meeting with Tony Blair. Conflicting schedules meant it was 15 February 1996 before Winning and Barry arrived at the House of Commons. Both men lingered in the public gallery, for that afternoon, Robin Cook attacked the government over the Scott Report into the sale of arms to Iraq, which was released that morning. The meeting took place in the offices of the Leader of the Opposition with Winning and Barry squeezed together on a sofa facing Blair, who was at his most congenial, over a coffee table. The conversation drifted through a range of topics including unemployment and the minimum wage, but Winning was most anxious to raise the issue of abortion. He had already examined Blair's voting record and was aware that on thirteen occasions he had voted to support a woman's right to abortion and that, in 1988, Blair had opposed the Alton Bill to restrict abortion to within eighteen weeks of conception, instead of twenty-eight weeks, unless the woman's life was threatened or the foetus was severely disabled. At the time, Blair had been lobbied by both his family's parish priest and constituents to support the bill, but articulated his opposition in an article in *The Times*:

> The inescapable consequence of the Alton Bill is that a woman will be made under threat of criminal penalties to carry and give birth to a child, perhaps severely disabled, that she does not want. I do not say she is right, in those circumstances, to have an abortion. But I cannot, in conscience, as a legislator, say that I can take that decision for her.[8]

When Winning raised the subject, Blair leaned forward and began paraphrasing his article in *The Times*, emphasizing different points with either an open hand or a clenched fist. He told Winning that he believed abortion was wrong, but that, in good conscience, he could not force his view on other women. He felt that the law was the wrong tool and that instead of legal force there should be public persuasion. It was Winning's view that Blair was sitting on the fence. He believed the Labour leader wished to be viewed as pro-life in his private life but was unwilling to take the political flak that would accompany any attempt to apply such a principle in public. Winning then asked: 'On what other policies do you apply such logic?' A question to which Blair had no answer, just a repetition of his previous response. As a result, Winning left their meeting disappointed and angry that Blair, a high-profile Christian, would make no attempt to tackle what he viewed as infanticide on a massive scale.

But what did Winning expect Blair to do? Repeal the abortion law rendering the very act illegal? No. He was aware of public pressure and that his political supporters would never permit such a proposal. In spite of Winning's public insistence in the past that the act be dealt with like 'any other form of murder' – a patently absurd idea – he knew a secular country would not tolerate a return to the butchery of backstreet abortions, especially when over 50 per cent of Scots Catholics were in favour of the current provision. What Winning wanted was a gesture, a review of current policy, as he explained: 'He could reduce the timescale for abortions, but he's unwilling to even do that.' Winning's belief was that Blair had suppressed his own views on abortion to further his political career:

I would hate to attribute that type of approach to him, that his political career is more important than this, but there has never been any attempt by him to lessen the grip on abortion that the Labour Party has. He has never made the slightest appeal to say 'go easy on this'.

What Winning viewed as a lack of consistency led him to cast doubts over the Prime Minister's personal faith. 'It is difficult to pass judgement on the bloke's spiritual life. The fact that he goes to Mass with his wife is a positive point as far as I am concerned.' But, as Winning then pointed out, mere attendance was not enough: 'Mr Smith was a Christian who went to church on Sunday. Mr Smith then went to hell for what he did on Monday.' Winning described Blair's attitude to abortion as: 'Take a superficial approach to things. If it gets hot, dodge the issue. Wash your hands of it.' The analogy of washing his hands is ironic as the cardinal was unfamiliar with Blair's sympathy towards Pontius Pilate, whom he regarded as the second most interesting character in the New Testament. On Easter Sunday 1996, Blair explored his views on Pilate in a newspaper article:

> One can imagine him agonizing, seeing that Jesus had done nothing wrong and wishing to release him. Just as easily, however, one can envisage Pilate's advisers telling him of the risks, warning him not to cause a riot or inflame Jewish opinion. It is a timeless parable of political life. It is possible to view Pilate as the archetypal politician, caught on the horns of an age-old political dilemma. We know he did wrong, yet his is the struggle between what is right and what is expedient that has occurred throughout history.[9]

Winning believed he could take the measure of a man in a single meeting and felt Blair had come up short. Six months later he took another opportunity to point out what he felt was expediency triumphing over what was right. The vocal religiosity of Tony Blair had inspired the BBC documentary strand, *Everyman*, to explore the connection between Christianity and Britain's political system. In his letter of introduction to Winning, who was invited to take part, the programme's producer, David Campanale, posed the question: 'Is the public being served up an opportunistic, watered-down Christianity for merely electoral reasons – an 'à la carte' approach which discards the unpalatable bits of the Church's historic teaching on faith and morals?'

The question had a resonance with Winning and he was impressed by the calibre of the contributors who included Dr Jonathan Sacks, the chief Rabbi, Melanie Phillips, a columnist he greatly enjoyed, and politicians such as Jack Straw and John Redwood, all of whom promised what he viewed as serious debate. Winning's contribution was conducted at the height of the Roddy Wright affair, and as his comments proved to be the most controversial, dominating the headlines in the week of transmission. It is important to be aware of exactly what he said:

I personally could be regarded as, sometimes referred to as, a left-wing person. I have never heard anyone call me a socialist. I said to Ian Lang, when he was Secretary of State for Scotland, 'Don't think that when I talk in public sometimes about a social conscience that I am a socialist.' I told the story about Jacques Delors where the politician said 'Jacques Delors isn't a socialist, he doesn't need to be. He is a Catholic and he is only applying the values of the gospel to the issues of today', and that's what I would be doing. So there's no need to be a socialist to do that.

New Labour does have a number of Christian politicians and yet it has consistently avoided condemning abortion. I don't believe you can just brush aside the absolute right to life and be prepared to stand up for other rights that are less important than that.

There is a life committee in the Labour Party, for example, and we had a terrible job a couple of years ago in Scotland; they were refused a stall at their annual conference, a pro-life group. And it was only because the Labour MPs in Scotland put their hands in their own pockets and paid for the stall that they got the stall. To me, this is – and it was said at the time – almost Fascist in the approach. And I'm afraid Mr Blair sort of washed his hands of it and still he says he doesn't agree with abortion but he would not condemn it, something like he doesn't want to condemn it or to have a policy on it.

And I asked him if he had a policy on theft. So there's an inconsistency there which belies a certain brand or a claim to have Christian values that to me is a sham. So I would be very wary. The Conservative Party has got some very good principles and in my dealings with members of the Conservative Party here in Scotland, the Secretaries of State, we have a good relationship.

I think the Christian faith of the Conservative Party stops somewhere along the line and the right-wing ideology takes over from it. But, again, I would not like to question the Christian conscience of any of those who claim to be Christians. I would like their credentials, I mean the credentials of these so-called Christians who are putting forward Christian principles in politics, I would like to see their credentials . . . without calling into question their sincerity. I want to see the whole picture.[10]

The two most inflammatory words were 'Fascist' and 'sham'. Winning was forever a fan of the broad-brush stroke on issues requiring a finer point, and this would lead to difficulties and accusations of offensive behaviour. The programme was to be broadcast on Sunday 28 October 1996, a fortuitous date as it fell just six days after publication of 'The Common Good'. The statement by the Bishops' Conference of England and Wales of guidance for voters in the following year's election was roundly accepted as favourable to New Labour at the Conservative government's expense. Tony Blair was so pleased by the document that he sent a letter of praise to Basil Hume, a point the Cardinal kept quiet for fear of further accusations of partisanship by the Catholic hierarchy. Yet if the bishops of England and Wales had blown up New Labour's balloon, their colleague north of the border now appeared with a pin.

In order to attract publicity for the programme, Winning's comments were issued to the press by the BBC on Friday 25 October, and sparked a round of front-page stories of the 'Cardinal Winning Attacks Labour' variety. New Labour's rebuttal was swift and to the point. A statement by Tony Blair was issued in which he said he 'profoundly disagreed' that how MPs voted should be a matter of party policy, insisting it had always been left to the conscience of each individual. 'The issue has never been pro- or anti-abortion but whether, by making abortion illegal, we do not simply drive the problem on to the back streets, which is the reason why the abortion law was reformed in the first place. That is a position taken by many practising Christians.' Alastair Campbell, as Blair's chief spokesman, asked why his boss had been so singled out, while John McFall, the Shadow Deputy Scottish Secretary, began a clarion call for an apology, insisting a red hat did not qualify Winning to call others Fascist.

On Saturday, Blair was forced to shore up his image by giving an interview to the *Sunday Telegraph*, where he was asked if the dictates of his private conscience would lead him to oppose abortion. Blair replied 'Yes', which allowed the paper to run a front page the following day that read 'Blair: I'm Against Abortion'. The paper then took him to task in an editorial for repeatedly going against his conscience and the views of his constituents by voting for abortion. 'Mr Blair apparently voted against his conscience in order to conform to conventional wisdom.' In Scotland, Labour MPs loyal to their leader began criticizing Winning's statements; Helen Liddell said her constituency was almost 100 per cent Catholic and those attending her surgery were 'outraged' at the cardinal's 'attack'. Tom Clarke branded it an 'ill-considered over-reaction' while John McFall continued his defence, this time calling the comments a 'gross insult'. In a series of anonymous briefings, Labour Party members promoted Winning as power-hungry – playing to the Vatican and anxious to succeed Pope John Paul II. Others pitched him in the unlikely colours of a true-blue Tory whose press secretary, Noel Barry, was a personal friend of John Major. A line more easily swallowed down south than up north.

Over the weekend, Winning was domiciled in the Vatican, staying at the new hotel built for use during the next conclave and, if his opponents were to be believed, already plotting his campaign to succeed to the seat of St Peter. In reality he was attending a meeting of the European Bishops and he perused each day's newspaper coverage as the front-page stories arrived by fax. They made depressing reading and Winning was in no hurry to return to Scotland and another few rounds with the Labour Party. A point he found baffling was Labour's confusion over why he had targeted Blair. In his mind it was simple: Labour was the only party to have incorporated a policy on abortion into their manifesto. Moreover, while previous party leaders such as Neil Kinnock and John Major had voted for abortion, neither was religious. Blair, on the other hand, had trumpeted his Christianity and was almost certainly set to be the next Prime Minister. Why not target him if it had the potential to push him into a defence of the unborn? The problem was, however, that Blair would not be bullied.

Winning was not scheduled to arrive back in Scotland until Tuesday evening and so a press conference was called for Wednesday morning. Meanwhile, the Society for the Protection of the Unborn Child (SPUC) and the Movement for Christian Democracy both faxed briefing papers to Winning's office, ammunition for the forthcoming fight. The MCD's fax included Blair's detailed voting record on abortion and a series of counter-arguments to dismantle Labour's defences. The MCD pointed out that while the party claimed a conscience vote, during the Alton Bill, party whips persistently reminded MPs of party policy and a number of those who voted for the bill, such as Frank Field, faced immediate attempts to deselect them. The fax from SPUC went on to highlight comments by Mo Mowlam, the Shadow Minister for Northern Ireland, who had stated that a Labour government would extend the Abortion Act to the province.

The following day, after Winning's return, Labour marshalled their forces. Donald Dewar, the party's chief whip, used an intermediary to contact a close friend, Mgr James McShane, a contemporary of the cardinal's and the parish priest of St Margaret's in Clydebank. Dewar was anxious to appease the situation and appealed to McShane to calm his archbishop down and avoid any further provocation. That evening, McShane spoke to Winning but to no avail. After McShane asked Winning to lay off Blair, Winning replied simply: 'Blair can take it.'

The press conference took place in the Eyre Hall in the Diocesan centre with Winning taking the same hot seat and peering over the same thicket of microphones as when he had handled questions on the Roddy Wright affair six weeks previously. In deference to Tony Meehan, the PR man whose advice he sought during the Roddy Wright affair and who had criticized him for wearing a grey shirt, which he felt lacked authority, the shirt Winning wore was black, presenting the picture of Catholic authority to the assembled press. Flanked by Fr Danny McLaughlin, Tom Connelly's deputy, Winning waded into battle. If New Labour were expecting a hint of retreat or a few placatory words, they were to be disappointed. Winning opened the conference by explaining that the reason for provoking the debate was to ask all political parties whether or not the Abortion Act of 1967 was appropriate for 1997. Asked if he intended to apologize for being specific to Tony Blair, he refused, insisting quite unashamedly that his comments were not personal. As with the *Daily Mail* article, Winning made a habit of making personal remarks then denying this was his intention. 'I have no intention of apologizing for something I did not do,' he explained before wading in once again regarding Blair's record on abortion. Noel Barry had already briefed the press using MCD's material, explaining that on twenty-eight pro-life issues Blair had been absent on fifteen occasions and had thirteen times given 'as we regard it, an anti-pro-life vote'. Winning then went on:

Tony says he's against abortion. But how can you be against abortion and vote for it on occasions? That's the point. The inconsistency of that line doesn't fill me with great confidence for the future. What I'm calling for is a discussion on this so that the Labour Party can clarify its stance on abortion. It is the only party that has an official line on abortion – since 1985 – and that is to promote the 1967 Abortion Act. How can you say that you are against abortion and that it's a matter of conscience and go out and vote for it?[11]

When asked directly if he could vote for Labour, Winning once again attempted to have it both ways, pointing out that he was 'not in the business' of telling people how to vote but based on the abortion issue alone he could not vote Labour. However, he quickly added: 'If I considered it on several issues, I consider the Labour

Party has done a great deal for this country.' This was not enough to stop the *Glasgow Evening Times* splashing on the cardinal, saying he could not vote Labour – an error corrected the following day.

There were those who strongly supported Winning's views. The two *Flourish* columnists gave their backing and Alex Salmond branded Labour's response as 'hysterical and impertinent', while George Galloway wielded his column in the *Daily Express* to insist the cardinal had a clear duty of faith to state that abortion was incompatible with Christian teaching. 'That is a Catholic religious Clause 4 which will never be ditched however old-fashioned some might think it is.' In England, Basil Hume lent a hand of support to his fellow cardinal, issuing a statement:

> I warmly welcome Cardinal Winning's statement today about the importance of the abortion issue and the need for the country to look again at the 1967 Abortion Act. He reinforces what I said in introducing the English and Welsh Bishops' statement 'The Common Good' last week, that respect for human life at all stages is 'the bedrock of our civilizations, and it is why abortion virtually on demand is one of the greatest scandals of our time.'[12]

Winning's comments had been personally problematic for Basil Hume. Where in the past Winning had envied Hume's emollient spirituality and felt incapable of reaching such peaks, the Archbishop of Westminster was now covetous of Winning's apparent autonomy within his own Bishops' Conference. As cardinals, both men were of equal stature but Winning, with his more pugilistic behaviour, was rapidly becoming a poster boy for England's Conservative Catholics. Privately, Hume had been unhappy with 'The Common Good' 's handling of the abortion issue as too insipid and had requested the committee compiling the document be more proscriptive. Clifford Longley, the former religious correspondent of the *Daily Telegraph*, initially co-drafted the document. Hume, however, had wanted his brother-in-law, Lord John Hunt, a former Cabinet Secretary, to do the job but was dissuaded on the grounds that it would look suspicious to the public. He was even more annoyed when the committee compiling the report insisted the paragraph on abortion which encourages people to raise their voice in protest against the rise in the practice but offers little more, would remain unchanged. After its publication, Hume came under considerable pressure from pro-life organizations such as SPUC which viewed him as unsupportive of their campaign.

Like all controversies over personal statements as opposed to concrete actions the cardinal's comments slipped from the news pages. Winning had refused to apologize and New Labour was still wounded. Privately, Winning was angry at the responses of Helen Liddell, John McFall and Tom Clarke, who he believed had been activated by remote control from Labour's headquarters in Millbank Tower, their buttons pressed by Alastair Campbell and not by any personal response to his own comments. A third meeting with Tony Blair was quietly arranged for the end of November.

Once again they met in Blair's office in the House of Commons. At the meeting Winning, in a reference to Campbell's alleged provocation of the MPs' retorts, told Blair to 'get his tanks off my lawn'. As a conciliatory figure, Blair attempted to build a bridge with Winning over the abortion issue but the cardinal was unable to move beyond what he viewed as a central paradox, the Labour leader's personal opposition but public support. Afterwards, Winning gave Blair a couple of issues of the *Catholic Medical Journal* containing articles on abortion: 'Read them yourself and don't tell George [Robertson] I gave them to you,' said Winning.

At the close of the meeting the two men shook hands. Winning then walked along the corridor, down the stairs, passed security, and left the House of Commons. It was a freezing November evening and Winning had once again walked out into the cold.

EIGHTEEN

A Right to Life

'When I needed it, you gave me a hand up, not a hand out.'[1]

ANONYMOUS WOMAN

'We cannot just say the Holy Father is very happy when somebody is very strong and clear, it has to be strong, clear and compassionate at the same time. I see that compassion in Cardinal Winning.'[2]

DR JOAQUIN NAVARRO-VALLS, SPOKESMAN FOR
POPE JOHN PAUL II

On a wet Sunday evening in late October 1996, Ronnie Convery, the religious affairs correspondent at Scottish Television, was sitting at home with his wife Anne when at nine o'clock, long after their two young children were in bed, the phone rang. The caller was Mgr Michael Conway, Convery's former chaplain at Glasgow University, who was in receipt of a request from Cardinal Thomas Winning. 'I'd like you to come and see me,' explained Mgr Conway. 'The Cardinal would like you to do a wee job for him.' Convery had not seen Winning since he had interviewed him about Roddy Wright six weeks previously but imagined the request would be to write a press release or help in the preparation of a religious report, the standard unpaid favour the Church made a habit of calling in from laymen of talent. He suggested the pair meet the following Saturday and was surprised when Conway insisted the matter was more pressing and asked that they meet that night. As Convery put down the phone and got his coat, he began to imagine the worst and said to Anne as he left: 'Surely not another catastrophe.'

When he arrived at Scotus College where Conway was currently rector, he found, not a second errant bishop, but an offer of a job. The Roddy Wright affair had been mishandled and the newspaper coverage about Fr Noel Barry and his alleged affair with Annie Clinton, though false, had been no less damaging. There was also the matter of the priest's subsequent revelations to Winning (dealt with in the next chapter), which had led the Cardinal to view his press secretary as fatally compromised, though he felt bound to support him publicly during the forthcoming lawsuit. In the meantime, he had begun to take soundings on a possible successor and two friends, Mgr Conway and Professor Eileen Anne Millar, a lecturer in Italian at Glasgow University, had suggested Convery. His CV marked him as a strong candidate, for he was fluent in Italian, the Church's working language; he had graduated with a first-class honours degree; his career in the media, both print and television, had marked him as a talented writer who was also at ease on screen; while his personal life, happily married with two children, allowed him to project an upstanding image. The job was presented by Conway as playing the role of Bernard Ingham to Winning's Margaret Thatcher and was enticing enough for Convery, who was a keen student of politics, to agree to meet the cardinal in a fortnight's time.

The meeting took place on the eve of Winning's departure to Rome where he planned to celebrate the twenty-fifth anniversary of his ordination as bishop in the company of his family, but instead of looking back, his mind was fixed on his next few years as cardinal and his desire to shape the political agenda and dislodge the issue of abortion from the rut into which it was jammed.

In the appointment of staff and the recruitment of collaborators, Winning leant heavily on the recommendation of people whom he trusted as well as on his own private intuition. He had a habit of bracketing people very quickly as 'one of us' or 'one of them' and Convery was slotted into the former category within minutes of his arrival at The Oaks. Winning assured him that he was well aware of the quality of his current position and the importance of Convery's securing a reasonable financial package if he was to be swayed. Before the matter reached such a stage, Convery had two important issues to discuss.

The first of these centred on Convery's own spiritual life as a supernumerary, as married lay members were known within Opus Dei, the Catholic religious movement which had attracted controversy within the wider Church on account of its secretive nature, elitist attitude and, to moderates, Catholic right-wing stance on certain issues.

The movement had been founded in 1928 by a Spanish priest, Mgr Josemaria Escriva de Balaguer (who was to be canonised in autumn 2002), as a pious association of clergy and lay people, and had taken its title from the Latin for 'work of God'. The concept was that members would embark on a rigorous spiritual programme that included daily Mass, weekly confession, and one hour of mental prayer each day – through which they would sanctify their work and 'bring their spirituality into their work place'.

The organization had since grown to include eighty thousand lay members, two thousand priests, and was now the most powerful of the new religious movements, with more senior Vatican appointments within its ranks, in comparison to their number, than the Jesuits, to whom Church historians compared them. (The charges levied against Opus Dei are similar in manner to those made against the Jesuits upon their formation during the Counter-Reformation.)

Loyalty to the Pope had been Opus Dei's mantra and in 1982 this was rewarded when John Paul II recognized the movement as a 'personal prelature', allowing it to operate across national and diocesan boundaries and outside the control of local bishops. To critics, Opus Dei was a divisive institution, one which verged on being a cult and which was anxious to recruit only the richest and smartest candidates whom they would then manoeuvre into places of influence.

Basil Hume had become so concerned at what he viewed as Opus Dei's indoctrination techniques that he precluded them from working with teenagers in the diocese of Westminster. One area of concern was the group's practice of self-mortification: Escriva regularly flagellated himself, although members could choose a milder form such as a cilice, a chain strapped round the thigh as an irritant, to be worn as a penance for sins. Yet to their supporters, Opus Dei was the living embodiment of Vatican II; laymen and -women who acted as a true witness to Jesus Christ.

Convery had been drawn to Opus Dei while a student at Glasgow University and was aware of Winning's initial hostility to the movement; a hostility he displayed towards anything he viewed as divisive or which smacked of ecclesiastical snobbery. When the organization had first opened a house in Glasgow, Winning had let it be known that he would keep a close eye on their practices but when Convery raised his membership now, Winning seemed untroubled. He had obviously been informed about it, and he asked Convery to explain what was involved. When Convery took Winning through the daily routine of Mass, diet of spiritual readings and dedicated time set aside for mental prayer, the cardinal seemed impressed, commenting that such dedication would be a welcome change.

Ironically, over the subsequent years, Winning was to develop a soft spot for Opus Dei, defending them publicly when they were attacked and commenting that 'their theology is my theology'. Convery, on the other hand, left the organization eighteen months later, declaring the rigorous lifestyle to be 'impossibly demanding'. This did not dampen the suspicions of Winning's critics, nor some of his supporters who believed Convery's influence was seen in a hardening of the cardinal's comments.

The second issue Convery raised was Noel Barry and his own reluctance to step on his toes. Winning explained that Convery's role would be complementary rather than competitive: working in the background, preparing speeches, conducting research and developing ideas, while Barry would continue to operate front of house. Although this differed substantially from what Mgr Conway had suggested, the offer still proved attractive, but as soon as Convery began to convey his enthusiasm, Winning began to backtrack. 'I can't promise anything, we'll have to find the money for it and I will have to go and pray about it. But I have a simple belief that if God wants it, it will happen.'

A fortnight later, Winning extended the offer. An official press release was issued announcing Convery's appointment as a current affairs adviser to the cardinal, yet because of his background in journalism, it was generally assumed he would also handle the press. The next day, the *Scotsman* published a leader welcoming his appointment on the grounds that the Church's PR was disastrous: 'Will Mr Convery have some wise things to say on great moral issues, and will the Cardinal be wise enough to listen to him on how the Church's case should be stated?' pondered the paper before concluding his success required 'perfect health' and the 'hide of a rhinoceros'. Convery found the column humorous but was touched when Winning called him at home, concerned in case the article had caused offence.

Meanwhile, Father Noel Barry had expressed his concerns privately to Mgr Tom Connelly that he was being squeezed out by Convery, but the pair nevertheless settled into an amicable working relationship with Convery redirecting any press calls to Barry's office and continuing to contribute articles to *Flourish*. As Convery had as yet no clearly defined job description, a former storeroom as an office and little to do, he was glad of the diversion *Flourish* offered. 'At the beginning, Winning felt I was underemployed and would give me things to read and I would panic, thinking this was very important, but it was just to keep me busy.'

The threat of indolence would no longer be a problem come March.

The General Election of 1997 coincided with the thirtieth anniversary of the 1967 Abortion Act, and for the first time in political history the public would be given the opportunity to vote for a pro-life party. As an alternative to what protesters saw as every political party's meek acquiescence of the status quo as regards the provision of abortion, their own party, the Pro-Life Alliance, was formed to provide an alternative. Their ambition was to field over fifty candidates, a number that would permit them access to a party political broadcast, in which they intended to use graphic footage detailing the effects of an abortion to a startled nation. The party, who would field ten candidates in Scotland, was inspired by Winning's strong stance in recent years and believed they would attract the Catholic vote. As Countess Josephine Quintavalle, the organizer with the alliance, pointed out: 'There is a strong Catholic vote in Scotland and traditionally that is a pro-life vote.'[3]

Unfortunately, this was no longer the case. While Catholics were still more likely to oppose abortion than were Protestants, atheists or agnostics, their opposition had greatly weakened. Between 1979 and 1992, the percentage of Catholics polled who felt that NHS provision of abortion had gone too far, fell from 46 per cent to 16 per cent, while those who believed provision was about right practically doubled, from 22 per cent to 41 per cent. Just as Catholics used birth control, divorced, remarried and 'lived in sin', to use the old colloquialism, all against the explicit rules of the Catholic Church, so many no longer viewed abortion as black and white but rather an excruciating decision in myriad shades of grey. The current reality of Catholic lay thinking was brought home to Winning in February 1997 when BBC Scotland broadcast a documentary, *Faith, Votes and Sanctity*, which set out to examine whether or not a Catholic voter would be swayed over a candidate's stance on abortion. A poll of 400 Catholics found that 68 per cent favoured a woman's right to choose and 51 per cent disagreed with the Church's public involvement in politics. Winning had been invited to take part but declined, allowing Noel Barry to speak on his behalf. When the poll was published he dismissed it as flawed and wrote to John Birt, the director general of the BBC, to complain.

As a priest, Winning had always opposed abortion but since being made a bishop and the subsequent discovery, while preparing his Episcopal coat of arms, that his father was illegitimate, his response was more personal. If he had been conceived a hundred years later to a poor servant girl and a reluctant father, Thomas Winning senior would have been lucky to have been born. The issue of abortion troubled Winning not only as a cardinal and a Catholic; it troubled him as a son. The question was what could be done about an issue that, like trench warfare, saw both sides dug in behind impregnable positions, convinced of their own right? Winning's idea was to climb out of the trench and walk towards those women who found themselves alone in 'no man's land'.

On the morning of Monday 3 March, Winning called Convery into his office to discuss a forthcoming speech. In six days time he was to address a rally for the Society for the Protection of the Unborn Child (SPUC) as he had done many, many times before. This time would be different. He wanted to make an impact. The event was to be held at Glasgow's Caledonia University on Mother's Day and with the General Election expected in a few months' time, Winning felt now was the time to raise their banner. The question was what could be said that had not already been said again and again? Convery was despatched to speak to Fr George Donaldson, a lecturer at Scotus College and an expert on the issue of abortion and bioethics, and he in turn suggested he read *The Hand of God* by Bernard Nathanson, an American doctor who had performed thousands of abortions, including one on his own child by his mistress, before a Damascene experience led him to argue against the practice. By the time Convery had returned from his research, he believed he had come up with an idea that would change Winning's image. He had read in *Familia et Vita*, an obscure Vatican journal, about the plan put in place by Cardinal John O'Connor of New York to offer financial help to women facing crisis pregnancies. Convery deliberately withheld the source of the idea as he was aware of Winning's dislike of O'Connor. The idea was not new as The Innocents, a pro-life organization, had long offered a similar service but, as Convery pointed out, the impact of such a statement of help from a cardinal would be invaluable. The next question to address was how much help exactly? Noel Barry, who had floated similar ideas in the past, was brought into the discussions and together the three men began to bounce around ideas. When Convery and Barry raised concerns that the Church might appear too generous, Winning argued that they were not dealing with a mass market. His offer would be to any woman who wanted to keep her child, but whose financial circumstances were pushing her towards having an abortion. It is incredible that no calculations were made, no funds accrued, nor even a rough mental note made of how much each woman might require; instead, the decision was made that the offer would be the major theme of Winning's speech and Convery was despatched to write it up. If the diocesan debt was the nadir caused by Winning's lack of interest in financial matters, then the Pro-Life initiative was its glorious summit. Only a man for whom money sat a long way down his list of priorities could have made such an offer, almost on the spur of the moment, without sinking into the inevitable mire of consultation and compromise.

Once the speech was prepared, the three men met again to discuss the publicity the offer could generate. They felt it was crucial that the offer was presented as stealing a march on the pro-choice opposition for the very reason that it offered a choice to women considering an abortion because of lack of funds. Convery and Barry were sure the story would be big and that the speech should be leaked to a Sunday newspaper to ensure that the dailies then covered the speech. A broadsheet was favoured over a tabloid on the grounds that it could give it in-depth treatment, but it was felt the *Observer*, the *Sunday Times* and *Scotland on Sunday* would provide the story with a negative spin. The most likely candidate to promote the story positively was the *Sunday Telegraph* whose editor, Dominic Lawson, had taken a persistently pro-life line, and although Winning was concerned by its small Scottish readership of twenty-five thousand, his advisers argued that by the end of Saturday night every paper would be carrying the story. John Clark, a former PA reporter-turned-freelance, was invited up to Clyde Street and the story and a copy of Sunday's speech was dropped in his lap.

The plan unfolded with only the slightest of wrinkles. The *Sunday Telegraph* splashed the story on the front page, but used the headline: 'We'll Pay You Not to Abort, Says Cardinal', a line that triggered a motif that would later develop into 'Cash for Babies', a reference to the previous government's 'Cash for Questions' scandal.

Before nine o'clock on Sunday morning, Winning received his first phone call from an individual who wished to donate £50,000. One hour later, an English woman called pledging the profit from her house sale. By the time Convery arrived at The Oaks to collect Winning, it was apparent to both men that they had triggered something special. Television cameras from the BBC and ITV were in place at Glasgow Caledonia University alongside a posse of newspaper reporters and such a media presence delighted the veteran members of SPUC who had grown weary of their message being of interest only to the Catholic media. Winning had been an indifferent speaker throughout his career, neither particularly charismatic nor eloquent, but he rose to the occasion, not simply delivering the speech, but preaching it. He began with a light allusion to his recent spats over abortion: 'It is an issue that I've once or twice highlighted in recent months, not necessarily to the liking of politicians of varying persuasions.'[4] He then moved on to tell the story of Bernard Nathanson. The mentality of devaluing life, Winning argued, was making serious inroads in society and after the unborn, the frail and elderly, the sick and the disabled would no longer be valued; it was against this 'Culture of Death' that he unveiled his bold new initiative:

Today I issue an open invitation to any woman, any family, any couple who may be facing the possibility of an unwanted pregnancy. I strenuously urge any person in that situation, of any ethnic background, of any faith, from anywhere, to come to the Archdiocese of Glasgow for assistance.

Today I can announce a new set of provisions that have been put in place to help you. Whatever worries or cares you may have, we will help you. If you need pregnancy-testing or counselling, we will help you. If you want help to cope with raising the baby on your own, we will help you. If you want to discuss the adoption of your unborn child, we will help you. If you need financial assistance, or help with equipment for your baby and feel financial pressures will force you to have an abortion, we will help you. If you cannot face your family, or if pressure in your local area is making you consider abortion, come to us, we will help you find somewhere to have your baby surrounded by support and encouragement. We will help you. And finally, if you have had an abortion, if you are torn apart with guilt, if your relationship has split up because of abortion, if you are suffering from post-abortion stress – come to us, we will help you.

This invitation, I repeat, is open to all. Irrespective of age, creed or colour. Today I urge anyone in that situation – let us help you to avoid making one of the biggest mistakes of your life. Call us at our archdiocesan headquarters from tomorrow onwards. We will help you in whatever way you need. I make this pledge today as a genuine and practical response from the archdiocese of Glasgow to this fundamental problem facing society.

Winning closed his speech by explaining how it was the work of organizations such as SPUC that had convinced Bernard Nathanson to change his mind and his practice and to transform himself into one of the most prominent Pro-Life advocates in America. 'Public opinion is turning. It may be slow, but it's turning. And I think that we have good grounds for hope that in the new millennium we will see the "Culture of Death" with which we are currently grappling give way to something new. Pope John Paul has a name for that something new too. He calls it a "civilization of life".'

Winning left the stage to a standing ovation and applause which would echo for weeks to come. After the event press photographers were insistent he pose with a baby and so Convery went through the audience. When a willing mother was found and the child procured, an audience member shouted: 'Make sure he's not a Jesuit, or we'll never get the kid back.' The photograph of Winning pulling faces for a dozy four-month-old girl appeared on the next day's front pages.

Despite Winning's assurance in his speech that 'a new set of provisions' had been set in place, at this stage this assurance was nothing but words. There was no office, no telephone line, no funds set aside, no manager in place – there was barely even a plan. Instead there was only Winning's belief that, in the words of St Teresa, 'all will be well; all will be well, all manner of things will be well'.

The person who would be given the task of transforming words into deeds had not even been informed. Roseann Reddy had been a member of SPUC for fifteen years, an interest that developed after the discovery that a close friend had had an abortion but had felt unable to discuss her decision. For the past few years, she had worked for the Archdiocese Pastoral Care Trust. On Sunday evening she returned from Mass and switched on the television to see her goddaughter held aloft by the Cardinal. Later in the evening, Peter Smith called to say: 'The Cardinal was thinking, would you like to run this for him?' Taken aback at the Church's lack of preparation, but aware that this was Winning's way, she joked: 'I was just thinking the Cardinal wasn't thinking.'

The response to Winning's initiative was mixed and, among the pro-choice organizations, openly hostile. A spokeswoman for the Abortion Law Reform Association argued the Church was applying 'unfair pressure on women'[5] to squeeze them through a difficult crisis, then 'dumping them'; the Birth Control Trust accused Winning of organizing a 'publicity stunt' backed by a 'bribe'; while a spokeswoman of the National Abortion Campaign insisted a celibate man was unfit to even participate in the debate of such an issue. Among the newspapers, the *Herald* performed a soft-shoe shuffle, praising Winning for his courage and Christian charity then chastising him for indicating that money is the only reason for abortions – a claim he had never made – before finally asking: 'Where on earth (or in heaven) will the financially tottering archdiocese of Glasgow find the resources to cope?' Noel Barry had argued with journalists that the issue was far more complex than merely giving people 'a blank cheque' or handing over 'a fistful of fivers', and that the financial offer had been overplayed at the expense of other provisions. Yet the financial offer was to remain the initiative's greatest strength. The *Daily Telegraph*, meanwhile, delivered a leader that read like a love letter: 'Little if any effort is made to offer advice to women who are thinking of having a termination on the options that are available – particularly adoption. It is this hole in the system that Cardinal Winning's initiative aims to plug. As such it could and should be welcomed, not just by anti-abortionists but also by charities, social workers, doctors and the government.'

The response that upset Winning the most emerged from the diocese of Westminster where Basil Hume described his fellow cardinal's initiative as a good lead and 'one we should all consider carefully'.[6] What Winning desired was unanimous backing and a thunderous back slap; instead, what he received was a polite, if distinctly cool, applause and a hint in the phrase 'consider carefully' that the lead might not be so 'good' after all. When informed of Hume's comment, Winning replied testily: 'What the hell does he mean by that?' In fact, Hume nurtured a twinge of jealousy over the autonomy that his northern neighbour exercised – Winning was able, almost at the drop of a hat, to launch a headline-grabbing initiative while in England and Wales Hume himself struggled to maintain a consensus. Then of course there was the issue of money: like everyone else, Hume had no idea how Winning could afford to make good his promise. The answer was provided by the generosity of strangers matched to the frugality of those women in need. The boldness of Winning's gesture had captured the imagination of people throughout Britain who wished to make donations, while those who sought his help wished no more than what would tide them over. Fears of the Church being asked to fund a child to their sixteenth birthday, like an absent father snared by the Child Support Agency, evaporated as quickly as the press puffed them out.

The day following Winning's speech, Monday 10 March, Roseann Reddy arrived at the diocesan offices shortly after nine o'clock to find a camera crew outside the office. Inside, Winning explained that he felt she was the most suitable person to coordinate the initiative. 'He was just unbelievably calm and yet there was nothing planned, there was not a scrap of paper. We had three women literally appear on that first day at the door. We took them downstairs to the counselling rooms and went from there.'

As Reddy prepared himself at one end of the building, Ronnie Convery was at the other taking a call from a businessman in the City of London who had read about the initiative in that morning's

Telegraph and wished to donate £40,000 in five annual payments of £8,000. He was not alone. Charitable donations were to arrive in such a flood that in two weeks over £250,000 would be collected and there was therefore no need to dip into the diocese's own pockets.

The first afternoon, Roseann Reddy received a call from a woman in obvious distress. A mother of three children, she was now pregnant with a fourth; a child neither she nor her husband felt they could afford to keep. In an incident of touching synchronicity, she had heard of Winning's initiative on the car radio while she and her husband returned from an initial appointment at an Edinburgh abortion clinic. Upon returning to her house, her children presented her with daffodils for Mother's Day and she realized how desperately she wished to have the child even though an abortion was now booked for the following Tuesday. On the Monday evening, Reddy drove to Edinburgh to meet the family and assess their needs. The woman's husband was in a low-paid job and she herself worked part-time as a cleaner, a position she would have to give up for the first few months if she was to keep the child, and it was this loss of income, combined with the additional expenses of a double-buggy, nappies and supplies which she feared would tip the family into penury. In her living room she broke into tears. Reddy, however, assured her that the Church would do all it could. In the end, and on paper, it did not seem that much – a double-buggy, a Moses basket, nappies and baby feed for the first couple of years, and a cash supplement to the couple's income during the weeks when the woman was unable to work – yet it was enough to save a child's life and lead a mother's gratitude to express itself in a note that would come to encapsulate the philosophy behind Cardinal Winning's Pro-Life Initiative, as it would come to be known: 'When I needed it, you gave me a hand up, not a hand out.'

Winning's Pro-Life Initiative was to earn him the sobriquet of 'hero of the Church', a title bestowed upon him by Archbishop Barbarito, the Papal Nuncio, when he attended the Bishops' Conference later that first week. There Winning's fellow bishops chose to adopt the initiative, under Winning's name. It was an issue on which they had, once again, not been consulted, but one which they heartily approved of. An example of Winning's control and authority over the Bishops' Conference is illustrated by his next step in the battle against abortion, for having now given assistance to women in crisis pregnancies he wished to reapply the pressure to the politicians. Where the Bishops' Conference of England and Wales's pre-election document, 'The Common Good', was compiled by a committee, and so judiciously prepared that even Basil Hume was unable to secure a stronger line on abortion, the Scots document, 'Throw Open the Doors to Christ', was written almost entirely by Ronnie Convery on Winning's instruction, enjoying only the slightest of tweaks by the six other bishops. In 'The Common Good', the issue of abortion was reduced to a single paragraph in which Catholic electors were reminded of Britain's acquiescence in the 'Culture of Death' and urged to 'raise our voices in protest', but whether or not this was to be done at the ballot box was entirely unclear. The Scottish document, by contrast, left little room for doubt, arguing that all other political issues such as housing, health or education, were all dependent on the right to life and that this issue should take precedence. The inspiration for the pastoral letter was a papal document, the papal encyclical *Evangelium Vitae*, read by Convery which argued the same point. 'Throw Open the Doors to Christ' was printed in April and disseminated throughout Scotland's parishes two weeks before the General Election on 1 May and if the fears of politicians had been realized and the Church truly had the ability to direct voters to place their tick next to the candidates they favoured, then the nine pro-life candidates standing in constituencies across Scotland would have enjoyed a huge increase in votes. But the Pro-Life Alliance's performance was a little less than dismal, pulling in 5,172 votes from nine seats, an average of 1.54 per cent of the vote per seat, except in East Kilbride where they accrued 2.4 per cent.

The General Election of 1997 which swept Labour to power in a landslide that also wiped out every Conservative MP in Scotland, appeared to confirm what had long been suspected – namely that the Catholic Church's power over voters was an illusion. The Church's pre-election statement had largely been ignored by the Catholic voter, but even so, Winning refused to view it as a waste of time, feeling that the Church had done all in its power to raise the issue, and that the rest lay in the hands of the Holy Spirit and the conscience of the new government.

For all his political heckling and political point-scoring, Winning's true triumph on the issue of abortion was the fact that he extended his hand to women in need, a gesture of such simplicity that it would be later be praised by Germaine Greer, the feminist academic, as providing 'real choice'. In *The Whole Woman*, her sequel to *The Female Eunuch*, she wrote: 'Cardinal Winning no doubt hopes the government will take over his responsibility and offer support to every child conceived. Feminists should share his hope.' Winning was surprised by her support and said he was grateful for it, but he could not help but comment to his aides that Greer had always struck him as resembling 'someone who had been dragged through a bush backwards'.

The issue of abortion would come to dominate the headlines in Scotland for the next two years but there was no visible evidence that the thousands of words in newsprint, radio reports and television broadcasts had any effect in changing the minds of those for whom the practice remained a necessary evil. In October 1997, the thirtieth anniversary of the legislation legitimizing the practice, Winning spoke out again, while Hume urged Tony Blair, the new Prime Minister, to reassess the legislation that permitted the largest number of abortions in Europe. In Scotland, the issue's prominence went on to attract the militant pro-life organization, Precious Life, a provocative Christian fundamentalist group who favoured picketing women's health clinics, the targeting of doctors and the public display of photographs depicting torn foetuses in buckets of blood – all to Winning's grave distaste. Yet in the first year of operation, his initiative assisted dozens of women and saw forty-one children born who otherwise might not have been. Over the next five years, only five women would visit the offices then proceed with an abortion, and four out of the five returned to the Church for counselling.

The death of Diana, Princess of Wales, on the night of Saturday 31 August was of little concern to Winning. He regretted the death of anyone before their allotted three score years and ten and felt briefly for her two sons, William and Harry, whom he included in his prayers that week, but in Clyde Street or The Oaks there would be none of the outpouring of grief witnessed so publicly throughout the rest of the country. In truth Winning was intimidated by royalty. He had been introduced to the Queen on a couple of occasions (both times at memorial services – one for the Lockerbie disaster, the other following the Gulf War) and he would describe her as someone 'to whom I have nothing really to say'. It was on these occasions that he felt his working-class roots fixed him to the spot. Once, he bypassed a royal reception at Windsor Castle in favour of a quick return to Archbishop's House in Westminster for a bowl of soup on the grounds that 'he couldn't be bothered', only to discover that the Queen had asked where he had gone.

The prominent emotion in Glasgow in the week between Diana's death and her funeral was anger, rather than grief, over what Winning considered a public snub to himself, and by extension Scotland's Catholics, over his seating arrangement at the Princess's funeral.

Winning had been informed that due to space restrictions he would be unable to sit with the other religious leaders such as Basil Hume, Dr Jonathan Sacks and members of the hierarchy of the Episcopal Church and the Church of England. In attempting to represent the geography of Britain, the Dean of Westminster, Wesley Carr, had Hume representing Britain's Catholics and the Moderator of the Church of Scotland representing Scotland. No amount of phone calls from Winning, delicately handled but forceful, would change his mind. He was apologetic but refused to budge. Winning, in turn, then refused to attend, a dangerous move that threatened a public backlash against him. Alex Salmond, leader of the SNP, was contacted in an attempt to put a little public pressure on the issue, but even his outraged comments accusing the funeral organizers of snubbing Scots Catholics were to no avail.

Two days before the funeral, Winning solicited the advice of Noel Barry, Tom Connelly and Ronnie Convery over whether or not he should attend, but first stated his own view that he should not. Each man said in turn that he should swallow his pride and attend. 'Do you really think so? I'm amazed you feel that way. But if you think so, I'd better go.'

In a volte-face, the speed of which stunned them, he picked up the phone to book the next flight to London. On Saturday, two hundred million people around the globe watched Elton John sing his reworked tribute to Marilyn Monroe, 'Candle in the Wind', and Winning, thanks to a last-minute change, was seated one row behind Tony Blair, the new Prime Minister. As Winning later recalled: 'It was the perfect position from which to keep an eye on him.'

NINETEEN

The Spin Doctor Who Came Unspun

> She came all the way to Preston
> Where in the Crest trousers are pressed on.
> It took two full days,
> But I was amazed
> That she pressed and pressed and pressed on.[1]
>
> FR NOEL BARRY AT THE COURT OF SESSION

> 'He's damaged goods now. He'll never operate front of house again.'[2]
>
> MGR TOM CONNELLY

When the call came, all Fr Noel Barry could think about was that he already had enough on his plate. In September 1996, with the Roddy Wright affair having spiralled out of control, he was facing his own demons. On a Monday morning, the *Sun* newspaper had cast aspersions about an improper relationship with Annie Clinton, a former headmistress, and although entirely false, the story had deeply damaged the Cardinal's press spokesman. Now a voice from the past threatened to sink him. When Noel Barry phoned the office on the day after the story ran to check for any messages, his secretary told him there was only one: a Caroline Keegans Brown had called, wishing to talk to him urgently.

Barry was taken aback. Caroline Keegans Brown was a former nun with whom he had had an illicit relationship while working as a young curate at St Ninian's, a large parish in the west end of the city. The couple had first met in 1981 when Caroline was a young member of the Franciscan order, and a mutual spark had ignited as Barry flirted during an invitation to tea. They did not meet again until 1984, after Caroline had left the order and had taken a post working with the handicapped in Bellshill, a small town in Lanarkshire a few miles from Winning's birthplace. A brief meeting after Mass and an exchange of phone numbers had led to coffee and, in the space of a few weeks, a love affair. The couple – he was twenty-eight, she was twenty-four – tried to meet as often as possible, kissing in a borrowed car or walking among the Campsie Hills that border the north of the city. On one occasion, they stayed out all night in order to watch the dawn break while they were in each other's arms. It was a confusing time for Barry, ordained only four years previously and already torn between a woman he loved and a vocation that, in his heart, he considered to be true. The couple went on to discuss marriage and opened a joint bank account in order to save towards a future in which they could be together. But instead of leaving the priesthood for marriage and children as so many of his predecessors had done, Barry broke off the relationship and remained to honour his vocation. The last time the pair had met was for a few awkward moments in 1992 when Caroline had dropped into the offices of *Flourish* with a photograph of her recent marriage to Patrick Brown, a residential childcare officer, asking for its publication.

After collecting her number from his secretary, Barry now returned the call, trying to suppress the queasy feeling of nausea. The conversation was brief and strained with little room for the social niceties. Brown said she was calling out of courtesy as she now planned to reveal their relationship to Winning. In light of what she had read in the *Sun*, Barry was patently unsuitable for his position. He was taken aback, but there was little he could do but assure her that she had to do what she thought best. After he put down the phone, he called Fr Peter Smith to ask if she had called. 'It's nothing,' Barry insisted. 'It's all nonsense.' The seed of denial was sown and the fruits would be bitter and public.

When Brown called Peter Smith, she did not explain her reason for requesting a meeting with the Cardinal, but from another source he already had a fair idea and so he arranged a provisional meeting with himself at The Oaks in order to discover the seriousness of her allegations. At the meeting on Wednesday 2 October 1996, Brown insisted that she had had a full sexual affair with Fr Barry and that he was entirely unsuitable for the prominent position he now held. Smith was understanding, but insisted that it would remain her word against his, and Barry had already denied any relationship. He asked if she had any evidence such as personal correspondence. Brown said she had a number of letters from Barry and promised to bring them to a second meeting with Winning. This meeting took place a few days later and was, unknown to either party, watched by the *Sun* which had received an anonymous tip-off that a former flame of Barry's was paying the cardinal a house call.

The meeting between Winning, Smith and Brown, who had also brought a friend along for support, took place in the living room of The Oaks where, only ten days before, Bishop Wright had confessed his secrets. Brown insisted that she had had a sexual relationship with Barry and wanted him expelled from his post as a press secretary. During the conversation, Winning was protective towards his priest. He asked Brown if she possessed any tapes and she said she did not. She also failed to produce the letters that she had told Smith she possessed. While Winning attempted to explain his position, that he could not in good conscience sack his priest over a disputed relationship, Brown broke down and said: 'I don't think you realize how difficult this is for me to come here.' According to Brown's later testimony in court, Winning replied: 'What do you want, tears?' Winning always denied making the statement, a position backed by Smith, but it was certainly well within character. As Mgr Tom Connelly commented later, 'You could hear Tom say that line a mile away.'

Brown was frustrated and angered and left when her attempts to brief Winning proved unsuccessful. The reason for Winning's behaviour was that, unknown to Smith, Barry had already spoken with the Cardinal. He admitted forming a relationship with Brown and contemplating abandoning the priesthood but denied breaking his vow of celibacy. Winning had pushed him a number of times, but Barry denied any sexual relationship and, in the Cardinal's words, the situation – unfortunate but far from uncommon for a young priest – was a 'misdemeanour, not a hanging offence'.

While confiding in Winning, Barry brazenly denied any form of relationship when speaking to Smith and insisted there were no letters either. Winning was reluctant to discuss what Barry had confided to him and never raised the subject with Smith on the grounds that such an issue discussed between a bishop and his priest should remain confidential.

At this point the only people to know of the existence of Caroline Keegans Brown, or so Barry thought, were Winning and Smith. The public had read of the erroneous allegations of a suggested affair between Barry and Annie Clinton, but for the moment, the existence of Brown was hidden. Barry felt under pressure from Annie Clinton to sue the *Sun* and later insisted he enjoyed the Cardinal's full support, but Winning remained unconvinced of the wisdom of such action. He was adamant that if Barry did sue, the archdiocese would be unable to offer any financial aid and Barry would be dependent on others. 'If you were to say I told Fr Barry to sue the *Sun*, you'd be wrong,' was his comment. However, his attitude remained that if Barry, through his own volition, did choose to sue the *Sun*, he would be as supportive as possible.

Barry, however, chose to fudge the issue. A fighting fund set up by Tom Cassidy, a journalist with the *Daily Record* who regularly helped to sub-edit *Flourish*, had been unsuccessful. Monsignor Tom Connelly contributed £1,000 but after contacting dozens of people the pot contained just £4,000. During his years of service for Winning, Barry had become notoriously unpopular with his fellow priests and many members of the media. A generous benefactor was required and so Barry contacted Brian Dempsey and told him that Winning wanted him to sue.

Dempsey and Barry had become close friends over the past eight years and the multimillionaire had attempted to talk the priest out of any legal action. 'You've a great opportunity here,' he told Barry one evening. 'Stand up in the pulpit at St Joseph's and say: "She's not a friend, she's one of my best friends. I have nothing to cover up. There is nothing sexual going on. I have a day off and I'm entitled to spend it without denying my vows." Then you should say to the *Sun*: "I'm a man of no means. I can't sue. I'm in a weak position and as a man of God I'm expected to turn the other cheek and do so willingly." You should turn it to your advantage.'[3] But Barry would not be swayed by Dempsey's advice and insisted legal action was his only option. When his benefactor quizzed him on the existence of any skeletons that might prove problematic, Barry made no mention of Caroline Keegans Brown and insisted that his cupboard was clean. Dempsey was bolstered by Barry's assurances and agreed to fund his legal case on the following conditions: that this was what the Cardinal wanted, that this was what Barry wanted, and that they were both quite clear that he believed they were wrong in their actions. He then lodged a substantial five-figure sum with the priest's lawyers, McSparran & McCormick of Glasgow, who also acted on occasion for the diocese of Glasgow. John McCormick was to give Barry the same advice as Dempsey, which was to play on his inability to sue, but Barry was insistent.

It had been said many times of Noel Barry that he had an eye for the bishop's crook and mitre, an ambition he persistently denied, saying that anyone coveting such a role 'needed their head examined' – the correct response in an institution that frowns upon ambition. Yet he was aware that Winning had been without an auxiliary bishop since John Mone's departure in 1988, and it had been a role colleagues felt he would have liked to fill.

Barry's critics insisted he had deliberately befriended the leader of Opus Dei in Glasgow, Xavier Bosch, on the grounds that the prelature was rumoured to have influence over the Congregation of Bishops, the Vatican office with the responsibility for handing out crooks and mitres, once again a statement Barry denied. But any ambition Barry might have nurtured to rise further within the Church he had served to the best of his abilities (temptations aside) for two decades was to collapse in public humiliation and private rejection by Winning, a man whom he had loyally served.

Born in London but raised in County Cork and educated first at the Scots College in Valladolid in Spain and later at Cardross and Newlands in Scotland, Barry was ordained in 1981 and had risen to the position of Winning's de facto spokesman on account of his abilities as a writer and political interests that paralleled those of his archbishop. As a close acquaintance of Alex Salmond and George Galloway, he kept Winning up to date with political gossip and, far from stirring him up, would often be responsible for calming him down. There was both a public and private side to Barry's relationship with Winning. On any occasion where the press were in attendance Barry would be bolted to his hip, chain-smoking cigarettes and growling down disrespectful questions. On two occasions they had gone on holiday together, including a trip with Tom Connelly to Brian Dempsey's home in the Cayman Islands.

The libel trial fell on an unfortunate date: the third week in December 1998 was Winning's Golden Jubilee, the fiftieth anniversary of his ordination as a priest. Ecclesiastical anniversaries were of great importance to him, lending themselves to an opportunity to celebrate with family and friends the goodness of God's grace. He had wished to celebrate the date in Rome at the Basilica of St John Lateran, the church of his ordination, but the cost to his niece and nephew and other family members had preyed on his conscience and instead a long weekend was organized at the Seamill Hydro on the Ayrshire coast. As December carried not only the long shadow of the court case, but a diary packed with Christmas preparations, the celebration was brought forward to the long September weekend. On the Saturday, Winning stole away with his nephew Edward to watch Celtic at Parkhead then returned that evening for a celebratory dinner. On the Sunday, Mass was celebrated in a private room with his grand-niece and grand-nephew fulfilling the role of altar servers.

Winning returned from the tranquillity of the rugged Ayrshire coast to the news that John King, the former director of social services, had been listed as a witness for the *Sun*'s defence. When Barry broke the news to him, Winning replied: 'That bastard, what the hell has he got to do with anything? It's just to cause us embarrassment.' The diocese had been alerted to King's involvement by a phone call from a former city councillor who had remained friendly with the former priest. He had then called Ronnie Convery and asked Barry to get in touch, but the priest refused and insisted King speak instead to his solicitor. The news, in the event, was positive with King explaining to John McCormick that he had no intention of appearing on the *Sun*'s behalf and that on the necessary dates he would be in America on a long-arranged golfing holiday.

On Tuesday 8 December, Annie Clinton and Noel Barry's libel case against the *Sun* began at the Court of Session in Edinburgh. The press were ready in attendance for what promised to be the court case of the year, involving not only sexual intrigue but also the Cardinal's right-hand man. Father Barry was first in the witness box for a testimony that would last three days and would dredge through his personal life with true diligence. The first day progressed smoothly with Barry determined to pitch the *Sun* as the work of the Devil complete with the whiff of sulphur. He first referred to the paper as the 'beast' and went on to say he had sensed a 'malignant force at work'. He insisted he and Clinton had a strictly platonic friendship and illustrated the distress suffered by the paper's intrusive tactics. After being disturbed at home and accused by a reporter of having an affair with the former head teacher, the story that subsequently ran had resulted in a number of anonymous abusive phone calls. He recalled how one man had shouted: 'You fucking bastards are all at it. It's about time you got your comeuppance.'[4]

The *Sun*'s defence was simple. Their lawyers argued that the newspaper did not imply any sexual relationship or secret affair and that instead the copy was consistent with a platonic friendship, just one that involved 'bizarre cloak and dagger' meetings, therefore they had no case to answer. A secondary strand to their defence was the destruction of Fr Barry as a credible witness on the basis that he had had a previous affair. On the second day of the case,

Neil Davidson, the newspaper's QC, examined Barry closely to
establish his vow of celibacy. When asked about previous sexual
relations, Barry insisted:

> I have not broken my vow of celibacy. I am as human as any man
> or woman in this room. I have never suggested I am anything other
> than a fragile human being. I am as human as the next person. I
> am as attracted [to others] as the next person. I would be a very
> poor priest if I were inhuman. I have never had sexual intercourse
> with a woman, nor with a man, while I have been a priest. I can
> assure you that it is not because there were times I would not have
> wanted that.[5]

At this point, Davidson stated: 'As far as you are concerned, you
have never had sexual relations with another woman?'

Father Barry answered: 'I have never had sexual relations with
another woman.'

Davidson then sprang his trap: 'If I were to suggest you have
had sexual relations with another woman, will you deny that?'

Before Barry had the opportunity to reply, his own counsel, Paul
Cullen, leapt to his feet and shouted: 'Do not answer that question.'
The intervention was to prevent the question of Barry's sex life
being raised. The reason was simple. For weeks in the run-up to
Barry's case, his lawyers had quizzed him closely on his relationship
with Brown. While Barry was prepared to admit to a relationship
– one that stopped short of sex – to his archbishop, he had dis-
sembled to his lawyers by insisting that there was nothing in Brown's
story. The truth of his relationship emerged only after the *Sun*'s
legal team faxed a copy of Barry's own letters to Brown through
to John McCormick's office at five o'clock on Friday 4 December,
just as he was leaving to attend the annual Archbishop's Ball. This
left only the weekend to restructure their case and grill Barry on
the actual facts, which he now insisted involved a love affair that
stopped short of sex. Back in the courtroom, Cullen attempted to
argue that such a line of inquiry was inappropriate. The jury was
then dismissed while the lawyers wrangled over each point. This

could only mean one thing: the *Sun* had access to Caroline Keegans Brown. Barry returned to St Joseph's parish house in a state of emotional distress.

The following week, the *Sun*'s lawyers revealed in court that they had copies of Barry's letters to Brown and the full extent of their affair was aired in court. On the witness stand Barry admitted falling in love with the former nun, but denied having sexual intercourse. 'I was passionately in love with the woman. Priests are not people of steel devoid of emotion. I am a human being, as open to feelings as anyone else. To fall in love is not a sin, is not a crime. But I took the decision to continue as a celibate priest.'[6] It was then revealed under examination that Barry and Keegans Brown had spent the night together at the Crest Hotel in Preston, near Blackpool, and, according to the *Sun*'s lawyers, the couple had sexual intercourse. There were two points of evidence, the first of which was a letter to Brown in which Barry had written: 'I want to thank you for giving me so much. I cannot begin to tell you how much it meant to me. I will treasure it always.' While the lawyers argued this referred to Brown's virginity, Barry insisted it referred instead to shared feelings and emotions. The second was a limerick Barry had written after the trip. The rhyme read out in court went:

> She came all the way to Preston
> Where in the Crest trousers are pressed on.
> It took two full days,
> But I was amazed
> That she pressed and pressed and pressed on.

Barry insisted that he was referring to a hurtful statement: 'That refers to what was, for her, a very hurtful statement I had made in the course of that night telling her I would not take off my trousers in this hotel room, and if I did it would be to press them on the trouser press.' Barry then sought to discredit Brown by pointing out her involvement with the *Sun*, and taking the moral high ground by insisting that, despite this, he forgave her. 'Although there are people who say that she has betrayed me dreadfully by involving herself with the *Sun*, the truth of the matter is I still love her . . . There are people who would say: "What kind of person is this?" I do not condemn her. I do not attack her. I regret deeply that I hurt her. In conscience I had no choice.'

During the case Winning could not bring himself to read the daily press coverage which, following Barry's testimony, included the headline in the *Mirror*: 'Cleric Tells of Secret Night with Nun.' The papers were left on his desk every day but he pushed them away unread. Noel Barry, meanwhile, was enduring an even darker night of the soul. The previous evening, after his testimony about Brown, he was visited by Dempsey who was furious that he should have been kept in the dark as to her very existence, especially considering he had funded Barry from his own pocket. As Barry, who was visibly distraught, talked of the damage he had done to the Church, Dempsey initially berated him over his secret, before realizing that his friend was in no condition to argue back and that his own behaviour was entirely unconstructive. The evening closed with Dempsey urging him to tell the truth, whatever its form, and saying that, regardless of the outcome, he would stand by him.

The evidence of Annie Clinton was potent and moving. The education adviser spoke of her distress at opening the front door in her dressing gown and being asked by a male and female reporter who told her they were from the *Sun*: 'Can you tell us about your affair with Fr Noel Barry?' The episode had a detrimental affect on her elderly mother who, two years after the story's publication, was still fearful of strangers. The paper had been tipped off about visits by Fr Barry by her neighbour, Barbara Lawson, who had hoped to buy herself a conservatory with the proceeds from selling her story, but in the event she was paid nothing, and later insisted her planned purchase had been a harmless joke.

Clinton told the court: 'What I did all my life was trashed and destroyed because of this article. It is what I am that has been ruined, what I represent, what I stand up for, it is all gone.'[7] She had refused to speak to the paper, which had been extensively briefed on the relationship by a third party, when first approached.

On Wednesday 16 December, Caroline Keegans Brown was finally called to the witness stand. The former nun, now a married mother of two, gave a detailed account of her relationship with Barry. After briefing the court on how they had first met and how their romance had blossomed, she insisted that the relationship had involved sex and that she had lost her virginity in January 1985 in the hotel in Preston. Her testimony was explicit. She described her bleeding after they first had sex and the priest's methods of birth control which had ignored the teachings of '*Humanae Vitae*'. 'He would wear condoms and always told me not to worry. He always withdrew.'[8] When asked about Barry's denial of any physical side to their relationship, Brown insisted that the priest had lied under oath. While Barry had attempted to present her as a Judas, she went on to reveal her unwilling involvement with the *Sun*, a situation she had done her best to avoid. She had refused to speak to the paper when first approached. When the lawyer to whom she turned for legal advice suggested she sell her testimony and wipe out her mortgage, she sought a second opinion. The new lawyer argued that by providing both a statement and evidence to the newspaper the case could well be settled out of court. In the meantime, the *Sun* had increased its pressure on her, warning her that a story could still be published about her involvement with Barry, behaviour that she viewed as a form of blackmail. So in court, stripped of her privacy and dignity and without a financial cushion on which to fall back, her only desire, as she explained, was to 'tell the truth'.

For the duration of the trial, Winning had dreaded the prospect of being called as a real witness. Barry's lawyers had listed the Cardinal as a witness, in part to avoid the indignity of his being listed as a witness by the *Sun*'s defence team. But as the trial progressed, with its revelations about Barry's private life, Winning became increasingly reluctant to take the stand. He was deeply concerned that in court he would be asked to reveal details he considered himself bound to keep private. In Winning's mind, anything discussed between a priest and his archbishop was similar to an exchange between a student and his spiritual director and should remain entirely confidential. He was also conscious of the repercussions faced by Keith O'Brien when he had taken the stand a few years previously when one of his priests faced child-abuse charges. The comments made by the Archbishop of St Andrews and Edinburgh had accidentally rebounded on him when the priest was found not guilty.

After the first few days, Winning had decided that, if called, he would refuse to speak and would request that the court understand his position – but if necessary he was willing to face jail for contempt of court rather than act against his conscience. Fate, however, intervened. Just as a compromise had been reached with the lawyers, enabling Fr Peter Smith to take the stand in his place, the case came to a sudden close. The jury deliberated for just one hour before returning their verdict in favour of Barry and Clinton. They may have doubted the priest's testimony, but they were aware that any previous relationship had no bearing on the case before them, which they viewed as clearly defamatory. Annie Clinton was awarded the sum of £120,000, while Barry received only £45,000 – less than half this amount. It was a gesture which was picked up by the priest's critics who were even now lining up to demand his dismissal. Hugh Farmer, editor of the *Scottish Catholic Observer*, stated: 'Even if Father Barry is to be believed when he says he didn't have sex, he still admitted to being in a hotel room in Preston with her. We have to ask, is this acceptable behaviour for a priest?'[9] A headline in the *Daily Record* asked: 'Was it Worth it, Father Noel?' To which the answer was an emphatic 'no'. Noel Barry may have felt he had no choice but to pursue the case, yet his victory was purely Pyrrhic. His reputation lay in ruins.

A public ceremony to celebrate the fiftieth anniversary of Winning's ordination was scheduled for Sunday 17 January 1998, the feast day of St Mungo, patron saint of Glasgow, and a suitable distance from Christmas and the misery of Barry's court case. Winning was now seventy-three, but a healthy lifestyle and judicious use of a running machine on which he exercised every day had served to strip a decade from his appearance. As the cathedral was too small to contain the two thousand invited guests, an altar was erected in the city hall, where Winning concelebrated Mass with Cardinal Basil Hume and Cardinal Cahal Daly, the former Primate of All Ireland. Among the guests sat Donald Dewar, the Scottish Secretary, and Alex Salmond, leader of the SNP, who both listened as Winning used his twenty-minute homily to defend the family, an institution he considered under threat. 'Husband, wife and child in a stable environment. The sooner society returns to that model, the healthier it will be.'[10] In a precursor to what would become Winning's most formidable campaign, he spoke out against the gay lobby. The speech had been heavily trailed in the previous Friday and Saturday newspapers, with Ronnie Convery briefing the media of the Cardinal's intended target. In the speech's most controversial passage he said:

> 'There are well-organized and resourced forces at work in our society, hell-bent, I see, on destroying that Christian family. To those people I say, you will not succeed in destroying the Christian Church's commitment to the family – whether you use all-out assaults on the institution of marriage or try to trick us under the guise of political correctness into accepting all sorts of lifestyles which are quite simply unacceptable to the Christian.'[11]

The attendance of Noel Barry, together with over a hundred of the diocese's priests, could be read either as a show of solidarity or a public display of how far he had fallen. Formerly Winning's right-hand man, his position in the back row on the far left of the altar, a fair distance from the principal celebrant, spoke volumes. The *Sunday Times* had run a story sourced to Tom Connelly on an unattributable basis that Barry would no longer act as Winning's press secretary, but, prior to the service, the Cardinal dismissed the suggestion as 'absolute rubbish' and described his priest as 'a man of good standing'. He had no interest in washing his dirty linen in public, but all press calls were now referred to Ronnie Convery. After a civic reception at the City Chambers and the presentation of a new portfolio by Pat Lally, the Lord Provost, the guests drifted home, some anxious to catch Winning's appearance that evening on Scottish Television's *First Minister*, a documentary strand allowing various individuals the fantasy of running the new Scottish executive. Winning's contribution was predictable but heartfelt: abolition of student fees, public purse payments to stay-at-home mums, and the abolition of Trident and nuclear weapons. The most novel contribution was a school for politicians where new members of the Scottish parliament could be briefed on economics, ethics and education.

The question of what to do with a broken spin doctor and a loyal priest was a source of confusion to Winning. There was an assumption within the Church in Glasgow that Barry should be despatched straight away and allowed to re-establish himself in a distant diocese where the echoes of his unfortunate limerick and the name Caroline Keegans Brown would not reach. If he had been an ordinary diocesan priest, he might have been permitted to stay, but the maintenance of his current high-profile role was impossible. Tom Connelly had advised Winning not to take any immediate action lest the Church be presented as dancing to the media's tune and he had privately suggested to Barry that he wait a couple of months before requesting an indefinite leave of absence. 'Then you are going on your own terms,' explained the older priest.

At the end of January, Brian Dempsey and his girlfriend invited Barry to join them at his holiday home in the Cayman Islands, thinking that the hot sun and warm waters would aid his recuperation. Barry, burnt out and deeply depressed, accepted. A decade of six-, sometimes seven-, day weeks spent juggling the editorship of *Flourish*, a busy parish and press duties for a demanding employer had left him weary and in great need of a break. The only matter to be settled was what he would do when he returned. Barry wanted his position as parish priest at St Joseph's to remain open, but Winning wished his press spokesman to depart without ties and he had already begun, as early as January, a period of steady disengagement. He began insisting that he had never appointed Barry as his press spokesman and that the priest had purloined the title. This was a stance that made him appear both petty and churlish. Whatever the title, be it cheekily borrowed or officially bestowed, Barry had fulfilled an essential task, one which now fell on the shoulders of Ronnie Convery to whom Winning said: 'I'm sorry about all this. I hadn't meant this to happen.'

In order better to facilitate Barry's removal, Winning enlisted the assistance of Brian Dempsey to help explain his position. A departure date of Saturday 25 July was negotiated but Barry was under the impression he was to return to St Joseph's; it was only the day before his departure that he discovered this was not the case. Winning was insistent that he give up his position as parish priest to allow a new man to be appointed. Winning also insisted he see Barry's farewell sermon. He felt it was insufficiently contrite and hinted at a return in a few months, when in reality it would be years. Once again, Dempsey was despatched to calm troubled waters.

From the lectern of St Joseph's, Barry found the brief speech difficult to deliver without the accompaniment of tears:

The past year has been the most exhausting of my life. More and more I've felt the need to regain my energies – physically, mentally and spiritually. Some months ago I discussed the way I was feeling with the Cardinal. He has given me permission to take an indefinite period of leave beginning next week to allow me to get fully fit. I've been deeply touched and humbled by the support you have given to me and by the friendship and, indeed, the care you have extended to me. I want to thank you for that. And I think the best way I can begin to repay you is not only by apologizing for thoughtlessness, and for faults and failings on my part, which I do, but to take time to revitalize myself for the work which will be given to me on my return.[12]

At the end of the Mass, the priest wept openly, comforted by his parishioners. Barry's exile to Dublin, to a flat paid for once again by Dempsey, was to last two and a half years. Not until after Winning's death was he permitted to return and to perform, in Glasgow, the duties for which he was ordained. The crux of their estrangement was Winning's doubt over the validity of Barry's court testimony, coupled with the fear that his cupboard was not entirely clear of skeletons and that his return would trigger a fresh bout of tabloid interest. Barry believed his concerns were entirely misplaced, as the media silence that greeted his eventual return would prove, and so for two years he struggled to extract funds on which to live and endured a string of broken promises about the date of his return. Meanwhile, Winning wished to wipe the slate clean of Barry's fingerprints. A new editor, Vincent Toal, was appointed to *Flourish* and both George Galloway and Alex Salmond were dropped as columnists on Winning's instructions, without a note of thanks for their years of contributions. Winning also instructed Toal to dispense with the services of Tom Cassidy, who had laid out the monthly newspaper for the last fifteen years. When Cassidy wrote to Winning to express his disappointment at the manner of his dismissal, the Cardinal replied, in a bizarre letter, that his appointment had been made by Barry and had not been with his approval. In fact, Cassidy's position preceded Barry's own appointment as editor, a point he made in response. Cassidy dismissed Winning's next letter, in which he attempted to fudge the issue, and chose to let the matter lie. Barry had no choice but to do the same. His long period in limbo was tortuous and poorly handled by Winning, but served to rekindle Barry's pilot light for the priesthood. After all the mistakes and media attention a less committed character would have abandoned his collar and, like so many others before, he would not have returned to quietly do the work to which he was called.

TWENTY

The Opinion that Dare Not Speak its Name

'I deplore homosexual acts. I hesitate to use the word "perversion" but let's face up to the truth.'[1]

CARDINAL THOMAS WINNING

The creation of a Scottish parliament within the first term of the new Labour government – the first in 292 years since 'the parcel of rogues', as Robert Burns described those parliamentarians who, in 1707, sold out his nation's independence in return for a chest of gold – was to provide Thomas Winning with the opportunity to play politics on a playing field that, at long last, was level.

The reduction of the system of government from a large and remote entity situated five hundred miles south in the heart of Westminster to a smaller, indigenous parliament in Edinburgh was to the cardinal's overwhelming advantage. As he had grown in stature from archbishop to cardinal, so the institution over which he wished to exert an influence had shrunk. No longer would he be locked out of discussions, unable to access ministers or civil servants, all the while watching enviously as Basil Hume breezed up and down the corridors of power. Now he, too, would take his place at the table, scrutinize policy, argue for improvements, and voice his concern for the common good. Yet the fact that within a single year, from the parliament's first sitting, he would be so disillusioned with the infant institution that he would brand it an 'utter failure', illustrates the fact that politics was a profession to which, though he was passionate about it, he was not best suited. All those years spent locked outside had served to strengthen his lungs for shouting, but reduced his capacity to reason and compromise. The gift of subtle nuance and manoeuvrability was absent from his armoury, which at times appeared to consist only of a verbal battering ram.

However, in the run-up to the first Scottish parliamentary elections in May 1999, Winning seemed to embrace subtle statecraft, adeptly positioning his pieces in order to best promote victory for the Scottish National Party. Alex Salmond, the SNP leader, was the man he wished to take the title First Minister, not Donald Dewar, then Secretary of State for Scotland, whose general distaste for religion irritated Winning and who remained a crucial cog in New Labour, the party with whom he had grown deeply disillusioned.

In September 1997, the Scottish people had voted overwhelmingly for the creation of a Scottish parliament with tax-raising powers, and six months before the inaugural elections, Winning chose to reveal his subtle support for independence and the SNP.

The occasion was a speech on 5 October 1998 in Brussels to an audience of civil servants and MEPs invited by the Commission of Bishops' Conferences of the European Community (COMECE). On the surface, the speech, entitled 'A New Scotland in a New Europe', was a straightforward report on the issue of nationalism in Scotland at a time when nationalism was a dirty word across Europe, raising the spectre of bloodshed throughout the Balkans, the violent anti-immigrant rhetoric of the Northern League in Italy, or the Front National in France. This provided Winning with a veil of deniability against the inevitable accusations of political favouritism. The views expressed in the speech had been discussed during a series of private meetings with Salmond stretching over the past two years, but the SNP leader was unaware of the cardinal's plans and was told only a day before the speech's debut that he might enjoy its contents.

The speech was filmed by BBC Scotland who were alerted to its value by that morning's edition of the *Herald* which broke an embargo to reveal the contents under the headline: 'Winning Praises Nationalist Rebirth'. Winning went on to do just that, stating:

> Democrats can be assured that the emerging sense of nationhood and political nationalism in Scotland is unique in European terms. It is mature, respectful of democracy, and international in outlook. Why should this be so? Quite simply because it is emerging in uniquely fortuitous circumstances. What we are seeing is the rebirth of ancient nationhood in a cradle of modern democracy. An old-as-yet-new nation is taking its place once more on the world stage with its legal system, democratic institutions, respect for human rights, educational facilities and all the rest already in place. Few other nations can have emerged on to the world stage in recent centuries in quite such auspicious circumstances. Of course, the new Scottish parliament will not be fully sovereign. Westminster will remain the ultimate authority. But recent polls show an increasing openness among Scots to the possibility of full independence – probably around ten years from now. Certainly younger voters seem to back this option.[2]

The speech delighted the nationalists and appalled the government, who were deeply concerned about the rise in SNP support and feared that the Scottish parliament, the 'unfinished business', as the late John Smith, the former Labour leader described it, might finish the union. Where Winning saw a party 'mature, respectful of democracy and international in outlook', the Labour government perceived only 'wreckers', those who would take a hammer and chisel to the bonds that had united the two nations for nearly three centuries.

Yet it was not to be. Despite Winning's invitation to the SNP leader to address the Catholic Headteachers' Association of Scotland one week before the election in yet another sign of political anointment, the party failed to win control of the parliament despite support at an all-time high. Instead, they watched as a Labour and Liberal Democrat coalition, led by Donald Dewar, emerged with its hands on the reins of power.

*   *   *

The Opinion that Dare Not Speak its Name

On 1 July 1999, crowds gathered along the Royal Mile in T-shirts and sunglasses to catch a glimpse of the Queen in an open carriage as she trundled along the route to the Assembly Hall, high on the Mound where the new parliament would temporarily be in residence. As thousands of Scots waited in anticipation of the march of fledgling members of the Scottish parliament, dignitaries and senior MPs bearing the greetings of Westminster, Winning was inside a neighbouring hall renewing a series of old acquaintances.

Gordon Brown, the Chancellor of the Exchequer and a politician Winning had long admired, was also waiting for his name to be called to join the forthcoming procession and the two men fell into conversation. Brown, a son of the manse, who shared many of the cardinal's concerns on social justice, complimented him on the Church's role in Jubilee 2000, the international pressure group urging the cancellation of all Third Word debt. Winning accepted the compliment only to raise a perennial complaint – the Scottish Church's lack of access to the civil servants and the ministers of Westminster. Brown agreed with Winning but added that he believed the Scottish parliament would greatly ease past tensions. Winning then moved on to speak first with the Moderator of the Free Church of Scotland before being approached by a diffident man in scuffed desert boots and a red C&A sports jacket. Brian Souter, the chairman of Stagecoach, the international rail and bus company, had that year been listed by the *Sunday Times* with his sister Anne Gloag, as Scotland's first billionaire, but in sartorial terms the businessman was strictly bargain basement, often carrying business papers not in a leather briefcase but a plastic carrier bag. Souter was an evangelical Christian and a keen admirer of Winning's stance on abortion and his pro-life initiative, a point he was quick to make before he went on to thank him for his moral leadership. Winning was in a jovial mood and, sensing Souter's nervousness, put him at his ease by rubbing the lapel of his jacket and commenting: 'I've never touched a millionaire before.' A few minutes later, Winning's name was called for him to take his seat inside the new parliament, while Souter and other VIPs would watch the proceedings on CCTV in a secondary venue. As Winning departed,

Souter shouted: 'I may be a millionaire, but you've got the better seat.'

From the public gallery, Winning watched as the Queen bestowed upon the parliament a silver mace inscribed with the words: 'wisdom, justice, compassion, integrity'. He listened as First Minister Donald Dewar captured the day in a single sentence: 'Today there is a new voice in the land, the voice of a democratic parliament.' He was moved, almost to tears, as Sheena Wellington set the mood in song by her bittersweet rendition of Burns's 'A Man's a Man'.

The previous January, Winning had taken part in a thirty-minute documentary for Scottish Television entitled *First Minister*. The role of First Minister was now filled, but Winning was soon to move into the unofficial position of Leader of the Opposition. The opening of the Scottish parliament closed with a brilliant fireworks display, a harbinger of the political dynamite that would blow up the following autumn, throwing Thomas Winning and Brian Souter into a potent partnership.

The death of Basil Hume a few weeks previously, on 18 June, after a short battle with cancer which he had borne with formidable grace, was to leave Winning as Britain's only cardinal and illustrate his paradoxical approach to power.

On a personal level, Hume's death saddened him greatly, and the death of yet another contemporary turned the spotlight on his own mortality, but he took the opportunity to release a lengthy appreciation to the press praising his versatility in administering to both prince and pauper and altering the Catholic Church in Britain for the better: 'That is due, in no small measure, to Basil Hume the establishment figure, Basil Hume the diplomat, Basil Hume the wise counsellor, but most of all because of Basil Hume, the holy monk.'[3]

On a professional level, Winning used the opportunity of Hume's funeral to express his concerns to the English hierarchy, gathered as they were to mourn their lost leader, about their decision to pursue the possibility of taking up the government's offer of seats in a reformed House of Lords. While the English Catholic Church appeared anxious to join their Anglican counterparts in scrutinizing legislation, Winning was appalled at the very thought which he described as 'madness'. In spite of his strong political opinions and rigorous attempts to influence policy, he believed strongly the Church must remain outside the political process – a view shared by the Vatican, to whom the English hierarchy planned to write for permission to explore how, if at all, they could accept such an offer. Privately, Winning could understand his neighbours' desire, after centuries of prejudice, to be assimilated as part of the Establishment, but it was an ambition he could not condone. In the event, the English Church was to let the offer pass by.

After fulfilling his final engagements in July, Winning slipped away for the month of August to the little cottage Dr Anna Murphy owned in a village in Donegal. In the whitewashed house, which had a large garden and sea view, Winning spent his time in a new pursuit he described as 'pottering' – not the manufacture of glazed vases, but the idle flicking from one relaxed activity to another. He walked, read the newspaper cover to cover, and tried a single round of golf during which his swing displayed serious signs of rust, his back ached and, by the fifth hole, he had had enough, commenting: 'Maybe the game's passed me by.' Guests were invited by turn throughout the four weeks and included Mrs McInnes, his sister and his niece, together with her husband and children, followed by his nephew and his family. The holiday offered a window to retirement and for once Winning, now seventy-four, liked what he saw. Previous holidays had been spent in perpetual motion characterized by packed days and visits to the local diocesan office to examine their system of operation, but this year he returned proud of his new-found appetite for relaxation.

At the Edinburgh International Festival in August 1999, James Mac-Millan, the celebrated Scottish composer (who is also a Catholic), gave a controversial lecture, entitled 'Scotland's Shame', in which he insisted that the country was blighted with endemic bigotry and that Catholics continued to suffer persistent discrimination. In an impassioned speech he utilized the term 'sleep-walking bigotry' to capture the steady, persistent and, often ignored, quality of the condition. The reaction among the press and other Catholic commentators was hostile. MacMillan was accused of displaying the country's dirty laundry in front of foreign guests, gathered for the city's myriad festivals, and over-hyping a problem that was but an echo of the roar it once had been. Yet the lecture was seismic enough to reopen a debate scuffed and worn by decades of being kicked about. A book of essays was commissioned and edited by Professor T. M. Devine, author of *The Scottish Nation*, entitled *Scotland's Shame?*, which reacted to MacMillan's accusations both positively and negatively, depending on the outlook of the contributor. But it was a debate from which Winning was removed, both physically and, curiously, emotionally. He had been on holiday in Ireland when MacMillan made his speech and was uncontactable for comment. In private, he sympathized with the composer's view but, having lived through the 1930s, he felt tremendous progress had been made and that what remained was merely the silt at the bottom of the barrel.

Pockets of fierce anti-Catholicism still existed in Glasgow and while it is standard to argue that there are bigots on both sides, what is rarely accepted is that there is greater violence in speech and in act by sections of the Protestant community directed against the Catholic community, than vice-versa. As Dennis Sewell points out in his book *Catholics: Britain's Largest Minority*, while Orange Lodge bands sing songs with lyrics such as 'Fuck the Pope and the Virgin Mary', there is no Catholic comparison. The victims of violence after an Old Firm match are more likely to be Celtic fans, whatever their actual denomination, than Rangers fans and there has been no Catholic equivalent of Donald Findlay, the prominent QC who was filmed singing anti-Catholic songs with lyrics such as 'We are up to our knees in Fenian blood. Surrender or you'll die' at a Rangers post-victory function. Yet, despite this, Winning knew such feelings would take time to drain from the city's psyche and so instead he focused his determination on that element of insti-tutionalized sectarianism: the Act of Settlement. The fact that, prior to his death, the Scottish parliament had voted unanimously in support of its repeal and the Prime Minister hinted that it was under review, led him to the firm conclusion that progress had truly been made.

In Scotland, the parliament had tripped up in its first few weeks as the new MSPs debated little other than their own pay and holidays, a situation that quickly triggered a cloud – no surprise, given the Scottish summer – over what comedian Billy Connolly had already dismissed as the 'pretendy parliament'.

Inside Dewar's cabinet, the Blairites were anxious to flex the parliament's muscles and lead the way in the development of new policies for a new Scotland, but unfortunately the policies would have found greater favour among the chattering classes of Islington than up a tenement close in Easterhouse.

Wendy Alexander, the Minister for Community, the brightest of the new politicians and a woman groomed by Dewar as his potential successor despite her relative youth, wished to promote the repeal of Section 28 of the Local Government Act, a piece of legislation over which the average voter would only scratch their head in ignorance.

Introduced by Margaret Thatcher in 1988, Section 28 may have been dusty and relatively unknown but to the gay community it was a mark of prejudice they wished removed. The law specifically prevented the 'promotion' of homosexuality by local authorities and had been introduced to the statute books in response to ex-plicit material found in the classrooms of schools under the control of various liberal London councils in the mid-1980s. While a promise to repeal Section 28 could be found within the Labour Party's manifesto, there had been no mention of any such plans during the party's campaign for the Scottish parliament earlier that year where the same policy exists under a different title: Section 2a. (Throughout the forthcoming debacle both politicians and

protestors used Section 28, Section 2a and Clause 28 almost inter-
changeably.) Alexander was supported in the Cabinet by Dewar's
chief of staff, John Rafferty who, since leaving the archdiocese in
1993, had grown in stature and influence within the Labour Party.
Rafferty had been a long-time 'fixer' for Dewar, having organized
a strong campaign for the then Shadow Scottish Secretary against
the Poll Tax, while more recently he had earned the Prime Minister's
respect by revitalizing the party's Scottish election campaign. When
he arrived in March, the Scottish Labour Party was riddled with
infighting and ill-prepared to face a strong campaign by the SNP.
Rafferty, however used ruthless determination to carve out a substantial victory. As chief of staff he now attracted attention for
his empire building including an analysis in *Scotland on Sunday*
that presented pictures of both Dewar and Rafferty and posed the
question: 'So which of these two men is really running Scotland?'

The Catholic Church was perceived as an obvious threat to a
peaceful removal of Section 28 and in order to smooth out potential
problems, Rafferty paid a return visit to Clyde Street in early
October. This was only his second visit to the offices since working
for the diocese six years before. He had been invited to a drinks
party in 1998 to celebrate the erasure of the diocesan debt almost
five years to the day since his own five-year-plan had been implemented. As a few bottles of red and white wine were shared among
staff in the accounts and estates department, Winning had approached Rafferty and offered his appreciation. 'I'll be for ever in
your debt,' said the cardinal, to whom Rafferty replied in jest: 'Have
you not learned anything? You've not to be in debt with anyone.'
Eighteen months on Rafferty had come not so much to collect as
to remind, but as Winning was in Rovigo, accompanied by Ronnie
Convery, to speak to the Italian pro-life movement, the meeting was
with Peter Smith (now a monsignor) and Tom Connelly. Rafferty
explained how the Minister for Community was to announce the
repeal of Section 28, and that this would be followed by a three-
month period of consultation and the Church would have an important say in what would appear in the revised guidelines. Connelly
and Smith listened attentively as Rafferty closed with a request

for a temperate response before adding: 'Let's not go to war with each other.'

While Rafferty approached the Church, Wendy Alexander called Ron Mackenna, the political editor of the *Daily Record*, Scotland's largest tabloid newspaper. The paper was to be offered an exclusive on condition the story was sensitively handled. Mackenna agreed to speak to the *Record*'s editor, Martin Clarke, a former editor of the *Scottish Daily Mail*, who had transferred his Home Counties sensibilities to the nation's most powerful redtop. While Clarke was anxious to highlight the implications of the change, his reporter argued that he had a deal he was reluctant to break. Mackenna filed the story before travelling to Dublin where the First Minister was visiting the Taoiseach but that night he was confronted by John Rafferty and David Whitton, Dewar's press spokesman, who brandished a faxed copy of the *Record*'s front page and demanded to know: 'What the fuck is this?' Mackenna could only argue that he had written the story straight as he gazed at Clarke's headline: 'Gay Sex Lessons For Scots Schools'. The motif for a protest movement had been set in bold type.

The article explained that Section 28 would be removed with the introduction of the Ethical Standards in Public Life Bill scheduled to go before the new parliament early in 2000 with a final vote in June. Under the previous law it was deemed an offence for schools or teachers to promote homosexuality or tell pupils that such sexuality was acceptable in a family relationship. Wendy Alexander's argument was that restrictions such as this had led to an increase in bullying, which only the law's removal could tackle, and that any public fear of the promotion of a homosexual lifestyle to impressionable young children was unwarranted as any such practice would be blocked by existing controls and child protection systems. Instead of promoting homosexuality, the executive was removing, in her words, a 'vindictive and unjust piece of Tory legislation'.

The government were not without their supporters. The STUC, the Scottish Parent Teacher Council and the Educational Institute of Scotland were all quick to praise their plans. In truth, the decision to remove Section 28 was ideologically motivated. Hints of teachers with hands bound in red tape unable to prevent the bullying of children over their sexuality out of fear of prosecution were spurious at best. The motive was to remove all barriers or stigma tagging gay men or women as in any manner different. Winning believed this move was a reward to the gay movement for their long support of the Labour Party during the eighteen years of Conservative government.

Winning was first briefed on the repeal of Section 28 after he returned from Rome in early November, and while he was suspicious and uncomfortable with the government's plans, releasing a statement to this effect, he showed greater concern over a second bill scheduled to pass through the parliament – the Adults with Incapacity Bill – which he viewed as opening a back door to euthanasia. Winning dismissed Rafferty's visit as an attempt to 'buy off' the Church with the promise of consultation and yet when he travelled through to Edinburgh, he did not even raise the issue. In early December, Winning had had an appointment to say prayers at the Scottish parliament, a daily act of worship, that, in collaboration with other religious leaders, he had fought to secure in the face of Dewar's secular opposition. John Rafferty had arranged that on the day, the cardinal would arrive early for a cup of tea and a chat with the First Minister. When Winning, accompanied by Ronnie Convery and Peter Smith, had been ushered into Donald Dewar's large office with its worn leather chairs and view over Edinburgh, the First Minister made a point of looking the cardinal in the eye and insisting the executive had made the decision to remove the clause over concerns about discrimination. 'We intend to make more than adequate provision and there will be no matter about which parents should be concerned,' said Dewar. 'We are more than happy to talk.' At this point, Rafferty reminded Winning of his meeting with Smith and Connelly and suggested that a supplementary meeting be arranged between Winning and Dewar. Winning replied. 'John, that would be great.' As far as the executive was concerned the brief meeting had gone well and in their view Winning appeared to have grown increasingly comfortable with their plans. Instead, the cardinal was merely keeping his own counsel, as he believed a brief meeting before prayers was unsuitable to discuss the subject in depth.

The catalyst for what would become a long and fraught campaign against repeal was not the cardinal but a more unlikely candidate: Brian Souter. The businessman, who was a member of the evangelical congregation, the Church of the Nazarene, had read the plans announced by the Scottish Executive with increasing discomfort. His concerns grew as he read a booklet, entitled *Bankrolling Gay Proselytism: The Case for Extending Section 28*, produced by the Christian Institute, a religious think-tank based in Newcastle. The booklet articulated what Souter believed was an admirable case against scrapping the law in order to protect children from unsuitable material, but the trigger that transformed private concern into public action was a column in the *Daily Record* by Tom Brown, a senior journalist and leader writer who enjoyed the ear of the government. On 16 December, he delivered an unseasonable attack on the abolition of Section 28, which he viewed as serious abuse of power. He wrote:

> Suppose you are given a present in true Christmas spirit – you are made Santa Claus Minister with the power to do good. Who are the first people you would want to help? Children? The shivering old folk? Poor families? The homeless or homosexuals? How did they get priority? When did Scotland vote for Pink Politics? How come an insidious minority with a perverse agenda commands the attention of a new minister? When Labour was voted into power in the Scottish Parliament, it did not campaign on a manifesto to promote homosexuality in schools. We're not told about a hidden policy to expose our children to harmful propaganda. Communities Minister Wendy Alexander was not given a mandate for a 'personal crusade' that flouts the wishes of parents, Churches and the majority of the people she represents. Scrapping Section 28 of the Local Government Act may be a trendy New Labour thing to do. But there is no need for

it, except to establish the politically correct 'cred' of herself and her mentor, First Minister Donald Dewar.

As Souter remembered: 'That was the signal we needed. It was a focal point to stand against the parliament.' Twelve days later, on 28 December, he called Jack Irvine, the managing director of Media House, a public relations company, and his personal PR man. Irvine was at home in his luxury detached villa in the affluent Glasgow suburb of Whitecraigs, packing in preparation to see in the new millennium with his wife and children in Manhattan.

'What do you make of the Section 28 plans?' asked Souter. Irvine waffled. The subject had been on the fringe of his radar but he had no in-depth knowledge. 'Have you read Tom Brown in the *Record*?' added Souter before going on to explain his concerns over the potential repercussions of repeal. 'We need to draw a line in the sand. Do you think you could do it?' Souter then explained that he did not wish to be up-front in the campaign, but would bankroll it from behind the scenes to a cost of £500,000. Souter was conscious that he was intruding during the holidays and so asked Irvine to think it over and contact him when he returned. Over the next five days in New York, the idea distracted Irvine. Two nights before his return and a day after Times Square had exploded in a riot of paper streamers and people, Irvine awoke in his hotel room in the Waldorf Astoria and got up to fetch a glass of water. Once again Souter's idea dominated his thoughts. Irvine was convinced the result would be a head-to-head battle with a new government over the ideology of sex and religion and it was going to be huge. Irvine went back to bed smiling.

On 11 January 2000, Jack Irvine drove to Perth and the national headquarters of Stagecoach. Souter wished to go ahead with a campaign to be called 'Keep the Clause' ('Secure the Section' not being so snappy), and pondered commissioning a poll to discover what actual support for abolition existed in Scotland. Irvine was more concerned with the reaction of the country's press. The *Scotsman* and the *Herald* were dismissed as too ideologically liberal and with a combined circulation of around 200,000, inconsequential compared to the might of the tabloids. Back in the Glasgow office of Media House, Irvine contacted Bruce Waddell and Ramsay Smith, the Scottish editors of the *Sun* and the *Daily Mail* to gauge their reaction to Souter's plans and after receiving a favourable response he moved on to Martin Clarke at the *Daily Record*. Both men had had their differences in the past, but when Irvine asked Clarke his views on Section 28, Clarke said he was appalled at the plans. The following day, 12 January, all three newspapers splashed on Souter's campaign to Keep the Clause.

The initial plan was for the businessman to donate £500,000 to the School Boards Association as funds for a campaign to retain the clause, but when the organization's steering committee had second thoughts it became apparent the work would now be handled by Media House.

The situation was unprecedented in Scottish politics. In a scenario that echoed James Goldsmith's Referendum Party, a businessman worth hundreds of millions (a drop in share price had taken Souter and Gloag out of the billionaire bracket) was spending lavishly to prove a political point, namely that the Scottish people were almost entirely unsupportive of the government's planned repeal.

The consultation period closed on 14 January with 90 per cent of responses critical of change, while MSPs who favoured repeal admitted the volume of mail was 2–1 against. Yet this was not enough to stop members of the executive dismissing Souter as 'a homophobic bus driver' while gay rights groups launched a campaign to boycott his buses.

Prior to announcing the campaign, Souter had briefed his board members on his plans. There was to be no discussion; the decision was personal and a matter of conscience and any backlash would have to be endured. A number of board members had deep reservations. While they could applaud their chief executive's Christian commitment, it counted for little against share prices and a market where image was all.

The weekend of 15–16 January was one of the most difficult periods of Brian Souter's life. The Sunday newspapers, particularly the *Sunday Mail* and the *Sunday Herald*, were aggressive in their opposition to his intervention and at home in the family's large country house in the village of Crieff, Souter felt under siege with even the television offering no respite as both teletext and the news slots carried further criticism of his plans. He believed with the fervour of a fundamentalist that he was carrying out God's work but he feared the repercussion on his four children hinted at in hate mail.

Earlier in the morning of that same Sunday, during an interview* ostensibly on the first few years of his priesthood, Winning raised the subject of Section 28. He was angered by the hostile coverage of Souter's plans and what he described as 'the deafening silence' from the moral majority. He expressed a grave distaste for the euphemistic terms in which the debate had been couched:

> The truth of Section 28 is that it is sodomy. For anyone to deny that this is not a perversion is nonsense. The Universal Catechism calls it an act of grave depravity. It is condemned by all the world's religions. I don't know what the purpose is of somebody to make it appear wholesome. A government paper on bullying makes no mention of homophobic bullying so why do they want to repeal this act?

During the conversation, Winning expressed frustration at the lack of public figures willing to speak out against the repeal. Later that afternoon, he called Brian Souter at home. He began by inquiring after the well-being of both Souter and his family and then, alluding to the Roddy Wright affair, explained he knew how they felt and that he would shortly be offering his public support. As Brian Souter remembered: 'It was our darkest hour and his phone call was just perfect.'

Later that evening, Winning was joined at The Oaks by an old friend who also held strong views on homosexuality and together

*With the author.

they discussed Souter's campaign. The next morning, Monday 17 January, Winning was on a visit to a community centre in Bellshill. He had decided in the car en route that if asked he would speak out about his frustrations. Convery was concerned as he knew that without a prepared script, Winning was liable to slip into trouble. He offered to keep the TV reporter and camera crew from STV (with whom he had once worked) back, but Winning was insistent. He wanted to speak. Winning's comments would later be dismissed as an off-the-cuff gaff but they had been carefully thought through and were spoken with deliberate intent and so, standing on what was a bitterly cold winter morning, he uttered one of the most controversial statements by a British senior Church leader in decades.

Asked if the Catholic Church would accept money from Souter to run a campaign, Winning said that the Church would not, but that he approved of Souter's actions: 'I welcome with interest his involvement. I have only met him once, many months ago, and I am happy with his Christian commitment.'[4] Winning went on to say that he was concerned about the material that could be placed in schools once the law was lifted and that he felt it unfair that any criticism of homosexuality was tagged as 'homophobic', a position he described as 'absolute rubbish'. He then moved to the crux of the issue:

I might say also that there is an organization of Catholic homosexuals called Courage and their membership pledge to live according to the teachings of the Catholic Church. That is all we want. Not according to the teachings of the Catholic Church for everybody, but to keep the lifestyle that is going nowhere out of society. I hesitate to use the word perversion, but let's face up to the truth about this situation. Are we now being asked to say what was wrong before is now right and they can go ahead and do it? It is bound to affect society, it is bound to affect the transmission of things that we don't want. It is bound to affect the promotion of a lifestyle that is contrary to everything – natural law, not just religion.

After speaking to the TV reporter from STV, he went on to expand on his view with the newspaper journalists present. 'I deplore the homosexual act, sexual acts performed by homosexuals, and the Church has always deplored them. I am not prepared to tell the Scottish public that they are right, when before they were wrong, morally wrong.'

He also tackled the silence of the many:

> What pains me is that the silent majority is so silent that the silence is deafening. I wish to God they would speak up. But when they do say something about it you are accused of homophobia, which is absolute rubbish. I have no objection to anybody. I'm supposed to love my neighbour and I try to do as much as I can. But I will not stand for this kind of behaviour.

On Donald Dewar, he said: 'I would like Donald Dewar to come out with a statement saying: "This is the policy of the Scottish Executive with regard to homosexuality" and to emphasize the protection of children.'

On gay groups, he said:

> I will support Mr Souter in his stance and welcome interest in the debate. Gay rights groups always claim it is impossible to promote homosexuality. That is rubbish. It is promoted every day by promoting the lifestyles of gay people. Children do not have to be born homosexual to adopt a homosexual lifestyle. When do children decide to be gay? This material will encourage that lifestyle.

The comments were incendiary, but from where did they come? The answer is a deep mixture of personal background, traditional Church teaching and a recent disturbing experience. There can be little surprise that a seventy-four-year-old man from the heartland of industrial Lanarkshire could harbour such an opinion of homosexuality. The fact that it sprang from the lips of a Prince of the Church, whose sworn duty is to uphold the teachings of the Catholic Church, should have diminished further any hint of surprise, yet those who felt the statement was singularly lacking in compassion had a valid point. Winning's views on homosexuality were set in stone: the practice of gay sex disgusted him. While in public he could articulate the standard Christian line of loving the man and detesting the sin, in private, he found the separation to be difficult indeed. In Winning's mind, homosexuality was a lifestyle choice that was evil and he remained unconvinced by medical research that advocated the condition as present at birth, though he was swayed slightly by the existence of effeminate young boys or, as he referred to them in the argot of the playground, 'sissies'.

As the archbishop of a large diocese, he was aware of the existence of gay priests and would handle any crisis with the same care and compassion as he would a clergyman caught in a relationship with a woman, or one who was an alcoholic or submerged in a deep crisis of faith. Yet while other dioceses in Scotland chose to admit gay men as seminarians on the understanding that they, like their heterosexual colleagues, abide by the rule of celibacy, Winning would not. He was concerned by the temptations of an all-male environment and had no wish to place extra pressure on a gay man as he viewed the priesthood as difficult enough.

To critics, Winning's beliefs had been fossilized and supported by the teachings of the Catholic Church and, in particular, communiqués from the Congregation of the Doctrine of the Faith. While the catechism of the Catholic Church views homosexual practice as an 'act of grave depravity', a declaration published by the CDF went further. The author was Cardinal Joseph Ratzinger, nicknamed 'the German panzer' for his ability to steamroller over anyone with the Pope's blessing. In '*Homosexualitatis Problema*' – (a letter, published in 1986, to the bishops of the Catholic Church on the pastoral care of homosexual persons), he wrote: 'Although the particular inclination of the homosexual person is not a sin, it is more or less a strong tendency ordered toward an intrinsic moral evil and thus the inclination itself must be seen as an objective disorder.'

The argument was drawn from the New Testament, in which Paul condemns homosexual relations, and was backed by Church tradition and the ideas found in systematic theology which Ratzinger used to argue that homosexuality upsets God's plan for male-female complementarity. The Pope had also expressed the teaching, in his encyclical 'Veritatis Splendor', that the homosexual condition had an intrinsic evil. A major concern Winning shared with the Vatican was the increase in gay rights organizations and what he saw as their unjust demands for equality. In his eyes, and those of the Church, a lesbian or gay couple would never be on par with a male-female marriage and any elevation of their position led to a corresponding reduction in the value of heterosexual marriage. As a member of the Pontifical Council for the Family, this was a fight to which he was deeply devoted.

A final ingredient in Winning's psyche at this time was the memory of an incident involving a gay priest and thousands of images of hardcore pornography which he had found repulsive. In February 1999, a priest in the offices of the Scottish Marriage Tribunal contacted Winning after the personal computer of Fr Jim Nicol, the tribunal president, was found to contain thousands of images of hardcore gay pornography. During the investigation, Winning had little choice but to view many scenes of oral sex, buggery and images of Fr Nicol receiving fellatio from a young man in his flat above the tribunal offices. Father Nicol was later removed from his office but Winning found the images deeply troubling. The Pontifical Council for Communications articulates the pernicious nature of pornography and there is little doubt that a cardinal is as susceptible to recurring images of unpleasant sights as an ordinary member of the public.

Winning viewed his statement as a marker that had to be laid down. Archbishop John Foley, the American head of the Pontifical Council for Social Communications, once said of him: 'Like good art, good morals begin with the drawing of a line. Cardinal Winning draws that line.'[5] The media coverage that followed was intense. In Scotland, the story led the evening news on both STV's Scotland Today and the BBC's Reporting Scotland, while the statement made the front page of many of the following day's newspapers. *The Times* went a step further, insisting that Winning had called homosexuals 'perverts' and though Ronnie Convery was quick to fire off a letter of complaint, to critics this was simply meddling in semantics. The editorial of the *Herald* declared that the repeal of Section 28 would nurture tolerance, 'the law as it stands is a barrier to furthering tolerance', meanwhile, the *Scotsman* insisted Winning had 'fallen below the standard of compassion and tolerance demanded from the holder of his office'. The conservative press was understandably more supportive with the *Daily Mail* explaining: 'Cardinal Winning wants the silent majority to rise up. What a pity it takes a Catholic, and a Scot to boot, to spell out what the Anglican Church should be saying!'

To those who had worked closely with gay men and women the statement was viewed as outrageous and extremely damaging. In the living room of his town house in the centre of Edinburgh, Bishop Richard Holloway, leader of the Scottish Episcopal Church, could only shake his head in dismay as he watched the news footage of Winning's statement that evening. One week before, Holloway had accused the Labour administration of allowing the Catholic Church to dictate the nation's moral agenda. John Cairns, the Moderator of the Church of Scotland, privately believed that someone should take Winning on, and so accused him and supporters of Section 28 of wishing to perpetuate a law that, as he believed, 'creates fear and a certain stigma against certain people'.[6] Yet in this belief Cairns found himself in opposition to the Kirk's powerful board of social responsibility who favoured retention. Among the most articulate critics was John Rafferty who was now readjusting to his fall from grace. One month earlier, Dewar's chief of staff had been forced to resign after it emerged that he had wrongly briefed a journalist that Susan Deacon, the Health Minister, had received death threats from Christian pro-life extremists. At home in South Queensferry, and between jobs, he was asked to write an article for the *Scotsman* on Winning's statement and so he drew comparisons between the Act of Settlement's discrimination against Catholics and Section 28: 'Is it not too much for the Cardinal to be consistent?

Discrimination, bigotry and sectarianism are never right. Why, then, is the Cardinal so out of step with modern thinking, and the thinking of many Catholic parents, on the issue of homosexuality?'[7]

The article went on to examine the ideas of the former Jesuit priest John J. McNeill, a radical proponent of homosexual pastoral care, who left the priesthood rather than conform to Church teaching, and ended with the quote: 'Perhaps Cardinal Winning will preach that homophobia is a sin?' There was one point on which both men agreed. Why, asked Rafferty, 'is it that the parallel legislation for England also abolishing Section 28 is now at a very advanced stage in its passage through parliament, with hardly an intolerant whimper south of the border?' This was a question for which Winning also wanted an answer, and so when contacted by Charles Moore, the editor of the *Daily Telegraph* and a Catholic convert, to write an opinion piece following on from his 'perversion' comment, he chose to light the fiery cross, the old Highland symbol of warning. In the article, Winning described the shock he felt when examining material he believed would be permitted within schools once the act was repealed. The examples he cited included role-playing games in which thirteen-year-olds imagine they are a homosexual 'coming out', or a gay married man caught having sex in a public toilet or a transvestite cabaret artist. He wrote: 'So far in England and Wales, it seems that there is a strange silence on this, but I cannot believe that Christians south of the border are any less concerned than those living north of Gretna.' He then went on to point out the lack of support among the Scottish public for such plans and cast doubt on the politicians' democratic mandate:

I can think of no other issue on which politicians are so spectacularly out of touch with the view of the man and woman in the street. If they are not reminded of that fact, they will push ahead with ever more damaging and immoral proposals. That is why it is so important for all who are worried about the danger of homosexual proselytism to speak up – and to speak up quickly. To do nothing is silently to consent. In the face of an increasingly militant and vocal 'gay rights' campaign, Scotland, and indeed the United Kingdom as a whole, needs the protection offered by Section 28.[8]

The article appeared on Wednesday 19 January, the same day Winning arrived in London for an official reception at the Houses of Parliament. He had been invited five months previously by Dr John Reid after the Labour MP's appointment as the first Catholic Secretary of State for Scotland and it was a gesture that delighted Winning. For over twenty years he had watched jealously as each new Moderator of the Church of Scotland was fêted during an annual function at the House of Commons. In the three years since Labour's victory, Tony Blair had made no gesture towards Scotland's cardinal and, despite their previous hostilities, Winning was irritated by what he viewed as a persistent snub. The visit offered the potential for an exchange of olive branches for, as Winning said three days previously, 'I hope he at least pops his head round the door. If not, then that's it. We're finished.' Informed spectators would have assumed their relationship had withered on the vine three years before but Winning, as a man of God, believed in the triumph of hope over experience. Once again he would be let down.

Winning and Convery had flown from Glasgow to Heathrow where a ministerial Rover collected them for the drive into central London. As Peter Tatchell, the organizer of Outrage, the gay pressure group, had planned a protest against Winning, the pair were brought through a back entrance to Dover House, the Secretary of State's official London residence.

At the initial reception attended by a number of Scottish MPs including Gordon Brown, Dr Reid took the opportunity to praise his guest's candour but hinted that he had recently gone too far. Winning, he said, had been a dynamo for constitutional change, but he could not have it both ways: be seen to campaign for a Scottish parliament then launch a drive against a legitimate decision. As Reid told the gathering: 'He has espoused some policies which have sometimes brought him into conflict with contemporary thinking. He had been a determined advocate of the Scottish parliament. Herein lies the paradox: those who champion that right do so in the full knowledge that they will sometimes come into conflict with the decisions made.'[9]

Blair did not attend, sending his apologies instead, but the Prime Minister could not resist a dig at Winning as he watched from the public gallery during Question Time. When asked by Jimmy Hood, a Scottish Labour MP, to guarantee that homosexuality would not be encouraged in schools, Blair replied: 'We believe it is right for schoolteachers and others to be able to explain to children properly the facts of life. Some people may make political capital out of it. I think it is a sensible change. I think it is a right change and I would hope we could get a maturer debate on it than we have had in certain quarters.'

After Question Time, Dr Reid was highly embarrassed and was profusely apologetic to Winning and anxious to dismiss the idea that he had been set up. Over drinks in a side function room Reid explained that it was a rogue question Blair did not expect but Winning was adamant that no apology was necessary.

The following day, Thursday 20 January, Winning flew to Malta. Before departing he visited the office to discover over one hundred letters of support and only a handful of hate mail. The reception he received in the town of Valetta on the devoutly Catholic Mediterranean island was to be equally positive. The success of his pro-life initiative had spread across Europe and led to an invitation to address the Catholic Families movement, but instead of focusing on past success, he warmed to his new theme and again spoke out against gay rights advocates. Winning had a taste for analogies that involved the Second World War and in the case of his Maltese audience, whose island home had been heavily bombarded, he believed such comparisons were particularly pertinent. In his speech he discussed how the island's position left the populace vulnerable to television broadcasts from a host of countries, whose contents were often 'utterly alien to the noble Christian traditions of the good people of Malta'. Towards the end of the speech, Winning discussed a new threat, 'the threat to equate homosexual partnerships with marriage', and went on to praise the new coalition that was forming in Scotland to fend off the menace. 'All over Europe an active and militant homosexual lobby is pushing for greater power and the threat to the Christian family is real.'

Winning at no point equated the gay lobby to the Nazis, nor mentioned the word, but his allusions to the Second World War and his discussion of 'the new threat' appeared to lend themselves to such an interpretation, one the media, who were passed the speech on the Friday, were only too anxious to use. *Scotland on Sunday* ran the headline: 'Gay Lobby Compared to Nazis in New Broadside by Winning', an error for which they were forced to apologize the following week and carry the unexpurgated portion of the speech from which they had injudiciously quoted. But if the newspaper had erred then so too had Winning, who should have appreciated the potential consequences of such a speech. On Sunday he issued a clarifying statement in which he said: 'I regret any offence caused by the misreporting of what I said in Malta.' Martin Pendergast, chairman of the Roman Catholic Caucus of Lesbian and Gay Christians Movement, said the intemperate language Winning had used that week would incite violence against homosexuals. The most virulent criticism of Winning came from a former ally. George Galloway was asked his opinion of Winning's comments on *Holyrood*, the BBC's Sunday discussion programme, to which he replied:

> I was disgusted by it. I am a person who had long-admired Cardinal Winning. I have worked with him on many projects ... But I was disgusted by the use of this word, which could have dripped from the lips of any raving bigot and Cardinal Winning had no business using such a word. He ought to know the atmosphere it would create. Cardinal Winning is not fit for the great office that he holds.

Galloway's criticism staggered Winning, who on many occasions had supported Galloway through trying times both political and personal. The MP instantly became a former friend, an invisible man to Winning. Eighteen months later, when Galloway spotted Winning in Glasgow Airport and approached him to say hello, the cardinal walked straight past him. At the time, Convery retorted that Pope John Paul II would be a better judge of Winning's capability, while a spokesman for the Keep the Clause campaign was more biting. 'A prince of the Church has little to fear from the clown prince of the Labour Party.'

There were some within the Catholic Church who believed Winning had made a serious error of judgement by using the word 'perversion'. Father Jimmy Breslin, the parish priest of St Bride's in Cambuslang, had spent twenty years giving pastoral care to gay people and he insisted Winning had endangered his work. Winning had little interest in Breslin's work in the neighbouring diocese of Motherwell, and he had never visited a meeting of gay Catholics during his twenty-six years as archbishop.

In Edinburgh, Fr Steve Gilhooley used his column in the *Edinburgh Evening News* to complain about the cardinal's stance, while six days after he uttered the words, Fr Gordon Brown, an Edinburgh priest, outed himself as gay in order to voice the views of, as he said, a considerable number of gay Catholic priests in Scotland.

A Scottish chapter of We are Church, an international liberal pressure group, was set up in response to Winning's words but to little effect. The response of two of his closest female friends carried considerably more weight. Susan McCormack rang him up to say: 'You've gone too far this time, Thomas Joseph.' When Winning began to shout back, she promptly hung up. Dr Anna Murphy spoke to him the evening after his comments were broadcast and found him at first concerned that he had made a verbal blunder. 'He is strongly motivated by guilt and that was what that first night was about,' said Murphy. 'That term and the way he used it worried him greatly.' If this was truly the case, it was a side he only revealed to her.

Whatever private doubts Winning harboured over his initial statement, he made sure that they were battened down for what was shaping up to be a long campaign. Winning had failed to consult the Bishops' Conference before making his statement and a number of bishops were privately appalled at what he had said. Bishop John Mone of Paisley and Archbishop Keith O'Brien were among the most uncomfortable about the cardinal's use of the word 'perversion'. As president of the Bishops' Conference, Winning wanted a statement released protesting the repeal, but a number of bishops objected to the initial wording and consequently the final draft was two paragraphs shorter. The compromise document read as follows:

> To take away a law which prohibits the promotion of homosexuality and replace it with 'guidelines' risks leaving our children extremely vulnerable to the message that a homosexual lifestyle is an equally valid moral choice to marriage. We ask all people of goodwill to pray for our legislators in their different tasks. We pray we can build a Scotland of justice for all – free of bigotry and intolerance, but ever mindful of God's law and morality.

Winning felt angry, betrayed and unsupported by his fellow bishops during the campaign, but there was one on whom he could rely: Bishop Mario Conti of Aberdeen, his eventual successor. On a number of occasions during his darkest times he was heard to say: 'Thank God for Mario.' A full five days before the statement from the Bishops' Conference was read out from pulpits across the country, Conti had already backed Winning with a strong letter to the *Herald* that hinted at a possible solution of a law for a law. 'We are in favour of retaining Section 28 – unless and until another legal instrument is put in its place protecting the unique role of the family in Scottish society.'

The clash of ideologies over Section 28 was to continue until the summer but a new battle front opened in February that would allow both sides to claim victory. If Section 28 was to be repealed, and few within the opposition campaign believed they would succeed in its prevention, one law should be replaced by another. If a law prohibiting the promotion of homosexuality in schools was to be scrapped then a law obliging teachers to highlight the importance of marriage should be inserted in its place. Winning believed this to be a suitable compromise offering children the same degree of protection as they currently enjoyed under Section 28 without using terminology that a minority found offensive. The executive, however, had no intention of giving up ground. The elevation of marriage to a paradigm was unacceptable to those within the executive that saw the institution as outdated and increasingly anachronistic in the new Scotland of single parents and co-habitees. To venerate marriage in law was to denigrate almost half the nation's family units. 'Marriage' in the collective eyes of the executive had become an ugly word.

By the end of February, a gap existed between Scotland and England and Wales. In the south, the quiet pressure put on Education Minister David Blunkett by Vincent Nichols, then Catholic Archbishop-elect of Birmingham, and the Rt Revd Alan Chesters, the Anglican Bishop of Blackburn, had resulted in the government agreeing that the 'importance of marriage' would be taught in classrooms. In comparison, Scottish children would be taught only the 'value of a stable family life', the only wording to which Donald Dewar was agreeable. The Catholic Church declared Scotland to be suffering a 'moral poll tax', a reference to Margaret Thatcher's controversial legislation of the 1980s which was pioneered in Scotland before being inflicted on the rest of the country. While Dewar insisted the language was 'inclusive, tolerant and non-judgemental', Winning argued that marriage was now considered 'so unpolitically correct that it can't even be mentioned for fear of offending certain pressure groups'. He continued:

> Stable family life is not defined and therefore could be interpreted to include homosexual or lesbian domestic arrangements. If councils are to promote such arrangements then that is a new danger to family life. Heterosexual marriage is not even mentioned. The implicit message is that marriage doesn't matter. The institution has been debased.[10]

Winning and his fellow protestors wished 'marriage' to be enshrined in law; the government, meanwhile, was offering 'stable family life' in unenforceable guidelines. Only the bloody nose of a by-election defeat, a protest of increasing hostility towards the government and the voice of over one million dissenters would shift their position.

On 16 March, Labour lost an MSP seat in a by-election in Ayr to the Conservatives, who had campaigned with vigour on the retention of Section 28. In England, Winning's call to the silent majority to rise up in protest had triggered a rebellion in the House of Lords led by Baroness Young, which, at the end of March, succeeded in blocking the government's plans. In consequence, the language of Tony Blair grew increasingly frustrated and aggressive. At the Scottish Labour Party Conference on 10 March, he described protestors as 'a phoney threat' and, two weeks later during Question Time on 29 March, as 'prejudiced against gay people'.

The consequence in the gay community of the Keep the Clause campaign cannot be ignored. A rise in homophobic abuse was reported, the Gay and Lesbian Switchboard recorded a 20 per cent rise in calls, and in February, the Scottish Executive released statistics which illustrated that gay bashing in Edinburgh was four times the national average. In spite of the fact the material was collated prior to the launch of the campaign, Peter Tatchell accused both Winning and Brian Souter of 'having queer blood on their hands'.[11]

On 8 March, Tatchell succeeded in climbing on to the stage at St Mary's Catholic Church hall in Croydon where Winning was delivering the annual Charles Cobb Memorial Lecture. Winning stepped back and waited while Tatchell was escorted from the hall. Four days later, Bishop Holloway, a close supporter of Tatchell, used his retirement speech to accuse Winning of 'harsh intolerance' towards homosexuals. Winning was unconcerned; he had long since dismissed Holloway as an authoritative Christian leader on account of his radical views and in private he frequently referred to him as 'Hollowhead'.

*   *   *

415

Monsignor Tom Connelly returned in March from a three-month sabbatical spent visiting his brother, a British High Commissioner in Tonga, to find relations between the Church and State at their nadir. Even Connelly who, prior to his departure had described Susan Deacon, the government minister, to the press as a 'nutcase', was appalled at how deep Winning had waded into domestic politics. 'Our job is to preach the gospel, not fight politicians,' he said in exasperation. He then attempted to pull the Church back from any direct involvement with Brian Souter's Keep the Clause campaign. Connelly was determined that when the businessman announced the funding of a £1 million referendum of every eligible voter – almost four million – the Church should make no statement to influence prospective voters.

The referendum was not without its problems. Gallup refused to take part, wounding its credibility, and although ICM Research stepped into the breach, every error that occurred was magnified under the existing press scrutiny. Some people received multiple ballot forms, others received none, and, in a small number of cases, the dead received a ballot form to the distress of the living. Richard Holloway tore up his paper in the pulpit and urged fellow worshippers to return their envelope empty to further increase Souter's overheads. A senior union representative said he would wait until he had run out of toilet paper before putting the ballot form to an alternative use.

When contacted by the media and asked how the Church felt Scots should vote, Connelly did not comment and insisted instead that it was not the Church's position to guide people on such a matter.

During this period in early May, Winning was in Newfoundland, where he was leading a retreat at the invitation of the Canadian Bishops' Conference, but upon his return he swept aside Connelly's attempts at restraint. Media House requested that the Cardinal write a personal letter of support to Souter which could be conveniently leaked to the *Daily Record*. Winning was happy to oblige.

The letter read:

I wanted to drop you a short line to offer my support in this difficult time. In recent weeks you have been subjected to some quite unacceptable press coverage, which must have been difficult for both yourself and your family. If it is any consolation, many, many people have mentioned to me how much they admire your courage in standing up for traditional marriage-based family and for Christian values. It must be clear to the politicians that any repeal of Section 28 will be carried out in outright defiance of the will of the people of Scotland. Such a situation is sadly very far from what we all hoped for last year at the birth of the Scottish parliament. Many of us believed that the New Scotland would be built on the best of our traditions: the family, creativity, humour, openness, hard work and generosity. We could never have foreseen that the marriage-based family would be one of the first casualties.

The referendum's result was in Souter's favour, which was to be expected, but it was the extent to which people had taken the trouble to reply that disturbed politicians: a total of 3,970,712 ballot papers were posted and 1,260,846 papers were returned; 1,094,440 favoured retention, 166,406 favoured abolition. Wendy Alexander dismissed the outcome and said: 'Less than one third of Scots back his position',[12] but in private her confidence was badly shaken. Repeal would be pushed through, but the executive knew it could no longer ignore the protestors' wishes and in May it was announced that the sex education guidelines would be statutory and marriage would appear in the wording.

On 5 June 2000, Winning sat in his office on Clyde Street and wrote a short letter of resignation. The following day was his seventy-fifty birthday, the day upon which, under canon law, bishops are instructed to resign. The letter was one Winning hoped the Vatican would not accept. Cardinals, if in good health, were encouraged to remain in office until their eightieth birthday. A few years earlier, prior to the diagnosis of cancer, Basil Hume had pleaded to be able to retire to his beloved Ampleforth Abbey, but his request had been rejected. Winning had little doubt that his position was secure and did not like to ponder life beyond the Church and so the letter was short and perfunctory. He merely stated that, in line with paragraph 1 of canon 401, he was offering his resignation and that he had tried to implement the changes of Vatican II. Emotion was reserved for a bad-tempered interview he gave to the *Scottish Catholic Observer*, ostensibly to reflect on his seventy-five years, but Winning restricted his focus to the past twelve months, demolishing the entire Scottish parliament when he meant to train his criticism on the executive.

> I was enthusiastic but I almost feel ashamed of them now. I am ashamed of our politicians and the way they have behaved and the things that they have done over the last year. I think it has been an utter failure. I defended them for months in different parts of the press and media and I said they needed five or ten years to give them credibility. I still think that, but I don't think the achievements of the last year are anything to be proud of. They have given me the impression that there is a very liberal agenda out there and come hell or high water they are going to see it through.

In justifying his statement months later, Winning insisted that hyperbole was necessary to attract attention. He compared the Scottish parliament to an 'unruly class of kids' to whom it is sometimes necessary to raise one's voice and said: 'Unless you say "For God's sake shut up and listen to me", you are not going to be heard.'

At the time of the interview, Winning's comments could have been presented as another example of his 'everyman' status. A recent ICM poll revealed that only one in three Scots held the view that devolution had benefited the country. But Winning was no 'everyman' and his comments were injudicious. As Donald Dewar was recovering from a heart by-pass operation, it was left to Jim Wallace as deputy First Minister to reply to his criticism. 'I respect Cardinal Winning, but to respect him doesn't mean I agree with him. I think the parliament has been remarkably successful.'[13]

There were other Catholics who, upon hearing Winning's comments, could only hold their heads in their hands. 'The Cardinal is expected to have an opinion,' said Tim Duffy, spokesman for the Scottish Catholic Justice and Peace Committee. 'But it would be useful to get rid of the "leader of the Catholic Church in Scotland" tag.'[14] Alex Salmond, loyal to the last, argued that Winning was referring to the executive, and a few weeks later he met him for lunch – to which he brought a bottle of Scottish parliament whisky. Salmond handed it over to Winning and said: 'You can now say something good has come out of the Scottish parliament.'

Winning softened his stance when asked to contribute an article on the parliament to the *Spectator*, but still succeeded in being drawn into a dispute with Sir Elton John. In his article, Winning once again expressed his view on homosexuality stating: 'Gay sex is wrong, because such behaviour is not good for the human person. Far from liberating a person it ensnares them in a lifestyle that can never respond to the deepest longings of the human heart.' In a letter to the magazine, the singer and composer of some of the greatest love songs of the twentieth century retorted, 'Cardinal Winning and his ignorance are totally representative of why people are turning away from the Church. I am astonished to be told by Cardinal Winning that my sexuality is not good for me. From what practical perspective does he form this point of view?' He concluded his letter by stating: 'The reality is that homosexuals have no choice and no amount of hectoring or hypnosis can make us change.' Ronnie Convery deflected the singer's attack in a haughty tone: 'We should say that Sir Elton's views are eminently predictable. The Cardinal would not wish to dignify them with a response.'

Section 28 was finally repealed in Scotland on 21 June with the passing of the Ethical Standards in Public Life Bill. In a private interview, Winning said of the repeal: 'If that is democracy, then I am no longer a democrat.' Though Winning failed in Scotland, he had started something which was to succeed in England and Wales, where the legislation, twice halted by the House of Lords, was later abandoned by the government. On 26 June, Winning wrote to congratulate Baroness Young on her efforts:

Please be assured, however, of my admiration and gratitude for all you have achieved in recent months in the House of Lords . . . May I take this opportunity to wish you every success in the months ahead in your struggle to achieve proper protection for our children from inappropriate sex education.[15]

The pair had hoped to meet at a private dinner held at Brian Souter's home in Crieff the previous weekend but Winning had been unable to attend and had sent Ronnie Convery in his place. In conclusion, Winning insisted he had no regrets over his handling of the whole affair and confessed in private that he felt guided by the Holy Spirit to speak in such blunt and direct terms. If he had alienated a proportion of young, liberal Catholics, his stature among other faiths, in particular Scotland's Moslems, and those among the English middle classes, had grown. Stature brings its own burden and in September Winning found himself satirized as the scheming Cardinal Patrick Doollan in *Boiling a Frog*, the latest crime novel by Christopher Brookmyre, an author of rising popularity. The Scots cardinal folded within the pages of his fiction pays a PR man to destabilize the government with sex scandals, allowing him to create a climate of sexual prurience. When told of the novel, Winning laughed and asked: 'And does he succeed?'

TWENTY-ONE

A Twilight Moment

'I didn't denigrate you. We're all adults. We can speak as adults.'
THOMAS WINNING

The chorus of 'Flower of Scotland', the nation's unofficial anthem, was impromptu but as the last lines echoed around the audience hall, they set the seal on an occasion of stirring symbolism. On 4 December 2000, the First Minister of Scotland, Henry McLeish, was introduced by Thomas Winning to Pope John Paul II in the great audience chamber of the Vatican. The visit was to celebrate the four hundredth anniversary (which fell the following day) of the founding of the Scots College by Pope Clement VIII, but, taken as a tableau, the scene illustrated the triumph of Scottish Catholicism over a past charged with prejudice. Where adherents to the faith had entered the twentieth century isolated, hunched and despised, the twenty-first century saw them rise to be embraced as equal partners. Among those who had travelled to Rome and paid their respects to the stooped figure clad in white were John Reid, the first Catholic Secretary of State for Scotland, and the Rt Revd Andrew McLellan, Moderator of the Church of Scotland; a public symbol that old enmities – at least between the Churches, if not all their followers – had long since been laid to rest.

The image of the nation's most senior politicians almost bowing to the Pope, who remained seated due to his infirmity, would have caused riots seventy years before and still caused a little discomfort to those who believed the government gave too much credence to

421

what they viewed as a fading religious rump. Yet after the antagonism of Section 28, the new First Minister, who had succeeded Donald Dewar after his untimely death two months previously, was anxious to restore relations to a better balance. Winning, meanwhile, was keen to savour the occasion. He was back in Rome, in the bright chill of winter, and was reminded of his ordination and the harsh landscape he had trodden since then. As he said of the visit: 'It reminds all of us how far the Catholic community has come over the centuries until today when we can play a full and active role in the life of the nation.'[1]

Winning was greatly to enjoy his few days as host. The actual anniversary was celebrated with a morning Mass and lunch at the Scots College but the festivities had extended for almost a week, beginning on the feast of St Andrew, 30 November, and concluding with a visit to the tomb of Clement VIII in the basilica of St Mary Major on 6 December.

During the six years since Winning had been made a cardinal, the frequency of his trips to Rome had increased but their enjoyment did not diminish. In Rome, neither his dress nor attitude were indicative of the position he held. While other less senior priests wore long dark frock coats, he favoured an anorak from C&A. On one occasion, he became involved in a casual conversation with a young Canadian Dominican brother in a coffee shop on the Via della Conciliazione. At the end of the conversation, when the man discovered Winning's true identity, he dropped on one knee and kissed his ring – to the cardinal's evident embarrassment. In Rome, Winning could be remarkably casual. On another occasion, he encountered a pair of English bishops. While in conversation with them, he spotted that the buttons on one of their tunics were undone. As it was a bitterly cold day, he proceeded to button them up.

Ever since he had received the red hat there were those who suggested Winning could have been a candidate for Pope – Andrew I. Prior to deciding he was unsuitable even to wear the red hat, George Galloway had claimed he might one day wear the white. In reality, such sentiments were akin to those of Ally McLeod, manager of the Scottish football team, who, when asked what he planned to do after the World Cup finals in Argentina in 1978, replied: 'Retain it [the cup].' But musings on his candidacy for Pope were no more than fanciful nonsense. As a child, sitting on his front step, his future unwritten, Winning may have dreamed of being the first Scottish pope, but when he reached the position where the role had become a possibility, however slim, he viewed it as one would a nightmare. On one visit to the Vatican shortly after he became a cardinal, Winning was shown the *stanza delle lacrime* – the room of tears – where, in the event of a conclave, three white robes in sizes small, medium and large, would sit in readiness for the new pontiff. As he stood in the room Winning shuddered at the very idea of such responsibility. When asked about his candidacy, he replied: 'There are much greater men than me. I don't consider it a viable option.'

Fifty years as a priest had failed to shake Winning's belief in the basic tenets of the Catholic faith, but when it came to matters of presentation, he felt there was room for considerable improvement. The issue of '*Humanae Vitae*' and the prohibition on the use of contraceptives had troubled him in recent years. While he passionately believed that the act of physical love must always be open to life, he believed that prostitutes, who were not involved in an act of love and were forced into the profession through poverty and/ or drug addiction, should be allowed protection. Winning was aware such an argument was riddled with holes and could be extended to include those partaking of a casual affair and so he kept his opinion quiet. When asked publicly about the issue, he maintained the party line. Ironically, when arguments were made by Church figures that married men or women who were accidentally infected with the HIV virus through a blood transfusion should be permitted to use contraceptives to protect their partner, Winning disagreed, stating that abstinence, in such a case, was essential. In line with many celibates, Winning believed sex was overemphasized. Society, he believed – in an opinion backed by ample evidence – was 'sex mad'.

It was for this reason that he believed now was not the time to tackle the issue of clerical celibacy. In principle, Winning had no qualms about the issue of married priests, a tradition that extended back less than one thousand years, but to have married priests in the Catholic Church as a reaction to the dictates of a global society that treated the sexual act with contempt was inadvisable. He addressed the issue in a lecture on the future of the Catholic Church in March 2001 at St Aloysius Church, where he said: 'Is it not important to remind people that family life can be surrendered so as to be a sign that there is something higher than this present life? At a time when there is great turbulence about sex and all its implications, is this really the best time to abandon the celibate life freely accepted and offered for the Kingdom of God?'

When first asked to express his vision for the Catholic Church in the twenty-first century, in a talk at St Aloysius Church in Glasgow as part of their regular series of Aloysius' Gonzaga Lectures, Winning compared his task to that of Michelangelo as he contemplated the decoration of the Sistine Chapel: where to begin? He had no desire to see another revolution, a Vatican III as some, such as Cardinal Martini of Milan, had called for. Almost forty years on, the radical concepts of Vatican II, such as the universal call to holiness, had still not embedded themselves in the hearts of the laity, and re-opening Pandora's box would lead to further confusion. He had no desire to see the ordination of women, on the grounds that such a change was in his opinion against the deposit of faith, the inviolate teachings left to the Church by Christ. Yet his encouragement of women to fulfil their calling was impressive. When Roseann Reddy, the organizer of his Pro-Life Initiative, expressed a desire to enter the religious life, but was unable to locate an order to suit her charism, he permitted her to found her own, the Sisters of the Gospel of Life, of which she is one of only two members.

Winning believed the Church had survived a century of persecution unparalleled in history, yet the 'anti-God' philosophies of Fascism, Nazism and Communism had been replaced by a subtler form of persecution, 'a religious indifference, apathy and a gradual elimination of religion from public life and policy'. He believed the laity – 'that sleeping giant' – must be roused and inspired to carry their faith into the world and that this was only possible through greater animation and renewal in the parish, which he believed was the beating heart of the Church. The fall in Church attendance across Western Europe was evidence that people had forgotten the importance of Mass and so the cornerstone of the Church's efforts, Winning felt, must be 'a rediscovery of the Eucharist, its meaning and its essential role in our lives'. Winning concluded his speech with a strong call in which he sought to characterize the Church of the new millennium in four words: living, free, courageous and involved:

> Living, because she will continue to confront the men and women of the new century with a coherent and vibrant message which makes moral and intellectual demands on them, demands which produce good fruits. Fruits of love and compassion and solidarity and faith.
>
> Free, because never before has the Church been more free of the shackles of temporal power than she is today. And, freed from these golden shackles, she can make her voice heard loudly and clearly, even in the face of worldly power.
>
> Courageous, because the Church will increasingly be called to be a sign of contradiction to society and all it holds dear. That means the Church must be prepared to face down the values of this world and denounce oppression, immorality, sin and its structures even when doing so earns a crown of martyrdom – literal or metaphorical.
>
> And involved, because the Church purified will be a Church at the heart of the world – involved in the day-to-day struggles of all peoples, especially the marginalized, those without a voice and those who are excluded.
>
> This is the Church of the future that I can begin to see emerging . . . a purified Church, a renewed Church, a brave Church, a humble Church.[2]

In his speech, Winning touched only lightly on a key concern, that of collegiality, as he argued that: 'I do not believe the structures of the Roman Curia are a burning issue to the ordinary men and women trying to live out their Catholic faith in the world.' They were, however, to him. Ever since Winning had received a snippy letter from the curial department responsible for Catholic education, chastising him, as an auxiliary bishop, for daring to suggest a particular canon law was no longer applicable, he had harboured a mild dislike for the bureaucrats of the Church. Over the years he had been the recipient of a number of letters inquiring about practice and behaviour from the curia; these were usually triggered by the letter-writing campaigns of organizations such as Catholic Truth, who viewed Winning as scandalously liberal.

The Vatican's perception of Winning was of a strong defender of the faith, but an uninspired thinker. An indication that the curia held one in high regard was if one was invited to take on the role of a reporter at a synod. This involved collating information and helping to draft the final reports, and was an invitation Winning never received. Yet the foundation of the Pro-Life Initiative had accrued him great respect. When the news broke, while he was attending the Synod for Europe in October 1999, that among the recipients of financial assistance was a pregnant twelve-year-old girl, Winning received a round of applause. In Britain, however, he received brickbats and accusations of gross irresponsibility. What became a cause of controversy in Britain was worth a mark of respect in Rome. Yet it was during this particular synod that Winning's attitude towards the curia hardened.

The Second Synod for Europe was a discussion forum that stretched over three weeks, and among its findings was that the European Union was a part of God's grand design. As a tribute, the 'founding fathers of Europe', Alcide De Gasperi of Italy, Robert Schuman of France and Konrad Adenauer of Germany, were to be considered for canonization.

The synod had moved smoothly for Winning until the final week when a press conference given by Keith O'Brien provoked outrage from curial cardinals. The Archbishop of St Andrews and Edinburgh had made candid comments on the curial officials' attempts to stifle debate on issues such as married priests. He went further and admitted to tensions between the curia and diocesan bishops over issues such as the forgiveness of sins, general absolution, the Mass, and clerical speculation over a successor to Pope John Paul. O'Brien's statements were true, but in the secretive atmosphere of the Vatican, to air them in public was almost unforgivable. A degree of embarrassment was heaped on Winning's head when O'Brien, while answering a question about papal successors, said that he would often ask questions of Winning such as, 'Who's that guy Tettamanzi?' and that Winning would reply: 'He's the wee fat guy'[3], while pointing him out.

Winning's response was swift and supportive. In his opinion the blame did not lie with O'Brien but with the Holy See's press office, who had allowed the press conference to deviate and whose press officer was unequipped to deal with the media. As Cardinal Jan Schotte, General Secretary of the Synod of Bishops, fulminated and called a final press conference to denounce O'Brien's comments, Winning arranged a meeting with Dr Joaquin Navarro-Valls, director of the Holy See's press office, to ask for help in sparing O'Brien any further embarrassment and in discovering how best to minimize the fallout. He then wrote a note of apology to Cardinal Tettamanzi, claiming O'Brien now regretted his comments, though he admitted to O'Brien later: 'He *is* wee and fat.'

There was to be one final embarrassment, however. At the synod's close, as Winning was kneeling down to pray, a curial cardinal leaned over and whispered in his ear: 'Be sure and pray for forgiveness for your brother bishop.'

In March 2001, Winning was excited by the news that an Extraordinary Consistory had been called to discuss the Pope's apostolic letter, '*Novo Millennio Ineunte*', which had been published in January and in which John Paul II had drawn on the pastoral experience of the Jubilee year and looked towards the future of the Church. Winning considered the letter to be one of the Pope's finest and noted with glee the criticism of 'careerism' among the curia. Winning had been a member of the Pontifical Council for the Family for six years and had attended any number of synods, yet the Extraordinary Consistory offered the glimmer of so much more; the potential for a free and frank exchange of ideas among the 155 cardinals who would, in time, choose the next Pope. The Secretariat of State had announced the consistory in late February, allowing the world's cardinals only ten weeks to clear their diaries for the four-day event and prepare responses to the twenty-one bullet points for discussion. As was typical of many Vatican conferences, the exact nature and layout of the consistory was unclear. What was known was that there would be six three-hour discussion sessions, five in general assembly and one spent in small groups, yet it was unclear who would be permitted to speak and on what topics.

As this was Winning's first Extraordinary Consistory, he was rigorous in his preparation. Like a schoolboy faced with essay questions, he prepared a response to each of the twenty-one bullet points, but knew precisely on which topic he wished to speak. He planned to make an attack on the curia and the lack of collegiality and consultation that existed between them and the Bishops' Conferences around the world.

The issue, which had simmered for so long, had reached boiling point during the last two years over what Winning viewed as the disrespectful treatment by the curia of the International Commission on English in the Liturgy (ICEL) chaired by Maurice Taylor, his old college friend and the Bishop of Galloway. The role of ICEL was to prepare new English translations of Catholic texts such as the missal, but their work had become a battleground between the liberal and conservative wings of the Church over their avoidance of gender-specific pronouns and attempts to produce texts that were more accessible and inclusive. The previous year, ICEL and Taylor's chairmanship had been dismissed as inadequate by Cardinal Jorge Medina Estevez, head of the Congregation for Divine Worship and the Discipline of the Sacraments, the curial department in charge. In a letter to Taylor, Estevez had accused the organization of acting with 'undue autonomy' and demanded a root-and-branch reform.

For two years, Winning had repeatedly requested a meeting in Rome with Estevez to petition on ICEL's behalf and discuss a document the Congregation was currently preparing on their instructions on how translations of liturgical texts should be handled. The document, entitled '*Liturgiam Authenticam*', was the result of years of secret work by the Congregation, and the presidents of the English-speaking Bishops' Conferences, who were denied access, feared it would be used to attack ICEL. In total, Winning had made a dozen attempts to speak with Estevez, in order to discuss the document, but he had been persistently stonewalled.

One week before the Extraordinary Consistory, the document was released – unannounced – on the Holy See's website. Winning was angered, not only by the disrespectful manner of its distribution, flying, as it did, in the face of all attempts at collegiality, but by its contents which, though applicable to all language translations, appeared to go out of its way to skewer ICEL. The document insisted that all English translations maintain close fidelity to the Latin original, that they display a 'sacred style' of language, and that they retain the masculine pronoun when speaking of God. Winning began to redraft the text of his speech.

In order to lend as much weight as possible to his words, Winning faxed a draft of the speech to the Bishops' Conferences of England and Wales, Canada, Australia, New Zealand, America and South Africa, and asked for their consent to speak in their name.

On Saturday 19 May, Winning flew to Rome and settled into a suite at the Santa Marta, the new hotel constructed within the Vatican for use during the next conclave. He was to have been accompanied by Paul Murray, the assistant director of the Pastoral Plan, but Murray had been delayed and was unable to fly out until the following day. As Rome was host to every cardinal in the world, the Santa Marta was full and so Murray was relegated to the Scots College. The two men finally met up in Winning's room at around eight o'clock on Sunday evening.

Winning displayed a mixture of excitement and nerves. Upon

arrival in Rome, he had learned that he would be allowed to speak on a matter of his own choosing, but he had also decided to address a second matter. The Extraordinary Consistory was taking place during the traditional month for Confirmations and this year, in particular, Winning had been struck by parents' lack of knowledge or interest in the Church. He now wished to include this observation and so, for over an hour, Murray sat at the desk each room provided and rewrote the speech on the laptop he had brought along for the task, while Winning looked over his shoulder. Just before ten o'clock, Winning suggested they finish the evening off with dinner at one of the restaurants on the Borgo Pio.

Murray rose early the following morning, finished incorporating the last few corrections, and then faxed the final draft over to Winning at the Santa Marta. Winning had also risen early to check his pigeonhole at the hotel as the last few faxed responses of support from the Bishops' Conferences drifted in.

The Extraordinary Consistory opened on the morning of Monday 21 May 2001 with Mass, followed by a series of speeches which Winning found frustrating. Cardinal Bernardin Gantin, Dean of the College of Cardinals, called on the consistory to be carried out in a 'collegial spirit', but instead of a serious critique on the state of the Church, Winning found himself listening to bland platitudes as cardinal after cardinal rose from his seat to praise the Pope, insist all was well and quote his own encyclicals back to him.

The consistory, like all Vatican conferences, was held behind closed doors with no media present in order to encourage honest discussion, but many present were reluctant to take the opportunity provided. There were exceptions, however. Cardinal Martini of Milan argued that the rules of the regular synods required revision, a point supported by Cardinal Achille Silvestrini, a veteran of the curia, who agreed that there was 'dissatisfaction' and that they were becoming 'monologues without debate or without response'. Winning sat through two days of speeches, and dined out each evening with college staff, before he was permitted to speak on the final day. Since the Pope was detained on Wednesday morning at his weekly public audience, the cardinals broke into small groups and were reunited in the afternoon. Murray had called Winning on Wednesday morning to wish him good luck and found him rather anxious. 'It's good to know a cardinal can still get nervous,' said Murray. It was early in the afternoon when Winning finally rose to speak. At first he raised his concerns over poor Mass attendance and said the Church was responsible for simply allowing guilt to dictate attendance.

We depended too much on weekly Mass attendance as a grave moral obligation. We have taken it for granted for too long that people would keep coming to Mass on Sunday, that they would regard the Eucharist as the source and summit of the Christian life. We can't take it for granted any more. The re-establishment of the Sunday celebration of the Mass as a norm in the Catholic community, therefore, needs to be the top priority for the new century.

He then moved on to tackle his key point. Speaking in English while the cardinals listened as his comments were translated into ten languages, Winning made his point:

My particular concern is with relationships between the Roman Curia and the Episcopal Conferences. The Apostolic Constitution, Pastor Bonus [John Paul II's Constitution of June 1988], rightly defines the function of the Roman Curia as a service, or diakonia. It is a service to the Holy Father in whose name the various dicasteries [Curia subdivisions] act, but it is also a service to the College of Bishops.

As diocesan bishops, we value greatly the insight, the pastoral concern and support we receive from the heads and collaborators of the various dicasteries here in Rome. I personally have experienced very warm and friendly meetings with many members of the Curia.

On occasion, however, tensions can and do arise. I know I speak for many bishops when I express my disappointment that the diakonia and collegiality of Pastor Bonus have, of late, not been evident in certain situations involving the Roman Curia and the Bishops' Conferences. I emphasize that such tensions are more due to misunderstandings and poor communication than to ill will and divergent ecclesiologies. I wish to suggest very strongly that a primary way of fostering the full potential of the Roman Curia is the need for greater consultation and dialogue between Bishops' Conferences and the Curia.

An essential element in genuine dialogue is that full information is available to those engaged in it. To engage in fraternal dialogue, particularly before the publication of documents of far-reaching importance and with grave pastoral implications, is not to undermine or interfere in the work of the dicasteries. Rather it is in the interests of the whole Church as well as being the expression of the fraternal and collegial spirit which is the legacy of the Second Vatican Council.

If we are sincere in practising the principles of collegiality and subsidiarity, there have to be consultation and exchange of views prior to the publication of major Church documents. When such dialogue is lacking, misunderstandings arise and when, without due dialogue, major documents are published which appear to be contrary to previously established policies, these misunderstandings give rise to serious concerns, even to questioning the very reasons for the document and its canonical validity.

Moreover, given our modern communications technology, it is disappointing that major documents are released unannounced on the Internet. Not only does this mean that the bishops find themselves relying on others to bring these documents to their notice, but the secular media are able to deal with the contents of the documents before bishops have been properly briefed, causing misunderstanding and confusion among the People of God.

I offer these thoughts in the spirit of openness and sincerity and my plea today is that any communication blocks which may exist between the Bishops' Conferences and the Roman Curia will be examined and cleared so as to allow a full, free and genuine dialogue and collaboration.

The Church we all love is ill served by attitudes of fear and distrust. This is a plea from the heart reflecting the minds of the Presidents of nine English-speaking Conferences of Bishops, and all the members of my own Bishops' Conference.

The speech caused great offence to Cardinal Estevez who, quite correctly, read it as a direct rebuttal to his treatment of ICEL and the manner of the publication of '*Liturgiam Authenticam*'. Winning was relieved when two cardinals approached him afterwards and praised his words. At the end of the day, Winning and Cardinal Murphy-O'Connor walked to the café within the building for an espresso. Murphy-O'Connor had only received his red hat that February and wished Winning to introduce him to a number of other cardinals and soon they were joined by Cardinal Desmond Connell, the Archbishop of Dublin. In the café, Winning was approached by Estevez, who was visibly angry and said: 'You denigrated me in there.' He then began to complain about the difficulty of his job, that it was forced upon him against his wishes. Winning had no time for either his evasions or his self-pity and was brisk in his response. 'I didn't denigrate you. We're all adults here. We can speak as adults.' At this point Estevez turned and walked off. After his departure, it was left to Connell to break the silence. 'You were a bit hard on him there, Tom.' Winning felt he had been merely stating the facts, but Connell explained: 'You told him to grow up.'

Winning saw little point in arguing. The confrontation had soured what would be his final visit to Rome and leave him chewing on the consequences during the last few weeks. He tried to content himself with the knowledge that he had bravely stated the opinions of his peers. At the daily press conference, Dr Navarro-Valls, who would later be accused by one *Newsweek* journalist of making misleading statements about the consistory, made no mention of Winning's provocative speech, which he viewed as too inflammatory. After a difficult day, Winning moved from the Santa Marta to the Scots College for his final night in Rome. Four students were celebrating their *Lectorate* and *Acolytate* – they were being made lectors and acolytes, further stages in their progression to the priesthood – and Winning administered the blessing during Mass and presented them each with a volume of the Gospels. The service was followed by a meal in the dining hall and a second presentation. Nello, a former employee of the college, responsible for ordering supplies, had recently retired and had been invited back for a celebratory dinner and the presentation of a silver quiach (presentation bowl) and crystal decanter. Winning appeared lost in thought, picked only occasionally at his food, and when the college staff retired to the common room for a whisky, he slipped off to bed.

He had less than one month to live.

If there was one thing which could shake off the gloom cast by the consistory it was Celtic Football Club. For decades Winning had been a devoted supporter, resisting all arguments that he should lay aside his passion for the club in the greater interest of ecumenism, and for the last ten years those few hours spent in the stand at Parkhead had become his only source of recreation. Like any football fan, Winning had fallen in and out of love with the club in which he held shares through the Scanlan Trust, set up by his predecessor, and which he as archbishop now controlled. He had endured a tortuous relationship with Fergus McCann, the Canadian multimillionaire who had rescued the club from almost certain financial ruin and ran it as a successful business for five years during the mid-1990s, but with little cup success. McCann had failed to persuade Winning to sell his shares and, although in public the archbishop had supported the businessman's 'Boys Against Bigotry' campaign, in private their relationship was strained. Winning enjoyed telling an anecdote about how he had confronted McCann in his office about the club's decision to permit fans to marry on the centre spot and how the businessman had ordered him from the room declaring bluntly that as he did not instruct the Archbishop on how to run the Church, he would not stand by and be told how to run a football club. Winning would cap the anecdote by explaining how he had prayed for McCann, who was himself a devout Catholic, when he went home that evening. (When word reached McCann of Winning's tale, a source close to him said he dismissed it as nonsense.) Winning was in the habit of writing to the club's official newspaper, *The Celtic View*, to express his disappointment at articles that he felt were incompatible with the team's Catholic image, such as features about players moving in with their girl-friends or having children conceived outside the marital bed.

By the close of the 2001 season, McCann had long since left the club and the business success that the Canadian had made of Celtic was now followed up by success on the field. Winning and his nephew Edward had watched as Martin O'Neill, the team's new manager, had won the League, the League Cup, and now had reached the final of the Scottish Cup, scheduled for Saturday 26 May. Two tickets for the sell-out match had been provided by Brian Quinn, chairman of the club, and at three o'clock Winning took his seat to see Celtic win the treble: the first time the club had won every domestic award in thirty-two years.

The sun was out, the sky was azure-blue, and each of the three times Celtic scored the two men leapt from their seats and hugged. The post-match celebrations were restricted to a whisky at The Oaks as Winning, ever diligent, had a sermon to prepare.

TWENTY-TWO

A Good Fight Fought

'As for me, my life is already draining to its close and the time of my departure is at hand. I have fought a good fight, I have finished my course, I have kept the faith.'

ST PAUL

Death disturbed Thomas Winning more than one would expect of a man of the cloth who believed God was waiting beyond the veil. God waiting was, in fact, what worried him. A new generation of Catholics, and indeed Christians, accept the afterlife as a casual fact, one stripped of the unpleasantness of Hell or even the peril of Purgatory, but, for Winning, a place in Heaven must first be earned and even he, after fifty years of service to God, felt his access was not yet guaranteed. Winning could never quite escape from the image of God as a judge who weighs one's life. Yet as much as the concept of death disturbed him, the physical process of dying distressed him more. There are priests whose quiet presence is a comfort to the terminally ill, but it was a category into which Winning did not fall. The duty of visiting priests in their final days caused him a greater upset than he would ever admit. As one priest commented: 'He hated you to die on him. When he visited the sick, all he wanted to hear was that you were getting better.'

On one occasion Winning described a recent visit to an elderly priest. The man had sat on the edge of his bed with his shoulders hunched and had struggled to raise his head – when he did, it was to say, 'Tom, I just want to die.' After telling the story Winning shuddered, as if someone had already walked upon his grave. Fear of incapacity and the slow, steady and tortuous decline that had afflicted both Donny Renfrew and Gerry Rogers crept into his thoughts. Until his final year, Winning's standard homily at a funeral for a fellow priest had focused on the life the man had led. Evidence that he underwent a spiritual change was apparent in the final year of his life when he began to state: 'If we asked the deceased, "Do you want to come back?" their response would be: "I want you to come where I am now."' 'Listening to the sermons it was as if he were analysing himself; instead of reflecting on what we lost in life, he began to reflect on what we gained in death,' commented Mgr Peter Smith.

Yet the subject of death never quite lost its sting. When Mgr Smith chose to redesign Glasgow Cathedral's crypt on the grounds that the next guest would be a cardinal and the library shelves on which lay the coffins of his predecessors had grown rather crowded, he did so during Winning's month-long holiday in August 1999, so his boss need never know. Unfortunately, the work ran late and when Winning returned early, he asked what was the cause of the commotion to the rear of the cathedral. When Smith reluctantly explained, Winning fell silent and responded with a simple: 'Oh.'

For many years, Winning had refused to even prepare a will, despite Smith's pleading, on the grounds that he had once read an article which stated the average person died within five years of signing such a statement and he had no desire to tempt fate. He finally relented in 1997. In spite of the good health he enjoyed, Winning's thoughts increasingly turned to his own demise and he would often reflect of his grand-nieces and grand-nephews: 'I'll never see them grow up.' His intuition was to prove correct.

On Friday 8 June 2001, five days after Winning celebrated his seventy-sixth birthday with a family dinner at Roma Mia, a small Italian restaurant two miles from The Oaks, he had his first heart attack. The day had begun at the funeral of the sister of a close friend, Mgr James McShane, after which Winning drove back to Clyde Street to complete a number of tasks. Ten priests in the diocese were celebrating their golden jubilee, fifty years since their ordination, and Peter Smith had purchased each a congratulations card for Winning to sign. Winning had also made the decision to move a priest to a new parish and had briefed him over lunch on what he wished him to achieve. He then planned to drive home to change, before heading on to Mount Carmel pastoral centre for a 3.30 p.m. session of discussions on the future of the Pastoral Plan. Father Cappellaro had arrived from Italy and Winning was keen to spend as much time as possible nursing his pet project into what was approaching its twentieth year.

He felt a wave of sickness overtake him as he left the building and walked towards the car park. He felt close to gagging but as the sensation seemed more akin to food poisoning rather than anything cardiovascular, he proceeded to drive home. The traffic after lunch was heavier than usual and it took Winning almost twenty-five minutes to complete the three-mile journey, during which nausea was joined by a crippling pain in his chest. By the time he reached The Oaks, he had begun to hyperventilate through panic. After struggling through the front door he alerted Mrs McInnes who dialled 999. An ambulance was despatched from Victoria Infirmary and a few minutes later Winning was being stretched onboard, accompanied by his housekeeper, who had left a message for Peter Smith, which in fact failed to reach him. After Winning's admittance to the cardiac unit, he was recognized by a nurse who was friends with his niece Agnes. Shortly after three o'clock, Agnes received a phone call that her uncle was seriously ill. Where other family members had given up pleading with Winning to ease up on his workload, Agnes had persisted and it was a phone call she had long dreaded. She phoned Clyde Street and told Peter Smith that she had been informed that her Uncle Thomas was in the hospital. Smith insisted there had been a mistake, as the cardinal had left an hour ago in good health and was probably at Mount Carmel as they spoke. To put Agnes's mind at ease, he said he would contact the pastoral planning centre but when Paul Murray, the assistant director, told him Winning had not yet arrived, alarm bells began to ring.

Smith next called the Victoria Infirmary. A nurse passed him on to a consultant who explained it was hospital policy only to answer questions from blood relatives and so he was unwilling to either confirm or deny Winning's admittance. Smith was irritated but, as a natural bureaucrat himself, he understood procedure must be maintained. 'Monsignor Clancy, the Vicar General, and myself are going to come down right away,' replied Smith, and when the consultant made no attempt to dissuade him, he was sure Winning had been admitted. Ronnie Convery then phoned Fr Stephen Hannah, the hospital's chaplain, and asked him to make his way to Winning's bedside and administer the Sacrament of the Sick.

The first to arrive was Edward McCarron. When he saw his uncle in a private room lying with his eyes closed, his hands clasped, and with the dark-suited Fr Hannah praying by his bedside, he feared he was too late and burst into tears. Winning had closed his eyes in relief at Hannah's arrival and also to concentrate on the prayers which eased his mind and soul to an extent he could never have imagined during all the years when the roles were reversed. When he heard Edward, he opened his eyes and said: 'Don't worry, I'm all right.'

A few minutes later Peter Smith and Jim Clancy arrived and were relieved to find their boss sitting up in bed and still in possession of his childish wit. When a nurse introduced herself as Jane, he quipped: 'I'm Tarzan.' By the time Margaret and her daughter Agnes arrived that evening, Winning was in a position to explain personally how he had suffered a minor heart attack from which he was expected to make a full recovery. He presented himself as the sick patient who was getting better. The medical staff, however, were insistent that the attack should be read as a warning, a shot across the bow, and that Winning make every effort to reduce his workload. Eighteen-hour days and six and a half day weeks were no longer suitable. He was not a young man and the heart attack had finally punctured the youthful vitality he had so long expressed and which led friends to quip that the attic of The Oaks contained a blackened portrait in the manner of Oscar Wilde's Dorian Gray. An aid to recovery was the bounteous supply of 'get well' wishes, cards and flowers that steadily filled his room to overflowing. On Wednesday, Ronnie Convery visited Winning and pointed to hundreds of cards, little messages of hope from across the diocese, the country and the world. 'Therapy,' said Winning. 'That's my therapy.'

Winning was discharged, seven days after admittance, on 15 June. His heart had settled back into a strong, steady rhythm and his diary had been swept clear until late November. Before departing the hospital, he made a short tour to thank staff for their kindness and care and to visit a number of fellow patients who had attempted to visit him but had been unable to penetrate the 'ring of steel' erected by nurses concerned their patient was in danger of overexertion. Crossing the threshold of The Oaks was a moving experience for Winning who, while waiting for the ambulance a week before, had feared he would not do so again. To greet him was Keith O'Brien, Archbishop of St Andrews and Edinburgh, while Mrs McInnes, still recovering from the shock of almost losing her closest companion, was in the kitchen making tea.

Over a pot of tea and biscuits, O'Brien brought Winning up to date with Church affairs and advised him to get as much rest as possible. He was conscious of how tired Winning looked and did not linger for a second cup and instead bade him farewell. Smith left with O'Brien, but promised to return the following morning to say Mass. Winning walked both men to the door and said he wanted to visit the oratory for a few minutes to thank God for allowing him to come home. Unable to kneel, he sat in front of the crucifix and bowed his head in prayer.

There were to be three other visitors that first evening. Fathers Paul Conroy, Paul Murray and Juan Baptista Cappellaro arrived to say goodbye as the Argentinian was returning to Rome the following morning. The trio spent less than an hour updating Winning on the recent sessions on the Pastoral Plan and, conscious of his enthusiasm for the project but his need to rest, they had deliberately decided against bringing any paperwork. They did, however, discuss the conclusion of their conference which was that a special event was required, one which would unite the entire diocese, reanimate their faith, and remind the people of their responsibilities. The last question all four considered was what form it should take.

The following morning, Winning was brought breakfast in bed – tea and a warm roll – together with the morning newspapers, the *Herald*, the *Scotsman* and the *Daily Record*. He rose after nine o'clock and dressed in his standard off-duty uniform of a white shirt, open at the neck, and grey cardigan. Peter Smith arrived at half past eleven to say Mass and laid down the rules: Smith would say Mass each morning until Winning felt able to concelebrate, then after a week or so, Winning would say Mass and Smith would concelebrate. That Saturday morning Smith stood at the altar, broke the bread and praised God. Winning and Mrs McInnes sat side by side, a quiet congregation of two. Afterwards, Winning and Smith talked for a couple of hours. The cardinal was relieved to be home and his spirits were raised. When the talk turned to the newspaper coverage of his illness, Winning said it had been like reading his own obituary. Smith laughed. 'That reminds me. The *Daily Telegraph* called for information. You've given them a fright. They realized they didn't have an obituary for you.'

'Stuff that,' replied Winning, and gave a theatrical shudder.

At around half past two, Smith left and explained that he would not return until the following afternoon, as he had to drive to Burntisland to deliver a speech on the cardinal's behalf. Winning had been invited over a year ago to deliver a speech to the Bible Society to mark the four-hundredth anniversary of the King James version of the Bible. The invitation of a Catholic cardinal to the anniversary of an event sparked by the Reformation was a source of pride to Winning and he was pleased Smith was to deliver the address in his absence. As Smith left the house and began crunching up the gravel drive, he turned round to see Winning standing in the doorway, waving goodbye.

Later that afternoon, Edward called. The children, who had been kept away from the hospital, were anxious to see their great uncle and a provisional arrangement had been made to visit that afternoon. Edward, however, was reluctant to arrive without first checking Winning's condition and found him anxious to postpone for one more day; as he explained: 'I'm just dead tired.'

On Sunday 17 June, Winning awoke at around seven o'clock. Breakfast was brought in at eight and when Mrs McInnes came up to clear away his plate, he told her that he was getting up. She argued that there was no need, that he had been told to get some rest and so rest he should. Winning, sitting up in bed, said: 'They say I've to get up. I'll be OK. I can rest just as easily sitting downstairs as I can sitting in my bed.' Mrs McInnes knew there was no point in arguing and so, sighing, she went back down to the kitchen to wash up. When she had completed her task, she realized that towels washed the day before were now dry and she decided to put them back in the airing cupboard on the upstairs landing. The cupboard was only a few feet from Winning's bedroom and as she put the last of the towels away she heard a noise. Moving towards the door she knocked a couple of times as was customary and said: 'Father'. After a few more knocks, and a second 'Father', with still no response, she pushed open the door.

Thomas Joseph Winning lay sprawled on the bed in his pyjamas. He had apparently swung his legs out from under the blankets and attempted to stand up. His heart had given out and he had collapsed back on to the bed. Mrs McInnes sensed he was dead, but ran to the phone to call an ambulance, then later Agnes, followed by Peter Smith, who took the call on his mobile as he drove to Burntisland. Mrs McInnes said: 'The medics are here but he's gone, Peter, he's gone.' In Motherwell, Edward had just returned from a morning jog when he took Agnes's call. 'It's happened again,' was all she said. In spite of the best efforts of paramedics and emergency staff at the Victoria Infirmary, Winning was beyond recovery.

When Edward arrived at the hospital with Mgr James Clancy, they listened to the doctor's explanation. They were then led into the emergency treatment room where, on the table, Winning lay covered to his neck in a green gown. Edward was struck that in all his years of attending funerals or memorial services he had never seen a priest cry, but Clancy was unable to stop the tears and neither was he. After a few minutes the pair left to allow Fr Stephen Hannah to say the prayers of the dead. 'By your glorious power give him light, joy, peace in heaven, where you live for ever and ever.' On his hospital records, a worn brown manila folder, the time of death is recorded at 9.55 a.m. on Sunday 17 June 2001. The Feast of Corpus Christi: the Body of Christ.

Winning feared the power of the press and the punishment they might mete out upon his death and the pain it would cause his family. 'I worry what they'll say when I'm gone,' he once said to Convery. It was a groundless fear that blew away like smoke from a thurible. When the Press Association and the BBC released news of his death shortly after ten o'clock, a number of members of the media were visibly upset. The press conference held in the hall at Clyde Street, where so many of Winning's media campaigns were launched or defended, was a subdued affair, with as many reporters keen to pass on their condolences as gather the necessary facts. When Peter Smith arrived to open his office in preparation for the conference, he found a get-well fax on the machine from Cardinal Lopez Trujillo in Rome.

That evening Scottish Television devoted a thirty-minute news programme dedicated to Winning's life and the next morning's newspapers were generous in their appraisal. 'Death of a Moral Warrior', declared the *Scotsman* in a banner headline, before praising Winning in its editorial: 'Thomas Winning consciously and pragmatically led his people from being tacit outsiders, ethnically and religiously, in a Scotland politely but firmly riven with a sectarian divide, to become part of mainstream society.' The *Herald* declared: 'Another great Scot is gone, a man of the people, but first of all a man of God' in their editorial, which praised his recent defence of asylum seekers but criticized his comments on Section 28 and the Scottish parliament. 'It was not always possible to agree with Cardinal Winning; indeed, he would have looked suspiciously on anyone who did,' the paper declared before insisting that in a secular society the voice of the Church was increasingly necessary.

Politicians lined up to praise his name. In the words of Gordon Brown, the Chancellor, he was a 'a great Scot and a great Christian'. Henry McLeish, the First Minister, said: 'Scotland had lost one of her greatest sons', while Alex Salmond paid tribute to a 'fearless fighter for the poor and dispossessed'. Even the Prime Minister had a few warm words for the man the *Daily Telegraph* described as 'a thorn in his flesh'. A statement issued by Tony Blair's office read: 'His energy, commitment and passionate defence of the core values of the Catholic Church were recognized by all.'

As dictated by tradition, Winning was prepared for a period of lying in state. On the evening of Monday 19 June at six o'clock, his coffin was carried from a hearse that had collected him from the funeral home to the Clyde Street offices. As a private tribute, Edward was later to slip the ticket from the recent Cup Final into the coffin shortly before they left for the diocesan offices. In a touch of which Winning would have approved, the coffin was delayed to coincide with live coverage for Scottish Television's evening news bulletin. That evening a private prayer service took place for the cardinal's family and was led by Mgr Clancy. The following morning at eight o'clock, and for the next six days, over five thousand visitors queued along the crash barriers that sat outside the office and waited for their few minutes alone with their archbishop.

The Eyre Hall had been decorated fittingly. The coffin containing Winning sat in front of a large wooden crucifix, flanked by flowers and two members of the Knights of the Holy Sepulchre, who stood in white cloaks, ceremonial berets and white gloves. In the dark wooden coffin Winning was robed in vestments of ivory and gold, with the archbishop's mitre on his head, wooden rosary beads laced through his fingers, and the gold ring given to him by the Pope on his finger. In tribute to his personality there were two comical touches: the socks he wore were scarlet red, the uniform of a cardinal. He had sworn he would only ever wear them once when receiving his red hat. At the foot of the coffin was an incongruous object, a white fireman's hat, a present from Strathclyde Fire Brigade, who had made him an honorary firemaster. When he had been given it, he had joked that it was the only white hat he was likely to receive.

In order to allow the participation of as many friends, parishioners and priests in Winning's funeral there were two ticketed events. On the evening of Sunday 24 June, a service of vespers was offered which began with the carrying of the cardinal's coffin into the cathedral while a piper played a lament. During the private service, closed to the media, Archbishop Keith O'Brien paid tribute to his colleague and reflected on what would take place the following day, commenting that it was akin to a state funeral. 'If Tom was here he would say, "With you involved, Keith, it will be a state."' But the description was no exaggeration. The funeral of Cardinal Winning the following morning was attended by Prince Edward, representing the Queen, four cardinals – the principal celebrant Cardinal Murphy-O'Connor, Archbishop of Westminster, Desmond Connell of Dublin, Cahal Daly of Armagh and Adrianus Simonis of Utrecht – as well as the Papal Nuncio, Archbishop Pablo Puente. Outside the cathedral in Clyde Street two thousand people gathered to watch a big-screen presentation of the events inside the church, which was also relayed to six other packed churches throughout the diocese.

So many threads of his life were united in the celebration of his departure. The priests he had so long ruled over processed in snow-white chasubles, three hundred of them, parting like a river left and right as they reached his coffin, many stopping to touch it in a fond farewell. As Peter Smith had helped organize his life, so he coordinated his death, wearing headset earphones to choreograph everyone's move. As the Pope had signalled his praise with a red hat, so he spoke through his nuncio, declaring: 'We have lost a friend on earth, but have gained one in heaven, who will be our guide and beacon.'[1] As his sister Margaret and her family had supported and encouraged him during his lifetime so they did in his death. The tears of his nephew as he carried his uncle towards the crypt were identical to those shed upon witnessing his uncle receive his red hat. A young girl who had read the scripture at the Scottish Exhibition Centre at the Mass following his return from

Rome with the red hat, now repeated the task seven years later. Jane, the nurse to whom he had played Tarzan, represented the staff of the Victoria Hospital. Bishop Devine, his former auxiliary, spoke of having dreaded any attempt to capture Winning in words, a man he described as 'a superstar of the Catholic Church in the twentieth century', and his homily closed with the simple words: 'Tom, thank you for being you.'

After the service the congregation, princes of the Church, bishop and priests, old friends, new acquaintances, family young and old, wandered out into the sunshine to talk of his life. The crowds lingered on awhile before beginning to drift off. Some to the pubs in the vicinity where men who had never darkened the door of a church in decades had watched the funeral on television, putting down their pints to shake hands with their fellow patrons during the sign of peace. On the giant electronic television screen was a memorable image of Winning. It was a freeze-frame of footage shot during his visit to Rome in 1994 to collect his red hat. In a packed St Peter's Square, surrounded by supporters, Winning smiles while biting his lip, an attempt to suppress his evident delight, but he can contain it no longer. In a display more reminiscent of an Olympic medal winner or jubilant footballer, he thrusts his hand holding the hat into the air, puts his head down and smiles broadly. The caption told the viewer everything they did not need to know: Cardinal Thomas Joseph Winning: 1925–2001.

Epilogue

Seven days after his death, I met Winning in my dreams, a ghost in a grey cardigan. A biographer's dream of his subject is a common occurrence. Before embarking on his life of Samuel Johnson, James Boswell was visited in a dream by the great writer and critic, an experience that left 'a deep and pleasant impression on my mind'.[1] Until that evening Winning had filled too many of my days to intrude into my nights. (I did also, however, once dream of meeting Tony Blair in a restaurant in Tuscany, where he agreed to share his views on the thorn in his side, an offer rescinded at daybreak.)

When I dreamed of Winning, I found myself in the living room of The Oaks, sitting opposite my subject, who was dressed simply in black trousers, a white open-necked shirt and, of course, the grey cardigan. In the warm, fuzzy logic of dreams I said how delighted I was to see him, but that I had heard he was dead. He did not go so far as to quote Mark Twain's 'reports of my death have been greatly exaggerated', but that lay at the core of his response. We began to talk, but I do not know of what, when quite suddenly I found myself in the grounds of a house, partially obscured by mist. I was alone when, one by one, people appeared – both men and women. When asked where Winning was they could only point towards the house. I then found myself on the upstairs landing of The Oaks, outside the room in which he died. The corridor now seemed interminable, flanked on both sides by locked doors leading to room after room. Winning was nowhere to be found, so once again I set off in search of him.

I am conscious of the imagery the dream aroused, in particular Jesus's description of heaven: 'In my Father's house there are many rooms', but I do not believe I witnessed Winning in his 'just reward'; it was, instead, the conjurings of an overactive brain. Yet the idea of the search lingered long. After three years, hundreds of hours of interviews, and a tale that extends from the 1840s to the present day, what did I find? Who was Thomas Joseph Winning and what did he achieve in his lifetime? Just as no painter ever captured a true likeness of Cardinal Winning, so no obituary or tribute conveyed the true complexity of his character. Winning described the portrait in oils which hangs in Eyre Hall as 'too Robert Mitchum', and the cardinal has too often been portrayed as the tough guy. In truth he was a man of many paradoxes. He was a man of God who struggled to express his spirituality, a politician without an electorate; a reformer who encouraged greater democracy in a dictatorial manner; an admirer of the Pope who wrestled against the control of his curia. He was a man firmly of his time, who rose above circumstances to become 'one of Scotland's greatest sons'. He was undoubtedly greater than the sum of his constituent parts, as Winning's legacy becomes porous when held too closely to the light.

His twenty-seven years as Archbishop of Glasgow were a curate's egg. He dispensed with the chauffeur and formal robes of previous 'prince bishops', climbed down from the pedestal and walked among his parishioners. He embraced modern methods of communication and launched what remains a successful diocesan newspaper. The only criterion on which he felt he should be judged as archbishop was how successfully he implemented the changes of Vatican II. Undoubtedly he achieved much, altars were turned around, Latin was replaced by the vernacular, but in his attempts to spiritualize and animate the diocese, his reach proved greater than his grasp. For over twenty years he clung to the Pastoral Plan as a method of urging parishioners to take their Christianity out of the Church and on to the streets, but cast in even the most sympathetic light the project consumed far greater resources, time and goodwill than its achievements would ever merit. By importing a communitarian model which flourished best in the mountain villages of South America into an individualist and industrial society, Winning took on the role of Sisyphus. After two decades the boulder was no nearer the summit, priests were exhausted by the effort, and those who stood in the way were crushed. Father Cappellaro, the Pastoral Plan's godfather in Italy, believed Winning singularly failed to convince his priests and was unable subsequently to connect with the laity. By the time of his death, Winning had alienated many of the senior priests of the archdiocese and, while having an official College of Consulters, he took his advice from just three men: Mgr Peter Smith, Fr Paul Conroy and Ronnie Convery. Then there was the debt, whose legacy was a culture of distrust and disappointment directed towards Clyde Street. Yet, in spite of such circumstances, Winning was loved by the majority of Catholics in the diocese, not feared or merely respected, but held in genuine affection. This was a real achievement in comparison to previous archbishops.

The political achievements of Thomas Winning were limited. During the 1980s he was too closely associated with the Labour Party and too violently opposed to the essence of Thatcherism, which he felt was inherently selfish, to achieve political gain. The ascension of New Labour to power corresponded with his estrangement from Tony Blair and a determination to take him to task at each opportunity. It is arguable that Winning could have achieved more with a carrot than a stick. While he himself remained locked out of Downing Street, Cardinal Hume was a regular visitor whose private chats over tea achieved more than Winning's public bellowing. Winning was so conditioned by the role of the outsider that he found it impossible to alter his style of politics. Vocal condemnation of student fees, the bombing of Kosovo and abortion achieved little. Instead, what Winning achieved was an illusion of power. In Scotland, his stature had grown as a cardinal while politics had shrunk from Westminster to Holyrood. He was a large fish in a smaller pond. Even in Scotland, his condemnation of Section 28 failed to prevent the legislation from being repealed. However, his call against the repeal did trigger a bandwagon in England and Wales where the law remains upheld, though change is imminent.

Thomas Winning was a deeply spiritual man who struggled throughout his life to overcome the rigidity and distance of his priestly formation. The black shirt and white collar might as well have been a chain-mail shirt and suit of armour for all the physical and emotional connection it allowed. For too long Winning was among the world but disconnected from it. During his life the active spirituality of the Movement for a Better World worked a personal miracle, he grew within the suit of armour until he no longer clanked and the iron thinned until it became skin. Like an alcoholic who discovers AA and is convinced everyone else is a drunk, so Winning, redeemed by MBW, attempted to force such a particular salvation on others.

So what were Winning's achievements? They are elusive and not easily defined. His greatest achievement was a consistent courage to stand and boldly state what he believed at a time when such rigidity and unvarnished certainty were rare and welcomed by a majority who felt bereft of a voice amid a chorus of political correctness. His clear statements attracted the media and raised his profile at a time when few other religious leaders were visible. In Scotland he succeeded in becoming the public face of Christianity, an incredible achievement in a country that previously harboured such hostilities to his faith. In truth he was aided by the dissembling of the Church of Scotland and the rules that require the Moderator to change each year. Ironically for a man who paid only lip service to ecumenism, his fight to retain Section 28 was to create the most impressive ecumenical movement in recent years, attracting the widespread support of the Church of Scotland, the Free Church of Scotland, Muslims, Sikhs, Baptists and the Jewish community. Upon his death, the United Free Church of Scotland praised him for speaking 'for many other denominations in Scotland and beyond',[2] Baptists praised his fearless stand, while a Muslim leader explained: 'What we loved most about your great Cardinal was his sincere way of speaking up with no compromise.'[3] Through his strength and actions the Catholic Church in Scotland rose in stature from a despised sect to part of the mainstream. In truth, the Catholic Church was aided by its enemy, secularism, for as society became less interested in religion, so it lost interest in old prejudices and prohibitions.

Winning's greatest achievement, and perhaps what he will be best remembered for, is the introduction of the Pro-Life Initiative. At the time of writing, over four hundred and fifty children have been born to mothers who received aid. It would be naïve and opportunistic to say Winning's work saved their lives, yet there remain a handful of children, no more than four or five, whom staff believe would not exist now without Winning's practical assistance. The Jewish people have a saving: 'He who saves a single life, saves the world entire.' Winning has certainly saved a life.

In one of my final interviews with Winning, he agreed that on occasion he overemphasized a point for dramatic effect. 'Sometimes you just have to shout: "Shut up and listen to me!"' He was effective, in that everyone did listen, though they might not agree and rarely acted on such forceful advice, but through his efforts the Catholic Church and, more importantly, Catholic culture and values, had a voice. He inflated the importance of organized religion at a time when it was minimal, through the perfect combination of position and personality. Winning was a man who believed God had given him a second chance. A failure who had almost bankrupted his diocese, he rose from the ashes of the archbishopric to take on the new role of cardinal. He used the red hat and the extra weight attached to his words to influence the very culture of Scotland and, to a lesser extent, England and Wales. Few in Britain will be able to think about the issue of abortion without recollecting his active assistance, while the poor have lost an able advocate with his death.

He was a man who struggled to build Christian communities out of the loneliness of modernity. As a schoolboy, he said he wished to leave the world a better place than he found it. Upon his death, it was said: 'Scotland is a better country for his life and work.'[4] An image of Winning, which formed during the writing of this book, was of a man shouting into a tempest: 'Here I stand.'

The world as it is – hostile, uncharitable, greedy, promiscuous and violent – was swirling all around him. His achievement was not that the storm abated or changed course, but rather that he continued to stand, unbowed, shouting and rallying others to his cause.

NOTES

Full details of primary and secondary sources are given in the Bibliography. I have not included sources where it is obvious from the text that the person being quoted was interviewed by the author. A full list of interviewees appears in the Acknowledgements. Where the source is given in the text, I have not repeated the attribution.

CHAPTER ONE In the Beginning . . .
1 'The Papists (are like) . . .' Quoted in T. M. Devine, *The Scottish Nation 1700–2000*
2 'Priests were savagely assaulted . . .' Quoted in John Cooney *Scotland and the Papacy*

CHAPTER TWO Blairs Bound
1 'The master has recalled me . . .' Quoted in Thomas Winning's diary, 1943

CHAPTER THREE To the City by the Tiber
1 'Perhaps the most intimate quality . . .' Quoted in Thomas Winning's article: 'The Scots College and Our Nation', *Scottish Catholic Observer*, 20 November 1964
2 'Would history have judged Pius . . .' Quoted in Thomas Winning's article in the *Daily Telegraph*, 5 October 1999
3 'He read a lot in bed . . .' Quoted in Vivienne Belton *Cardinal Thomas Winning: An Authorised Biography*
4 'We all assembled at . . .' Quoted in Vivienne Belton *Cardinal Thomas Winning: An Authorised Biography*
5 'Only the holes in the walls . . .' Quoted from 'Twenty-Five Years at the Villa' by William Clapperton in *The Scots College Magazine*
6 'He is waiting there . . .' Quoted in Ronald Knox's *The Priestly Life*

CHAPTER FOUR A Curate's Tale
1 'manifest an appalling lack . . .' Quoted from Thomas Winning's
A Treatise on the Law of Scotland Respecting Tithes

CHAPTER FIVE A Time to Die
1 ' A good, efficient secretary . . .' Quoted from Clifford Longley's
The Worlock Archive
2 'You can imagine a dedicated life . . .' Gerry Rogers quoted in his
obituary in the *Catholic Directory for Scotland*, 1976

CHAPTER SIX No One is Far Away
1 'We were a Church of Silence . . .' Fr John Fitzsimmons in author
interview
2 'I was out of my depth' Quoted in Michael Turnbull's *Cardinal
Gordon Joseph Gray: A Biography*
3 'How nice, a month's holiday in Rome' From *Cardinal Gordon
Joseph Gray: A Biography* by Michael Turnbull
4 'horse flesh for lunch' ibid.
5 'We rejoice that relations . . .' Pope Paul VI quoted in the *Scottish
Catholic Observer* and *Scottish Catholic Herald*, 20 November 1964

CHAPTER SEVEN A Better World
1 'A year as curate at Chapelhall . . .' Private information

CHAPTER EIGHT A Battered Mitre
1 'He was not happy . . .' Susan McCormack, interview with author
2 'That year I . . .' Thomas Winning, interview with author
3 'Bishop Winning's duty . . .' Gordon Gray quoted in the *Scottish
Catholic Observer*, December 1971
4 'In the encyclical . . .' Bishop's statement on '*Humanae Vitae*' in
Scotland and the Papacy by John Cooney (Paul Harris Publishing,
1982)
5 'The failure to recognize . . .' SLAM letter quoted in John Cooney,
Scotland and the Papacy
6 'so-called Catholic renewal . . .' Archbishop Scanlan quoted in
John Cooney *Scotland and the Papacy*
7 'Having explained the ruling . . .' Fr Gerard Hughes memo quoted
in the *Glasgow Herald*, 22 May 1972

CHAPTER NINE The New Archbishop

1 'He has no time for ordinary people . . .' Thomas Winning quoted in the *Scottish Catholic Observer*, 30 August 1974

2 'We live in a world . . .' Thomas Winning quoted in the *Scottish Catholic Observer*, 6 September 1974

3 'We do not subscribe . . .' Thomas Winning quoted in Vivienne Belton's *Cardinal Thomas Winning: An Authorised Biography*

4 'My dearly beloved brothers . . .' Thomas Winning quoted in the *Scottish Catholic Observer*, 23 May 1975

5 'I don't say come to my side . . .' Revd James Matheson quoted in the *Scottish Catholic Observer*, 23 May 1975

6 'If we are to have one . . .' James Matheson quoted in the *Scottish Catholic Observer*, 27 February 1976

7 'Christians who take an active part . . .' Ecumenical letter quoted in the *Scottish Catholic Observer*, 2 November 1976

8 'Gerry Rogers accepted this one final cross . . .' Thomas Winning quoted in the *Scottish Catholic Observer*, 22 August 1975

CHAPTER TEN Glasgow's Miracle

1 'You are bold to say . . .' John Spottiswoode quoted, in *St John Olgilvie S.J.*, edited by Christopher Carrell

2 'You act like a hangman . . .' ibid.

3 'Is it treason . . .' ibid.

4 'by damning my soul . . .' ibid.

5 'I do not think . . .' Prof. William Barclay quoted in the *Scottish Catholic Observer*, 21 May 1976

6 'That way of thinking . . .' Moderator Dr James Matheson quoted ibid.

7 'Patient, friendly . . .' Thomas Winning quoted ibid.

8 'The saint that we venerate . . .' Pope Paul VI quoted in *Scottish Catholic Observer*, 22 October 1976

CHAPTER ELEVEN Tough Talking

1 'We fought a war . . .' Thomas Winning quoted in the *Glasgow Herald*, 3 February 1978

2 'When people are uncertain . . .' Prince Charles quoted in *The Times*, 1 July 1978

3 'astonishing, mean and unbecoming . . .' Revd John Gray quoted in the *Scotsman*, 3 July 1978

4 'I think it is a pity . . .' Revd Robert Woods quoted in the *Daily Telegraph*, 3 July 1978

5 'con trick' Thomas Fouhy quoted in the *Glasgow Herald*, 22 May 1978

6 'the Christian believer is a simple person . . .' Joseph Ratzinger quoted in John L. Allen's *Cardinal Ratzinger: The Vatican's Enforcer of the Faith*

7 'The last state was worse . . .' Basil Hume quoted in Peter Stanford's *Cardinal Hume and the Changing Face of English Catholicism*

CHAPTER TWELVE When Peter Met Andrew

1 'let Scotland flourish . . .' John Paul II quoted in the *Glasgow Herald*, 2 June 1982

2 'I am very much for non-violent . . .' Revd David Cassells quoted in *The Times*, 2 April 1982

3 'I am sure there will be violence . . .' Pastor Jack Glass quoted in *The Times*, 2 April 1982

4 'What must be urged . . .' Church of Scotland's Inter-Church Committee quoted in the *Herald*, 30 April 1982

5 'The Pope can't arrive at Heathrow . . .' Basil Hume quoted in *The Times*, 15 May 1982

6 'The sinking of the *Belgrano* . . .' Basil Hume quoted in the *Guardian*, 15 May 1982

7 'To quote a phrase used . . .' Derek Worlock quoted in the *Herald*, 18 May 1982

8 'Prepare your bombers . . .' Archbishop Lopez Trujillo quoted in Peter Hebblethwaite's *The Next Pope*

9 'I have to say that far . . .' Derek Worlock quoted in Clifford Longley's *The Worlock Archive*

10 'We are not asking him to come . . .' Cardinal Casaroli quoted in Clifford Longley's *The Worlock Archive*

11 'When self-indulgence is at work . . .' Pope John Paul II quoted in *The Pope Teaches: The Pope in Britain – The Complete Text*, CTS, 1982

12 'And so from this . . .' Professor John McIntyre quoted in the *Glasgow Herald*, 2 June 1982

13 'I am profoundly grateful . . .' Pope John Paul II quoted in the *Glasgow Herald*, 2 June 1982

14 'Today marks another significant . . .' Pope John Paul II quoted in the *Glasgow Herald*, 3 June 1982

CHAPTER THIRTEEN The City of God

1 'The Pastoral Plan was our Cuba . . .' Fr Philip Tartaglia interview with author

2 'The guy was a prophet . . .' Dr Anna Murphy interview with author

3 'only with . . . consensus . . .' Thomas Winning quoted in *Flourish*, December 1984

4 'Priests need to stop . . .' Mgr Tom Kleisser quoted in *Flourish*, June 1986

5 'My father is a loving God . . .' Winning's prayer diary

6 'The Christian Just War . . .' Thomas Winning quoted in *Speeches and Sermons on the Gulf War*, Glasgow Archdiocese

CHAPTER FOURTEEN The Collection Plate

1 'What can you get for 64p? . . .' Thomas Winning quoted in *Flourish*, March 1988

2 'As if they never existed' Private information

3 'dead duck' Private information

4 'clean breast of the whole thing' Private information

CHAPTER FIFTEEN The Red Hat

1 'It's about time that something . . .' Mario Conti quoted in the *Scottish Catholic Observer*

2 'Jesus Christ came to bring good news . . .' Thomas Winning in *Scotland on Sunday*, 17 October 1993

3 'I would say that Archbishop Winning's instinct . . .' Joseph Devine in the *Glasgow Herald*, 18 February 1994

4 'To all of you . . .' Thomas Winning in *Flourish*, December 1994

CHAPTER SIXTEEN The Affair of the Errant Bishop

1 'Crisis! What Crisis?' Thomas Winning quoted in Raymond Boyle and Peter Lynch's *Out of the Ghetto*

2 'Tom Winning is a religious leader . . .' Jim Sillars in the *Sun*, quoted in Raymond Boyle and Peter Lynch, *Out of the Ghetto*

3 'horrendous' Ileene McKinney quoted in the *Daily Record*, 23 September 1996

4 'I am physically and spiritually unable . . .' Roddy Wright quoted in the *Daily Mail*, 17 September 1996

5 'I am very, very shocked and saddened . . .' Basil Hume to *BBC News*, 19 September 1996

6 'Open Letter to Editors' quoted from the *Herald*, 27 September 1996

CHAPTER SEVENTEEN The Thorn on Labour's Rose

1 'Nobody can dismiss . . .' George Galloway in author interview

2 'My role is not to tell . . .' Thomas Winning quoted in Raymond Boyle and Peter Lynch, *Out of the Ghetto*

3 'most crimes committed . . .' Andrew Dewar Gibb quoted in Tom Gallagher *Glasgow: The Uneasy Peace*

4 'The Scots are a dying people . . .' George Malcolm Thomson quoted in his work *The Re-discovery of Scotland*

5 'The Labour for Life ban is more . . .' Thomas Winning in the *Daily Mail*, 20 February 1995

6 Letter from Tony Blair from Thomas Winning's private files

7 'rock bottom . . .' Noel Barry speaking anonymously to the *Sunday Mail*, 30 April 1995

8 'The inescapable consequences . . .' Tony Blair in *The Times*, 19 January 1988

9 'One can imagine him agonizing . . .' Tony Blair in the *Sunday Telegraph*, 7 April 1996

10 *Everyman* documentary quoted in the *Herald*, 28 October 1996

11 'Tony says he's against abortion . . .' Thomas Winning in the *Glasgow Herald*, 30 October 1996

12 'I warmly welcome . . .' Cardinal Hume quoted in press release from files of Catholic Church's media office in Glasgow

CHAPTER EIGHTEEN A Right to Life

1 'When I needed it, you gave me a hand up . . .' Note written to Roseann Reddy

2 'We cannot just say . . .' Dr Joaquin Navarro-Valls in author interview

3 'There is a strong Catholic vote . . .' Josephine Quintavalle in the *Scotsman*, 6 January 1997
4 'It is an issue . . .' Winning quoted in his pro-life speech from files of the Archdiocese of Glasgow
5 'Unfair pressure on women . . .' Jane Rowe to *Scotland on Sunday*, 9 March 1997
6 'One we should all consider carefully' Basil Hume quoted in *The Times*, 10 March 1997

CHAPTER NINETEEN The Spin Doctor Who Came Unspun
The material for this chapter is comprised of both interviews and the daily reports of the court case.

1 'She came all the way to Preston . . .' Quoted in the *Herald*, 11 December 1998
2 'He's damaged goods now . . .' Mgr Tom Connelly in author interview
3 'You've a great opportunity here . . .' Brian Dempsey quote. Private information
4 'You fucking bastards . . .' Noel Barry quoted in the *Scotsman*, 10 December 1998
5 'I have not broken . . .' Noel Barry quoted ibid.
6 'I was passionately . . .' Noel Barry quoted in the *Scotsman*, 11 December 1998
7 'What I did . . .' Annie Clinton quoted in the *Scotsman*, 12 December 1998
8 'He would wear . . .' Caroline Keegans Brown quoted in the *Edinburgh Evening News*, 17 December 1998
9 'Even if Father Barry . . .' Hugh Farmer quoted by the *Daily Record*, 19 December 1998
10 'Husband, wife, child . . .' Thomas Winning quoted in the *Herald*, 18 January 1999
11 'There are well-organized . . .' Thomas Winning quoted ibid.
12 'The past year has been . . .' Noel Barry quoted in the *Sunday Times*, 25 July 1999

CHAPTER TWENTY The Opinion that Dare Not Speak its Name

1 'I deplore homosexual acts . . .' Thomas Winning speaking to STV, 17 January 1999

2 'Democrats can be . . .' quoted from speech by Thomas Winning provided by files of the Archdiocese of Glasgow

3 'That is due . . .' Thomas Winning's article in the *Herald*, 19 June 1999

4 'I welcome with interest . . .' Thomas Winning speaking to STV, 17 January 1999

5 'Like good art . . .' Archbishop John Foley in author interview

6 'creates fear . . .' Revd John Cairns in the *Sunday Times*, 14 November 1999

7 'Is it not too much . . .' John Rafferty writing in the *Scotsman*, 19 January 2000

8 'I can think of no . . .' Thomas Winning writing in the *Daily Telegraph*, 19 January 2000

9 'He has espoused some policies . . .' John Reid in the *Sunday Mail*, 23 January 2000

10 'stable family life . . .' Thomas Winning quoted in the *Daily Mail*, 25 February 2000

11 'having queer blood . . .' Peter Tatchell in the *Daily Mail*, 7 February 2000

12 'Less than one third . . .' Wendy Alexander in the *Daily Record*, 31 May 2000

13 'I respect Cardinal Winning . . .' Jim Wallace in the *Daily Mail*, 2 June 2000

14 'The Cardinal is expected to have an opinion . . .' Tim Duffy in *Scotland on Sunday*, 4 June 2000

15 'Please be assured . . .' Thomas Winning's letter to Baroness Young dated 26 June 2000, provided by Baroness Young (letter given by her to the author)

CHAPTER TWENTY-ONE A Twilight Moment

1 'It reminds all of us . . .' Thomas Winning in the *Scotsman*, 5 December 2000

2 'Living, because . . .' Thomas Winning quoted in his speech, 'The Catholic Church in the Twenty-first Century', provided by the archdiocese of Glasgow

3 'Who's that guy Tettamanzi . . .' Keith O'Brien in *The Times*, 30 October 1999

CHAPTER TWENTY-TWO A Good Fight Fought
1 'We have lost a friend on earth . . .' Pope John Paul II quoted in the *Scotsman*, 26 June 2001

Epilogue
1 'a deep and pleasant . . .' James Boswell quoted in *Boswell's Presumptuous Task*
2 'for many other denominations . . .' Revd Archibald M. Ford, Moderator of General Assembly United Free Church of Scotland, quoted in *The Cardinal: Official Tribute* (Lindsay Publications, 2001)
3 'What we loved most . . .' Dr A. Majid Katme, Islamic Concern, quoted in *The Cardinal*, ibid.
4 'Scotland is a better . . .' Prof. John Haldane, Dept of Philosophy, University of St Andrews, quoted in *The Cardinal*, ibid.

PUBLICATIONS CONSULTED
The *Scottish Catholic Observer*
Flourish
The *Tablet*
The *Innes Review* 1950
The *Scots College Magazine*
The *Catholic Times*
Christian Order
L'Osservatore Romano
The *Scotsman*
The *Herald*
The *Daily Record*
The *Times*
The *Daily Telegraph*
The *Sunday Telegraph*
The *Sunday Times*
The *Sunday Mail*
The *Daily Mail*
The *Daily Express*

BIBLIOGRAPHY

Abbott, Walter M., *The Documents of Vatican II* (Geoffrey Chapman, 1966)

Allen, John L., *Cardinal Ratzinger: The Vatican's Enforcer of the Faith* (Continuum, New York, 2000)

Allen, John L., *Conclave* (Doubleday, New York, 2002)

Baty, Nick, *Archbishop Cormac and the Twenty-first-Century Church* (Fount, London, 2000)

Belton, Vivienne, *Cardinal Thomas Winning: An Authorised Biography* (Columba Press, Dublin 2000)

Bernstein, Carl & Politi, Marco, *His Holiness: John Paul II and the Hidden History of Our Time* (Transworld Publishing, London, 1996)

Boyle, Raymond & Lynch, Peter, *Out of the Ghetto: The Catholic Community in Modern Scotland* (John Donald, Edinburgh, 1998)

Butler, Carolyn, *Basil Hume: By His Friends* (Fount, London, 1999)

Butler, Carolyn, *Faith, Hope & Chastity: Honest Reflections From the Catholic Priesthood* (Fount, London, 1999)

Carpenter, Humphrey, *Robert Runcie: The Reluctant Archbishop* (Sceptre, London, 1996)

Catholic Directory for Scotland (John S. Burns, Glasgow, 2001)

Collins, Paul, *Papal Power: A Proposal for Change in Catholicism's Third Millennium* (Fount, London, 1997)

Coogan, Tim Pat, *The Troubles: Ireland's Ordeal 1966–1996 and the Search for Peace* (Arrow, 1996)

Cooney, John, *Scotland and the Papacy: Pope John Paul II's Visit in Perspective* (Paul Harris Publishing, 1982)

Copleston, F. C., *Aquinas: An Introduction to the Life and Work of the Great Medieval Thinker* (Penguin, London, 1991)

Cornwell, John, *Hitler's Pope: The Secret History of Pius XII* (Viking, London, 1999)

Cornwell, John, *A Thief in The Night: The Death of Pope John Paul I* (Viking, London, 1989)

Cornwell, John, *Breaking Faith: The Pope, The People, and the Fate of Catholicism* (Viking, London, 2001)

Devine, T. M., *The Scottish Nation 1700–2000* (Allan Lane, London, 1999)

Devine, T. M., *Scotland's Shame? Bigotry and Sectarianism in Modern Scotland* (Mainstream, Edinburgh, 2000)

Dilworth, Mark, *St John Ogilvie 1579–1615: An Illustrated History of His Life, Martyrdom and Canonisation* (Third Eye Centre, Glasgow 1979)

Dues, Greg, *Catholic Customs and Traditions: A Popular Guide* (Twenty Third Publications, Connecticut, 1993)

Duncan, Robert, *Wishaw Life and Labour in a Lanarkshire Industrial Community 1790–1914* (Motherwell District Council, 1986)

Elder, Fraser & Gilfeather, Martin & Wilkie, George, *Always Winning* (Mainstream, Edinburgh, 2001)

Ellman, Richard, *Oscar Wilde* (Penguin, London, 1988)

Feldman, Christian, *Pope John XXIII: A Spiritual Biography* (The Crossroad Publishing Company, New York, 2000)

Gallagher, Tom, *Glasgow: The Uneasy Peace* (Manchester University Press, 1987)

Hebblethwaite, Peter, *The Next Pope: History in the Making* (Fount, London, 2000)

Herman, Arthur, *A Guide to the General Assembly of the Church of Scotland* (The Saint Andrew Press, Edinburgh, 1986)

Isaacs, Jeremy & Downing, Taylor, *The Cold War* (Bantam Press, London, 1998)

Kemp, Arnold, *The Hollow Drum: Scotland Since The War* (Mainstream Publishing, Edinburgh, 1993)

Knox, Ronald, *The Priestly Life* (Sheed & Ward, London, 1959)

Küng, Hans, *The Catholic Church: A Short History* (Weidenfeld & Nicolson, London, 2001)

Linklater, Magnus & Robin Denniston, *Anatomy of Scotland: How Scotland Works* (Chambers, Edinburgh, 1992)

Longford, Frank, *The Bishops: A Study of Leaders in the Church Today* (Sidgwick & Jackson, London, 1986)

Longley, Clifford, *The Worlock Archive* (Geoffrey Chapman, London, 2000)

Bibliography

Martos, Joseph, *Doors to the Sacred: A Historical Introduction to the Sacraments in the Catholic Church* (Triumph Books, Missouri, 1991)

McBrien, Richard, *Encyclopedia of Catholicism* (HarperCollins, New York, 1995)

McCaffery, John, *The Friar of San Giovanni: Tales of Padre Pio* (Darton, Longman & Todd, London, 1978)

McCoy, Alban, *An Intelligent Person's Guide to Catholicism* (Continuum, London)

McCluskey, Raymond, *The Scots College Rome 1600–200* (John Donald, Edinburgh, 2000)

MacGill, Patrick, *Children of the Dead End* (Berlinn, Edinburgh, 1999)

Matthews, Eugene, *Counting My Joys* (Eugene Matthews, Girvan, 1990)

Miles, Jack, *Christ: A Crisis in the Life of God* (William Heinemann, London, 2001)

Naughtie, James, *The Rivals: The Intimate Story of a Political Marriage* (Fourth Estate, London, 2001)

A Pilgrim People: Diocese of Motherwell, 1948–1998 (John S. Burns, 1998)

Rawnsley, Andrew, *Servants of the People: The Inside Story of New Labour* (Hamish Hamilton, London, 2000)

Reese, Thomas, J., *Inside the Vatican: The Politics and Organization of the Catholic Church* (Harvard University Press, Cambridge, 1996)

Reid, Harry, *Outside Verdict: An Old Kirk in a New Scotland* (Saint Andrew Press, Edinburgh, 2002)

Rentoul, John, *Tony Blair Prime Minister* (Little, Brown, London, 2001)

Smart, Aileen, *Villages of Glasgow Volume 2* (John Donald, Edinburgh, 1996)

Stanford, Peter, *Cardinal Hume and the Changing Face of English Catholicism* (Geoffrey Chapman, London, 1999)

Storr, Anthony, *Feet of Clay: A Study of Gurus* (HarperCollins, London, 1997)

Stourton, Edward, *Absolute Truth: The Catholic Church in the World Today* (Viking, London, 1998)

Sewell, Dennis, *Catholics: Britain's Largest Minority* (Viking, London, 2001)

Thomson, George Malcolm, *The Re-discovery of Scotland* (Routledge, London, 1928)

Turnbull, Michael, *Cardinal Gordon Joseph Gray* (Saint Andrew Press, Edinburgh, 1994)

John Paul II, Chronicle of a Remarkable Life (Dorling Kindersley, London, 2000)

Rome: Eye Witness Travel Guide (Dorling Kindersley, Great Britain, 1993)

Ward, Keith, *God: A Guide for the Perplexed* (One World, Oxford, 2002)

Weigel, George, *Witness to Hope: The Biography of Pope John Paul II* (HarperCollins, New York, 1999)

Wellburn, Andrews, *The Beginnings of Christianity: Essene Mystery, Gnostic Revelation and the Christian Vision* (Floris Books, 1991)

Wright, Roddy, *Feet of Clay: The Autobiography of the Former Bishop of Argyll and the Isles* (HarperCollins, London, 1999)

Thomas J. Winning, *Tithes in Pre-Reformation Scotland* (Pontifical Gregorian University, Rome, 1953)

Willis, Garry, *Why I am a Catholic* (Houghton Mifflin Company, Boston, 2002)

Willis, Garry, *Saint Augustine* (Weidenfeld & Nicolson, London, 1999)

INDEX